RECONCEIVING THE SECOND SEX

Fertility, Reproduction and Sexuality

GENERAL EDITORS:

David Parkin, *Fellow of All Souls College, University of Oxford*
Soraya Tremayne, *Co-ordinating Director of the Fertility and Reproduction Studies Group and Research Associate at the Institute of Social and Cultural Anthropology, University of Oxford, and a Vice-President of the Royal Anthropological Institute*
Marcia Inhorn, *William K. Lanman Jr. Professor of Anthropology and International Affairs, and Chair of the Council on Middle East Studies, Yale University*

RECONCEIVING THE SECOND SEX
MEN, MASCULINITY, AND REPRODUCTION

Edited by

Marcia C. Inhorn, Tine Tjørnhøj-
Thomsen, Helene Goldberg, and
Maruska la Cour Mosegaard

Berghahn Books
New York • Oxford

First published in 2009 by

Berghahn Books
www.BerghahnBooks.com

Library of Congress Cataloging-in-Publication Data
Reconceiving the second sex : men, masculinity, and reproduction /
edited by Marcia C. Inhorn, ...[et al.]
    p. cm.—(Fertility, reproduction and sexuality ; v.12.)
Includes bibliographical references and index.
ISBN 978-1-84545-472-2 (alk. paper)
ISBN 978-1-84545-473-9 (alk. paper)
1. Men—Psychology. 2. Men—Sexual behavior. 3. Masculinity.
4. Human reproduction. I. Inhorn, Marcia Claire, 1957–
HQ1090.R43 2009
306.874'201—dc22   2009013894

British Library Cataloguing in Publication Data

A catalogue record for this book is available
from the British Library.
Printed in the United States on acid-free paper

ISBN 978-1-84545-472-2 Hardback
ISBN 978-1-84545-473-9 Paperback

CONTENTS

FIGURES

Introduction

THE SECOND SEX IN REPRODUCTION?
MEN, SEXUALITY, AND MASCULINITY

Marcia C. Inhorn, Tine Tjørnhøj-Thomsen, Helene Goldberg, and Maruska la Cour Mosegaard

In *The Second Sex* (1952 [1949]), French feminist Simone de Beauvoir argues that women's marginalization emanates from their association with reproduction. Because of their responsibility for pregnancy, parturition, breastfeeding, and childcare, women are excluded from positions of power within male-dominated patriarchal cultures. As a feminist "call to arms," *The Second Sex* generated multiple responses. It encouraged some second-wave feminists to rethink the motherhood mandate, arguing that the reproductive essentialization of women served as a fundamental obstacle to their advancement. However, other second-wave feminists embraced reproduction as the ultimate source of women's power—power that never could be shared by men, the so-called nonreproductive sex. Put another way, because men do not give birth, their power lies elsewhere in social life, making them disinterested and uninvolved in matters of human reproduction. Today, this assumption of men's disengagement from reproduction remains largely untested, but it is widely held in feminist, social science, population policy, and lay circles. Indeed, as we enter the new millennium, men are viewed as "the second sex" in reproduction.[1]

Men's reproductive marginalization is abundantly apparent in the scholarly literature on reproduction (van Balen and Inhorn 2002).

Extensive social science research, particularly by cultural and medical anthropologists and science and technology studies scholars, has explored women's reproductive lives, their use of reproductive technologies, and their experiences as mothers and nurturers of children (e.g., Becker 1994, 2000; Edwards 1993; Edwards et al., 1993; Franklin 1997; Franklin and Ragoné 1998; Ginsburg and Rapp 1995; Inhorn 1994, 1995, 2003; Kahn 2000; Layne 1999; Ragoné 1999; Rapp 2000; Stanworth 1987). As noted by Marcia C. Inhorn (2006a) in her recent review of the anthropological literature, more than 150 ethnographic volumes have been devoted to women, reproduction, and women's health in the past twenty-five years, with nearly two-thirds of those volumes published since the beginning of the new millennium. Meanwhile, few, if any anthropological texts, have explored men's reproductive concerns, with the exception of a volume on men and childbirth in the United States (Reed 2005), a volume on men and masculinities in Latin America (Gutmann 2003), and a volume on men and contraception in Mexico (Gutmann 2007).

To date, there are no ethnographic monographs on such major topics as male infertility; male sexuality and the use of new pharmaceuticals for erectile dysfunction; men's use of contraceptive technologies; men's use of assisted reproductive technologies, including donor sperm; men's experiences of sexually transmitted infections; men's experiences of vasectomy; men and prostate health; or men and reproductive health in general. Although several new journals are devoted to men's health (e.g., *International Journal of Men's Health, Journal of Men's Health and Gender*), the empirical literature is scant compared to that devoted to reproduction in women. Most of the published anthropological work on men and reproduction focuses on male infertility, mainly men's reactions to sperm donation (e.g., Becker 2002; Birenbaum-Carmeli, Carmeli, and Casper 1995; Birenbaum-Carmeli, Carmeli, Madjar, and Wessenberg 2002; Birenbaum-Carmeli, Carmeli, and Yavetz 2000; Inhorn 2004, 2006b; Nachtigall et al. 1997; Schmidt and Moore 1998). Men influence women's reproductive lives and health in a variety of ways (see Dudgeon and Inhorn this volume), but it is rarely explored how women influence men's reproductive lives. Instead, when men are included in reproductive health studies, the focus is generally on the consequences of their actions for women's reproductive lives and well-being.

But are men truly so disassociated from reproduction? Our volume challenges this assumption, arguing that the marginalization of men as the second sex in matters of reproduction is an oversight of considerable proportions. Rather, "reconceiving the second sex" requires bringing men back into the reproductive imaginary, as reproductive partners, progenitors, fathers, nurturers, and decision makers. Men contribute not only their gametes to human procreation, but are often heavily involved and invested in most aspects of the reproductive process, from impregnation to parenting. Furthermore, men have their own reproductive issues and concerns, which may be connected to but also separate from women's reproductive health and well-being. That men may be major contributors to women's reproductive health and the health of their offspring is also overlooked when men are left out of the reproductive equation. Thus, men need to be reconceived as reproductive in their own right, an insight that is long overdue.

To our knowledge, this volume represents the first attempt by anthropologists to examine men as reproducers. Feminist and kinship theorists within anthropology (e.g., Collier and Yanagisako 1987; Franklin and McKinnon 2002; Ginsburg and Rapp 1995; Martin 2001; Ortner 1974; Rosaldo 1974; Rubin 1975; Strathern 1992a, 1992b, 1995; Yanagisako and Delaney 1995) have challenged scholars to place reproduction at the center of social analysis. This requires reembedding men within this analysis—to study "men *as men*," in the words of Matthew Gutmann (1997:385)—and, in so doing, to break the silence surrounding men's thoughts, experiences, and feelings about their reproductive lives in order to shed new light on male reproduction from a cross-cultural perspective. This book is explicitly global in scope, focusing not only on men in Euro-America, but also in regions ranging from the Middle East to Asia to Latin America. Heterosexual, homosexual, married, and unmarried men are featured as reproducers in this volume, their concerns ranging from masculinity and sexuality to childbirth and fatherhood. Thus, the scope of this volume is explicitly wide ranging in order to highlight the large number of reproductive topics in which men are often heavily implicated.

Masculinity, Sexuality, and Reproduction

Throughout this volume, the interplay of masculinity, sexuality, and reproduction becomes apparent. Although the contributors do not agree on one overarching definition of either masculinity or sexuality, we argue that exploring how ideas of masculinity and sexuality are embraced, experienced, conceptualized, challenged, and sometimes rejected in the context of reproduction is inherently important.

What is generally meant by the term "masculinity"? In his review article, "Trafficking Men," Matthew Gutmann argues that studies addressing "masculinity" have done so in a rather vague way, not clearly defining the anthropological use of the concept. He identifies four distinct notions of masculinity used in scholarly discourse:

1. masculinity as anything men think and do;
2. masculinity as anything men think and do to be men;
3. masculinity as reflected by some men being inherently more manly than others; and
4. masculinity as anything that women are not, emphasizing the central importance of male–female relations (1997:386).

Recent studies of masculinity have tended to focus on physical training, sports, education, wage earning, militarism, and father-hood (Ben-Ari 1998; Kanaaneh 2009; Lupton and Barclay 1997; Townsend 2002), with attention paid to regional and religious dif-ferences between masculinities (Brandes 1980; Gutmann 2003; Herzfeld 1985; Jones 2006; Lewis and O'Brien 1987; Ouzgane 2006; Ouzgane and Morrell 2005). However, the notion of hierar-chy and competition *within* masculinities is also important. Accord-ing to R. W. Connell, "We must also recognize the *relations* between different kinds of masculinity: relations of alliance, dominance and subordination. These relationships are constructed through prac-tices that exclude and include, that intimidate, exploit, and so on. There is a gender politics within masculinity" (1995:37). Connell introduces the notion of "hegemonic masculinity" to suggest that dominant masculinities also produce subaltern forms. Perhaps no-where is this clearer than in the realm of reproduction. Delaney (1991, 1998) and others (Bouquet 1996; Goldberg 2004; Yanagisa-ko and Delaney 1995) have argued that, within the shared Judeo-Christian-Islamic tradition, hegemonic masculine ideals are clearly reflected in reproductive imagery and practices. Notions of pro-creation, or "coming into being," are inherently gendered, placing more value on men, who are seen as created in the image of God, as genitors, and as divinely embodied in the life-giving "seed," or sperm. As a result, sperm and its imagined unique abilities to "trig-ger" conception (Martin 1991) have captured the scholarly and popular imagination (see Goldberg, Moore, and Oaks this vol-ume), including in media and Internet discourses connecting the abundant production of sperm to manhood. Indeed, the "failure" of sperm to impregnate poses one of the greatest challenges to he-gemonic masculinity. The lack of ability to "perform" or "to get my wife pregnant" bespeaks a powerful form of subaltern masculinity qua emasculation, which is clearly tied to the stigma and silence still surrounding male infertility around the globe (Becker 2002; Carmeli and Birenbaum-Carmeli 1994, 2000; Gannon, Glover, and Abel 2004; Goldberg 2004; Inhorn 2003, 2004; Shokeid 1974; Tjørnhøj-Thomsen 2005).

Although male infertility and impotency is not the same thing, their common conflation speaks to the connection among reproduction, masculinity, and sexuality in men's lives. As with masculinity, sexuality has at least four different meanings:

1. sexuality as male and female categories with physical differentiation based on the genitals;
2. sexuality as a set of learned behavior patterns tied to cultural ideas and expectations of how sex and gender (male and female) should be acted out or performed;
3. sexuality as "being sexual" and "having" sexual longings, orientations, and desires (e.g., lust, eroticism); and
4. sexuality as a fluid identity, to which a person subscribes and is ascribed by others (Pat Caplan 1987; also see Butler 1990; Gutmann and Mosegaard this volume; Kulick 1998; Weston 1993).

Although these varied meanings of sexuality should apply equally to men and women, the sexual lives of men seem to be a far more common subject in the social science literature than the reproductive lives of men. Especially since the arrival of HIV/AIDS, men have been studied as sexual creatures, while women continue to be framed in reproductive terms (Bolton and Singer 1992; Plummer 1995). Such a division unwittingly reproduces gendered stereotypes. For example, the one-sided focus on gay men's lives as merely sexual has had the effect of denying their lives as fathers and representing them as nonprocreative beings (Mosegaard this volume). Put another way, homosexuality and reproduction have been seen as mutually exclusive (Hayden 1995; Lewin 1993; Rich 1993; Weston 1991). For heterosexual men and men in general, the focus on male sexuality at the expense of reproduction has silenced central elements of masculinity, including what it means to be a man and a father. As Matthew Gutmann argues in his chapter in this volume, men's "sexual destiny" is more often than not taken for granted both in popular imagination and in gender studies, where scholars seldom question this assumption of uncontrolled male sexuality.

The scholars whose work is represented in this volume challenge this portrayal. Through their empirical studies, they argue that men's reproductive aspirations, roles, and capacities cannot easily be separated from men's sexual lives. The connections among masculinity, sexuality, and reproduction are reflected in men's interests and abilities as lovers, as producers of male reproductive gametes, as supportive contraceptors, and as impregnators and progenitors of desired offspring. Yet, these connections are not always seamless; some chapters in this volume explore how the interconnectedness of sexuality and reproduction is contested, renegotiated, and sometimes resisted in various cultural settings around the globe.

Studying such connections poses methodological challenges. Sex can only be formally studied through self-report, and physical reproduction occurs only through the bodies of women. Thus, certain aspects of sexuality and reproduction seem to be forever precluded from firm view (Butler 1993). In the realm of reproduction women become the central gatekeepers to knowledge through their roles in pregnancy, childbirth, and caretaking. Men inevitably become "othered" in this process, including by the many female anthropologists who, unwittingly perhaps, have treated men as the second sex in reproduction, not worthy of empirical investigation (Gutmann 1997; Inhorn 2006a; van Balen and Inhorn 2002).

Organization of the Volume

This volume is dedicated to overcoming the othering of men as central actors in the reproductive process. Men are connected to reproduction, theoretically and empirically, in fourteen chapters written primarily by anthropologists from four continents.

Part I. Masculinity and Reproduction

Part I introduces male reproduction from multiple theoretical perspectives, examining men as masculine subjects, as sexual beings, as reproductive partners, and as family decision makers. Masculinity and sexuality are the key themes of this section, with authors interrogating these concepts in multiple ways. In all cases, they challenge many untested assumptions about men's lives, including their presumed promiscuous sexuality, their uncontrolled fertility, and their lack of concern for their own reproduction or that of their reproductive partners. In this section, men are demystified as the second sex in reproduction and reconceptualized as multifaceted reproductive subjects with multiple needs, desires, and concerns for personal and familial well-being. Through exploration of common "mistakes" and "lies" about men and reproduction, as well as review of the existing literature on this subject, readers of the volume will gain foundational knowledge on a topic rife with stereotypes and misconceptions. This section serves as the backdrop for the empirical studies in the following sections.

In Chapter 1, "The Missing Gamete? Ten Common Mistakes or Lies about Men's Sexual Destiny," Matthew C. Gutmann argues that the woefully unmarked category of the "male heterosexual" has gone overdetermined and understudied. In the age of evolutionary psychology and the medicalization of all manner of (alleged) bodily processes, the belief in heterosexual men's hypersexuality has, in more than a few cultural contexts, become something of a totemic illusion that treats male sexuality as naturalized, fixed, and entirely distinct from female sexuality. Gutmann's chapter examines men's "sexual destiny," a topic taken for granted in the popular imagination, yet seldom studied by feminist and gender studies scholars. It poses the ten common "mistakes" or "lies" about men's sexual destiny that are still propagated in both popular and scholarly discourses.

In Chapter 2, "Killer Sperm: Masculinity and the Essence of Male Hierarchies," Lisa Jean Moore argues that sperm are attracting considerable media attention and social commentary—for example, through concerns about global declines in sperm count and accompanying web-based marketing of sperm-enhancing pharmaceuticals. Assisted reproductive technologies have rendered sperm more predictable and operational outside of male bodies but are nonetheless viewed ambivalently for reasons having to do with cost and masculinity. Thus, it is not a coincidence that new scientific theories have emerged to resituate semen as being composed of "active warriors" with highly organized and complicated divisions of labor. Several connections can be made between the increased knowledge about and control over sperm and the cultural anxiety men experience in contemporary societies. Using scholarship about hegemonic masculinity, this chapter explores the dialectical relationship between men's lived experiences and the production of masculinity through an analysis of how sperm is represented in the reproductive sciences.

In Chapter 3, "Gender, Masculinity, and Reproduction: Anthropological Perspectives," Matthew R. Dudgeon and Marcia C. Inhorn shift the focus from discourses of sexuality and masculinity to how men's reproductive health has become an explicit focus of population and development programs and policies. Anthropological research suggests that understanding men's reproductive health needs and problems requires investigation of both local biological and cultural variation. Taking a biosocial perspective on human reproduction, the chapter examines contributions from biological and cultural anthropology concerning men's reproductive health. Biological anthropologists have demonstrated important variations in men's reproductive physiology. Cultural anthropologists have explored intersections between masculinity and health, men's experiences of fatherhood, and reproductive problems such as infertility. The chapter explores the implications of both "local biologies" and "local masculinities," as rendered through anthropological approaches, for future research on men's reproductive health.

In Chapter 4, "Men's Influences on Women's Reproductive Health: Medical Anthropological Perspectives," Dudgeon and Inhorn examine the recent reproductive health initiative, which has emerged as an organizational framework that incorporates men into maternal and child health programs around the globe. The chapter begins by exploring the concept of "reproductive rights," examining the concept from an anthropological perspective. As part of this discussion, the question of "equality" versus "equity" is addressed, introducing anthropological perspectives on ways to incorporate men fairly into reproductive health programs and policies. The chapter goes on to provide a number of salient examples of men's relevance in the areas of contraception, abortion, pregnancy and childbirth, infertility, and fetal harm. For several decades, medical anthropologists have produced reproductive health research that explores male partners' effects on women's health and the health of children. This chapter summarizes exemplary research in this area, showing how medical anthropologists contribute new insights to the growing public health and demographic literature on men and reproductive health. The chapter concludes with thoughts on future areas of anthropological research that may improve understandings of men's influences on women's reproductive health.

Part II. Fertility and Family Planning

Part II interrogates men as contraceptors, family planners, and participants in pregnancy termination. Although men may impregnate women, they also contracept and may, in fact, consider family planning to be their major responsibility. The chapters in this section explore the development of family planning methods aimed at men and their willingness to adopt various forms of contraception, including hormonal methods. In addition, the authors in this section explore the degree to which men "control" the reproductive decision-making process, sometimes in ways that facilitate women's reproductive health. Although the notion that men are fully informed reproductive "partners" is questioned in this section, every chapter provides compelling evidence that men are important participants in the family planning process.

In Chapter 5, "Manhood and Meaning in the Marketing of the 'Male Pill,'" Laury Oaks documents the neglect of male hormonal contraceptive development despite the fact that, since the 1960s, female hormonal contraceptives have become available around the globe. This chapter examines the development and existing media coverage of the so-called male pill, including the benefits of and limitations to male hormonal contraceptive technologies; women's health advocates' positions on male hormonal contraceptive development; the increasing medicalization of the male sexual and reproductive body; the potential differential marketing of male hormonal contraceptives to men; and men's future role as contraceptive consumers. Particularly crucial to this discussion is the fact that hormonal contraceptives will not prevent sexually transmitted infections. Although women's health advocates may be hesitant to raise concerns about male hormonal contraceptive development, this chapter argues that it is necessary to promote health policies that take into account both women's and men's sexual and reproductive health.

Chapter 6, "Reproductive Paradoxes in Vietnam: Masculinity, Contraception, and Abortion," by Nguyen Thi Thuy Hanh, turns from men's role in contraception to that in abortion. Vietnam has one of the highest abortion rates in the world, and this chapter explores men's role in reproductive health care choices through case studies and in-depth interviews with couples seeking pregnancy termination at the Gynecology and Obstetrics Hospital of Hanoi. This study finds that although Vietnamese men—both married and unmarried—are involved in issues concerning reproductive health, they are not necessarily involved in the abortion decision-making process. Instead, they display relatively limited awareness of contraceptive methods and the effects of abortion on women's health. This chapter explores the paradoxical position of men as both empowered and powerless in the reproductive realm in Vietnam. In addition, the chapter discusses how information about various options is conveyed to couples, the communication between men and women, and ultimately how abortion affects women's health in Vietnam.

In Chapter 7, "Reproductive Politics in Southwest China: Deconstructing a Minority Male-Dominated Perspective on Reproduction," Aura Yen argues that culture and politics are crucial determinants of how indigenous men in rural China influence gender relations, reproduction, and development, sometimes adversely affecting women's reproductive health. This chapter examines how stratified social relations, as they reflect gender and class inequality, intersect with dominant Chinese reproductive health policies in an ethnic minority and purportedly "model contraceptive" village in Southwest China. Ascribed gender roles, hierarchical relations, and notions of "fate" sustain the power of male elders, who, by perpetuating a reproductive "myth" employed by the Chinese government and by utilizing their social position in order to foster their own families, prioritize their own reproduction and development over that of junior women. Under the male dominance of sexuality and reproduction, women's reproductive health problems are attributed to fate and are not viewed as problems to be rectified.

Part III. Infertility and Assisted Reproduction

Part III examines men's experiences of infertility and the variety of measures used to overcome this condition, ranging from painful genital surgeries, to assisted reproductive technologies, to gamete donation and adoption. Although more than half of all cases of childlessness involve a so-called male factor, male infertility remains deeply hidden and is considered one of the most stigmatizing of all male health conditions. Furthermore, the common conflation of male infertility with impotency leads to a kind of double stigmatization, even though the two conditions are usually separate phenomena. Behind this veil of secrecy, men around the world must cope with their infertility and seek methods to overcome it, often involving multiple forms of bodily objectification. The chapters in this section explore infertile men's sense of masculinity, their understandings of "weak" sperm, the problems of sexuality they may experience as sequelae of the infertility treatment quest, and the lengths to which they may go to produce biological offspring. The section also explores infertile men's alternative forms of family formation, including some men's eventual acceptance of "social" parenthood.

In Chapter 8, "The Sex in the Sperm: Male Infertility and Its Challenges to Masculinity in an Israeli-Jewish Context," Helene Goldberg takes readers to Israel, where there is a prevailing silence surrounding male infertility in both scholarly circles and clinical settings. This has led, in turn, to an unbalanced emphasis on women's infertility issues in the Israeli-Jewish population. This chapter questions the notion that assisted reproduction and reproductive technologies themselves are sexless. Rather, when the focus is shifted to infertile men rather than women, notions of sexual intercourse emerge as an important issue. In the context of male infertility, sexual intercourse is symbolically attached to sperm, and male infertility raises cultural notions of dysfunctional sperm, failed masculinity, and sexual impotence. Although male infertility and impotence are usually separate conditions, their conflation contributes to the silence surrounding the former.

In Chapter 9, "'It's a bit unmanly in a way': Men and Infertility in Denmark," Tine Tjørnhøj-Thomsen examines Danish men's perceptions of fatherhood and family life as well as their reactions and responses to their own infertility and childlessness. This chapter explores men's attempts to come to terms with their infertility, their use of reproductive technologies, and, in some cases, a form of fatherhood that does not involve a genetic connection to their offspring. Through the use of infertility narratives, this chapter illuminates infertile Danish men's thoughts, experiences, and feelings about their reproductive lives, their masculine identities, and their sense of authenticity as fathers.

In Chapter 10, "Male Genital Cutting: Masculinity, Reproduction, and Male Infertility Surgeries in Egypt and Lebanon," Marcia C. Inhorn examines why both fertile and infertile Middle Eastern men routinely undergo genital surgeries. These surgeries include varicocelectomy, a genital operation purported to remove infertility-producing varicose veins from the testicles; and testicular aspirations and biopsies, to draw sperm from the testicles for the purposes of assisted reproduction. In both cases, pain, swelling, and other complications may result. In the case of varicocelectomy, the surgery has little role in overcoming male infertility and has been subject to international critique. Yet, its popularity in the Middle East continues. This chapter highlights the reasons for the widespread practice of "male genital cutting" and includes stories of several Egyptian and Lebanese men, both fertile and infertile, who underwent testicular surgeries for the sake of their marriages and their future fertility. These men's willingness to "put their genitals on the operating table" bespeaks their desire to share their wives' suffering and signals changing marital and gender relations.

Part IV. Childbirth and Fatherhood

Part IV explores childbearing and fatherhood. Over the last few decades, interest in the "modern father" has increased in both the political and academic arenas. Modern family structures have given Western men the opportunity to parent in radically different ways than their own fathers (Gillis 1996; Townsend 2002), thus contributing to changing traditional conceptions of masculinity (Lupton and Barclay 1997). At the same time, fatherhood has not played a central role in studies and conceptualizations of masculinity. Although new and different forms of family and reproductive technologies have generated new and different modes of parenting and fathering, men have been relegated to the background of those studies (Franklin 1997; Inhorn 1994; Kahn 2000; Ragoné 1999). This section explores men's participation in pregnancy, childbirth, and fatherhood worldwide, arguing that changing forms of male participation may be leading to profound transformations in gender relations.

In Chapter 11, "'We are pregnant': Israeli Men and the Paradoxes of Sharing," Tsipy Ivry examines Israeli childbirth-education courses, showing how men participate in their partners' pregnancies and negotiate medicalized pregnancy by using notions from their own lives. For example, Israeli men explain pregnancy and childbirth by comparing it to their own physical hardships as soldiers. However, they also draw on the discourses of "natural birth" by employing TV-romanticized images of women from Third World countries giving birth without assistance. In so doing, Israeli men argue that the medicalization of pregnancy and childbirth is in the best interests of their "spoiled" pregnant partners, who are unable to withstand the physical tolls of labor and delivery. Thus, they encourage women to adopt medicalized forms of childbirth in order to prevent any pain or discomfort. This chapter questions this form of medicalization, by pointing to the paradoxes evident in Israeli men's ideals of "sharing." Although Israeli men expect to participate in the birth process, they may be doing so in ways that undermine women's best interests and reproductive health.

Chapter 12, "Making Room for Daddy: Men's 'Belly Talk' in the Contemporary United States," by Sallie Han, questions the assumption that because men's bodies are not involved and implicated in pregnancy in the same ways as women's bodies, the male partner's bond with the expected child is marginal and minimal. "Belly talk"—that is, speech and other communication, such as music and touch, that expectant parties direct to an expected child—allows men to become involved in the pregnant "feeling," or an emotional and sensory engagement with the pregnancy and the expected child. In this chapter, based on a study of pregnancy practices in an American Midwestern city, men's belly talk practices are described and analyzed. It is argued that belly talk and other male partners' practices during pregnancy must be understood within the context of an American political discourse on "family" that promotes the centrality of fathers in social life.

In Chapter 13, "Husband-Assisted Birth among the Rarámuri of Northern Mexico," Janneli F. Miller takes us to Northern Mexico's

Sierra Madre, where, until the middle of the twentieth century Rarámuri Indian women gave birth outdoors and alone. When the number of non-Rarámuri in the region rose dramatically and the forest was no longer considered safe, women began giving birth indoors. The change in birth place was accompanied by a change in birth assistant. Now, Rarámuri men often take an active role in their children's births, an involvement that continues in the work of shared child rearing. Although most observers have noted the profound sex segregation in this indigenous group, the private practice of husband-assisted birth points to changes in Rarámuri social life, including the strengthening of the husband–wife bond as the fundamental unit of social organization.

The final chapter, "Stories of Fatherhood: Kinship in the Making," by Maruska la Cour Mosegaard, highlights the little-known category of gay fatherhood. So far much attention has been given to lesbians and their motherhood, while gay fathers have been ignored in both political and legal discussions and in the scholarship on reproduction. Gay men act as fathers in multiple ways—as primary parents, as "donor dads," and as part-time caregivers. As parents, homosexual men both challenge and reproduce old ideas about the interconnectedness between sex and reproduction, and between partnership and parenthood. Although gay fathers are still quite invisible in popular and scholarly discourses, this chapter on gay fathers in Copenhagen, Denmark, aims to bring them into focus alongside the mothers of their children.

Taken together, these chapters provide evidence of the great variety of ways men around the world are participating in reproduction. Through this examination, we hope to successfully move men from the reproductive margins, thereby reconceiving their second-sex status in the anthropological study of reproduction.

Note

1. The argument that men are the "second sex in reproduction" was initiated by Goldberg (2004).

References

Becker, Gay. 1994. "Metaphors in Disrupted Lives: Infertility and Cultural Constructions Continuity." *Medical Anthropology Quarterly* 8(4):456–71.
———. 2000. *The Elusive Embryo: How Women and Men Approach New Reproductive Technologies*. Berkeley: University of California Press.

————. 2002. "Deciding Whether to Tell Children about Donor Insemination: An Unresolved Question in the United States." In *Infertility around the Globe: New Thinking on Childlessness, Gender and Reproductive Technologies*, ed. Marcia C. Inhorn and Frank van Balen. Berkeley: University of California Press.

Ben-Ari, Eyal. 1998. *Mastering Soldiers: Conflict, Emotions and the Enemy in an Israeli Military Unit*. London and New York: Berghahn Books.

Birenbaum-Carmeli, Daphna, Yoram S. Carmeli, and Robert F. Casper. 1995. "Discrimination against Men in Infertility Treatment." *Journal of Reproductive Medicine* 40(8):590–94.

Birenbaum-Carmeli, Daphna, Yoram S. Carmeli, and Haim Yavetz. 2000. "Secrecy among Israeli Recipients of Donor Insemination." *Politics and the Life Sciences* 19(1):69–76.

Birenbaum-Carmeli, Daphna, Yoram Carmeli, Yigal Madjar, and Ruth Wessenberg. 2002. "Hegemony and Homogeneity: Donor Choices of Israeli Recipients of Donor Insemination." *Material Culture* 7(1):73–95.

Bolton, Ralph, and Merril Singer, eds. 1992. *Rethinking AIDS Prevention: Cultural Approaches*. Montreaux: Gordon and Breach.

Bouquet, Mary. 1996. "Family Trees and Their Affinities: The Visual Imperative of the Genealogical Diagram." *Journal of the Royal Anthropological Institute* 2(1):43–66.

Brandes, Stanley 1980. *Metaphors of Masculinity: Sex and Status in Andalusian Folklore*. Philadelphia: University of Pennsylvania Press.

Butler, Judith. 1990. *Gender Troubles: Feminism and the Subversion of Identity*. New York: Routledge.

————. 1993. *Bodies That Matter: On the Discourse Limits of Sex*. New York: Routledge.

Caplan, Pat, ed. 1987. "Introduction." In *The Cultural Construction of Sexuality*. London: Routledge.

Carmeli, Yoram S., and Daphna Birenbaum-Carmeli. 1994. "The Predicament of Masculinity: Towards Understanding the Male's Experience of Infertility Treatments." *Sex Roles* 30(9/10):663–77.

————. 2000. "Ritualizing the 'Natural Family': Secrecy in Israeli Donor Insemination." *Science as Culture* 9(3):301–24.

Collier, Jane Fishburne, and Sylvia Junko Yanagisako, eds. 1987. *Gender and Kinship: Essays Towards a Unified Analysis*. Stanford: Stanford University Press.

Connell, R. W. 1995. *Masculinities*. Berkeley: University of California Press.

de Beauvoir, Simone. 1952 [1949]. *The Second Sex*. New York: Vintage Books.

Delaney, Carol. 1991. *The Seed and the Soil: Gender and Cosmology in Turkish Village Society*. Berkeley: University of California Press.

————. 1998. *Abraham on Trial*. Princeton: Princeton University Press.

Edwards, Jeanette. 1993. "Explicit Connections: Ethnographic Enquiry in North-West England." In *Technologies of Procreation: Kinship in the Age of Assisted Conception*, ed. Jeanette Edwards, Sarah Franklin, Eric Hirsch, Frances Pric, and Marilyn Strathern. Manchester: Manchester University Press.

Edwards, Jeanette, Sarah Franklin, Eric Hirsch, Frances Price, and Marilyn Strathern. 1993. *Technologies of Procreation: Kinship in the Age of Assisted Conception*. Manchester: Manchester University Press.

Franklin, Sarah. 1997. *Embodied Progress: A Cultural Account of Assisted Conception*. London and New York: Routledge.

Franklin, Sarah, and Susan McKinnon, eds. 2002. *Relative Values: Reconfiguring Kinship Studies*. Durham: Duke University Press.

Franklin, Sarah, and Helena Ragoné, eds. 1998. *Reproducing Reproduction: Kinship, Power and Technological Innovation*. Philadelphia: University of Pennsylvania Press.

Gannon K., L. Glover, and P. Abel. 2004. "Masculinity, Infertility, Stigma and Media Reports." *Social Science and Medicine* 59(6):1169–75.

Gillis, John R. 1996. *A World of Their Own Making: Myth, Ritual and the Quest for Family Values*. New York: Basic Books.

Ginsburg. Faye D., and Rayna Rapp, eds. 1995. *Conceiving the New World Order: The Global Politics of Reproduction*. Berkeley: University of California Press.

Goldberg, Helene. 2004."The Man in the Sperm: A Study of Male Infertility in Israel." MA thesis, Institute of Anthropology, University of Copenhagen, Denmark.

Gutmann, Matthew. 1997. "Trafficking Men: The Anthropology of Masculinity." *Annual Review of Anthropology* 26:385–409.

———, ed. 2003. *Changing Men and Masculinities in Latin America*. Durham: Duke University Press.

———. 2007. *Fixing Men: Sex, Birth Control, and AIDS in Mexico*. Berkeley: University of California Press.

Hayden, Corrine P. 1995. "Gender, Genetics, and Generation: Reformulating Biology in Lesbian Kinship." *Cultural Anthropology* 10(1):41–63.

Herzfeld, Michael 1985. *The Poetics of Manhood: Contest and Identity in a Cretan Mountain Village*. Princeton: Princeton University Press.

Inhorn, Marcia C. 1994. *Quest for Conception: Gender, Infertility, and Egyptian Medical Traditions*. Philadelphia: University of Pennsylvania Press.

———. 1995. *Infertility and Patriarchy: The Cultural Politics of Gender and Family Life in Egypt*. Philadelphia: University of Pennsylvania Press.

———. 2003. "'The Worms Are Weak': Male Infertility and Patriarchal Paradoxes in Egypt." *Men and Masculinities* 5(3):236–56.

———. 2004. "Middle Eastern Masculinities in the Age of New Reproductive Technologies: Male Infertility and Stigma in Egypt and Lebanon." *Medical Anthropology Quarterly* 18(2):162–82.

———. 2006a. "Defining Women's Health: A Dozen Messages from More Than 150 Ethnographies." *Medical Anthropology Quarterly* 20(3):345–78.

———. 2006b. "'He won't be my son': Middle Eastern Muslim Men's Discourses of Adoption and Gamete Donation." *Medical Anthropology Quarterly* 20(1):94–120.

Jones, Adam, ed. 2006. *Men of the Global South: A Reader*. London: Zed.

Kahn, Susan Martha. 2000. *Reproducing Jews: A Cultural Account of Assisted Conception in Israel*. Durham and London: Duke University Press.

Kanaaneh, Rhoda Ann. 2009. *Surrounded: Palestinian Soldiers in the Israeli Military.* Stanford: Stanford University Press.

Kulick, Don. 1998. *Travesti: Sex, Gender and Culture among Brazilian Transgendered Prostitutes.* Chicago and London: University of Chicago Press.

Layne, Linda L., ed. 1999. *Transformative Motherhood: On Giving and Getting in a Consumer Culture.* New York: New York University Press.

Lewin, Ellen. 1993. *Lesbian Mothers: Gender and Power in American Culture.* Berkeley: University of California Press.

Lewis, Charlie, and Margaret O'Brien, eds. 1987. *Reassessing Fatherhood: New Observations on Fathers and the Modern Family.* London: Sage.

Lupton, Deborah, and Lesley Barclay. 1997. *Constructing Fatherhood: Discourses and Experiences.* London: Sage.

Martin, Emily. 1991. "The Egg and the Sperm: How Science Has Constructed a Romance Based on Stereotypical Male–Female Roles." *Signs* 16(3):485–501.

———. 2001. *The Woman in the Body.* Berkshire: Beacon Press.

Nachtigall, R. D., J. M. Tschann, S. S. Quiroga, L. Pitcher, and G. Becker. 1997. "Stigma, Disclosure, and Family Functioning among Parents of Children Conceived through Donor Insemination." *Fertility & Sterility* 68(1):83–89.

Ortner, Sherry B. 1974. "Is Female to Male as Nature Is to Culture?" In *Woman, Culture and Society*, ed. Michelle Zimbalist Rosaldo and Louise Lamphere. Berkeley: University of California Press.

Ouzgane, Lahoucine, ed. 2006. *Islamic Masculinities.* London: Zed.

Ouzgane, Lahoucine, and Robert Morrell, eds. 2005. *African Masculinities: Men in Africa from the Late Nineteenth Century to the Present.* New York: Palgrave.

Plummer, Kenneth. 1995. *Telling Sexual Stories: Power, Change and Social Worlds.* London: Routledge.

Ragoné, Helena. 1999. "The Gift of Life: Surrogate Motherhood, Gamete Donation and Constructions of Altruism." *In Transformative Motherhood: On Giving and Getting in a Consumer Culture*, ed. Linda L. Layne. New York: New York University Press.

Rapp, Rayna. 2000. *Testing Women, Testing the Fetus: The Social Impact of Amniocentesis in America.* New York: Routledge.

Reed, Richard K. 2005. *Birthing Fathers: The Transformation of Men in American Rites of Birth.* New Brunswick: Rutgers University Press.

Rich, Adrianne. 1993 [1980]. "Compulsory Heterosexuality and Lesbian Existence." In *The Lesbian and Gay Studies Reader*, ed. H. Abelove, M. Barale, and D. Halperin. New York: Routledge.

Rosaldo, Michelle Zimbalist. 1974. "Woman, Culture and Society: A Theoretical Overview." In *Woman, Culture and Society*, ed. Michelle Zimbalist Rosaldo and Louise Lamphere. Berkeley: University of California Press.

Rubin, Gayle. 1975. "The Traffic in Women: Notes on the 'Political Economy' of Sex." In *Towards an Anthropology of Women*, ed. Rayna R. Reiter. New York: Monthly Review Press.

Schmidt, Matthew, and Lisa Jean Moore. 1998. "Constructing a 'Good Catch,' Picking a Winner: The Development of Technosemen and the

Deconstruction of the Monolithic Male." In *Cyborg Babies: From Techno-Sex to Techno-Tots*, ed. Robbie Davis-Floyd and Joseph Dumit. New York: Routledge

Shokeid, Moshe. 1974. "The Emergency of Supernatural Explanations for Male Barrenness among Moroccan Immigrants." In *The Predicament of Homecoming: Cultural and Social Life of North African Immigrants in Israel*, ed. Shlomo Dreshen and Moshe Shokeid. Ithaca: Cornell University Press.

Stanworth, Michelle, ed. 1987. *Reproductive Technologies: Gender, Motherhood and Medicine*. Cambridge: Polity Press.

Strathern, Marilyn. 1992a. *After Nature: English Kinship in the Late Twentieth Century*. Cambridge: Cambridge University Press.

———. 1992b. *Reproducing the Future: Anthropology, Kinship and the New Reproductive Technologies*. Manchester: Manchester University Press.

———. 1995. "Displacing Knowledge: Technology and the Consequences for Kinship." In *Conceiving the New World Order: The Global Politics of Reproduction*, ed. Faye D. Ginsburg and Rayna Rapp. Berkeley: University of California Press.

Tjørnhøj-Thomsen, Tine. 2005. "Close Encounters with Infertility and Procreative Technology." In *Managing Uncertainty: Ethnographic Studies of Illness, Risk and the Struggle for Control*, ed. Vibeke Steffen, Richard Jenkins and Hanne Jessen. Copenhagen: Museum Tusculanum Press.

Townsend, Nicholas. 2002. *The Package Deal: Marriage, Work, and Fatherhood in Men's Lives*. Philadelphia: Temple University Press.

van Balen, Frank, and Marcia. C. Inhorn, eds. 2002. *Infertility around the Globe: New Thinking on Childlessness, Gender and Reproductive Technologies*. Berkeley: University of California Press.

Weston, Kath. 1991. *Families We Choose: Lesbians, Gays, Kinship*. New York: Columbia University Press.

———. 1993. "Lesbian and Gay Studies in the House of Anthropology." *Annual Review of Anthropology* 22:339–69.

Yanagisako, Sylvia, and Carol Delaney, eds. 1995. *Naturalizing Power: Essays in Feminist Cultural Analysis*. London: Routledge.

Part I.

MASCULINITY AND REPRODUCTION

Chapter 1

THE MISSING GAMETE?
TEN COMMON MISTAKES OR LIES
ABOUT MEN'S SEXUAL DESTINY

Matthew C. Gutmann

The French philosopher Simone de Beauvoir writes in *The Second Sex* that "biological facts [provide] one of the keys to the understanding of woman." Yet, she quickly adds, "I deny that they establish for her a fixed and inevitable destiny" (1970 [1949]:29).[1]

This revolutionary thesis that detached female bodies from female destinies has been a cornerstone of feminism and women's studies for several decades, sometimes captured in the aphorism that biology is not destiny. Since *The Second Sex*, our understanding of the biological facts have become more complex (see, for example, Anne Fausto-Sterling's *Sexing the Body* [2000]). Some hallowed truths about bodies have been more difficult to dislodge than others. This chapter examines the notion of men's sexual destiny, a topic widely taken for granted in the popular imagination yet sadly and oddly seldom examined by feminist and gender studies scholars. This volume is an important step toward rectifying that situation.

Beliefs revolving around men's sexually rapacious appetites are found worldwide. In academic circles today, evolutionary psychologists claim to have uncovered the primal motives of male licentiousness—a built-in compulsion on the part of males of the species to spread their seed. In his primer to this new science of evolutionary psychology, Robert Wright goads, "Can anyone find a single culture in which women with unrestrained sexual appetites *aren't* viewed as more aberrant than comparably libidinous men?" (1994:45). Lest we blithely dismiss such biologistic and universalist claims (or their widespread popular counterparts), we still must reckon with the dearth of good scholarship—feminist or otherwise—on male (het-ero)sexuality and reproduction. By not studying male sexuality and reproduction, we have left unchallenged the conclusion common to evolutionary psychologists that, with respect to sexuality, "male li-cense and (relative) female reserve are to some extent innate" (46). And in case there is any confusion regarding the shortage of studies on male heterosexuality and reproduction, this situation is not the product of some reverse feminist bias against men but the general totemization of male sexuality. In an age of evolutionary psychology and the medicalization of all manner of (alleged) bodily processes, the belief in men's hypersexuality has, in more than a few cultural contexts, become something of a totemic illusion treating male sex-uality as naturalized, fixed, and entirely distinct from female sexual-ity. Indeed, many feminist theories of gender inequality help pro-vide the framework within which we are now able to develop the study of men, sexuality, reproduction, and masculinity as integral to a more general project of exploring the history and diversity of gender/sexuality systems in the world.[2]

Further, we might do well to remember Anthony Giddens's (1983) double hermeneutic, by which he means that, unlike the subjects of study in the natural sciences, social scientific conclu-sions about society and social groups have an impact on the people studied. What health researchers say about male sexuality, for ex-ample, even if simply by implication, can and does have a chain of consequences among those we seek to represent. That so enormous and everyday a topic as male heterosexuality and reproduction has gone largely unnoticed in anthropology and the other social sci-ences shows both the importance and urgency of the task at hand, because left underexamined and underanalyzed it is too easy to rely on facile biologisms that reduce men and their sexualities to man and his sexuality.

In short, if we settled (or began to unsettle) the matter of wom-en's bodily destiny over fifty years ago, why is the myth of men's sexual destiny still so pervasive in popular culture, and why does it remain largely unchallenged in scholarly venues?

A clue to the answer to this question may lie with what Car-ole Vance (1999 [1991]) has termed "the cultural influence model," in which cultural differences provide a patina of sexual diversity spread over primordial male and female bodies. This speaks to the central dilemma in Western sexuality research in the last hundred years: the interaction between material bodies and cultural meanings in the course of periodic licking, sucking, inserting, enveloping, topping, and bottoming one another. In Vance's formulation, the cultural influence model is utilized to describe the sexuality of both men and women so that "sexuality is seen as the basic material—a kind of universal Play Doh—on which culture works, a naturalized category which remains closed to investigation and analysis" (44). With the cultural influence model, one may encounter a range of mutually exotic and/or repugnant sexual practices cross-culturally, but each is but a script on the basic, underlying corporal essence of human beings. As a friendly amendment to Vance's critique of the view that culture is a mere epiphenomenal influence on sexuality, I would add that in feminist research—though certainly not in the popular imagination—the male body, even more than the female body, is still considered in too many ways to come factory-loaded with a predictable Play-Doh hard drive.[3]

The notion of sex drives, urges, and impulses, for instance, has been repeatedly challenged and explored in sophisticated feminist literature on women's sexualities. For a similar corpus of work among men, only queer theory and studies of same-sex sex can make any claim to wide-ranging, complex, and nuanced treatments of sexualities. It is time to queer our dull understanding of male heterosexualities; that is, to consider the woefully unmarked category of the male heterosexual that, despite and perhaps because of its hidden dominance in models of sexuality, has nonetheless too long gone overdetermined and understudied. And as we do this, we should keep in mind R. W. Connell's cautionary judgment regarding social constructivists:

> They face, as a group, difficulties about the bodily dimension of sexuality. Bodily processes and products—arousal, orgasm, pregnancy and birth, menarche and menopause, tumescence and detumescence, semen, milk and sweat. . . . Placing an emphasis on the historicity of sexuality, as Foucault and his followers do, often marginalizes these matters (1997:63–64).

We must not continue to ignore the confluence of biological and cultural parameters on sexuality and how these factors feed and transform one another.

The anthropological gambit of first gaining conceptual clarity in the social margins has served us well, but it is now necessary to bring lessons learned to a study within the margins. In successive

conceptual waves—first closely linking sex(uality) and gender systems (Rubin 1975), then splitting them apart and not just analytically (Rubin 1999 [1984]), with more recent linking of sexuality and
gender again in a feminist post-Freudian synthesis (Segal 1994)—we
have learned about narrowly treating sexuality as biology and gender as culture. This is important because if male sexuality is the biological given and the rest of what we do with it is the gendered fluff,
then the wide range of manly sexual desire, dread, pleasure, worry,
obsession, fantasy, experience, and practice is merely lying there to
be dutifully discovered and documented and not much more.

Relatively little has been written, for example, about heterosexual men not enjoying sex, not enjoying it often, and not missing
sex when they do not have it. Reports on such topics are exceptional indeed. Among the rare accounts, in an attempt to refute the
"Freudian thought . . . that each person has a certain innate amount
of sexual energy which must be expressed in some fashion." So
wrote Karl Heider among the Grand Valley Dani in Indonesia. In the
1960s, when he conducted his fieldwork, there was a standard four-
to-six-year postpartum sexual abstinence. What is even more note-
worthy is that no one showed any signs of unhappiness or stress as
a result of such celibacy (Heider 1976:195). Among the *hijras* in India, Nanda writes that their "emasculation is their culturally defined
'proof' that they do not experience sexual desire or sexual release as
men" (1990:29).[4] And in research on changing gender identities and
practices in Mexico City, a male friend confessed to me, "I'll tell you
honestly, sex has just never been as important to me as it seems to
be for a lot of other guys" (Gutmann 2006:144). Yet the very shortage of such accounts cross-culturally can lead us blithely to assume
that (a) most men are not like this and (b) we know what most men
are like with respect to sexuality and reproduction.

Anthropologists may infrequently take perverse pleasure in re-
cording the polymorphous philandering of males and females of all
ages, shapes, and kinds.[5] They may be keen observers of sexual variety and breadth, and retain a phobic allergy to ideal types and the
norms of normativity. Yet, they may harbor the suspicion that most
heterosexual males feel and behave a certain way, say, with an innate sex drive. The usual way around this predicament in contemporary cultural anthropology is to focus on the local and avoid any
presumption of panhuman experiences, that is, by recourse to anthropology's localist conceit—that "beliefs and practices are sui ge-
neris in every locale at every point in history." This orientation has
been particularly important and necessary in response to the medicalization of human bodies and biomedical declarations regarding

corporal normality and pathology (see Scheper-Hughes 1994). As someone who has spent a good part of the last twenty years in central and southern Mexico, I am acutely aware of the perils of generalizing for regions, much less the populations of entire nation-states and, still less, larger groupings of people when it comes to sexuality, reproduction, men and masculinity, or much else. My purpose in this chapter is to raise a series of questions I hope will be relevant in more than one historical and cultural context.

As a way to explore pertinent ideas and poke fun at these misconceptions, I offer the following list of "common mistakes and lies" about men, sexuality, and reproduction.

Reproduction and Reproductive Health Only Concern Women

Obviously, many readers know better than to think reproduction is for women alone. However, it may be worth noting that this reality is less obvious than it should be, as evidenced by the fact that in some of the recent and important collections on reproduction and gender and health, the editors were unable to include articles dealing substantially with men and reproduction (see, for example, Ginsburg and Rapp 1995; Sargent and Brettell 1996).[6] To highlight the missing presence of men from discussions of reproduction, Meg Greene and Ann Biddlecom titled their 2000 review essay "Absent and Problematic Men: Demographic Accounts of Male Reproductive Roles" (also see Dudgeon and Inhorn 2003; and Inhorn 2002, 2003, 2004). That men have been absent from studies of reproduction is itself problematic. The trick now is to incorporate men into this field without losing sight of the politics of reproduction.

Fortunately, in discovering this missing link (gamete?) in the history of reproduction and sexuality, we are able to build on the existing substantial literature on topics like women and reproduction,[7] fatherhood and men's "prior involvement,"[8] and men who have sex with other men. To be sure, the inclusion of men in any field is more than a matter of adding men and stirring the mixture, though even that can be a start. Among the issues deserving early attention in this endeavor are a few mentioned below.

With ingenuity and not a little flair, queer theorists and second-wave feminists have embarked on the task of marking male heterosexuality as normative and nothing more. As we have learned from Rich's (1993 [1982]) classic essay on "compulsory heterosexuality," the taken-for-granted category of male (hetero)sexuality has long

been employed as a stand-in, the unmarked, for all forms of sexuality. Yet analytically outing heterosexual men from their unmarked
closets, or, showing them to have particular and not universal kinds
of sexualities, was in many ways all that was done. Until recently, in
feminist scholarship they have analytically remained in the shadow
of the closet, albeit rather naked in their heteronormativity.[9]

The issue is not only how best to represent the views and experiences of the population of men who are engaged in reproduction in
some manner or another, and the women and men in their lives, or
how to discuss the diversity of male heterosexualities in relation to
reproductive rights, behavior, and technologies. The challenge is to
develop this field without losing the key insights from feminism and
queer theory regarding inequality and privilege, in particular the real
corporal and societal constraints women and men face. In the case
of men, we might ask what would be the obverse of the following
characterization by Segal: "The complexity of the social is ignored,
reduced to generalizations about fixed relations of power—as though
to be less powerful in society, as mothers so often are, is to be, and to
be perceived to be, simply submissive and powerless" (1994:148–49).
What about men perceived to be powerful? Are they automatically
so in all contexts, including the most sexually intimate?

Finally, surprisingly few gender studies in the social sciences focus on both men and women. Although the either/or approach has
advantages in some contexts for some topics of inquiry (for Latin
America, see Gutmann 2003), it also has severe drawbacks when
one is examining a subject such as reproduction.[10] In the burgeoning literature on birth and midwives, for example, men seldom are
given more than a passing reference despite the central role they
may play before, during, and after childbirth.[11] With respect to infertility, men have long been treated as irrelevant, or if incorporated
into studies, they were the ones refusing to consider the possibility that they had the problem. Significant work in this area is just
beginning (see Inhorn 2002, 2003, 2004; Kahn 2000).[12] Following
international conferences in Cairo in 1994 and Bejing in 1995, the
intersection of politics and reproduction and the incorporation of
men into reproductive health matters have received state sanction
in most parts of the world. As necessary as these shifts may be and
as good as it may be to involve men in the scholarship on reproduction, as in the development field and the shift from Women in
Development to Gender and Development, risks are involved (see
Chant and Gutmann 2000). Within anthropology, it is only in HIV
research that men, sexuality, and reproductive health have been
studied and discussed extensively.[13]

Reproductive Health Only Concerns Women in General and Men and Women with AIDS

The AIDS epidemic made men relevant to reproduction and sexuality, at least insofar as the health of men and their sexual partners were concerned. Initially considered a health issue for gay men and men who had sex with men but did not self-identify as gay—in the patronizing language of public health, these men were flagged collectively as a significant "risk group"—and especially when epidemiological studies showed a geometric growth of the contagion in parts of southern Africa and the Indian subcontinent, heterosexual men and their foreskin hygiene, sexually transmitted infections (STIs), and dry-sex idiosyncrasies came under closer scrutiny. As elsewhere in the world, reproductive health and sexuality in Latin America was spawned by AIDS campaigns for medications and safer sexual practices.

The relationship among male heterosexuality, bisexuality, and homosexuality is of central concern in studying men, sexuality, and reproduction for a variety of reasons, not the least of which are the theoretical deficiencies in existing models of heterosexuality. How do studies of male (homo)sexuality jibe with male (hetero)sexuality and with human sexuality in general? Nancy Chodorow has examined the psychoanalytic literature and concluded that, lo and behold, "psychoanalysis does not have a developmental account of 'normal' heterosexuality (which is, of course, a wide variety of heterosexualities) that compares in richness and specificity to accounts we have of the development of the various homosexualities and what are called perversions. . . . most of what one can tease out about the psychoanalytic theory of 'normal' heterosexuality comes by reading between the lines in writings on perversions and homosexuality" (1994:34; also see Segal 1994, 1997). Commonplace assumptions and clichés about heterosexuality, however, continue to abound.

Recent public health attention in some parts of the world—to problems like testicular and prostate cancer (especially affecting younger and older men respectively), erectile dysfunction (a problem that grows with time and pharmaceutical solutions), and premature ejaculation—addresses certain reproductive health concerns by men regardless of sexual orientation. Yet, emphasizing male analogues to female gynecological problems will only take us so far in developing our conceptual toolkit regarding male sexualities. To give texture and vigor to the study of men, sexuality, and reproduction, we must find ways to extend and develop the feminist and queer literatures on sexuality—including bisexuality—so that if male heterosexualities are no longer seen as compulsory, neither are they necessarily and generally understood as compulsive.

Male Reproduction Equals Male Sexuality (and Vice Versa?)—or, a Biological Solution to the Reproduction of the Species

It may be a coincidence that penises and testicles can be sites of physical arousal and sexual pleasure, and are also closely involved in male fertilization. But the fact remains that for the vast majority of men's lives, penises and testicles are not in high states of excitation. The erect penis is not the default.[14]

Clearly, one of the main problems with this equation of male reproduction and sexuality is that it leaves out all forms of sex between men, one more confirmation of masculinity as homophobia (see Kimmel 1994). Understanding men who have sex with other men as, yet again, an elided category involves more than the straightforward recognition that men have sex with each other without any thought of procreation. In the history of sexuality studies, the notion of activity and passivity among men who have sex with each other also has become prevalent as a proxy analytical framework for heterosexual-reproductive sexuality. These terms link male and female heterosexuals to tops and bottoms among men who have sex with other men. Here, too, we may learn from the recent ethnography (see, for example, Parker 1999) of emerging homosexualities that makes clear how the active/passive dichotomy can cause more conceptual problems than it resolves. This is a valuable lesson, because until recently male (hetero)sexuality has been associated too often and too cavalierly with activity (and aggression), in contrast to women's passive and aggrieved (hetero)sexuality (Gutmann 2003; Segal 1994, 1997).

Still, same-sex male sex is not the only kind of nonproductive sex that takes place; not only does sex between men and women usually not result in pregnancy, but most sex between men and women is intentionally "nonreproductive." This lends further weight to not reducing all discussions of male sexuality to male reproduction, just as it is important not to reduce male reproduction to male reproductive health problems like erectile dysfunction, low motility of sperm, and impotence. Questions of pleasure and desire (and lack thereof), of emotional comfort (and discomfort), of fantasy (and fear)—all these factors are at play in and throughout men's sexual and reproductive lives.

A recent study of men who frequent strip clubs in the U.S. state of North Carolina provides yet more evidence why male sexuality must be separated from male reproduction and even basic male sex acts. In her book, Katherine Frank (2003) describes why some men may spend hundreds of dollars each week *not* to have sex with women, and in the process uncovers how, instead of direct sexual release, men pay to look at and spend time with strippers. Frank argues that for many men, the strip clubs provide a space where their feelings of psychological powerlessness are given safe haven from the social world, in which they have acknowledged authority.[15]

In short, as the extensive and extensively cited literatures on same-sex sex, transvestism, and transgender politics illustrate, separation of male reproduction and sexuality as analytic categories is indispensable. The more difficult riddle is how and when to recombine these categories, and not just for analytic purposes, in order to explore the lives of billions of men for whom reproduction and sexuality are connected in everyday and palpable ways. It is apparent that activities like sexual intercourse and other sexual activities between men and women have been stunningly avoided and/or ignored in scholarship. One might expect anthropologists to be interested in such activities for their habitual and ritualized qualities alone.

It is sometimes said that men's reproduction is contingent on their sexuality—and more specifically on their achieving erections—in ways not true for women.[16] Nevertheless, to carry this argument to its logical conclusion, unless one were to argue that all erections are the same—and that all erections arise for the same reason—it is as foolish to exaggerate such features of male sexuality as to consider them wholly distinct from the ways women's reproduction can be contingent on their sexuality. For both men and women, it would seem that the most salient issue is not alleged universal physiological manners of responding to sexual stimulation but what causes what kinds of responses in what cultural contexts, and when, how, and why.

Men Do Not Take Responsibility for Birth Control

This assertion may not be a real mistake, much less a wholesale lie. Many men do not take responsibility for contraception and never have or will.[17] Further, who among men is demanding birth control for men? Internationally, the only coherent social movements among men that are identified with "men as men" are the multithreaded struggles for gay rights and freedoms. In particular countries, of course, there are organizations professing to advance the rights of men, like the U.S. right-wing Christian Promise Keepers. Yet, in none of these movements are men seeking to gain more control over their fertility through male hormonal implants, silicone injections in their vas deferens, or other methods of contraception, nor are men as a cohesive social force demanding more condoms and more vasectomies for the masses.[18]

Missing in Mexico, as in most parts of the world, is a history of men's participation in preventing pregnancies. To what extent have men's experiences paralleled those described by Schneider and Schneider (1996) in nineteenth- and twentieth-century Sicily, where the practice of *coitus interruptus* was widely practiced and regarded as an eminent sign of respectability? Given that before the introduction of chemical methods, the "reverse gear" (as it was called in Italy) was also a primary contraceptive technique in Mexico, we would do well to learn the extent to which *coitus interruptus* "had less to do with an ascetic renunciation of pleasure than with empowerment," gaining purchase on life and love (162).

Meanwhile, women in Mexico sometimes describe the contraceptive situation as *las mujeres ya saben de eso* (women are the ones who know about that). Women in Mexico *cuidarse*, they "take care of themselves," when they employ one or more methods to prevent pregnancy. It is unclear how often this situation exists because women and not men become pregnant, or because men by nature will not share responsibility for family planning, or because the contraceptive options available on the global market are overwhelmingly those that women must ingest, insert, or inject. There are, in fact, few birth control options for men. Why? To what extent are culture and physiology, for example, implicated in the lack of male contraception? Experiments with male hormonal birth control and temporary silicone plugs for the vas deferens have not led to development and marketing for the enormous population of men presumably availing themselves of contraceptive options for women.[19]

Widespread ignorance, misinformation, and unfounded fears are at least as significant as some unbridled and peculiarly Mexican machismo in understanding the reasons few men in Oaxaca get vasectomies. According to many of the men I met and interviewed in vasectomy clinics between 2001 and 2005, lack of knowledge is one reason. Some men and women learn about vasectomies from public service announcements on television, the radio, or newspapers, and from brochures at family planning clinics or the nurses and doctors working in these clinics. Word of mouth, especially from one man to another, is often the most convincing method of publicizing the procedure. In addition, many Mexican health clinics paint advertisements on their outside walls to publicize their clinic's ability to perform vasectomy surgeries, thus promoting male participation in this form of permanent contraception.

Yet in most clinical situations I encountered in Oaxaca, in state-run family planning promotion efforts, vasectomy is presented as a matter of individual choice and not in the context of the overall relations between men and women, in which men seldom assume primary responsibility for contraception. The official brochures, for example, do not compare vasectomy with tubal ligation for women, the latter being a far more invasive and temporarily debilitating procedure. The approach to vasectomy is that this method of birth control is available should a man choose to avail himself of this service. Not surprisingly, perhaps, for men who do choose a vasectomy, acquiring one can be difficult.

It is a mistake to discount all together the active participation and empathy of any men in contraception. One conclusion from my vasectomy research in Oaxaca is the great relief men express when they no longer have to worry about the women they have sex with getting pregnant. Not insignificantly, several women in the same study reported a similar release from the pregnancy worries they had experienced throughout their sexually active lives. When comparing statistics of men's participation in what are often considered more "male forms of birth control" like condoms and vasectomy, the figures vary tremendously from country to country (and sometimes from region to region within countries). Do these numbers represent something fundamental about cultural attitudes and practices with respect to male sexuality? Can we, to recall the comments made to me by a National Science Foundation official, in a meaningful sense correlate contraceptive prevalence among men to particular national "machismo and nonmachismo cultures"?

Ultimately, the involvement of men in contraception is not just a matter of individual choice, of machismo and nonmachismo cultures, nor a matter of men versus women—those who inseminate during spasms that last a few seconds versus those who potentially will carry a fetus for nine months. To explain what Latin American scholars Barbosa and Viera Villela (1997) call "the introduction of a contraceptive culture" and what Colombian anthropologist Mara Viveros Vigoya (2002) calls "the female contraceptive culture," in which women worldwide are overwhelmingly responsible for birth control, we must not only look at negligent and roguish men who seek to absolve themselves of responsibility for preventing pregnancies (see also Barbosa and Di Giacomo do Lago 1997). We also must look at the role of governments in population control, family planning, and reproductive health and sexuality campaigns, the Catholic Church, the United Nations Population Fund, the International Planned Parenthood Federation and its local affiliates, the Population Council, and the Ford, MacArthur, and Rockefeller foundations and their roles in creating a female contraceptive culture. Just as decisively, we must examine the part played by the pharmaceutical industry in demarcating the limits of what is considered by their research scientists to be biologically possible and feasible for ensuing marketing strategies. Clearly, some of these institutions have played a much stronger role in finding ways to move beyond the so-called fertility regulation, to buck the tide of the female contraceptive culture, to involve men, and to develop a comprehensive approach to women's health.

As a final point with respect to men and contraception, it would be a shame to forget that before the days of the pill many men played a larger part in preventing reproduction, and that condoms and withdrawal were significant features in more heterosexual sexual encounters than in most circumstances today. This is not the current situation, when sixty-one percent of all "women of reproductive age" worldwide who are married or in a consensual union are using contraception (United Nations 2003).

Men's Sexual Impulse Is a (Natural) Given

This enormous topic is so freighted with popular lore it is difficult to know how to begin unraveling the mistakes and lies. Perhaps one place to start would be to ask where the gay gene went. One answer, of course, is that it never existed and therefore had nowhere to go. More substantially, the research proclaiming the discovery of the gay gene was hopelessly flawed because it rested on a social construct (knowledge and consensus as to who is gay in the first place) and then attempted to trace backward to find some genetic similarity among such people. The attributive and ascriptive aspects of gayness, whatever that might be, are impossible to tease apart. Also problematic is what Roger Lancaster calls "genomania and heterosexual fetishism" (2003). As he explains, "I do not believe that homosexuality is really susceptible to even 'good' biological research. As a complex, meaningful, and motivated human activity, same-sex desire is simply not comparable to [genetically related] questions like eye color, hair, color, or height" (256).

The futile quest for the gay gene is relevant to the question of male sexual impulses insofar as they are similarly naturalized. In

1968, Mary McIntosh helped free us from seeing homosexuals as having "a condition"—in the language of the day, she emphasized instead that homosexuals play social roles. With heterosexual men, it seems we have not advanced much in our understanding to the extent they are viewed—albeit today with the imprimatur of evolutionary psychology and hormone level testing—as having their own kind of homogeneous sexual condition. For example, it is truly extraordinary that we have so few feminist studies on men and rape—the motives, contexts, and histories—and the relationship of power and sexuality to understanding it.[20] Further, early second-wave feminism inadvertently contributed to the problem of biologistic reasoning. More specific, Lynne Segal notes the "theoretical inadequacy of the scientifically respectable but nevertheless reductive model of sexuality in use in these early feminist writings, based upon the idea of drives and their repression or release" (1994:41).

In the course of exploring the pervasive influence of notions in Mexico regarding an intrinsic and totemic sexuality among men, I have found that the stereotype of "real men must procreate to prove themselves men" is linked historically to the state-sponsored pronatalism that developed after the Mexican revolution in the 1910s. It then accelerated lasting until the early 1970s, during which the Mexican nation was generally conflated with men and masculinity (see Gutmann 2006). In addition to the totemization of male sexualities continuing unabated in the twenty-first century, this national natural history has played an important role in contemporary shibboleths and truisms regarding what men in Mexico sexually want, do, seek, and need.

One implication of the totemization of male sexuality for the subject of men and reproduction is to promote a mechanistic understanding that "men's participation in the reproductive process is, in effect, limited to their contribution of sperm" (Marsiglio 1998:50). Marsiglio's 1998 study is among the few devoted to analyzing the relationship between men, sexuality, and reproduction, albeit largely based on U.S.-related data. His book is in many respects a subtle examination of "procreative man," and Marsiglio is careful not to overstep the limits of our knowledge about these topics. Yet, though the reader may think she or he knows what Marsiglio really means by "limited to their contribution of sperm," I wonder if this is the most helpful way to formulate the matter. The cultural influence model at play here allows Marsiglio to speculate that, because men do not carry the fetus for nine months, it leads to men's "indifference" to pregnancy and even a general "alienation from the reproductive process," which is only now being slightly mitigated by new technologies like ultrasound, which allows men (in some classes and countries) to visually experience the fetal growth and impending birth of their children (51).

Such an approach to studying men, sexuality, and reproduction is too culturally circumscribed and ultimately supports the notion that narrowly conceived notions of biology inevitably trump all else, though undoubtedly it has a rehabilitated ring of truth today, when the role of genetic testing to establish paternity is forcing some "deadbeat" dads to acknowledge their paternal responsibilities. Even paternity, including in societies espousing normative nuclear families, has ultimately proved itself not so very reducible to consanguinity and still less should male sexuality ever be reduced to neural firings and blood flows.

Love Has Nothing to Do with Men, Sexuality, and Reproduction

The claim may be patently ridiculous, but after taking stock of most scholarship on these subjects, one could well be left with this impression. Part of the fault may lie with Foucault (1980), for whom love was conspicuously absent, but the lack of attention to love and the like, especially with respect to men and their sexual and reproductive life histories, is a glaring omission.[21] Obviously, terms like "love" must be thoroughly contextualized culturally and historically, yet the difficulty of such an enterprise does not explain our prior reluctance to undertake this task. Instead, and following on naturalized assumptions about male sexuality, we may have unintentionally assumed that love, for men, is not relevant to the study of sex and reproduction. As absurd as this may seem, it is hard to otherwise explain our scholarly lapse.

One indication of how skewed our perspective on love and sexuality may be is illustrated by the language generally used to discuss reproductive health, whether related to women, men, or both. In brochures and medical texts, contraception is generally presented in rather negative terms, as when we talk of population and birth *control*, fertility *regulation*, family *planning*, and pregnancy *prevention*. If there is, at least for some on some occasions, a joy in sexuality that does not result in procreation and even, god forbid, reproduction, it might be worth attending to the complex meanings such pleasures might entail.

Men Will Do What They Do Sexually and Reproductively Regardless of Women's Intervention

The inclusion of men in studies of reproduction reflects, in part, scholarship catching up with reality. The conceptual and empirical obstacles to this inclusion are many, and here I call attention to a particular weakness in studies of men and masculinities that has caused problems more generally than simply with respect to reproductive matters: the absence of substantial research that documents and theorizes the influence adult women have on adult men. There are many studies showing the influence of women on male children. There are studies on the influence of adult men on adult women. But there are precious few that examine what mothers, sisters, wives, and other women say and do in the lives of their men. If nothing else, this omission feeds the notion that men in their daily lives are not responding in good measure to the negotiations, entreaties, threats, and seductions initiated by women.

The ad folks on Madison Avenue know better than to accept this conclusion. Following the 1998 initial advertising campaigns that were aimed more squarely at men by announcing the advent of Viagra on the global market, newer drugs like Cialis and Levitra have made pointed use of women to promote the idea that "if you want to have sex and your male partner suffers from erectile dysfunction, get him to try this pill." During my research of contraceptive decision making in Oaxaca, I discovered the influence of women on men. Of the few men opting for vasectomies, many made reference to their wives' experiences with contraception, pregnancy, and childbirth and offered that their primary reason for sterilization was, "It's my turn to suffer." Even long-term topics of interest in reproductive health studies of women might be restudied to examine the relationship of women to men. These include postpartum sexual taboos, as well as giving serious attention to the fact that the meanings and experiences of such strictures for men are not often acknowledged by more than a sly, sneering wink about male resentment and sexual frustration. There is more to be explored on these and related topics.

The shifting sands of feminist conceptualizing about similarities and differences in men's and women's sexualities undoubtedly is part of the picture here. To the extent that root differences are expected and given emphasis, it seems there is a tendency to assume that when left to their own sexual devices, men are at most subject to female restrictions but not truly amenable to change, including at the behest of women. If the influence of adult women on adult heterosexual men is a subject of study in ethnographic research, we will find evidence of men reporting trepidation and diffidence, and not just confidence and disrespect in their sexual and reproductive relations with women.

It is rather easy to ridicule erectile dysfunction as one more sob story from men unsatisfied with their sex lives with women; it is more difficult to develop rich and nuanced ethnographic examinations of topics like impotence and prostitution that are more often the object of jokes than serious study. Cornwall's mention of the impact that accusations of impotence in southwestern Nigeria can have on men is too brief and too rare: "Laughed at by his colleagues and accused of being impotent for not wanting to chase women, he struggled to become a man in their terms, learning to mask his shyness with alcohol and eventually to blot out his disquiet" (2003:238). The implications of the stigma of impotence are too often ignored or glossed over. Odd as it might seem, studies of men seeking female prostitutes are even more unusual, as if the only subject worthy of careful attention in such relations are the experiences of the women, and the only point of controversy is whether these women more exemplify victims or agents.[22]

We Can Accurately Study Sexual Practices

Without a doubt, the principal complicating factor in any research on sexuality is the uncomplicated fact that people may not wish to tell the truth, they do not remember the truth, they misremember, and they lie, and it is often impossible to tell if and when one of these conditions pertains. The central conceptual conundrum of research on sexuality is therefore the extent to which these kinds of problems severely and irremediably limit what can be known in this realm. As frustrating as it may be to admit that certain parts of human existence in some profound way might be unknowable, no amount of wishing it were not so and no amount of variables that run through multiple regression analyses will make it otherwise. Because we researchers cannot jump into bed with people and would not want to in most cases, and if we did we would hopelessly skew subsequent events, we must seek indirect ways to study who does what to whom, how, and when. And we must rely to a great extent on self-reporting. Undoubtedly, there are ways to compare quantitative, survey research with oral histories, for instance, in order to gain a better idea about sexuality and reproduction. But there are limits to our abilities to chart this terrain.

We can also invent ways to get a rough fix on how often people are probably doing a range of things to each other. If we extrapolate from condom sales, for example, we might assume we have an approximate count of how often men engage in ejaculatory forms of sex. Yet what can condom sales actually tell us? For example, what can we learn about men, masculinities, sexualities, and reproduction from the fact that sales are higher in Tokyo and Buenos Aires than they are in Topeka and Budapest? Without a local cultural perspective on the meanings of condom use in particular locales and without understanding global pharmaceutical marketing practices and their local impact, such comparisons are doomed to the realm of speculation far more than many researchers are comfortable admitting.

Traditional Men Approach Reproduction and Sexuality Differently Than Modern Men

The polarity of traditional/modern makes as much sense with respect to men as a group as does active/passive with regard to sexual behavior—that is, not very much at all. There is no such thing as a traditional man, and there never has been, despite the fact that the term is frequently used as shorthand to describe what is presumably a consistent set of attitudes and practices associated by the labeler as premodern—men who want many children or men who do not utilize some form of modern, artificial birth control. Among the many problems with this formulation is that it is rooted in stereotypes of imagined social relations and ideologies from the past far more than it is grounded in actual knowledge of these phenomena. To speak of traditional men implies they come from a changeless and uniform cultural milieu, in comparison to those men involved in the rapidly transforming "modern world."

This traditional/modern man dichotomization is particularly harmful for the analysis of men, sexuality, and reproduction. It easily can lead to false assumptions about men's sexual relations with women (some might describe a man as sexually traditional if he shows little concern for women's sexual pleasure) or why men may not practice birth control (it might be held that traditional men are less willing to use certain forms of contraception). Such a conceptual framework fails to incorporate diversity, change, and contestation among the very populations we modernists too haphazardly brand as traditional, even as we make unwarranted assumptions regarding the sexual proclivities and practices of our own families and friends.

We await a well-grounded study of the modern sex habits of members of university communities.

Sometimes a Cigar Is Just a Cigar

Sadly, this is no longer the case and not simply owing to the indiscretions of Bill Clinton and Monica Lewinsky. When writing of women and female bodily realities, Simone de Beauvoir inadvertently taught us something about male bodies and fixed destinies. Assumptions about men's bodies and sexuality, reproduction, and masculinity have remained surprisingly overdetermined in subsequent decades of feminist scholarship on gender and sexuality. So perhaps we need to return a bit not only to de Beauvoir but even to Sigmund Freud, who still might have a thing or two to teach us about not following biomedicalized models of male sexualities, reproduction, and masculinities. (And, no, one must not overlook the fact that Freud, in his characteristically self-contradictory fashion, also helped to promote active men and passive women and cigars that never could be smoked.) We might remember that the physics and chemistry of sex do not tell us very much about desire and pleasure, or even domination and submission, the very issues that have everything to do with understanding men's sexualities and reproductive lives—or at least they should.

Acknowledgments

My gratitude to the editors of this volume for the invitation to participate in this exciting collection. Apologies and thanks to Eduardo Galeano for cribbing the subtitle of his 1982 essay, "Literatura y cultura popular en América Latina: Diez errores o mentiras frecuentes." I have learned from fertile dialogues about masculinity, sexuality, and reproduction over the years (some many, some few), with Ana Amuchástegui, Philippe Bourgois, Stanley Brandes, Carole Browner, Sylvia Chant, Raewyn Connell, Benno de Keijzer, Orlandina de Oliveira, Gil Herdt, Michael Higgins, Marcia Inhorn, Michael Kimmel, Roger Lancaster, José Olavarría, Richard Parker, Lynn Stephen, and Mara Viveros. Thanks to all. Robin Tittle kindly tracked down some material for this and other projects. Funding for my research on vasectomies, AIDS, and men's reproductive health in Oaxaca, Mexico, has been generously provided by a fellowship from the National Endowment for the Humanities and various small faculty grants from Brown University. An earlier version of this essay appears in Gutmann 2007.

Notes

1. She goes on to argue that such biological facts "are insufficient for setting up a hierarchy of the sexes; they fail to explain why woman is the Other; they do not condemn her to remain in this subordinate role forever" (de Beauvoir 1970 [1949]:29).
2. On the relation of feminism to masculinity studies, see the fine collection by Gardiner (2002).
3. I do not count advice columns in skin magazines as a scholarly venue.
4. To be sure, in the present discussion of men's sexuality and reproduction, the case of the hijras may be inherently problematic because hijras do not define themselves as heterosexual but see themselves as neither men nor women. Nonetheless, of those born male, some undergo castration, and it is this process that Nanda and others like Cohen (1995) discuss in relation to sexuality, sexual desire, and sexual pleasure, which is relevant here. See also Higgins and Coen (2000) on similar issues raised by transvestite prostitutes in Oaxaca, Mexico.
5. Freud (1962 [1905]) of course coined the term "polymormously perverse disposition" to reveal, among other things, that human sexuality does not begin with puberty but can be found throughout infantile experiences as well.
6. See also Greenhalgh's discussion of population studies (1990, 1996).
7. In addition to Ginsburg and Rapp (1995), see especially Browner (2000), Browner and Sargent (1996), and Clarke (1998).
8. For extensive bibliographies regarding fatherhood in the social sciences, see Townsend (2002) and Marsiglio and Pleck (2005).
9. And if we cannot treat heterosexuality as a singular entity, what of heteronormativity? Can we speak of heteronormativit*ies*?
10. Carrillo (2002) is one of the exceptions to this generalization, as his study deftly explores sexuality among men and women, straights and gays, in Guadalajara, Mexico, in the time of AIDS. In my own work I have possibly too often focused on men, though I have always tried to incorporate as central to the study of masculinities the ideas and experiences of women in their relationships with men. See, for instance, Gutmann 1997, 2003, 2005, 2006, 2007.
11. The activities of men in certain tribal societies during their wives' pregnancies and the births of their children—known in the anthropological literature as "couvade"—has received periodic and limited attention. See, for instance, Munroe, Munroe, and Whiting (1973) and Paige and Paige (1981).
12. On anthropological studies of infertility more generally, see also Inhorn and van Balen (2002). For the best anthropological demography collection to date on men and fertility, see Bledsoe, Lerner, and Guyer (2000).
13. One possible exception is the literature on circumcision. See, for example, the discussions of circumcision in Bloch (1986), Heald (1999), and Bilu (2000).

14. And when it is, a condition known as priapism, this is cause for imme-
    diate medical attention.
15. It would be interesting to know if men's depictions and rationalizations
    of their presence at strip clubs would be different when reported to
    other men or even women who were not themselves strippers, includ-
    ing with respect to feelings of control over women.
16. Though as Laqueur (1990) has famously shown, for a long time in
    Europe it was believed that in order to conceive, women too had to
    orgasm.
17. For a pioneering collection on the anthropology of contraception, see
    Russell, Sobo, and Thompson (2000).
18. Regarding research for a male hormone pill, see Oudshoorn (1994,
    2003, 2004). At this juncture, many researchers have concluded that
    the development of male contraception that does not simultaneously
    help prevent sexually transmitted infections would be irresponsible.
19. For more on research regarding male contraception, see Marsiglio
    (1998:75–85).
20. For a recent collection critiquing evolutionary-psychology models of
    rape, see Travis (2003) and especially articles by Kimmel (2003) and
    Martin (2003). For a discussion of the Darwinian origins of modern
    thinking about men's sexual nature, see Lancaster (2003:86–90).
21. An exception here is the work of Jennifer Hirsch (2003).
22. For exceptions, see Hart (1994) and Brennan (2004).

References

Barbosa, Regina Maria, and Tania Di Giacomo do Lago. 1997. "AIDS e dire-
    itos reprodutivos: para além da transmissão vertical." In *Políticas, Institu-
    ições e AIDS: Enfrentando a Epidemia no Brasil*, ed. Richard Parker. Rio de
    Janeiro: Jorge Zahar.
Barbosa, Regina Maria, and Wilza Viera Villela. 1997. "A Trajetória Feminia
    da AIDS." In *Quebrando o silêncio: Mulheres e AIDS no Brasil*, ed. Richard
    Parker and Jane Galvão. Rio de Janeiro: Relume-Dumará Editores.
Bilu, Yoram. 2000. "Circumcision, the First Haircut and the Torah: Ritual
    and Male Identity Among the Ultraorthodox Community of Israel." In
    Imagined Masculinities: Male Identity and Culture in the Modern Middle East,
    ed. Mai Ghoussoub and Emma Sinclair-Webb. London: Saqi Books.
Bledsoe, Caroline, Susana Lerner, and Jane I. Guyer, eds. 2000. *Fertility and
    the Male Life Cycle in the Era of Fertility Decline*. Oxford: Oxford University
    Press.
Bloch, Maurice. 1986. *From Blessing to Violence: History and Ideology in the Cir-
    cumcision Ritual of the Merina of Madagascar*. Cambridge: Cambridge Uni-
    versity Press.
Brennan, Denise. 2004. *What's Love Got to Do with It? Transnational Desires and
    Sex Tourism in the Dominican Republic*. Durham: Duke University Press.
Browner, Carole. 2000. "Situating Women's Reproductive Activities." *Amer-
    ican Anthropologist* 102(4):773–88.

Browner, Carole H., and Carolyn F. Sargent. 1996. "Anthropology and Studies of Human Reproduction." In *Medical Anthropology: Contemporary Theory and Method*, ed. Carolyn F. Sargent and Thomas M. Johnson. Westport, CT: Greenwood.

Carrillo, Héctor. 2002. *The Night Is Young: Sexuality in Mexico in the Time of AIDS*. Chicago: University of Chicago Press.

Chant, Sylvia, and Matthew C. Gutmann. 2000. *Mainstreaming Men into Gender and Development: Debates, Reflections, and Experiences*. Oxford: Oxfam.

Chodorow, Nancy. 1994. *Femininities, Masculinities, Sexualities: Freud and Beyond*. Lexington: University of Kentucky Press.

Clarke, Adele E. 1998. *Disciplining Reproduction: Modernity, American Life Sciences, and "The Problem of Sex."* Chicago: University of Chicago Press.

Cohen, Lawrence. 1995. "The Pleasures of Castration: The Postoperative Status of Hijras, Hankhas, and Academics." In *Sexual Nature Sexual Culture*, ed. Paul R. Abramson and Steven D. Pinkerton. Chicago: University of Chicago Press.

Connell, R. W. 1997. "Sexual Revolution." In *New Sexual Agendas*, ed. Lynne Segal. New York: New York University Press.

Cornwall, Andrea A. 2003. "To Be a Man Is More Than a Day's Work: Shifting Ideals of Masculinity in Ado-Odo, Southwestern Nigeria." In *Men and Masculinities in Modern Africa*, ed. Lisa A. Lindsay and Stephan F. Miescher. Portsmouth, NH: Heinemann.

de Beauvoir, Simone. 1970 [1949]. *The Second Sex*. Trans. H. M. Parshely. New York: Bantam Books.

Dudgeon, Matthew R., and Marcia C. Inhorn. 2003. "Gender, Masculinity, and Reproduction: Anthropological Perspectives." *International Journal of Men's Health* 2(1):31–56.

Fausto-Sterling, Anne. 2000. *Sexing the Body: Gender Politics and the Construction of Sexuality*. New York: Basic Books.

Foucault, Michel. 1980. *The History of Sexuality: Volume I: An Introduction*. Trans. Robert Hurley. New York: Vintage.

Frank, Katherine. 2003. *G-Strings and Sympathy: Strip Club Regulars and Male Desire*. Durham: Duke University Press.

Freud, Sigmund. 1962 [1905]. *Three Essays on the Theory of Sexuality.* Trans. James Strachey. New York: Basic Books.

Galeano, Eduardo. 1982. "Literatura y cultura popular en América Latina: Diez errores o mentiras frecuentes." In *La cultura popular*, ed. Adolfo Colobres. Tlahuapan, Puebla, Mexico: Porrúa.

Gardiner, Judith Kegan, ed. 2002. *Masculinity Studies and Feminist Theory: New Directions*. New York: Columbia University Press.

Giddens, Anthony. 1983. *Studies in Social and Political Theory*. London: Hutchinson.

Ginsburg, Faye D., and Rayna Rapp. 1995. "Conceiving the New World Order." In *Conceiving the New World Order: The Global Politics of Reproduction*, ed. Faye D. Ginsburg and Rayna Rapp. Berkeley: University of California Press.

Greene, Margaret E., and Ann E. Biddlecom. 2000. "Absent and Problematic Men: Demographic Accounts of Male Reproductive Roles." *Population and Development Review* 26(1):81–115.

Greenhalgh, Susan. 1990. "Toward a Political Economy of Fertility: Anthropological Contributions." *Population and Development Review* 16(1):85–106.

———. 1996. "The Social Construction of Population Science: An Intellectual, Institutional, and Political History of Twentieth-Century Demography." *Comparative Studies in Society and History* 38(1):26–66.

Gutmann, Matthew C. 1997. "The Ethnographic (G)Ambit: Women and the Negotiation of Masculinity in Mexico City." *American Ethnologist* 24(4):833–55.

———. 2003. "Discarding Manly Dichotomies in Latin America." In *Changing Men and Masculinities in Latin America*, ed. Matthew C. Gutmann. Durham: Duke University Press.

———. 2005. "Scoring Men: Vasectomies and the Totemic Illusion of Male Sexuality in Oaxaca." *Culture, Medicine, and Psychiatry* 29(1):79–101.

———. 2006. *The Meanings of Macho: Being a Man in Mexico City.* 2nd ed. Berkeley: University of California Press.

———. 2007. *Fixing Men: Sex, Birth Control, and AIDS in Mexico.* Berkeley: University of California Press.

Hart, Angie. 1994. "Missing Masculinity? Prostitutes' Clients in Alicante, Spain." In *Dislocating Masculinity: Comparative Ethnographies*, ed. Andrea Cornwall and Nancy Lindisfarne. London: Routledge.

Heald, Suzette. 1999. *Manhood and Morality: Sex, Violence and Ritual in Gisu Society.* New York: Routledge.

Heider, Karl G. 1976. "Dani Sexuality: A Low Energy System." Man (N.S.) 11:188–201.

Higgins, Michael J., and Tanya L. Coen. 2000. *Streets, Bedrooms, and Patios: The Ordinariness of Diversity in Urban Oaxaca: Ethnographic Portraits of the Street Kids, Urban Poor, Transvestites, Discapacitados, and Other Popular Cultures.* Austin: University of Texas Press.

Hirsch, Jennifer S. 2003. *A Courtship after Marriage: Sexuality and Love in Mexican Transnational Families.* Berkeley: University of California Press.

Inhorn, Marcia C. 2002. "Sexuality, Masculinity, and Infertility in Egypt: Potent Troubles in the Marital and Medical Encounters." *Journal of Men's Studies* 10(3):343–59.

———. 2003 "'The Worms Are Weak': Male Infertility and Patriarchal Paradoxes in Egypt." *Men & Masculinities* 5(3):236–56.

———. 2004. "Middle Eastern Masculinities in the Age of New Reproductive Technologies: Male Infertility and Stigma in Egypt and Lebanon." *Medical Anthropology Quarterly* 18(2):162–82.

Inhorn, Marcia C., and Frank van Balen, eds. 2002. *Infertility around the Globe: New Thinking on Childlessness, Gender, and Reproductive Technologies.* Berkeley: University of California Press.

Kahn, Susan Martha. 2000. *Reproducing Jews: A Cultural Account of Assisted Conception in Israel.* Durham: Duke University Press.

Kimmel, Michael S. 1994. "Masculinity as Homophobia: Fear, Shame, and Silence in the Construction of Gender Identity." In *Theorizing Masculinities*, ed. Harry Brod and Michael Kaufman. Thousand Oaks, CA: Sage.

———. 2003. "An Unnatural History of Rape." In *Evolution, Gender, and Rape*, ed. Cheryl Brown Travis. Cambridge: MIT Press.

Laqueur, Thomas. 1990. *Making Sex: Body and Gender from the Greeks to Freud.* Cambridge: Harvard University Press.

Marsiglio, William. 1998. *Procreative Man.* New York: New York University Press.

Marsiglio, William, and Joseph H. Pleck. 2005. "Fatherhood and Masculinities." In *Handbook of Studies on Men and Masculinities*, ed. Michael S. Kimmel, Jeff Hearn, and R. W. Connell. Thousand Oaks, CA: Sage.

Martin, Emily. 2003 "What Is 'Rape'? Toward a Historical, Ethnographic Approach." In *Evolution, Gender, and Rape*, ed. Cheryl Brown Travis. Cambridge: MIT Press.

Munroe, Robert L., Ruth H. Munroe, and John W. M. Whiting. 1973. "The Couvade: A Psychological Analysis." *Ethos* 1:30–74.

Nanda, Serena. 1990. *Neither Man nor Woman: The Hijras of India.* Belmont, CA: Wadsworth.

Oudshoorn, Nelly. 1994. *Beyond the Natural Body: An Archaeology of Sex Hormones.* New York: Routledge.

———. 2003. *The Male Pill: A Biography of a Technology in the Making.* Durham: Duke University Press.

———. 2004. "'Astronauts in the Sperm World': The Renegotiation of Masculine Identities in Discourses on Male Contraceptives." *Men and Masculinities* 6(4):349–67.

Paige, Karen E., and Jeffery M. Paige. 1981. *The Politics of Reproductive Ritual.* Berkeley: University of California Press.

Parker, Richard. 1999. *Beneath the Equator: Cultures of Desire, Male Homosexuality, and Emerging Gay Communities in Brazil.* New York: Routledge.

———. 2003. "Changing Sexualities: Masculinity and Male Homosexuality in Brazil." In *Changing Men and Masculinities in Latin America*, ed. Matthew C. Gutmann. Durham: Duke University Press.

Rich, Adrienne. 1993 [1982]. "Compulsory Heterosexuality and Lesbian Existence." Reprinted in *Culture, Society and Sexuality: A Reader*, ed. Richard Parker and Peter Aggleton. London: UCL Press.

Rubin, Gayle. 1975. "The Traffic in Women: Notes on the 'Political Economy' of Sex." In *Toward an Anthropology of Women*, ed. Rayna Reiter. New York: Monthly Review.

———. 1999 [1984]. "Thinking Sex: Notes for a Radical Theory of the Politics of Sexuality." Reprinted in *Culture, Society and Sexuality: A Reader*, ed. Richard Parker and Peter Aggleton. London: UCL Press.

Russell, Andrew, Elisa J. Sobo, and Mary S. Thompson, eds. 2000. *Contraception Across Cultures: Technologies, Choices, Constraints.* Oxford: Berg.

Sargent, Carolyn F., and Caroline B. Brettell, eds. 1996. *Gender and Health: An International Perspective.* Upper Saddle River, NJ: Prentice Hall.

Scheper-Hughes, Nancy. 1994. "Embodied Knowledge: Thinking with the Body in Critical Medical Anthropology." In *Assessing Cultural Anthropology*, ed. Robert Borofsky. New York: McGraw-Hill.

Schneider, Jane C., and Peter T. Schneider. 1996. *Festival of the Poor: Fertility Decline and the Ideology of Class in Sicily, 1860–1980.* Tucson: University of Arizona Press.

Segal, Lynne. 1994. *Straight Sex: Rethinking the Politics of Pleasure*. Berkeley: University of California Press.

———, ed. 1997. *New Sexual Agendas*. New York: New York University Press.

Townsend, Nicholas W. 2002. *The Package Deal: Marriage, Work and Fatherhood in Men's Lives*. Philadelphia: Temple University Press.

Travis, Cheryl Brown, ed. 2003. *Evolution, Gender, and Rape*. Cambridge: MIT Press.

United Nations. 2003. "World Contraceptive Use 2003." www.un.org/esa/population/publications/contraceptive2003/WCU2003.htm.

Vance, Carole. 1999 [1991]. "Anthropology Rediscovers Sexuality: A Theoretical Comment." Reprinted in *Culture, Society and Sexuality: A Reader*, ed. Richard Parker and Peter Aggleton. London: UCL Press.

Viveros Vigoya, Mara. 2002. *De quebradores y cumplidores: Sobre hombres, masculinidades y relaciones de género en Colombia*. Bogotá: Universidad Nacional de Colombia.

Wright, Robert. 1994. *The Moral Animal: Evolutionary Psychology and Everyday Life*. New York: Vintage Books.

Chapter 2

KILLER SPERM: MASCULINITY AND THE ESSENCE OF MALE HIERARCHIES

Lisa Jean Moore

Seminal Proliferations: The Shattering Release

A normal healthy man makes as many as 1,500 sperm a second. That's 90,000 a minute; 5.4 million an hour; 130 million a day; almost 50 billion a year. At that rate, it would take no more than a fortnight for that one man to make a sperm for every fertile woman on the planet. The world's men produce up to 286,000,000,000,000,000 sperm a day: if you could stop the little blighters from wriggling and align them all end-to-end, the line would stretch for many millions of kilometers—enough to encircle the Equator thousands of times or to reach further than the Sun.

—Bob Beale, Australian science writer, www.bob.beale.org

Sperm and spermatic imagery abound in scientific, cultural, and political arenas. As the above quote illustrates, there appears to be endless fascination with the real or imagined capabilities of this proliferating and endless resource. Although semen is understood in biological terms as a mixture of prostaglandin, fructose, fatty acids, and one percent sperm cells, there are numerous other ways to understand this substance. Though it can be seen as technology and commodity (Moore and Schmidt 1999), biology textbooks describe it as a sexual aggressor (Martin 1991), children's books as a "friendly tadpole" (Moore 2003), sex workers as "hazardous waste material" (Moore 1997), and DNA forensic texts as "proof of crime" and "little soldiers" (Moore and Durkin 2004). This chapter is a part of a larger quest to create a formal, grounded theory of semen as multiply constructed in our social worlds (Moore 2007).

Often, these representations of semen socially reproduce the existing gendered and raced power structures from which they emerge. Increased knowledge about and control over sperm is dialectically related to cultural anxieties about heterogeneous definitions of masculinity within the West (particularly the United States) during the twentieth and twenty-first centuries. There is traffic among scientific realms of sperm science, popular expressions of men's changing social, political, and economic positions, and social and health policies that attempt to maintain a limited definition of fatherhood. This chapter explores sperm's reproductive trajectory within the discourse of biological sciences and infertility industries. First, I briefly situate my work within a theoretical framework of feminist science and technology studies as well as within masculinity studies. I define and describe what I mean by the term "masculinity crisis." Next, I outline my methodology. The remainder of the chapter offers an analysis of history of sperm as a cultural, scientific, and reproductive object read in juxtaposition to recent scholarship and popular accounts lamenting the decline of male dominance and changing ideals about masculinity.

Theoretical Backdrop: Masculinity Studies and Scientific Representations

> Masculinity is realized here not as a monolithic entity, but as an interplay of emotional and intellectual factors—an interplay that directly implicates women as well as men, and is mediated by other social factors, including race, sexuality, nationality and class (Berger, Wallis, and Watson 1995:3).

Masculinity studies encompasses the work of certain interdisciplinary scholars who aim to disturb the taken-for-granted and essential notions of masculinity as arising from obviously "natural" male bodies. Guided by masculinity studies, I continue to examine how gender emerges from the "natural" fluids of men and the "natural gendered order" (Moore 2007; Moore and Durkin 2004). Gender is represented in scientific narrative by relying on tropes and

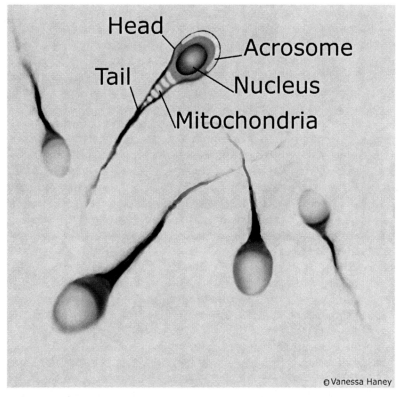

Figure 2.1. Digital image of sperm cells. By Vanessa Haney. Used with permission.

metaphors from fables, traditional stories, and familiar imagery. I view sperm and semen representations as both signifiers and speech acts of different types of masculinity, such as the fierce competitor, the benevolent father, the impotent wimp, the good catch, and the masculine threat, to name a few.

Although it is possible that the masculinity represented by sperm exists in real-lived human experiences (both male and female), these representations also are ideal types of masculinity begging for a performance. The definition of masculinity is not concrete, consistent, and fixed; because members of society participate in multiple, ongoing interactions within the contours of masculinity and femininity, this process is fluid and changes depending on historical circumstances. The images or representations are sometimes unintentionally meant to instruct or incite actual men and women. Thus, there is assumed traffic between the ideal type of masculinity and the performance of it. In other words, the normative conceptions of masculinity are simultaneously produced and consumed by the public (many of whom are men), and in turn this public performs its masculinity in light of these normative conceptions.

Although there are many versions of masculinity, not all masculinity is created equal. R. W. Connell, an Australian men's studies scholar, has coined the term "hegemonic masculinity" to refer to a type of masculinity dialectically constructed in relation to subordinate masculinity and femininity. This ascendancy of hegemonic masculinity is supported by the social structures in which masculinity is embedded—religion, politics, urban space, and popular culture. Hegemonic masculinity helps to explain that though different images of sperm and semen exist in different social worlds, thus producing different versions of masculinity, some of these versions elevate certain types of men—heterosexual, white, middle class, reproductive, monogamous men, above women and other types of men—homosexual, of color, lower class, nonprocreative or sterile, and nonmonogamous.

In addition to the masculinities literature, I situate my work within the scholarship of social/cultural studies of science and technology studies and medicine (STS&M). Within this realm, there has been considerable interest in representations over the past decade. Visual images have been particularly useful in the construction of the kinds of objectivities central to modern Western sciences. Feminist analyses of the work of images in science begin from both different and similar premises. The difference is that feminists, among whom I situate myself, centrally locate sex, gender, and sexuality (Braidotti 1997). The similarity is that feminists and others examine how the activities of scientists are organized, produced, and manufactured as products of the so-called objective knowledge. Distinctively, feminists ask how visual and textual images may benefit science and scientists, how images of masculinity or femininity may rely on existing power differentials between the sexes or races, and how sciences intervene in gender; for example, by providing new ways of "doing" masculine and feminine (West and Zimmerman 1987).

In my near-decade of researching sperm representations, I have been intrigued by the changing role of men in our society. With both fascination and irritation, I read pop culture's accounts of how men have suffered from the feminist movement, especially the women's self-help health movement. Frustrated young men in my women's studies classes often exclaim how confusing everyday life has become due in part to feminism, expressing concerns ranging from employment to childrearing and, most important, dating. Movies like *Fight Club* (1999) or popular books such as *Stiffed: The Betrayal of the American Man* (Faludi 1999) and *The War Against Boys: How Misguided Feminism Is Harming Our Young Men* (Hoff-Sommers 2000) are trendy illustrations of masculinity repositioned. Several connections can be made between the increased knowledge about and control over sperm and the cultural anxiety men experience in contemporary societies.

Through my use of STS&M, I explore how sperm becomes a kind of elixir that helps to generate not only "life" through reproduction (and technology) but also whole sets of social practices in the realms of science and gender relations. The power of reproductive sciences to thereby *naturalize* hierarchical social relations is considerable because of their privileged epistemological position as "official" knowledge. In interpreting the ways sperm cells are deployed by differently interested actors and institutions, my work interrogates the dialectics of the consequences (intended and unintended) of manipulating sperm and the perpetual legitimation crises of masculinities in the twenty-first century. What I mean by legitimation crises of masculinities is how the terms of what it is to be legitimately masculine are volatile and consistently verified, challenged, and regulated. As knowledge about and technological manipulation of men's bodies—particularly their fluids—changes, the terms of what is considered a legitimate masculinity must adapt.[1]

Examining scientific renderings of sperm, my work intends to expose the essence of male hierarchies. Remarkably, these gendered hierarchies are inherently unstable *and* self-sustaining. In other words, it is amazing how gender hierarchies are ubiquitous and enduring while constantly in crisis. Changes in social structure and social relationships are constantly attempting to redefine what it means to be a man and what constitutes the realm of legitimate masculinity.

Methodology

Focusing my analytic lens on sperm provides interesting perspectives to interpreting how sperm "is spent," "reabsorbed," "swims," "spurts," "careens," and "crashes" through ducts, penises, vaginas, test tubes, labs, families, culture, and politics. I understand semen as a boundary object (Star and Griesemer 1989)—that is, the same object, semen, is brought into different arenas, and its flexibility allows it to be used for local purposes and inscribed with local meaning by different social worlds (Clarke 1991). Meanings about semen accrue through practices and uses, and these meanings blend into one another.

Although this study does not claim to be exhaustive or representative of the entire realm of semen science, I attempt to gather and triangulate data from a range of sources. Data sources include scientific historical documents of biomedical discovery and recasting of sperm and semen (c. 1600–2004, written in or translated into English), discourse about the fatherhood rights movement (1970s), and narrative evidence of the traffic between biological accounts of sperm and social accounts of men, through weblogs and popular texts. Dimensions were interrogated, such as the description of sperm or semen, the frequency of references to sperm, the verbs used to animate sperm, and images of sperm. Furthermore, as the president of the board of directors of a sperm bank for six years in the 1990s, I have tremendous fieldwork experiences (however, I was not an active researcher during that time for reasons of patient confidentiality).

These data are analyzed based on a modified-grounded theory methodology.[2] According to Anselm Strauss, a key developer of grounded theory, it is through one's immersion in the data that these comparisons become the "stepping stones" for formal theories of patterns of action and interaction between and among various types of data. By triangulating data sources about sperm representations over the past ten years (scientific texts, health and social policy recommendations, children's books, popular accounts, and semen-banking practices and promotional materials), I am able to establish various points of comparison to explore multiple concepts about sperm in different environments. Working with my analytic memos written about these sperm representations, I am able to establish interrelationships between concepts. "Theory evolves during actual research, and it does this through continuous interplay between analysis and data collection" (Strauss and Corbin 1994:273). My methodology combines grounded-theory techniques with content and discourse analysis as a way to develop theoretically rich explanations and interpretations of semen. In this fashion, I am able to track both the frequency of certain terms and representations as well as the interpretative meaning and significance of these images. Similar to other qualitative research, content analysis can be *exploratory* and *descriptive*, enabling limited insight into why significant relationships or trends occur. The aim is not toward standardization of facts into scientific units, but rather an appreciation and play with the range of variation of a particular phenomenon. Outliers, representations that do not fall neatly into the most common themes and concepts, are useful because they enable analysts to capture the range of variation and dimensions of the concepts. This process builds an understanding of the diversity of human experience, such as the range and significance of spermatic representations in science as illustrated below.

Scientific Production of Sperm

Many of the earliest sperm scientists (predominantly men) envisioned semen as the key to reproduction; sperm was a cell embodying a preformed individual, the homunculus. These scientists marveled at the sperm cells' powerful agency and self-contained role in reproduction. However, through the "progress" of technological and scientific innovation and the skillful manipulation of semen, sperm cells become merely raw materials that can be technologically procured, amplified, and even "programmed" for predictability.

Harnessing the potential of semen has been pursued in biomedicine for over four centuries. In 1550, Bartholomeus Eustacus recommended that a husband guide his semen toward his wife's cervix with his finger in order to enhance the couple's chances of conception; this was the first recorded suggestion in Western medical literature that humans could control their reproductive capabilities by manipulating semen. But this suggestion was made without the aid of a microscope or other scientific understandings about semen and sperm. Some of the first scientific ideas about the form and function of sperm were developed in the seventeenth century. This theory of preformation asserts that within each primordial organism resides a miniature, but fully developed, organism of the same species. Clara Pinto-Correia, a Portuguese biologist, analyzes the origins of embryology by reviewing competing theories of preformation, spermism versus ovism (1997). Battles between the ovists—those who believed the preformed entity is in the egg, and spermists—those who believed the preformed entity is in the sperm cell, are highlighted to depict different scientific constructions of how these cells embodied individual replicants of humans. Pinto-Correia ties these scientific advances to religious doctrines and social practices of the time whereas "both the old and New Testament seemed to agree on God's profound distaste for any hint of sperm waste. By the seventeenth century, these brief passages from scripture had echoed in Western morals in numerous invasive and influential ways, so the issue was certainly not to be treated lightheartedly" (80).[3]

Within many academic and social worlds, the spermists were considered the victors in the battle. This resulted in the seventeenth-century belief that women were "mere vessels" in the case of human reproduction. By the nineteenth century, the consequences were also significant for men, as writers believed in what historian Barker-Benfield has called the "spermatic economy," in which men were to exercise sexual restraint lest they waste and damage their seed and deplete their physical integrity. Although medieval and early modern clerics interpreting the biblical story of Onan found the fruitless "spilling of seed" to be a capital crime, the scientific validation of the spermatic economy accounts, in part, for the proliferation of antimasturbation tactics in nineteenth-century Western civilization. A Swiss physician, Samuel Tissot, took the exclusively medical view, arguing that the unnatural loss of semen weakened mind and body and led to masturbatory insanity (his book, published in 1758, was reprinted in 1905). Furthermore, the laws of the "spermatic economy" accorded that masturbation would take away from the impulse to perform the civilizing work that was the true manly calling. Contemporarily, this belief about semen loss reverberates in admonitions to athletes to abstain from sex before games, as depletion of semen is depletion of energy and vitality.

In the 1670s, a single scientific innovation—the invention of the microscope—revolutionized the natural sciences and provided an entirely new perspective for semen scientists. Antoni van Leeuwenhoek and his medical student Mr. Ham were able to define sperm cells as based on physical observation. Leeuwenhoek's own description of spermatozoa, or animalcules, as he called them, indicates his excitement about this breakthrough, as he marvels at the effort spermatozoa make to move minuscule spaces.

> Immediately after ejaculation . . . I have seen so great a number that . . . I judged a million of them would not equal in size a large grain of sand. They were furnished with a thin tail, about 5 or 6 times as long as the body, and very transparent and with the thickness of about one twenty-fifth that of the body. They moved forwards owning the motion to their tails like that of a snake or an eel swimming in water; but in the somewhat thicker substance they would lash their tails at least 8 or 10 times before they could advance a hair's breadth (Leeuwenhoek, as quoted in Kempers 1976: 63).

This first scientific description of sperm, "the discovery," is linked to phallic imagery of snakes and eels swimming furiously rather than, for example, cells rhythmically undulating. In 1694, building on Leeuwenhoek's work, researcher Nicholas Hartsoeker theorized the umbilical cord was born from the tail of the spermatozoa and that the fetus sprouted from the head of a sperm cell embedded in the uterus (Spark 1988). It was not until 1824 that it was discovered that animalcules, or small cells in seminal fluid, fertilized female eggs.

During the 1930s, again through use of microscopes, G. L. Moench named fifty variations in sperm morphology with terms such as microsperm, megalosperm, puff-ball type of cell, and double neck. In his *Human Sex Anatomy* (1949), well-known reproductive researcher Henry Latou Dickinson describes semen as "a fluid that is grayish white rather than milky; upon ejaculation its consistency resembles a mucilage or thin jelly which liquefies somewhat within three minutes after emission, later becoming sticky" (81). The linguistic cues about sperm are working on the cultural and historical understandings of masculinity. For example, Dickinson assures readers that semen is not "milky"—perhaps suggesting breast fluid—but that it is a "mucilage" or strong adherent substance.

From these humble beginnings, semen representations and manipulations have proliferated from the "low-tech" donor insemination, intracervical, or intrauterine, to the "high-tech" intracytoplasmic sperm injection (ICSI), where a single sperm cell is injected into an oocyte. The parameters of semen analysis from the original microscopic visions have expanded and now include volume, pH, viscosity, sperm density, sperm motility, viability, and sperm morphology. Each technological conception of semen enables new disciplinary and scientific strategies to further measure, define, control, and use sperm. It is necessary to stress how these innovations of human sperm are not isolated events but part of sweeping technical innovations and interventions into human reproduction. Typically, women bear the brunt and the blame of infertility treatments, but male bodies can be impacted in reproductive sciences (Mason 1993).

Many of the innovations in sperm research emerge from an attempt to understand the medicalized condition of male infertility, generally defined as less than twenty million/ml sperm density. In 1929, scientists Macomber and Sanders developed "spermatozoa count," or sperm count, as the first diagnostic tool to be used in the detection of male infertility. However, social mores were an obstacle to efficient scientific research on sperm, as was historically the case in the reproductive sciences (Clarke 1998). From 1930 to 1945, masturbation was not an acceptable method for collecting semen samples; thus, scientists had to collect samples through the use of rubber or skin condoms used during intercourse. Historically, sperm count has been used as an evaluation of infertility in men, however, "this no longer is sufficient, for recent advances in endocrinology, genetics, immunology and embryology have established a broader base for the differential diagnosis of male infertility" (Spark 1988:126). Imaging technologies, such as electron microscopes and other devices, create new opportunities to produce scientific knowledge (often read as truth) about sperm. For example, biochemists can measure the components of human seminal plasma; one textbook lists thirty-five different elements with referent anatomical production mechanism (Adelman and Cahill 1989).

Through innovation, technical manipulation of semen is accompanied by well-crafted, value-laden discourses about the product (sperm) and its producers (men). The Internet provides a new venue for sperm representations and explanations of high-tech fertility services. Using the pull-down menu of variables depicted on the California Cryobank's Web site, individuals are encouraged to concoct a dream daddy composed of the most desirable characteristics imaginable. Of course, this individual's sperm may not be available, but visitors are enticed to fantasize about that perfect semen sample to produce a gifted, attractive, and healthy baby—one that seems to precisely mirror social stratification writ large. So how does the possibility of creating a downloadable dream daddy further exacerbate the crises in masculinity? Social actors, such as physicians, health policy officials, and politicians, who in effect preserve existing gendered hierarchies and hegemonic masculinity, create policies and procedures that keep certain men from participating in semen banking (e.g., those of short stature [below 5'10"], high school dropouts, or those who have had sex with men since 1979). Thus, certain aspects of gendered hierarchies are retained during types of social changes in biological reproduction—the tall, well-educated, heterosexual man.

To continue the escalation of crisis, the emergence of new players into the assisted reproductive technologies enterprise creates new social changes threatening existing power relations. ManNotIncluded.com, a British sperm virtual marketplace, is the latest and perhaps most transparent of alterative reproductive practices. Although the manipulation, marketing, and merchandizing of sperm to serve clients' needs and desires is not new, the deliberate and unequivocal nonnormative promotion is.[4] Truly transgressive to the social and biological reproductive narratives, this service boasts that over 5,500 anonymous male donors and over 3,000 single women and lesbians have been registered for potential matches and future inseminations. But the service has not been without controversy; as Josephine Quintavalle, director of Comment on Reproductive Ethics, urged, "The whole idea must be vigorously resisted, and men must see this initiative for what it is—yet another attack on their role in society. The male must not be reduced to a vial of anonymous sperm, and the rights of children to enjoy real fathers must be protected."[5] Ironically, the technological innovation that enabled "infertile" men to reproduce is exploited to eliminate certain men from the same process.

As the above example illustrates, perceived assaults on hegemonic masculinity often lead to adaptations in social practices, which in effect maintain dominant hierarchies. By allowing only some men to give sperm, other men are ranked as inferior or lacking masculinity. But how has sperm emerged as a reproductive actor? By beginning with scientific representations of semen, not only can we witness the "discovery" of sperm, but we also can recognize that this discovery is embedded within tropes of masculinity.

In sum, the act of discovering and refining "sperm" and "semen" is a contextually and temporally situated activity. As demonstrated above, the interpretations of historical renderings of sperm by scientists represented sperm and men as primarily, if not singularly, powerhouses of procreation. As sperm science moves through time and men become more knowable and masculinity reconfigured, representations of sperm change but retain historical imagery. How sperm becomes known is based on who defines it, under what social circumstances, and for what purposes.

Do Speed and Shape Really Matter?

The demands and expectations that men and their fertility provide awesome reproductive possibilities appear in a variety of cultural artifacts, including Genesis 9: "And God blessed Noah and his sons, and said unto them, Be fruitful, and multiply, and replenish the earth." Intensified efforts to scientifically comprehend human semen appear to be within the evolutionary logic of scientific progress, whereby the truth of semen is more clearly revealed and determined by biomedical science. Measuring and evaluating the shape and speed of sperm is one of a number of scientific mediations aimed at constructing the pathologies of sperm. One example of how knowing, naming, and diagnosing semen's pathological forms is produced in interaction with existing beliefs about "pathological" men is evident in an infertility textbook for medical practitioners. A chapter encompassing sophisticated techniques for medically managing infertility is titled "Coping with the Hopelessly Infertile Man" (Spark 1988). The use of the terms "coping" and "hopeless" indicate the threat to masculinity that is assumed by the lack of fertility. For example, the pejorative vernacular of "shooting blanks" refers to men's inability to deliver live ammunition (fertile sperm) when using a gun (their penis).

There has been an ongoing debate in the fields of epidemiology, toxicology, and infertility regarding the increasing rate of men's infertility, and men exposed to environmental and occupational toxins have reported consistently higher rates of infertility (Schrader, Turner, and Simon 1991; Whorton, Krauss, Marshall, and Milby 1977; Wyrobek et al. 1983). Using data from the 1930s through the 1990s, Caroline Cox's 1996 article "Masculinity at Risk" traces the decline in sperm counts of healthy men exposed to pesticides. In addition, a man's exposure to chemotherapy, ulcer, and blood-pressure medications, as well as alcohol, marijuana, and anabolic steroids, has been demonstrated as lowering sperm counts. Furthermore, scientific claims based on research from sixty-one studies indicate that lower sperm counts are prevalent in our global environment, which is riddled with toxic pollutants (Swan and Elkin 1999).

Similar to other social, physical, and environmental problems, solutions to male factor infertility have been pursued assiduously within the medical industrial complex and all of its affiliated biotechnological accessories. As a medicalized condition, curing the individual's body has been the main objective in overcoming infertility. Treatments of male infertility were originally not successful, and the rise of donor insemination was established as the most popular alternative to male-factor infertility for heterosexual couples. By using the fresh ejaculate of a fertile male or by freezing another male's semen, semen can be immediately used or reanimated for insertion into females. Of course, the use of fresh ejaculate is not as likely an option for most individuals, due to logistical and prevailing social and sexual health norms. For example, by 1990, in response to the AIDS crisis and the resulting hysteria, semen banks had adopted the six-month cryopreservation standard, now a requirement of the American Fertility Society's guidelines. This policy enabled the donor to be retested for HIV before releasing the semen for insemination purposes. Frozen semen has thus become the standard for donor insemination. Many research studies describe a cult of secrecy or shame around male infertility because of the link between infertility and a lack of masculinity (e.g., Bharadwaj 2003; Daly 1999; Lee 2003; Mason 1993; Nachtigall 1993; also see Tjørnhøj-Thomsen and Goldberg, both this volume).

There are interesting parallels to consider between reports of the global declines in sperm production and global masculinity "under threat." Discourse analysis demonstrates the ways popular accounts conflate male infertility with impotence, where a low sperm count is conflated with a lack of potency. A headline from *The Independent* attests: "Why today's man is losing his virility" (Gannon, Glover, and Abel 2004).

The two most common assessments of sperm's relative health are motility and morphology testing. Sperm motility can be measured quantitatively by counting the numbers of inactive sperm and/or qualitatively by assessing the type of movements sperm make. When describing motility, "The swimming velocity of sperm is just such that the hydrodynamic *drag* on the sperm body equals the flagellar *thrust*" (Katz 1991:416). The use of human ingenuity to measure the distance and speed of sperm movement has been remarkable. Some recent methods used to measure sperm motility have been kinematics of flagellar undulations, computerized method, laser doppler velocimetry, and microchip assessment. In his clinician's guidebook to diagnosing qualitative motility problems, Spark instructs that "sperm appear to move as if befuddled. They possess no purposeful forward motion and occasionally exhibit circular or erratic movement patterns" (1988:130).

If you were to microscopically examine a sample of semen from most men, you would find that the sperm are polymorphic, meaning that there are several different shapes and sizes of sperm cells. In addition to morphology, other parameters for semen analysis (Adelman and Cahill 1989) include volume, pH, viscosity, sperm density, sperm motility, and viability. So, do size and shape matter? Clearly, as the technology advances and scientists create new tools, size and shape may only be a problem for those without access to biomedical technologies. In sum, with this increased knowledge about and control over sperm (identifying and creating solutions to male factor infertility), the standard of what counts as masculinity has adapted.

One of the most innovative procedures available since 1992 (Beaubien 1995) is intracytoplasmic sperm injection (ICSI), which is performed by a physician selecting a sperm cell from the testes or epididymides for direct injection into the egg. Now subfertile men, as well as men with an infertility diagnosis, are able to participate in human reproduction. Notably, to bypass male infertility, the woman's body must be treated through implantation of embryos. It is important to note that due to ICSI, sperm count is no longer as significant a measurement of fertility in men. Men who historically might have been diagnosed as infertile or subfertile due to low sperm count now can contribute sperm to the formation of an embryo.

As I have read research on and popular accounts of ICSI, it was interesting to note the celebratory spin used to emphasize the impact of ICSI on infertile men. It is not unlike the marketing messages used in ads for Rogaine and Viagra: "Hallelujah, you too can feel like a man again." The widespread use of ICSI is considered by some sperm banks to be a potential threat to their livelihood. However, the advent of ICSI also could be seen as a boon to the sperm-banking industry. As experts in the cryopreservation of sperm, these banks could use ICSI as an opportunity to expand their range of services. Furthermore, this technology has the potential to make men unnecessary in reproduction. Based on the fact that cryopreserved sperm has no known expiration date, sperm banks across the globe have hundreds of thousands of vials of semen with millions of sperm cells encapsulated in each vial, and ICSI only requires one sperm cell per injection in ovum. The implication is that for the purpose of reproduction, actual men could be considered redundant. Of course, this interpretation of ICSI has revolutionary potential for the creation of families, the roles of men and women, and the organization of social power. How could actual men respond to this notion that previously procured sperm could be used to reproduce without them? Could this free-agent sperm cell now be a threat to actual men?

The discourse of paternal deprivation has been employed to create spurious social psychological correlations between a child's lack of relationship to the biological father to the child's individual suffering. Clearly, paternal deprivation is tacitly used to state how men experience loss when denied the chance to be fathers. The author, activist, and the founder of the National Fatherhood Initiative, David Blankenhorn, wrote the highly influential *Fatherless America* (1996), which essentially lays the blame for major Western social problems at the feet of fatherlessness. The book explores the different "cultural scripts" of various types of fathers—deadbeat, step, and so on—but the chapter most relevant to the present discussion is titled "The Sperm Father."

> The Sperm Father completes his fatherhood prior to the birth of his child. His fatherhood consists entirely of the biological act of ejaculation. He spreads his seed, nothing more. He is a minimalist father, a one-act dad. Neither a New Father or an Old Father, he is an unfather, leaving no footprints or shadows. . . . His is the fatherhood of the one-night stand, the favor for a friend, the donation or sale of sperm (176).

The author repeatedly states that good fatherhood is possible only through a "healthy" heterosexual marriage. The Sperm Father is thus highly problematic for the development of good children and a good society. Sperm Fathers—or is it the use of the sperm itself?—threaten the core of all notions of fatherhood and can topple the father's position, as "to make room for the Sperm Father is also to insist upon the essential irrelevance of all fathers" (177). Furthermore, Sperm Fathers can single-handedly create dreadful, social situations for many generations. "A society of Sperm Fathers is a society of fourteen-year-old girls with babies and fourteen-year-old boys with guns" (184).

According to Blankenhorn, this advent of the Sperm Father is a postmodern phenomenon and a large part of a cash nexus. It becomes obvious fairly quickly that what Blankenhorn finds morally objectionable is the creation of nonheterosexual families and not the actual use of donor semen. He indicates it is morally acceptable for sperm to be sold to infertile couples, but the growing use of this sperm for unmarried women is detrimental to society. One of his closing remarks, his twelve points for social change, includes the following:

> State legislatures across the nation should support fatherhood by regulating sperm banks. New laws should prohibit sperm banks and others from selling sperm to unmarried women and limit the use of artificial insemination to cases of married couples experiencing fertility problems. In a good society, people do not traffic commercially in the production of radically fatherless children (233).

Responding to technological innovations that create sperm cells as commodities, social actors must adjust to sperm's new potentials. ICSI and sperm banks create new avenues for sperm to be deployed. Therefore, it is important to consider what type of normative model of family and parenthood Blankenhorn is attempting to resurrect in his fairly unsubstantiated text. By linking the creation of an ethically superior society, "a good society" (288), with said society's restriction of sperm to certain acceptable individuals, we have witnessed the transformation of sperm to a state-controlled substance that should only be available to certain state-sanctioned citizens.

Honorable Death—Kamikaze Sperm

> Social changes require heterosexual men to relinquish certain aspects of power and privilege that they enjoyed in the context of the traditional nuclear family. Most men no longer have sole economic power over their families. Similarly, most men must accept some degree of responsibility for childcare and household tasks. The majority of heterosexual men no longer have full-time wives to buffer the stress of balancing work and family roles. Within this new context of power sharing and

role sharing, heterosexual men have been moved from the center to the margins of many versions of family life. In our view, the societal debate about gender differences in parenting is, in part, a reaction to this loss of male power and privilege. We see the argument that fathers are essential as an attempt to reinstate male dominance by restoring the dominance of the traditional nuclear family with its contrasting masculine and feminine gender roles (Silverstein and Auerbach 1999:399).

As has been stated in many social commentaries, men and boys and sperm and semen are under attack. It is not a coincidence that in these times of ambivalent use of reproductive technologies that render sperm more predictable and operational outside of male bodies, new scientific theories emerge to resituate semen as composed of active warriors with highly organized and complicated divisions of labor. Below, I present an analysis of the theories in Robin Baker and Mark Bellis's *Human Sperm Competition: Copulation, Masturbation and Infidelity* (1995). I have read this work as an attempt to resurrect sperm (and men) like a phoenix from the ashes.

Sperm competition is a scientific theory that has been in existence for about thirty years and has been most commonly applied to nonhuman animals. It is based in evolutionary biology and provides explanations for how multiple male ejaculates, primarily from different progenitors, compete to fertilize the eggs of a single female (for recent research on sperm competition, see Birkhead and Moller 1998). Baker and Bellis have taken sperm competition several steps further and applied the scientific principles (through the generous extrapolation of animal models and behavior) to humans. They claim that human sperm competition is one of the key forces shaping genetics and driving human sexuality. Written in a casual and accessible style, with many illustrations and diagrams, this work depicts the crossover between hard science and pop science. Baker has experience in this genre, as he is also the author of the highly successful trade publication *Sperm Wars*, which relies on some of the same scientific claims.

Despite the criticism *Human Sperm Competition* and its theories and methodologies drew (Holden 1999; Short 1999), the book is still making a splash in the United States and Britain. The ideas of the sperm wars are taken very seriously by popular writers and physical anthropologists; these sperm theories serve as the biological basis for responding to the contemporary crisis of masculinity (e.g., Tiger 1999). The stated aims of this work are "a purely scientific understanding of the reproductive behavior of humans and other animals" and that "our research could revolutionize the medical approach to infertility" (xiv). However, the authors' interpretation of biomedical evidence is rife with sociobiological claims about how human behavior emerges from the seemingly conscious motivation of individual sperm cells. Within the pages of the preface, this book is "scientific," claiming that men and women are "programmed to behave" in predetermined ways "in sexual matters" (xii). For example, the authors propose the theory of human mate-guarding, whereby the male species shields the female in order to reduce the probability of sperm competition, based on their extrapolations from squirrel data. One claim from this data and a methodologically questionable survey (Birkhead 2000) performed by Baker and Bellis states "some form of mate-guarding behavior is a nearly universal feature of the sexual programming of modern male humans" (22). Furthermore, the book can be read as a relationship manual to aid in understanding the enigmatic opposite sex.

The risk of sperm competition is thought to have influenced many aspects of sexuality, not only concerning sperm and the ejaculate but innumerable other aspects of male and female anatomy and physiology. Thus, sperm competition may be argued to promote not only highly competitive ejaculates, but also to shape anatomical devices such as the penis and vagina, and to generate a whole array of copulatory behavior (Baker and Bellis 1995:1).

At its inception, this book uncritically presents sperm competition, extrapolating liberally from bioscientific research primarily based on nonhuman models, to grand theories of human behavior devoid of sociological insights. There are problematic statements, such as "a female who promotes sperm competition generally increases her chances of being fertilized by the male with the most competitive sperm. Whatever the origins of any difference in sperm competitiveness, the female can only benefit" (26). If females can only benefit from sperm competition from multiple partners, what happens in instances where multiple ejaculates are forced on women? Is this a rationale for rape? Or is it the basis for more "academic and scientific" explanations of rape based on sexual selection and evolutionary adaptiveness (see, for example, Thornhill and Palmer 2000)?

Reminiscent of feminist anthropologist Emily Martin's (1991) exquisite work deconstructing reproductive-textbook descriptions of fertilization as a romance between the sperm and the egg, Baker and Bellis, without self-reflexivity, create scenarios where sperm are anthropomorphized to the degree that they have almost superhuman agency:

> As an analogy, let us compare a person (=DNA) leisurely driving a car
> (=sperm) uncontested from A (=vagina) to B (=site of fertilization)
> with the same person in a rally car racing to arrive at B ahead of nu-
> merous other hostile competitors from one or more opposing teams
> (=sperm competition). In both cases only the car which arrives at B at
> precisely the right moment will receive a prize (=egg). However, the
> requirements, resources, and strategies necessary to attain a prize in
> the second scenario are infinitely greater than in the first even though
> in the first the person may stand a better chance of completing the
> journey (2).

Here, the masculine social world of car racing is used to bring to
mind speed, fierce competition, and danger. The choice of this example is not random; rather, these images are conjured from the
tropes of a historically situated, culturally specific hegemonic masculinity. In addition to sports-car racing tropes, World War II fighter
jets, football, and nuclear destruction are used to illustrate sperm
behavior. What can we learn from these analogies? Completing the
journey is not as important as getting there first. Sports cars are able
to capture the checkered flag faster than leisure sedans. These tropes
are used in sperm allegories about hegemonic male ideals, including
winning, competing, speeding, destroying, and attacking.

The crowning glory in *Human Sperm Competition* is the development of a theory called the Kamikaze Sperm Hypothesis (KSH),
which "suggests that animal ejaculates consist of different types of
sperm, each programmed to carry out a specific function. Some, often very few, are 'egg-getters,' programmed to attempt to fertilize
the female's eggs. The remainder, often the vast majority, is programmed for a kamikaze role. Instead of attempting to find and fertilize eggs themselves, their role is to reduce the chances that the egg
will be fertilized by sperm from any other male" (23).

Through their concept of KSH, Baker and Bellis provide a means
to rescue all morphs of sperm from the label of "useless" and to provide job descriptions for them all. "In the past, 'non-normal' sperm
have been considered to be unwanted passengers in the ejaculate;
unavoidable deformities that are a hindrance to conception. Our
Kamikaze Sperm Hypothesis argues otherwise. Each sperm morph
has a part to play in the whole process of sperm competition and fertilization" (251). That is, each morph is a part of a team in pursuit of
the larger goal of allowing the true, chosen sperm to fertilize the egg.
In a battlefield motif, all sperm work in a concerted effort to benefit
the chosen one's ability to capture the castle. Old and young sperm
are "recruited" from the ejaculate: normal and nonnormal morphs
have purpose. Although "younger" sperm cells may be more likely

to reach an egg, it is important to understand the ways the scientist delivers this information.

The authors discuss the credentials of these morphs of sperm in detail, using football or war analogies in their labeling and description of the "division of labor" sperm. For example, there exists chemical warfare in the acrosome on the sperm head, which "were in effect carrying a bomb on their heads" (275), and sperm engage in "head-to-head combat" (276). Because sperm occupy two primary status positions within KSH, Baker and Bellis provide readers with detailed typologies of each. Egg-getters are thought to be "macros," oval-shaped head sperm that are longer and wider than other sperm (275). In addition to the commonplace knowledge of the challenges of sperm achieving fertilization, according to the KSH, egg-getters must overcome even more tremendous obstacles. "Throughout the whole journey, the successful egg-getter has to avoid the seek-and-destroy attention of both sperm from other males and even 'family planning,' some from within its own ejaculate" (292).

The use of the term "kamikaze" appears to be an odd choice for scientists to use when developing a scientific theory of sperm. During World War II, Vice Admiral Takijiro Onishi, commander of Japan's First Air Fleet, selected volunteers from his troops to become suicide pilots to fly planes loaded with bombs into allied ships.[6] Called kamikaze (translated as "divine wind") fighter pilots, due to the high honor of such a mission, Admiral Onishi had more volunteers than planes—these were "real men." Do Baker and Bellis mean to suggest that this is a revered job in the division of labor of reproduction? Is the honor bestowed to the men who flew these self-sacrificing missions to be transferred to the valiant sperm that die during the mission to fertilize an egg? Is fertilization, then, a bombing mission where sex and violence are conflated once again?

Kamikaze sperm are subdivided into two specific groups: blockers and those that seek and destroy. Blockers prevent another male's sperm from the "cervical crypts." Coiled-tail, "old and dying sperm" are often blockers, as blocking is a "sedentary activity" (261). Images come to mind of aging football players blocking the competitors' access to the football/egg so that the spry quarterback can toss the football/egg to the rightful recipient—the fastest, fittest wide receiver who is gracefully avoiding collision with the competitors' player/sperm.

Seek-and-destroy sperm roam around, seeking another male's sperm, and through the use of "highly destructive proteolytic enzymes produced by their ascrosomal complex," incapacitate other sperm (23). The authors hypothesize that through an unknown mechanism, seek-and-destroy sperm from one male transform from oval-headed to round-headed, releasing their ascrosome to kill other sperm. This "chemical warfare" and "head-to-head combat" causes the transformed sperm to be less fertile and results in higher rates of mortality for all sperm (274). Seek-and-destroy sperm are identified in part by their shape: tapering, pyriform, and modal oval-headed. These representations also seem at least somewhat informed by computer/video games, another masculine pursuit—such as the 1980s favorite, Pac Man, which featured little creatures gobbling up other creatures.

Within the KSH, no sperm morph is unaccounted for in the division of labor and the quest to fertilize the egg. Even the old, sedentary, and dying sperm cells can go out with glory, by blocking access to other sperm. The competitive nature of men against men and sperm against sperm seems to echo the notion of hegemonic masculinity, whereby the most superior sperm will win and all men are born to fight. According to these authors, sperm (with no mention of the egg) is single-handedly responsible for the evolution of human sexuality, with no discussion of outliers such as lesbian and gay sexual identities, nonprocreative sexuality, or sophisticated technological manipulation of sperm. It seems these theories are a response to social changes and may also precipitate change. What type of social order is being invented or resurrected in this rendering of human sexual reproduction?

In *Standup Guy: Masculinity That Works* (1999), *Esquire* journalist Michael Segell studies male behavior through focus groups, which he calls "bitchfests" and "cocktalks" (quoted in Tierney 1999). He discusses the idea of sexual payback, whereby men bring women to climax but do not complete the sex act "all the way." "The only thing that's more enjoyable than having sex," one commodities trader explained to Segell, "is making a girl want it and not giving it to her" (quoted in Tierney 1999:84). Concerned over the difficulties of the dating scene for men and women between the ages of twenty-five to forty-four, Segell guides men to return to a new alpha male, a combination of traditional masculine qualities and emotional sensitivity as a means to restore a certain type of social order in the dating world and hence reproduction. What are the connections, if any, between the new alpha male and the egg-getter, blocker, and seek-and-destroy sperm?

Segell uses the work of sperm competition theory as a means of explaining male instinct to "keep a tightly clamped lid on the female libido" (84). In a matter-of-fact style, Segell writes,

Let's say your wife is out of town for a week on business with six male colleagues, all of whom make about ten times as much money as you. Even if you ejaculate every day she's away, you'll still release more spermatozoa when she returns to your eager, trembling arms than you did during any of the (presumable) emissions. You'll also begin to manufacture more sperm designed to compete with a rival's sperm whose sole function is to fertilize an egg. Scientists consider this a sophisticated psychophysiological adaptation to your unavoidable lapse in mate monitoring—or, put another way, to your possessive and suspicious nature (84).

Not surprising, much of Segell's book discusses the changing notions of fatherhood as they relate to what it is to be a standup guy in today's culture. He tracks how fatherhood has gone through changes and speaks of an almost-renaissance of fatherhood in which standup men want to be better fathers than their own, even with the added threat of optional single motherhood to eliminate fathers.

In *The Decline of the Males* (1999), Lionel Tiger, an anthropologist who coined the term "male bonding" in the 1960s, and argued, in the 1970s, that sexism was an evolutionary adaptation, explores how the birth control pill, women's role in the labor market, abortion, reproductive technology, and single motherhood have cut men out of reproduction. "This book is about an emerging pattern. Men and women may not discern it clearly, but the pattern underlies their experiences in industrial society. It is the pattern of growth in the confidence and power of women and the erosion in the confidence and power of men. More women are having children without men, and therefore more men are without the love of families" (2).

According to Tiger, maleness and masculinity are not produced or constructed within the culture but, rather, are inherent or inborn variables threatened by women's ascendancy. This ascendancy is demonstrated by women's reproductive "choices," whereby single motherhood is a threat to a man's ability to achieve love, connection, self-esteem, and well-being. In an article in the *New York Times*, Tiger asserts that "[m]en have been alienated from the means of reproduction. They don't feel they're rewarded enough by being family men, and there's no longer the coercion of religion or the law to discipline and motivate them. We won't solve the problem if we keep pretending that there's no difference between the sexes or shouting at men to behave more like women. We need new rules based on an understanding of the old rules of nature" (Tierney 1999:84). It is not surprising that Tiger cites in laudatory fashion the work of Baker and Bellis as evidence that men change their sperm production and

sperm's behavior to respond to these troubling sociocultural changes in women's contraceptive use and labor-force participation. Tiger
also links what he sees as increases in extreme forms of masculine
expression—"interest in sports and pornography"—as outlets for
masculinity to be expressed at times when men "feel otherwise ob-
ligated to repress their masculinity" (Tiger 1999:229).

In summary, many groups try to assert new gender rules or at
least recast the rules of previous generations. Some have characterized North American men's movements as being driven by nostalgia
for the heteronormative, male-dominated patriarchal nuclear family. Unfortunately, as depicted in some reactions to sperm science
and spermatic commerce, many familial representations are taken
as the version of a singular truth about biology and destiny. We must
remember that these are not arbitrarily produced representations,
and we must work to reinsert social analyses of the belief systems
these images recreate and perpetuate.

Fluid Tenacity

Sperm and semen do things to human bodies and social relations. This
chapter has traced the historical journeys of sperm from their fabulous
Western bioscientific discovery to their war-weary travails through
the vaginal crypt. Over time, sociocultural and scientific representations of sperm and semen have changed, but throughout, sperm and
semen have maintained definitions of tenacity, strength, and suprem-
acy. Much like the fluid of semen can leak on to different fabrics and
into different bodies and create social circumstances, the meanings of
semen are able to seep into our consciousness, transmitting the valid-
ity of certain gendered hierarchies. At times of relative stability in gendered social relations, when women have limited participation in public life and production of formal knowledge, representations of sperm
are fairly straightforward and primal. But as fascination with sperm
grows, so too do civil rights movements that enable more democratic
participation in scientific research and layperson practices. Sperm is
at the same time more interesting, complicated, and specialized, and
yet more programmable, deployable, and predictable. Its usefulness
has expanded in the increasingly technically sophisticated world of
infertility. As social changes escalate the production of heterogeneous
ways to be gendered and renovated gendered hierarchies, knowledge
about sperm has become more specialized and accessible.

Regardless of the triumph of scientific ingenuity to capture and
program individual sperm cells through their studies of human

sperm competition, scientists present sperm as having distinct personalities and jobs. The scientific practices that elevate sperm to the lofty heights of sole reproductive actor also transform sperm into a relatively easily accessible commodity. Real, embodied men become obsolete through the use of reproductive technologies. Certain men and women react to this spermatic marketplace by intensifying the efforts to defend against the "supposed" attack on fatherhood. Through a backlash against feminism, a battle cry is issued to the ranks of men to get up and defend their reign over the family. What better icon than a kamikaze sperm risking his life to give the egg-getter sperm better access to the egg, to represent the struggle of real men at times of social upheaval? Sperm can go down in glory as they retain their preeminence as the provider, protector, and rightful dominator of the family. It is not terribly surprising that theories of sperm competition rely on notions of nostalgic forms of masculinity and stereotypical macho men. It is, however, troubling how different scholars and laypersons have consumed this "scientific" theory as a means to further the agendas of certain types of oppressive and/ or regressive family structures.

As a consumer of scientific knowledge, it is important to ask how sperm/semen is rendered as knowable, paying particular attention to the intended and unintended assumptions about gender. The images or representations are meant sometimes unintentionally to instruct or incite actual men and women. Thus, there is traffic between the ideal type of masculinity and the embodied performance of "being masculine." Simultaneously, the meaning of masculinity is not concrete, consistent, and fixed; rather, because members of society participate in multiple ongoing interactions within the contours of masculinity and femininity, this process is fluid, and changes depending on historical and cultural circumstances.

Acknowledgments

The author thanks Matthew Schmidt, Monica Casper, and this book's editors for their helpful comments.

Notes

1. An example of a potentially threatening practice to masculinity through scientific knowledge and practices is demonstrated by innovations in semen banking. The emergence of cryopreservation, the necessary

technology for semen banking, dates back to 1776 Italy (Sherman 1979). In the United States, the first documented semen bank opened in 1950 at the University of Iowa; early banks were exclusively part of the university system until the early 1970s. The academic arena provided the materials, funding, and legitimacy to research, develop, and clinically apply these technologies, leading to the first work on humans in 1954 (Olson 1979; Sherman 1979). In 1972, commercial semen banks were established for men who would become infertile due to sickness or treatment, and heterosexual couples needing semen for reproduction. This new wave of semen banking converged with the modern birth control movement, which included an option for men—vasectomy. Currently, some men, specifically those vasectomized or undergoing chemotherapy, use semen banks as a storage facility (similar to a safety deposit box at a financial bank). This type of "fertility insurance" is marketed to alleviate fears of exposure to toxic substances harmful or lethal to sperm and/or men. For example, during the first Gulf War, there was a marked increase in semen storage requests (*Los Angeles Times,* 4 February, 1991; *Time,* 11 February, 1991). Although presumably not the intended audience, single women or couples (lesbian and heterosexual) use semen banks in order to reproduce.

2.   Grounded theory is a deductive process whereby analysts incorporate as much data as possible so the formative theories can be used as deductive tools. Through the writing and rewriting of analytic memos, grounded theory ultimately aims to incorporate the range of human experiences.

3.   At the close of the sixteenth century, Benedicti identified three main aspects of sperm waste: "1) Masturbation is unarguably a mortal sin— with its seriousness increasing along a sliding scale encompassing the different kinds of thoughts that masturbators summon up during the act, since thinking of a married woman is to commit adultery, thinking of a virgin is rape, thinking of a parent is incest; 2) masturbation should be condemned not only for being an act against nature but also for having been described as the object of God's wrath in scripture; 3) even to this rule some exceptions apply, the most complex ones concerning how to classify 'nocturnal pollutions' which depending on whether they are cause by a lascivious dreams, states of drunken stupor, agitations due to the ingestion of certain spicy foods, or number other causes have different degrees of severity" (Pinto-Correia 1997:81).

4.   Sperm banks are active participants in erasing the biological and social differences between sperm cells and the men donating them. "For example, a donor who likes to play the trombone, ballroom dance, and read Chaucer may culturally indicate healthier semen than a donor who enjoys slam dancing, riding Harley motorcycles, and body piercing. The Lamarckian assumption of the inheritance of acquired characteristics is both re-created and sustained in these catalogues. Through a dialectical process, semen banks invest semen with social characteristics" (Moore and Schmidt 1999:345).

5.   http://news.bbc.co.uk/2/hi/health/2062212.stm.

6. For an interactive history of kamikaze fighter pilots, see http://motlc. wiesenthal.com/text/x19/xm1943.html.

References

Adelman, Marilyn Marx, and Eileen Cahill. 1989. *Atlas of Sperm Morphology.* Chicago: ASCP Press Image.

Baker, R. Robin, and Mark Bellis. 1995. *Human Sperm Competition: Copulation, Masturbation and Infidelity.* London: Chapman and Hall.

Beaubien, Greg. 1995. "Progress against Infertility." *American Health,* September 14.

Berger, M., B. Wallis, and S. Watson, eds. 1995. "Constructing Masculinity." In *Contemporary Culture.* New York: Routledge.

Bharadwaj, Aditya. 2003. "Why Adoption Is not an Option in India: The Visibility of Infertility, the Secrecy of Donor Insemination, and Other Cultural Complexities." *Social Science & Medicine* 56(9):1867–80.

Birkhead, Tim. 2000. *Promiscuity: An Evolutionary History of Sperm Competition.* Cambridge: Harvard University Press.

Birkhead, Tim, and A. P. Moller. 1998. *Sperm Competition and Sexual Selection.* London: Academic Press.

Blankenhorn, David. 1996. *Fatherless America: Confronting Our Most Urgent Social Problem.* New York: Harper.

Braidotti, Rosi. 1997. "Generations of Feminists, or, Is There Life after Post-Modernism? Including Responses and a Discussion." *Found Object Six* (Fall):55–86.

Clarke, Adele. 1991. "Social Worlds Theory as Organization Theory." In *Social Organization and Social Process: Essays in Honor of Anselm Strauss,* ed. David Maines. Hawthorne: Aldine de Gruyter.

———. 1998. *Disciplining Reproduction: Modernity, American Life Sciences, and the "Problem of Sex."* Berkeley: University of California Press.

Cox, Caroline. 1996. "Masculinity at Risk." *Journal of Pesticide Reform* 16(2):2–7.

Daly, Kerry J. 1999. "Crisis of Genealogy: Facing the Challenges of Infertility." In *Dynamics of Resilient Families,* ed. Hamilton I. McCubbin, Elizabeth A. Thompson. Thousand Oaks, CA: Sage.

Dickinson, Henry Latou. 1949. *Human Sex Anatomy.* Baltimore: Williams and Wilkins.

Faludi, Susan. 1999. *Stiffed: The Betrayal of the American Man.* New York: Perennial.

Gannon, Kenneth, Lesley Glover, and Paul Abel. 2004. "Masculinity, Infertility, Stigma and Media Reports." *Social Science and Medicine* 59(6):1169–75.

Hoff-Sommers, Christina. 2000. *The War against Boys: How Misguided Feminism Is Harming Our Young Men.* New York: Simon & Schuster.

Holden, Constance. 1999. "No Evidence for the Sperm Wars." *Science* 286(5448):2265.

Katz, David. 1991. "Characteristics of Sperm Motility." *Annals of New York Academy of Science* 637(125):409–32.

Kempers, Roger. 1976. "The Tricentennial of the Discovery of Sperm." *Fertility and Sterility* 27(5):603–5.

Lee, Sammy. 2003. "Myths and Reality in Male Infertility." In *Inconceivable Conceptions: Psychological Aspects of* Infertility *and Reproductive Technology*, ed. Jane Haynes and Juliet Miller. New York: Brunner-Routledge.

Martin, Emily. 1991. "The Egg and the Sperm: How Science Has Constructed a Romance Based on Stereotypical Male-Female Roles." *Signs* 16(3):485–501.

Mason, Mary-Claire. 1993. *Male Infertility: Men Talking*. New York: Routledge.

Moore, Lisa Jean. 1997. "'It's like you use pots and pans to cook. It's the tool': The Technologies of Safer Sex." *Science, Technology and Human Values* 22(4):434–71.

———. 2003. "Billy, the Sad Sperm with No Tail: Representations of Sperm in Children's Books." *Sexualities* 6(3–4):279–305.

———. 2007. *Sperm Counts*. New York: New York University Press.

Moore, Lisa Jean, and Heidi Durkin. 2004. "The Leaky Male Body: Forensics and the Construction of the Sexual Suspect." In *Medicalizing Masculinity*, ed. Dana Rosenfeld and Chris Faircloth. Philadelphia: Temple University Press.

Moore, Lisa Jean, and Matthew Schmidt. 1999. "On the Construction of Male Differences: Marketing Variations in Technosemen." *Men and Masculinities* 1(4):339–59.

Nachtigall, Robert D. 1993. "Secrecy: An Unresolved Issue in the Practice of Donor Insemination." Transactions of the Fifty-Ninth Annual Meeting of the Pacific Coast Obstetrical and Gynecological Society. *American Journal of Obstetrics and Gynecology* 168(6):1846.

Olson, John. 1979. "Present Status of AID and Sperm Banks in the United States." *Human Artificial Insemination and Semen Preservation*, ed. Georges David, W. S. Price, and Wendel S. Price. Paris: International Symposium on Artificial Insemination and Semen Preservation.

Pinto-Correia, Clara. 1997. *The Ovary of Eve: Egg and Sperm and Preformation*. Chicago: University of Chicago Press.

Schrader, S. M., T. W. Turner, and S. D. Simon. 1991. "Longitudinal Study of Semen Quality of Unexposed Workers: Sperm Motility Characteristics." *Journal of Andrology* 12(1):126–31.

Segell, Michael. 1999. *Standup Guy: Masculinity That Works*. New York: Villard.

Sherman, J. K. 1979. "Historical Synopsis of Human Semen Cryobanking." In *Human Artificial Insemination and Semen Preservation*, ed. Georges David, W. S. Price, and Wendel S. Price. Paris: International Symposium on Artificial Insemination and Semen Preservation.

Short, Roger. 1999. "Human Sperm Competition: Copulation, Masturbation and Infidelity." http://numbat.murdoch.edu.au/spermatology/rsreview.html.

Silverstein, Louise B., and Carl F. Auerbach. 1999. "Deconstructing the Essential Father." *American Psychologist* 54(6):397–405.

Spark, Richard. 1988. *The Infertile Male: The Clinical Guide to Diagnosis and Treatment.* New York: Plenum.

Star, Susan L., and J. R. Griesemer. 1989. "Institutional Ecology 'Translations' and Boundary Objects: Amateurs and Professionals in Berkeley's Museum of Vertebrate Zoology 1907–39." *Social Studies of Science* 19(345):387–420.

Strauss, Anselm, and J. Corbin. 1994. "Grounded Theory Methodology: An Overview." In *Handbook of Qualitative Research*, ed. N. Denzin and Y. Lincoln. London: Sage.

Swan, Shanna, and Eric Elkin. 1999. "Declining Semen Quality: Can the Past Inform the Present?" *Bioessays* 21(7):614–22.

Thornhill, Randy, and Craig T. Palmer. 2000. *A Natural History of Rape: Biological Bases of Sexual Coercion.* Boston: MIT Press.

Tierney, John. 1999. "Suitable Men: Rare Species under Study." *New York Times*, June 7.

Tiger, Lionel. 1999. *The Decline of the Males.* New York: St. Martin's Press.

West, C., and D. Zimmerman. 1987. "Doing Gender." *Gender and Society* 1(June):125–51.

Whorton, D., R. M. Krauss, S. Marshall, and T. H. Milby. 1977. "Infertility in Male Pesticide Workers." *Lancet* 2:1259–60.

Wyrobek, A. J., L. A. Gordon, J. G. Burkhart, M. W. Francis, R. W. Kapp, G. Letz, L. V. Malling, J. C. Topham, M. D.Whorton. 1983. "An Evaluation of Human Sperm as Indicators of Chemically Induced Alterations of Spermatogenic Function." *Mutation Research* 115(4):3–148.

Chapter 3

Gender, Masculinity, and Reproduction: Anthropological Perspectives

Matthew R. Dudgeon and Marcia C. Inhorn

Since the landmark 1994 International Conference on Population and Development, in Cairo, Egypt, population and development programs and policies have increasingly adopted a "reproductive health" approach. Criticizing earlier initiatives for focusing on demographic goals such as population limitation rather than health needs, a coalition of feminist and developing country stakeholders advanced a platform that emphasized reproductive health, broadly defined, as a basic human right, rather than as a means to achieve population control through increasing contraceptive prevalence rates. As a result, reproductive health has come to refer to a spectrum of health concerns involving individual sexual and reproductive well-being and resting directly on a foundation of reproductive rights, including the right to have all sexual experiences as wanted ones, the right to control the timing and conditions of pregnancy, and the right to achieve healthy pregnancy, birth, and child health outcomes (Petchesky 2000).

Several antecedents influenced this shift to a reproductive health paradigm. First, classic demographic transition theory has failed to explain why population growth continues, often in the face of other indicators of economic development and despite falling fertility rates in many countries (Greenhalgh 1995; Handwerker 1986). Second, work by feminist groups has shown how population and development interventions that focus on demographic goals as a means to economic and social development often disregard or negatively affect the health of women (Dixon-Mueller 1993a). In particular, feminists in developing countries have pointed to major imbalances in reproductive health outcomes in First and Third World countries, suggesting the need to address population control within the context of holistic, comprehensive reproductive health care services (Corrêa and Reichmann 1994). Finally, the global HIV/AIDS pandemic has caused a fundamental rethinking of reproductive health programs, shifting attention from population control to sexual behaviors and practices that affect the transmission of sexually transmitted infections (STIs) among and between men and women (Dixon-Mueller 1993b; Parker, Barbosa, and Aggleton 2000; Vance 1991).

This shift to a reproductive health model has had important consequences for the ways men are conceived as participants in reproductive and sexual health. On the one hand, men are seen as important influences on the reproductive health of others. These influences are numerous and may involve direct effects, such as sexual violence or STIs, as well as more indirect effects, such as the mediation of resources available during pregnancy and childbirth. Because most human societies privilege men in both the private and public domains, men also structurally affect the reproductive health of others in ways women do not, namely through the positions of authority they occupy, the resources they control, and the sexual and reproductive norms they support or subvert. On the other hand, men traditionally have not been included in interventions targeting maternal-child health, contraceptive use, or other reproductive health problems (Collumbien and Hawkes 2000; Ndong, Becker, Haws, and Wegner 1999).

Men's lack of inclusion in these programs has been a result of a combination of factors. First, limited resources traditionally have focused on women, who obviously play a more direct role in pregnancy and childbirth and are often excluded by men from access to existing resources. In particular, women's access to birth control and prenatal and delivery care are often seen as key avenues for the empowerment of women. Second, assumptions about men's lack of involvement and interest in reproductive health have militated against men's inclusion in reproductive health programs. Finally, ideological issues have influenced research agenda. For example, lack of research and development on male contraceptives stems in part from assumptions about men's lack of desire for contraceptives and about the nature and importance of male versus female sexuality, including sexual satisfaction.

Importantly, the reproductive health model that was promoted post-Cairo emphasizes the reproductive health needs of all individuals, including men. Framing reproductive health in the language of human rights (Cliquet and Thienpont 1995), reproductive health programs emerging from the Cairo and Beijing platforms address male reproductive health as a fundamental human right. More specifically, several areas have been identified as important to consider in comprehensive approaches to men's reproductive health needs, including male contraceptive technology, reproductive-tract infections and STIs, male infertility and sexual dysfunction, male adolescent reproductive health, male reproductive aging, and occupational and environmental effects on male reproductive health (Mundigo 1998; Wang 2000).

However, given the broad definition of reproductive health stressed in these conference platforms, this list of concerns is largely biomedical in nature, potentially of more concern to health care providers than to individual men. Furthermore, this biomedical focus may prove inadequate to capture the range of issues men themselves may include in reproductive health definitions (Collumbien and Hawkes 2000). Though the reproductive health needs of men finally have been placed squarely on the research and policy agendas, there are still many unanswered questions about what constitutes male reproductive health, as well as the best ways to achieve it.

Increasingly, reproductive health policymakers (and their critics) have recognized the need for qualitative research to improve understandings of male involvement in reproductive health, as well as men's reproductive health problems (Drennan 1998; Mbizvo 1996; Presser and Sen 2000). One area of particular interest involves the cultural determinants of reproductive health. It is clear that culture, as a predominant system of beliefs and practices shared by a group, affects reproductive health outcomes. Discussion of culture in reproductive health initiatives to date has tended to focus on the beliefs and practices concerning the origin and treatment of reproductive health problems, particularly as they present barriers to biomedical intervention.

Because of its long tradition of research among non-Western populations and its qualitative research strategy of ethnography, the discipline of anthropology has been seen by many as a means to investigate local reproductive norms and problems, as well as to implement a gendered perspective that does not assume universal meanings of masculine and feminine. Anthropology has, to date, been characterized as a discipline suited to complement biomedical health interventions with qualitative knowledge that will improve the deployment of those interventions.

Anthropology is rapidly growing in this complementary role to international health efforts (Sargent and Brettell 1996; Vlassoff and Manderson 1998), and it has more to offer than local knowledge in the area of reproductive health. For one, medical anthropologists often have taken a critical stance toward international health efforts (Kleinman 1978; Lane and Rubinstein 1996; Morgan 1993), including men's incorporation into reproductive health interventions (Collumbien and Hawkes 2000). From this critical medical anthropological perspective, culture influences the very character of biomedicine, both as a Western discipline and as a form of health care now found in many non-Western sites around the globe (Inhorn 1994). Culture influences not only how individuals are treated for their reproductive health problems within given systems of medicine, but also how individuals living within local communities define and experience their reproductive health.

This chapter explores how anthropology, as a humanistic social science, is particularly well suited for assessing men's reproductive health needs through its emphasis on both the specificity and variability of those needs within local cultural contexts. Relying on a biosocial perspective, anthropologists who focus their research on reproduction generally argue that local biologies, as well as local cultures, influence men's reproductive health definitions and needs. Understanding men's reproductive-health needs requires framing men's health and well-being within local contexts, the traditional focus of anthropology.

This chapter examines the contributions of both biological and cultural anthropology to furthering our understanding of men's reproduction and reproductive health within an explicitly biosocial framework. The first part of the chapter examines recent empirical work in physical/biological anthropology, which has shown important variations in reproductive physiology within and between groups of men in different environmental contexts. This work, we suggest, indicates the need for further consideration of "local biologies," first defined by Lock as "an ongoing dialectic between biology and culture in which both are contingent" (1993:xxi). In exploring the cultural meanings surrounding menopause in Japan and North America, Lock suggests that Japanese women may experience menopause differently than North American women, in part because of higher average levels of phytoestrogens in Japanese diets, which may serve to mitigate the effects of estrogen decline at the climacteric. Because human reproductive physiology is under endocrinological control, human reproductive ecologists have come to recognize that both male and female reproductive physiologies are sensitive to local environments. Thus, local biologies must be considered when attempting to assess men's various reproductive health needs around the globe.

The second part of the chapter turns to contributions of cultural anthropology, with its ethnographic tradition of in-depth, field-based research and its central concept of culture. Cultural anthropologists have argued that gender is a key organizing principle of social relations, influencing both sex and reproduction. As part of this discussion, we consider recent anthropological research on men and masculinity, much of which falls outside of current conceptualizations of men's reproductive health. Nonetheless it forms part of the matrix of relations influencing men's (and women's) reproductive well-being.

Human Reproduction as a Biosocial Process

In addition to its social nature, reproduction is fundamentally biological, with necessary physiological requirements for its accomplishment and relatively well-defined biomedical parameters marking reproductive health and illness. Human gestation usually lasts nine months, with delivery before or after that point potentially indicating a reproductive health problem. However, as discussed below, some parameters of reproductive health exhibit variation in different human populations for men as well as women. Furthermore, different human groups subjectively value reproductive health states differently; for example, they may differently label collections of symptoms as reproductive illnesses, or they may attribute different causes to similar reproductive health problems.

A central argument is that human reproduction is a biosocial process (Harris and Ross 1987; Panter-Brick 1998). It is dynamic and changes over time, and it occurs at the intersection of human biology, ecology, and social and cultural context. Beyond the (current) necessity for the gametes of two differently sexed individuals—one male and one female—to interact in procreation, human reproduction is an inherently biosocial process in many ways. Trevathan (1996) argues that because of the shape of the birth canal and female pelvis, human reproduction has evolved to require assistance from another individual during delivery. Although caregiving practices during and after pregnancy vary—from the valuation of stoicism and solitary delivery (Sargent 1989) to the medicalized childbirth of many Western societies (Davis-Floyd 1992)—individuals besides the biological mother are usually involved in reproduction in all societies, and in some societies, reproduction is a socially collective effort.

Social collectives—households, lineages, and states—derive power and resources from the control and administration of reproduction. For example, in the Middle East and in many other patrilineal, pronatalist societies around the world, households and extended families consider children to be a source of both labor and family power (Inhorn 1996; Inhorn and van Balen 2002). Thus, childbearing is culturally mandated, and infertility is despised (Bharadwaj 2002; Feldman-Savelsberg 1999; Inhorn 1994, 1996, 2003a). Furthermore, different levels and mechanisms of collective social control have had different effects on reproductive health. For example, the focus of states on the vaccination of infants is a way of ensuring labor forces and lowering national health costs, although this focus often diverts limited resources from other health programs. Similarly, states may or may not invest in fertility-limiting technology in an attempt to control women's labor, including preventing them from occupying certain positions because of their reproductive status or potential (Bandarage 1997).

Apart from the more direct aspects of power related to control of labor and resources, biological reproduction occupies a key position in the reproduction of ethnic and other social groups. Anthropologists have emphasized the centrality of kinship as an ideological concept organizing social relations within groups, as well as the regulation of ethnic boundaries through the control of miscegenation (Bledsoe, Guyer, and Lerner 2000; Delaney 1991; Schneider 1968; Yanagisako and Delaney 1995). These organizing structures of kinship prove important for families and lineages and for political entities such as the state. In a powerful example, Das (1995) examines the attitude of the Indian state toward abducted women and children born of sexual violence following the violent creation of Pakistan. She argues that, though great variability existed in the "practical kinship" of community and family norms regarding these women and children—including in many cases acceptance and assimilation into the community—a patriarchal concept of Indian "national honor" drove the state's policy of forced repatriation.

Variation in Reproductive Physiology and Behavior

Although the importance of reproductive physiology is clear in a consideration of reproductive health, biological anthropologists have suggested that a biomedical perspective may be inadequate to explain reproductive physiology within a larger ecological context. Biological anthropology has made important contributions to understandings of reproductive health, primarily in the areas of reproductive ecology and behavioral ecology. Reproductive ecologists investigate reproductive functions and procreative decisions as influenced by ecological factors, including nutrition, seasonal variations, and workload. Such research has shown patterns in female reproductive physiology that vary by ecological context. For example, declining age at menarche in Western populations has been related to improved nutritional adequacy and lowered workload in adolescence (Wood 1994). Furthermore, rising rates of ovarian cancers in Western populations may be related to increased lifetime exposure to ovarian hormones. Such increased hormonal exposure is due to fewer, widely spaced pregnancies and shorter periods of breastfeeding, both of which lead women to ovulate more frequently over the course of their lives (Ellison 1999).

Reproductive ecologists' research on male reproductive physiology has begun to examine variation between groups of men (Campbell and Leslie 1995). For example, declining levels of testosterone in men as they age have been seen as a reproductive health problem in the West and thus are a common topic of discussion in popular men's-health literature, where testosterone decline is linked to age-related changes in frequency of sex, sex drive, muscle mass, and general function. Available data from non-Western groups suggest that the trajectories of decline in testosterone levels with age vary considerably across populations, with non-Western populations showing lower peak lifetime levels and more gradual declines (Bribiescas 2001; Ellison et al. 1998). For example, Worthman (1999) found that men in Nepal attain much lower peak lifetime levels of testosterone in comparison with American men but do not exhibit significant declines in testosterone with age. The implications of such variation in lifetime exposures to testosterone for health risks such as prostate cancer are presently unclear and warrant further investigation, which is beyond the scope of this research (Bribiescas 2001).

Examining the ecological influence on human reproductive choices has been the work of human behavioral ecologists, whose research is devoted to the ecological context in which human reproductive decisions and behaviors occur. In investigating reproduction within human systems of marriage, behavioral ecologists stress differences in male and female reproductive behavior produced by natural selection. They argue that

- men and women will tend to pursue different reproductive strategies (e.g., beginning and length of reproductive career, timing and frequency of mating, number of partners, and investment in offspring) (Borgerhoff Mulder 1992, 2000);

- individual men will pursue variations on this generalized pattern of male reproductive strategy, differing from one another at different points over the course of their lives (Hill and Hurtado 1996; Worthman 1995); and
- differences in mating strategy, fertility, and mortality between groups will be associated with ecological constraints, such as resource availability and distribution (Hill and Hurtado 1996; Hill and Kaplan 1999), which ultimately affect group subsistence patterns (Marlowe 2000; Sellen and Mace 1997, 1999).

Behavioral ecologists have made important contributions to understanding why certain marriage systems arise and persist in conjunction with subsistence mode; for example, why polyandry (marriage of one woman to multiple men) exists in only one percent of human societies, including Himalayan groups, where land shortage makes households viable only with multiple males. Such a perspective proves important for understanding conditions under which socially imposed monogamy (such as by religious institutions or states) may not lead to sexual or reproductive exclusivity.

Although debates exist over the relevance of evolutionary pressures to explanations of contemporary human reproductive patterns, all the aforementioned approaches highlight the fact that meaningful differences exist in the reproduction of men and women, of different men, and of men over the course of their lives. Even small differences in reproductive patterns can have profound effects on reproductive health outcomes; for example, different mean numbers of sexual partners per year can affect the incidence rates of an STI (Finer, Darroch, and Singh 1999). STI rates are also affected by the differences in patterns of sexual behavior between older and younger men (Olayinka, Alexander, Mbizvo, and Gibney 2000). In summary, insights from biological anthropology regarding men's reproductive physiology and behavior have been used to demonstrate physiological variation between and within populations and to describe local conditions under which men are more likely to invest in their partners and children. Rather than rigidly determining reproductive behavior or health, human biology exhibits flexibility in ecological context. Furthermore, biological anthropological research suggests the importance of gender particularly gender relations between men and women, as having a profound impact on reproductive health outcomes, including the well-being of women and children.

Gender Perspectives on Men and Masculinity

One of the more important shifts emerging from the Cairo and Beijing conferences has been the explicit adoption of the concept of gender as an important determinant of reproductive health. Borrowed from linguistics and deriving from work in feminist theory and humanistic social sciences such as anthropology, the concept of gender originally described aspects of behavior and identity usually ascribed to either men or women. Such attributes could not be determined by biological sex and thus were referred to as gender roles and identities (Kessler and McKenna 1978). However, the concept of gender has been extended by some theorists to describe a set of power relationships loosely organized around biological sex and related to (but not defined by) access to material resources and social status (Butler 1990). More specifically, in reproductive health research the concept of gender has been used to account for the different kinds of illnesses experienced by men and women (Lorber 1997; Moynihan 1998) and the inequities in health status between men and women, which are often attributable to power differentials (Sargent and Brettell 1996).

Ironically, perhaps, this "gender lens" only recently has focused on men, even though men have long been at the center of social scientific investigation and health research, often at the exclusion of women (Inhorn and Whittle 2001; Rosaldo 1974). Only recently have men as men—that is, as gendered agents, with beliefs, behaviors, and characteristics associated with but not dependent on biological sex—become subjects of theory and empirical investigation within the social sciences (Connell 1987, 1995; Seidler 1994), including in anthropology (Bourgois 1995; Gutmann 1997; Lancaster 1992). Although no single framework for the study of men holds, attempts have been made to explain general patterns in male identity and behavior. For example, the notion of masculinity has been used to refer to a differentiated set of roles and behaviors undertaken by men and involving ideas about self as they relate to these roles. Recently, theorists have stressed that individual men do not simply fill static roles and identities; rather, they must perform masculinity as an ongoing process drawing on existing sets of behaviors and ideas while allowing for innovation and change over time. Gilmore (1990), for example, argues that masculine identity and roles are more tenuous than feminine identities and roles, thus must be performed more vigorously. According to Gilmore, this need for greater performance of masculinity is the result of two realities. First, women can demonstrate their femaleness through reproduction, while men cannot demonstrate such a concrete realization of gender, relative to either other men or women. Second, throughout the world, women in family structures raise boys. But as boys become men, they must differentiate themselves from that feminine world, a separation young women need not make. However, such an argument is more descriptive than explanatory. Furthermore, it homogenizes men, thereby tending toward a unitary definition of masculinity defined in opposition to femininity.

Social scientists have pointed to the plurality of definitions of masculinity, even within a single social group. Masculinity is characterized as a plural set of gender identities or masculinities (Connell 1995), which are related to but not uniquely determined by biological sex. Given that there are different ways of being a man, Connell argues that masculinities are differently valued. "Hegemonic masculinities" are ideal types, which, though varying cross-culturally, exhibit general patterns. Hegemonic masculinities often concentrate ideal masculine attributes, including wealth, attractiveness, virility, strength, heterosexuality, and emotional detachment. Conversely, "subordinate masculinities" embody some of the opposites of these ideal attributes. Models of hegemonic masculinity, or ideal masculine behavior and identity, may distress the many men unable to achieve these ideals. Moreover, men may be conflicted about their desire to achieve hegemonic masculinity in ways that may motivate and affect their reproductive health behavior.

Connell (1995) notes that gender tends to organize three distinct but related domains—division of labor, exercise of power, and objects of desire. These three domains directly relate to men's reproductive health. Gendered divisions of labor affect men's differential access to work and income, as well as structure their reproductive risks through occupational exposures. Men's power in many societies ranges from institutionalized connection of masculinity with authority to the legitimization of sexual and reproductive violence. Finally, gender informs systems of desire, influencing the kinds of bodies deemed desirable and the conditions under which they are desired.

Approaches to men's involvement in reproductive health must account for broader social patterns that structure men's attitudes and behaviors regarding sex and reproduction. Men's effects on the reproductive health of others are diverse and often complex, ranging from direct effects, such as STI transmission and sexual violence, to mediation of resources available for women and children's health needs, to structural asymmetries that privilege men and maleness in arenas such as contraceptive technology development and infertility treatment. These influences may cross generations; with the onset of HIV/AIDS, researchers increasingly direct attention toward predictors of sexual risk behavior, including childhood abuse. Epidemiological studies suggest that men abused sexually during childhood are more likely to engage in risky sexual behavior than their female counterparts (Windom and Kuhns 1996). Men who report unwanted sexual activity in childhood also seem more likely to participate in risky behaviors in general (Tyler 2002); these behaviors, such as substance abuse, may increase HIV risk. Also, men who have sex with men have shown increased sexual risk-taking associated with a history of childhood abuse (Paul, Catania, Pollack, and Stall 2001), as have men at high risk for HIV transmission.

Handwerker (1989) applies an anthropological perspective to the question of childhood sexual abuse and its connections with later sexual risks, modeling these risks on gender differences in power between parents. In a survey of men and women in Barbados, he found patterns within power relationships between men and women, with some men exploiting women's economic dependence for sex, childbearing, and household services and authority. He argues that children growing up in such contexts begin their sexual careers earlier and remain sexually mobile into their thirties. Men who were physically, emotionally, and/or sexually abused as children, controlling for other important demographic variables, are significantly more likely to spread STIs.

As suggested by this research, men themselves experience the negative reproductive health effects of what Rubin (1984) calls the "sex/gender system," which roots gender not only in individual behavior, but also in social institutions and cultural norms. For example, the use of steroids for muscle building can be related to men's acquiescence to a sex/gender system in which size, athletic performance, and muscle mass signal superior masculinity. Many bodybuilders use steroids even when they know the use of such hormones is linked to health risks like testicular cancer (Klein 1995). It is important to point out that pursuits such as bodybuilding are not straightforwardly hegemonic or uniformly oppressive. Men and women actively participate in decisions about such body modifications and may feel empowered through their decisions, as has been documented about some women and cosmetic surgery (Davis 1995). However, in the United States, such decisions have increasingly become pathological obsessions as men become more and more subject to unattainable body ideals. Referring to an "Adonis Complex," Pope, Phillips, and Olivardia (2000) have suggested that men in the United States may feel threatened by women's entrance into traditionally male arenas of power, finding that the only way to "be a man" is by compulsive exercise and dieting regimes. At the same time, they note that many men may suffer in silence over body dysmorphia disorder and fail to seek serious medical attention.

Masculinity and Reproductive Health

Research in fields such as medical anthropology and medical sociology has begun to draw connections between gender and men's health (Browner and Sargent 1996; Doyal 2000; Krieger and Fee 1994; Lorber 1997; Moynihan 1998; Sabo and Gordon 1995; Sargent and Brettell 1996; Zeidenstein and Moore 1996). In general, such approaches argue that numerous aspects of health, ranging from accidental deaths to cardiovascular disease, are conditioned not only by differences between male and female physiologies, but also by the culturally specific, socially constructed gender roles and identities men and women perform. Courtenay (2000) argues there is a reciprocal relationship between masculinity and health, stressing that men's health problems are often produced by men's enactment of masculinity, and that cultural norms and expectations reinforce these enactments. In addition, some researchers have observed that certain aspects of health and illness help define hegemonic masculinity (Sabo and Gordon 1995). For example, certain markers of health are emphasized over others (e.g., men's muscle mass), markers that may not fit biomedical models for good health (Klein 1995). Moreover, illness in general may be characterized as unmasculine, and some disorders, such as infertility and erectile dysfunction, are seen as particularly emasculating (Inhorn 2002, 2003b; Webb and Daniluk 1999). In some cases, men's health disorders, such as benign prostatic hypertrophy, can be characterized as "culture-bound syndromes," given differential (and often profitable) emphasis in diagnosis and treatment by doctors and pharmaceutical manufacturers (McDade 1996).

Not surprising, many of the aspects of health most closely tied to masculinity involve reproduction and sexuality. Masculinity affects reproductive and sexual health insofar as sexual behaviors play key roles in defining gender roles and identities (Dixon-Mueller 1993b). Gender approaches stress the culturally constructed meanings of sexual practices (Vance 1991), in the main demonstrating that other- or same-sex sexual behaviors are not isomorphic with universal definitions of hetero- or homosexual, straight or gay identities (Herdt 1997; Lancaster 1992). In addition, attention has been drawn to the importance of particular sexual behaviors—many of them unhealthful for both men and women—for the performance of masculinity. Often listed among such practices are sexual promiscuity (Farmer, Connors, and Simmons 1996) and avoidance of contraceptives (Ward, Bertrand, and Puac 1992; Wingood and DiClemente 1998). These behaviors are theorized as being in a dialectical relationship with masculinity, with the behaviors both conditioned by and as part of the basis for masculine identities and roles.

In addition, cultural constructions of sexual behavior and sexual disorders shape the ways individual men experience their own masculinity. Anthropologists have demonstrated that culture-bound syndromes such as semen depletion (Bottéro 1991; Herdt 1997) or erectile dysfunction (Inhorn 2002; Potts 2000) depend not only on culturally specific understandings of human reproductive physiology, but also on a phallocentric perspective on human sexuality that deemphasizes other forms of male sexual expression and pleasure.

Given the connection of masculinity to reproduction, interventions targeting men's involvement in reproductive health, such as the promotion of condoms and sexual responsibility, must cope with sexual behaviors as they are embedded in masculine identity roles. Men and women often exhibit different patterns of sexual behavior, and similar patterns of sexual behavior affect men and women differently. In many societies, men's sexuality is sanctioned and encouraged, while women's sexuality may be closely monitored, constrained, and condemned (Nencel 1996; Pyne 1994). For example, in researching relationships in rural Haiti, de Zalduondo and Bernard (1995) argue that nonconjugal sexual relationships between men and women are not the product of men and women's individual or dyadic choices, but rather reflect their positions in a political and moral economy. Men are expected to have "flings," and women are expected to resist and ask for economic recompense. Although women do not depend completely on men economically and actually outproduce men in the fragile local economy, the returns on women's labor over time are small relative to men's returns, the latter being important in economic emergencies. Thus, non- and extra-conjugal sexual relationships make possible women's economic survival while putting them at greater risk for sexual harm (e.g., STIs) and for the birth of children outside of stable unions. The authors conclude that "far from being idiosyncratic results of male and/or female non-compliance to sexual and conjugal norms, non-conjugal sexual relations are predictable consequences of the interlocked sexual, economic, and moral premises that underlay male and female gender roles and men's and women's expectations regarding conjugality" (de Zalduondo and Bernard 1995:151).

Such research suggests that the connection between sexuality and reproductive health cannot be limited to an examination of sexual orientation or behavior alone, but must also account for shifting notions of masculinity, femininity, and gender relations within larger political, economic, and moral contexts. Gender organizes a system of health. For example, gender provides the structure, which is different across cultures, for what counts as a healthy male body, what physical ideals men should pursue, and what illnesses men should fear, ignore, accept, or endure. Moreover, notions of hegemonic masculinity do not refer simply to differences in ethnicity or socioeconomic status, but also to health and fitness—ideals that may or may not coincide with men's overall well-being. Men's reproductive health offers a particularly penetrating lens to explore this mutually reinforcing, but not necessarily health-promoting, relationship between gender and health.

Men's Pronatalism and Fatherhood

The relationship between men's intentions and desires for conception, pregnancy, childbirth, and fatherhood have not been studied extensively and hence are little understood, especially in international contexts. A male partner's intentions and desires have been shown to affect the timing of first pregnancy, women's desires in and prospects for becoming pregnant, partners' feelings upon learning of a pregnancy, and subsequent changes in women's evaluation of pregnancy wantedness both during pregnancy and the postpartum period (Joyce, Kaestner, and Korenman 2000; Zabin, Huggins, Emerson, and Cullins 2000). Indeed, understanding male partners' effects on intendedness of pregnancy may be important in explaining shifts in women's completed fertility rates around the world.

Anthropological research in a variety of settings has shown that men's desires for large families in pronatalist community settings marked by high fertility rates may be powerful factors in women's fertility decision making, effectively militating against fertility limitation campaigns. Furthermore, men's pronatalist desires are clearly connected to hegemonic concepts of masculinity in many societies.

This is best illustrated by examples from Latin America. The concept of machismo operates in variable ways throughout Latin America, affecting men's behavior regarding paternity and ultimately women's childbearing. According to Browner, "In Colombia it meant that a man who impregnated a woman had the right to deny paternity, abandon the woman, or insist on abortion. In contrast in the Oaxacan village [in Mexico], it generally meant that men imposed their desire for large families on their wives" (2000:783).

In urban areas of Mexico, poor men may be guided by national stereotypes of masculinity and machismo but must also reconcile themselves to the realities of life in poor barrios, which has required them to cooperate, both politically and economically, with women for survival, including through limiting family size. Indeed, Gutmann's (1996) work on changing concepts of masculinity in Mexico City provides several extended examples of men's attempts to make meaning of their experiences of fatherhood under difficult local economic and social conditions. Gutmann argues that some activities, such as work outside the home and childcare, have become less gendered, that is, less associated with either men or women over time. Cross-cultural studies have shown that, generally speaking, men tend to spend between 25 and 35 percent of the time that mothers do interacting with young children (Lamb 1987). However, in societies where men are involved in childcare, men are less inclined to display hypermasculine roles and aggressive competition (Coltrane 1994). A psychodynamic explanation holds that boys and adolescent males raised by men and women have less need to differentiate themselves from women as they mature (Gilmore 1990).

Generally speaking, men's fathering behaviors do not center on an investment in childcare during infancy and early childhood. Rather, men's investments as fathers are often tied to the concretization of access to sexual or economic resources from their female partners, their realization of broader social obligations to produce children for their families or communities, and their interest in the child's potential as an adult member of a social group (Browner 1986; Greene and Biddlecom 2000; Guyer 2000). Such diverse men's interests in fatherhood are linked to, but not captured by, a Western perspective on fathers that emphasizes, for example, genetic relationships and economic responsibility, or one based on negative examples of what fathers should not be (abusive, absent, adulterous, irresponsible).

Scholarly interests in the effects of individual fathers on children and families rose in the 1970s, with an emphasis on fathers' participation in infant care and childcare, bonding between father and children, preference for children, and effects on child development.

Five fathering functions were characterized and described as endowment, provision, protection, caregiving, and formation. In reviewing this literature on fathers, Tripp-Reimer and Wilson (1991) suggest it has led to two lines of anthropological investigation on father–child relationships: ethological primate studies in biological anthropology, and culture and personality studies in cultural anthropology.

In considering male parenting across species, primatologists have emphasized mating patterns and potential for male investment in child survival within social contexts. Among solitary primates such as orangutans and single-male/multifemale grouping primates such as gorillas, males have been observed killing other males' offspring. Orangutans are the only nonhuman primate group in which males engage in forced copulations with females. Among multimale/multifemale grouping primates such as baboons and chimpanzees, however, males may invest in the offspring of other males. Primatologists such as Smuts and Gubernick (1992) have demonstrated the importance of nonhuman primate social relations resembling friendship between males and females in mediating sexual access, as well as influencing maternal and infant health. The authors argue that male investment in infants is often not determined by genetic paternity, but instead reflects a male's social relationship with the infant's mother and the possibility for future mating opportunities. Nonhuman primate studies suggest that rather than a single model of primate paternity, a range of paternal behaviors exists related to broader social relations. Such findings from ethological primate studies are important for studies of human fathering in that they caution against simple biological determinism.

Cultural anthropologists, too, have emphasized the importance of social relations, such as division of labor, social status, and household arrangements, in determining the nature of family life and child well-being. In particular, the cultural and personality school of anthropology has emphasized the effects of early childhood experience with parents, as determined in part by these social structures, in determining adult behavior. Such a perspective focuses on the way culture reproduces itself, suggesting that parenting behavior is in part determined by cultural norms and values, which are then impressed upon children at early ages in ways that will affect their adult lives. Although the culture and personality perspective has been challenged as overly deterministic, the perspective has made valuable contributions in understanding cross-cultural patterns of fathering, such as the effects of father absence on offspring, ceremonies of male initiation, and male segregation at puberty (Tripp-Reimer and Wilson 1991).

Though very different, these diverse anthropological perspectives stress that fathers' relations with mothers and children are influenced by social structural factors. Fatherhood, and especially responsible fatherhood, will take on different meanings when different social structures prevail. Even within Western concepts of fatherhood, historians trace ideological changes over time. Economic shifts in the late eighteenth and early nineteenth centuries changed the role of fathers as collaborators within households in which they were seen as rulers to supporters of families who worked outside the home. More recent changes in the United States include a shift from single-income fathers as bureaucratic managers to more cooperative models as fathers face additional responsibilities in dual-income families (May and Strickwerda 1992).

Yet, such models represent normative, hegemonic, idealized, and potentially minority experiences of fatherhood. For the most part, the emphasis in research on fatherhood has been on the effects that fathers have on others, rather than on the effects of fathering on fathers (Tripp-Reimer and Wilson 1991). More recent research on fathers emphasizes how local contexts, along with broader ideological underpinnings, combine with men's individual attempts to define fatherhood experiences and expectations for themselves (Reed 2005; Townsend 2002). One study of expectant fathers in the United States reported that though men wanted to be involved in pregnancy, childbirth, and parenting, they found few models of men as parents to guide them, and they struggled on their own for relevance as fathers (Jordan 1990). Townsend (2002) examines a highly uniform cultural norm of American fatherhood—part of what he calls the "package deal"—which is composed of emotional closeness, provision, protection, and endowment. This cultural norm, he argues, provides a lens of meaning and anticipation for men's often contradictory experiences of parenting. In interviews with men who graduated from a Silicon Valley high school in 1972, he examines "the composition of, and internal contradiction within, a cultural model of successful male adulthood and fatherhood" (20) "to understand how [men] construct themselves as men and fathers in order to better understand their actions" (28).

Such studies have, for the most part, been confined to North American and European fathers; however, more studies have begun to investigate father–child relationships in non-Western settings. Hewlett's (1991, 1992) work among the Aka Pygmies, who exhibit more paternal care than any other human group, suggests that male caregiving for infants may be part of a generalized reciprocity between husband and wife. Hewlett develops an ecological family systems theory of paternal caregiving, arguing that shared communicative activity between partners leads to greater partner intimacy as well as increased infant care by fathers.

In reviewing literature on father involvement in developing countries, Engle and Breaux (1998) point out that more is known about father's absence than presence. They suggest that, in addition to a caring relationship and economic support, one of men's most important influences cross-culturally is not having children outside a partnership. They consider evolutionary, economic, ecological, and cultural explanations for why some fathers, such as those described by Hewlett, invest more in children, while other fathers do not.

Men's Experiences of Reproductive Impairment and Loss

Just as men's experiences of fathering are poorly understood, men's experiences of and attitudes toward reproductive impairment and loss are just beginning to be investigated. For example, in the burgeoning anthropological literature on infertility and the uses of assisted reproductive technologies (ARTs), men's experiences of their own or their wives' infertility have been underprivileged, despite the fact that male infertility factors contribute to more than half of all cases of infertility worldwide (van Balen and Inhorn 2002). Yet, a growing body of anthropological research suggests the profound impact of male infertility on masculinity. Because men often deem paternity an important achievement and a major source of their masculine identity, male infertility may have significant emasculating effects. In some parts of the world, such as the Muslim Middle East, men may compete with one another in the realms of virility and fertility such that men demonstrate masculinity by fathering children, especially sons. Similarly, men and women alike conflate men's sexual problems (e.g., impotence) with male infertility (Ali 1996, 2000; Lindisfarne 1994). Men failing as virile patriarchs are deemed weak and ineffective, and will often go to great lengths to hide their infertility from others, including their closest family members, even their wives (Inhorn 2002, 2003a, 2003b). In studies of male infertility in India, most men are so humiliated by their infertility and resultant lack of fatherhood that they would rather resort to donor insemination (DI) than adoption (Bharadwaj 2003). As long as wives are willing to collude in a family secret, infertile men using DI can maintain the social pretense that they have fathered a child with their own sperm.

These studies from India and the Middle East show that most men do not accept the idea of social fatherhood through adoption, making a resort to ARTs the only viable option (Inhorn and Bharadwaj 2003). Although social fatherhood is more acceptable in the West, where both adoption and stepfatherhood are relatively common, infertile men still grapple with the moral and emotional ambiguities surrounding the acceptance of donor sperm as a solution to their infertility (Becker 2002). In one comparative study of infertile men in Canada and Israel, the subjects felt they were expected to "compete" with another man, the sperm donor, who could easily substitute for them as a biological progenitor (Carmeli and Birenbaum-Carmeli 1994). Thus, the authors of this study suggest that infertility may have a "diffuse, total impact" on men, who may become a "target of ridicule" if their infertility becomes known to family and friends.

Even in the United States, where ARTs and infertility support groups are now widely available, men's infertility remains much more stigmatized than women's (Becker 2002), suggesting that male infertility has potentially profound consequences for men's sense of their own masculinity. In an article provocatively titled "The End of the Line: Men's Experiences of Being Unable to Produce a Child," Webb and Daniluk (1999) note that men's feelings of personal inadequacy constituted a major theme during interviews about their infertility. According to the authors, "[t]he participants used words and phrases like failure, useless, a dud, inadequate, not a real man, garbage, loser, and defective in reference to their self-perceptions as infertile men—men who were unable to 'give their wife a child'" (15). Some men attempted to compensate for their feelings of inadequacy by acting like "super jocks," having affairs with other women or throwing themselves into their work. In another study, men reported that their male physicians attempted to "smooth troubled waters" by referring to their infertility as "shooting blanks"—language that left men feeling separate and estranged from their somatic experiences (Moynihan 1998). In the West, both infertility and its treatment have been reported as resulting for some men in impaired sexual functioning and dissatisfaction, marital communication and adjustment problems, interpersonal relationship difficulties, and emotional and psychological distress (Abbey, Andrews, and Halman 1991; Daniluk 1988; Greil 1997; Greil, Porter, and Leitko 1990; Nachtigall, Becker, and Wozny 1992; van Balen and Trimbos-Kemper 1994).

Relatively little is understood about what happens to men (including infertile men using ARTs) who are able to father a child but whose partners experience a pregnancy loss through spontaneous abortion, stillbirth, or neonatal death. Findings from investigation of miscarriage in Western countries (Cecil 1996; Miron and Chapman 1994; Murphy 1998; Puddifoot and Johnson 1997) suggest that men are caught in a double bind. On the one hand, they feel the need to avoid showing emotion so they can support their partners through the physically difficult experience of pregnancy loss, including delivery of a dead or dying child; on the other hand, they experience similar emotions of the grief and loss experienced by their female partners. This is perhaps especially true as biomedical technologies, such as prenatal sonograms, have changed men's expectations of paternal bonding to unborn children (Morgan and Michaels 1999). Research clearly suggests that men's feelings about miscarriage and stillbirth are influenced by fetal-imaging techniques. In interviews with American couples who experienced a spontaneous abortion, Layne (1992, 1999) found that fetal imaging affected the personhood status men assigned to a fetus and provided, for both men and women, a previously unavailable mode of knowing about a fetus. Couples who had used fetal imaging prior to a pregnancy loss often reverted to religious belief systems as a way of making sense of the reproductive tragedy. Thus, sonogram images provided pictures of "angels" who had returned to heaven. Such studies exhibit how men's relationships with their own experiences of reproduction are mediated not only by their physical separation from pregnancy, but also by numerous systems of meaning—material, medical, and moral in nature—that may be artfully interwoven or ultimately contradict one another.

Conclusion

As men are more completely drawn into discussions of reproductive health, frameworks will be necessary to organize and hopefully explain the reproductive roles they play and the reproductive problems they experience. Given the centrality of sexuality and reproduction in human relationships, individual psychological explanations—such as motivations and desires—will likely be combined with explanations of structural shifts in social, economic, and political organization to account for kinds and distributions of different reproductive health patterns and problems. More nuanced theoretical approaches will help to account, for example, for the increased investment of some men in the reproductive health of their partners and offspring, with the simultaneously declining investment—or flight from fatherhood—evident in many parts of the world.

In conclusion, it is tempting to draw parallels to classic demographic transition theory to explain men's attitudes toward fertility, pregnancy, childbirth, and fathering. To be specific, a distinction could be drawn between the instrumental value of children and their intrinsic value; that is, children's value for other purposes relative to their value in themselves. Such an argument might run as follows: in high-fertility, high-mortality populations, children have higher instrumental and lower intrinsic value for men, insofar as children serve to contribute to parental wealth, ensure lineage and community viability as adults, and consolidate a man's position as a full and potentially prestigious member of a community. High intrinsic value for children may be mitigated by the high rates of early mortality. As mortality falls, and child survival is less tenuous, the intrinsic value of children will rise. Their instrumental value, meanwhile, will have historically fallen as mercantilist and capitalistic economic systems limit the economic contribution of children to their parents and families. Resulting falling fertility rates will both reflect and contribute to the increasing intrinsic value of children, allowing few children to be heavily invested in for personal fulfillment. At the same time, the decline in instrumental value will release some men from responsibilities for partner and child welfare, in that men's instrumental needs must be satisfied in ways not involving their children. In particular, men may pursue personal success and enjoyment outside the context of family life—delaying marriage, initiating divorce, using birth control, and limiting participation in childcare.

Such a perspective complements other anthropological perspectives on demographic transition, including Caldwell's (1982) wealth flows theory and Handwerker's (1986) theory of gatekeeping, as well as the work of LeVine (1988), who has argued that different parenting strategies exist in agrarian and urban-industrial groups (i.e., agrarian groups maximize numbers of surviving children, and urban-industrial groups reduce numbers of children to focus on imparting skills to them). This transition framework also incorporates a subjective component in the valuation of children rather than simply regarding children as part of a wealth flow or access to resources. Moreover, it could be used to explain developments in countries such as the United States, where the nuclear family has been shown to be eroding.

Using such a framework, several predictions can be made about men's attitudes toward reproduction and reproductive health. With the transition framework described above, one might expect an increase in the importance of individual child survival and investment in individual births, as well as investment in the reproductive health of women during, after, and between pregnancies. Furthermore, one might expect changes in men's subjective experience of reproductive health problems that interfere with healthy reproduction. These would include sexual dysfunction, infertility, spontaneous abortion and stillbirth, induced abortion, the birth of disabled children, and the reproductive health problems of their partners. Men in "pretransition" regimes would be expected to experience such reproductive health issues as social and economic problems, while men in "posttransition" populations would likely experience them as personal psychological problems.

The anthropological perspectives presented in this chapter, although resonating with such an explanatory framework, ultimately argue against such a "male transition" model. Such an explanatory model, though it provides a useful starting point for envisioning reproductive health, is overly unilinear and deterministic, and does not recognize the plural relationships, positive and negative, existing between men and others, including their reproductive partners, within any single social group. Ideals of masculinity, male sexuality, reproduction, and fathering also differ greatly among societies that have not yet or have only partially undergone demographic transition. This model projects Western sexual and reproductive mores such as monogamy, fidelity, and responsible fatherhood, within a historical, quasi-evolutionary trajectory.

An alternative, anthropological account of the kind proposed in this chapter would emphasize that men's subjective experiences of masculinity, reproduction, and fatherhood do not necessarily or invariably change over time as societies continue to "develop." Rather, concepts of manhood and masculinity, influenced by economic and social structures that simultaneously influence fertility regimes, have shifted with changes in those structures. Such changes may be caused by demographic transition, may accompany it, or may in fact cause it (Schneider and Schneider 1995), suggesting that the model described above would need to be carefully evaluated in local historical contexts.

In returning to the international health perspectives mentioned at the beginning of this chapter, we see anthropology positively influencing an evolving reproductive health paradigm incorporating men in several ways. First, the concept of local biologies suggests that men's reproductive health must be evaluated within context rather than against a Western norm that is likely neither representative nor optimal (Bribiescas 2001). Men's reproductive behaviors, rather than solely the product of individual decisions, occur within an ecological context that must be carefully investigated. Second, cultural anthropology demonstrates the paucity of information on the reproductive health of men and the processes by which men come to define and understand their own reproductive health needs. Far from a set of biomedical outcomes conceived of as separate from social constructions such as gender, reproductive health seems to play a part in actually defining systems of gender. Thus, anthropological studies must further address how reproduction and reproductive health affect other areas of men's lives, including their notions of masculinity.

Finally, as the meanings of masculinity change, so have the meanings of reproduction, in ways that ultimately affect the healthy reproduction of men and their families. Thus, understanding changing notions of gender and masculinity is a vitally important component of the reproductive health initiative in the new millennium, with anthropological research shedding new light on what it means to "be a man" in societies around the globe.

Acknowledgments

The original version of this chapter was published in the *International Journal of Men's Health* 2, no. 1 (2003): 31–56. Copyright © 2003 by the Men's Studies Press. Reproduced with the permission of the Men's Studies Press.

References

Abbey, A., F. M. Andrews, L. J. Halman. 1991. "Gender's Role in Responses to Infertility." *Psychology of Women Quarterly* 15:295–316.

Ali, K. A. 1996. "Notes on Rethinking Masculinities: An Egyptian Case." In *Learning about Sexuality: A Practical Beginning*, ed. S. Zeidenstein and K. Moore. New York: Population Council and International Women's Health Coalition Network.

———. 2000. "Making 'Responsible' Men: Planning the Family in Egypt." In *Fertility and the Male Life-Cycle in the Era of Fertility Decline*, ed. C. Bledsoe, S. Lerner, and J. I. Guyer. Oxford: Oxford University Press.

Bandarage, A. 1997. *Women, Population and Global Crisis: A Political-Economic Analysis*. London: Zed.

Becker, G. 2002. "Deciding Whether to Tell Children about Donor Insemination: An Unresolved Question in the United States." In *Infertility around the Globe: New Thinking on Childlessness, Gender, and Reproductive Technologies*, ed. M. C. Inhorn and F. van Balen. Berkeley: University of California Press.

Bharadwaj, A. 2002. "Conception Politics: Medical Egos, Media Spotlights, and the Contest over Test-Tube Firsts in India." In *Infertility around the*

Globe: New Thinking on Childlessness, Gender, and Reproductive Technologies, ed. M. C. Inhorn and F. van Balen. Berkeley: University of California Press.

———. 2003. "Why Adoption Is not an Option in India: The Visibility of Infertility, the Secrecy of Donor Insemination, and Other Cultural Complexities." *Social Science and Medicine* 56:1867–80.

Bledsoe, C., J. I. Guyer, and S. Lerner. 2000. "Fertility and the Male Life-Cycle in the Era of Fertility Decline." In *Fertility and the Male Life-Cycle in the Era of Fertility Decline*, ed. C. Bledsoe, S. Lerner, and J. I. Guyer. Oxford: Oxford University Press.

Borgerhoff Mulder, M. 1992. "Reproductive Decisions." In *Evolutionary Ecology and Human Behavior*, ed. E. A. Smith and B. Winterhalder. Hawthorne: Aldine de Gruyter.

———. 2000. "Optimizing Offspring: The Quantity-Quality Tradeoff in Agropastoral Kipsigis." *Evolution and Human Behavior* 21(6):391–410.

Bottéro, A. 1991. "Consumption by Semen Loss in India and Elsewhere." *Culture, Medicine, and Psychiatry* 15(3):303–20.

Bourgois, P. I. 1995. *In Search of Respect: Selling Crack in El Barrio*. Cambridge: Cambridge University Press.

Bribiescas, R. G. 2001. "Reproductive Ecology and Life History of the Human Male." *American Journal of Physical Anthropology* 33 (Suppl.):148–76.

Browner, C. H. 1986. "The Politics of Reproduction in a Mexican Village." *Signs* 11:710–24.

———. 2000. "Situating Women's Reproductive Activities." *American Anthropologist* 102(4):773–88.

Browner, C. H., and C. F. Sargent. 1996. "Anthropology and Studies of Human Reproduction." In *Medical Anthropology: Contemporary Theory and Method*, ed. C. F. Sargent and T. M. Johnson. Westport, CT: Praeger.

Butler, J. 1990. *Gender Trouble*. Berkeley: University of California Press.

Caldwell, J. 1982. *Theory of Fertility Decline*. London: Academic Press.

Campbell, B. C., and P. W. Leslie. 1995. "Reproductive Ecology of Human Males." *Yearbook of Physical Anthropology* 38:1–26.

Carmeli, Y. S., and D. Birenbaum-Carmeli. 1994. "The Predicament of Masculinity: Towards an Understanding of Male's Experience of Infertility Treatments." *Sex Roles* 30:663–77.

Cecil, R., ed. 1996. *The Anthropology of Pregnancy Loss: Comparative Studies in Miscarriage, Stillbirth and Neonatal Death*. Oxford: Berg.

Cliquet, R., and K. Thienpont. 1995. *Population and Development: A Message from the Cairo Conference*. Dordrecht, Netherlands: Kluwer.

Collumbien, M., and S. Hawkes. 2000. "Missing Men's Messages: Does the Reproductive Health Approach Respond to Men's Sexual Health Needs?" *Culture, Health and Sexuality* 2(2):135–50.

Coltrane, S. 1994. "Theorizing Masculinities in Contemporary Social Science." In *Theorizing Masculinities*, ed. H. Brod and M. Kaufman. Thousand Oaks, CA: Sage.

Connell, R. W. 1987. *Gender and Power: Society, the Person, and Sexual Politics*. Stanford: Stanford University Press.

———. 1995. *Masculinities*. Berkeley: University of California Press.

Corrêa, S., and R. L. Reichmann. 1994. *Population and Reproductive Rights: Feminist Perspectives from the South.* London: Zed.

Courtenay, W. H. 2000. "Constructions of Masculinity and Their Influence on Men's Well-being: A Theory of Gender and Health." *Social Science and Medicine* 50:1385–1401.

Daniluk, J. C. 1988. "Infertility: Intrapersonal and Interpersonal Impact." *Fertility and Sterility* 49:982–90.

Das, V. 1995. "Conceiving the New National Honor and Practical Kinship: Unwanted Women and Children." In *The New World Order: The Global Politics of Reproduction,* ed. F. D. Ginsburg and R. Rapp. Berkeley: University of California Press.

Davis, K. 1995. *Reshaping the Female Body: The Dilemma of Cosmetic Surgery.* New York: Routledge.

Davis-Floyd, R. 1992. *Birth as an American Rite of Passage.* Berkeley: University of California Press.

Delaney, C. L. 1991. *The Seed and the Soil: Gender and Cosmology in Turkish Village Society.* Berkeley: University of California Press.

de Zalduondo, B., and J. M. Bernard. 1995. "Meanings and Consequences of Sexual-Economic Exchange: Gender, Poverty and Sexual Risk Behavior in Urban Haiti." In *Conceiving Sexuality,* ed. Richard Parker and John H. Gagnon. New York: Routledge.

Dilorio, C., T. Hartwell, and N. Hansen. 2002. "Childhood Sexual Abuse and Risk Behaviors among Men at High Risk for HIV infection." *American Journal of Public Health* 92(2):214–19.

Dixon-Mueller, R. 1993a. *Population Policy and Women's Rights: Transforming Reproductive Choice.* Westport, CT: Praeger.

———. 1993b. "The Sexuality Connection in Reproductive Health." *Studies in Family Planning* 24(5):269–82.

Doyal, L. 2000. "Gender Equity in Health: Debates and Dilemmas." *Social Science and Medicine* 51(6):931–39.

Drennan, M. 1998. *Reproductive Health: New Perspectives on Men's Participation.* Baltimore: Johns Hopkins School of Public Health, Population Information Program.

Ellison, P. T. 1999. "Reproductive Ecology and Reproductive Cancers." In *Hormones, Health, and Behavior: A Socio-Ecological and Lifespan Perspective,* ed. C. Panter-Brick and C. M. Worthman. Cambridge: Cambridge University Press.

Ellison, P. T., S. F. Lipson, M. T. O'Rourke, G. R. Bentley, B. C. Campbell, and C. Panter-Brick. 1998. "Inter- and Intra-Population Variation in the Pattern of Male Testosterone by Age." *American Journal of Physical Anthropology* 105(Suppl.):80.

Engle, P. L., and C. Breaux. 1998. "Fathers' Involvement with Children: Perspectives from Developing Countries." *Social Policy Report* 12:1–21.

Farmer, P., M. Connors, and J. Simmons, eds. 1996. *Women, Poverty, and AIDS: Sex, Drugs, and Structural Violence.* Monroe: Common Courage Press.

Feldman-Savelsberg, P. 1999. *Plundered Kitchens, Empty Wombs: Threatened Reproduction and Identity in the Cameroon Grassfields.* Ann Arbor: University of Michigan Press.

Finer, L. B., J. E. Darroch, and S. Singh. 1999. "Sexual Partnership Patterns as a Behavioral Risk Factor for Sexually Transmitted Diseases." *Family Planning Perspectives* 31(5):228–36.

Gilmore, D. D. 1990. *Manhood in the Making: Cultural Concepts of Masculinity.* New Haven: Yale University Press.

Greene, M. E., and A. E. Biddlecom. 2000. "Absent and Problematic Men: Demographic Accounts of Male Reproductive Roles." *Population and Development Review* 26(1):81–115.

Greenhalgh, S. 1995. "Anthropology Theorizes Reproduction: Integrating Practice, Political, Economic, and Feminist Perspectives." In *Situating Fertility: Anthropology and Demographic Inquiry,* ed. S. Greenhalgh. Cambridge: Cambridge University Press.

Greil, A. L. 1997. "Infertility and Psychological Distress: A Critical Review of the Literature." *Social Science and Medicine* 45:1697–1704.

Greil, A. L., K. L. Porter, and T. A. Leitko. 1990. "Sex and Intimacy among Infertile Couples." *Journal of Psychology and Human Sexuality* 2:117–38.

Gutmann, M. C. 1996. *The Meanings of Macho: Being a Man in Mexico City.* Berkeley: University of California Press.

———. 1997. "Trafficking in Men: The Anthropology of Masculinity." *Annual Review of Anthropology* 26:385–409.

Guyer, J. I. 2000. "Traditions of Studying Paternity in Social Anthropology." In *Fertility and the Male Life-Cycle in the Era of Fertility Decline,* ed. C. Bledsoe, J. I. Guyer, and S. Lerner. New York: Oxford University Press.

Handwerker, W. P. 1986. *Culture and Reproduction: An Anthropological Critique of Demographic Transition Theory.* Boulder, CO: Westview.

———. 1989. *Women's Power and Social Revolution: Fertility Transition in the West Indies,* vol. 2. Beverly Hills, CA: Sage.

Harris, M., and E. B. Ross. 1987. *Death, Sex, and Fertility: Population Regulation in Preindustrial and Developing Societies.* New York: Columbia University Press.

Herdt, G. H., ed. 1997. *Same Sex, Different Cultures: Gays and Lesbians Across Cultures.* Boulder: Westview.

Hewlett, B. S. 1991. *Intimate Fathers: The Nature and Context of Aka Pygmy Paternal Infant Care.* Ann Arbor: University of Michigan Press.

———. 1992. "Husband-Wife Reciprocity and the Father-Infant Relationship among Aka Pygmies." In *Father-Child Relations: Cultural and Biosocial Contexts,* ed. B. S. Hewlett. New York: Aldine de Gruyter.

Hill, K., and A. M. Hurtado. 1996. *Ache Life History: The Ecology and Demography of a Foraging People.* New York: Aldine de Gruyter.

Hill, K., and H. Kaplan. 1999. "Life History Traits in Humans: Theory and Empirical Studies." *Annual Review of Anthropology* 28:397–430.

Inhorn, M. C. 1994. *Quest for Conception: Gender, Infertility, and Egyptian Medical Traditions.* Philadelphia: University of Pennsylvania Press.

———. 1996. *Infertility and Patriarchy: The Cultural Politics of Gender and Family Life in Egypt.* Philadelphia: University of Pennsylvania Press.

———. 2002. "Sexuality, Masculinity, and Infertility in Egypt: Potent Troubles in the Marital and Medical Encounters." *Journal of Men's Studies* 10(3):343–59.

————. 2003a. *Local Babies, Global Science: Gender, Religion, and In Vitro Fertilization in Egypt.* New York: Routledge.

————. 2003b. "'The worms are weak': Male Infertility and Patriarchal Paradoxes in Egypt." *Men and Masculinities* 5(3):236–56.

Inhorn, M. C., and A. Bharadwaj. 2003. "Reproductively Disabled Lives: Infertility, Stigma, and Suffering in Egypt and India." In *Disability in Local and Global Worlds*, ed. B. Ingstad and S. Reynolds. Berkeley: University of California Press.

Inhorn, M. C., and F. van Balen, eds. 2002. *Infertility around the Globe: New Thinking on Childlessness, Gender, and Reproductive Technologies.* Berkeley: University of California Press.

Inhorn, M. C., and L. K. Whittle. 2001. "Feminism Meets the 'New' Epidemiologies: Toward an Appraisal of Antifeminist Biases in Epidemiological Research on Women's Health." *Social Science and Medicine* 53:553–67.

Jordan, P. L. 1990. "Laboring for Relevance: Expectant and New Fatherhood." *Nursing Research* 39(1):11–16.

Joyce, T. J., R. Kaestner, and S. Korenman. 2000. "The Stability of Pregnancy Intentions and Pregnancy-Related Maternal Behaviors." *Maternal and Child Health Journal* 4(3):171–78.

Kessler, S. J., and W. McKenna. 1978. *Gender: An Ethnomethodological Approach.* New York: Wiley.

Klein, A. M. 1995. "Life's Too Short to Die Small: Steroid Use Among Male Bodybuilders." In *Men's Health and Illness: Gender, Power, and the Body*, ed. D. F. Sabo and D. Gordon. Thousand Oaks, CA: Sage.

Kleinman, A. 1978. "International Health Care Planning from an Ethnomedical Perspective: Critique and Recommendations for Change." *Medical Anthropology* 2(2):71–96.

Krieger, N., and E. Fee. 1994. "Man-Made Medicine and Women's Health: The Biopolitics of Sex/Gender and Race/Ethnicity." *International Journal of Health Services* 24(2):265–83.

Lamb, M. E., ed. 1987. *The Father's Role: Cross-Cultural Perspectives.* Hillsdale, NJ: Erlbaum.

Lancaster, R. N. 1992. *Life Is Hard: Machismo, Danger, and the Intimacy of Power in Nicaragua.* Berkeley: University of California Press.

Lane, S. D., and Rubinstein, R. A. 1996. "International Health: Problems and Programs in Anthropological Perspective." In *Medical Anthropology: Contemporary Theory and Method*, ed. C. F. Sargent and T. M. Johnson. Westport, CT: Praeger.

Layne, L. L. 1992. "Of Fetuses and Angels: Fragmentation and Integration in Narratives of Pregnancy Loss." *Knowledge and Society* 9:29–58.

————, ed. 1999. *Transformative Motherhood: On Giving and Getting in a Consumer Culture.* New York: New York University Press.

LeVine, R. A. 1988. "Human Parental Care: Universal Goals, Cultural Strategies, and Individual Behavior." In *Parental Behavior in Diverse Societies*, ed. R. A. LeVine, P. M. Miller, and M. M. West. San Francisco: Jossey-Bass.

Lindisfarne, N. 1994. "Variant Masculinities, Variant Virginities: Rethinking 'Honour and Shame.'" In *Dislocating Masculinity: Comparative Ethnographies*, ed. A. Cornwall and N. Lindisfarne. London: Routledge.

Lock, M. M. 1993. *Encounters with Aging: Mythologies of Menopause in Japan and North America*. Berkeley: University of California Press.

Lorber, J. 1997. *Gender and the Social Construction of Illness*. Thousand Oaks, CA: Sage.

Marlowe, F. 2000. "Paternal Investment and the Human Mating System." *Behavioural Processes* 51:45–61.

May, L., and R. A. Strickwerda. 1992. "Fatherhood and Nurturance." In *Rethinking Masculinity: Philosophical Explorations in Light of Feminism*, ed. L. May and R. Strickwerda. Lanham, MD: Rowman and Littlefield.

Mbizvo, M. T. 1996. "Reproductive and Sexual Health: A Research and Developmental Challenge." *Central African Journal of Medicine* 42(3):80–85.

McDade, T. 1996. "Prostates and Profits: The Social Construction of Benign Prostatic Hyperplasia in American Men." *Medical Anthropology Quarterly* 17:1–22.

Miron, J., and J. S. Chapman. 1994. "Supporting Men's Experiences with the Event of Their Partners' Miscarriage." *Canadian Journal of Nursing Research* 26(2):61–72.

Morgan, L. M. 1993. *Community Participation in Health: The Politics of Primary Care in Costa Rica*. Cambridge: Cambridge University Press.

Morgan, L. M., and M. W. Michaels, eds. 1999. *Fetal Subjects, Feminist Positions*. Philadelphia: University of Pennsylvania Press.

Moynihan, C. 1998. "Theories of Masculinity." *British Medical Journal* 317:1072–75.

Mundigo, A. I. 1998. "The Role of Men in Improving Reproductive Health: The Direction Research Should Take." In *Reproductive Health Research: The New Directions, Biennial Report, 1996–1997*, ed. J. Khanna and P. F. A. Van Look. Geneva, Switzerland: World Health Organization.

Murphy, F. A. 1998. "The Experience of Early Miscarriage from a Male Perspective." *Journal of Clinical Nursing* 7(4):325–32.

Nachtigall, R. D., G. Becker, and M. Wozny. 1992. "The Effects of Gender-specific Diagnosis on Men's and Women's Response to Infertility." *Fertility and Sterility* 54:113–21.

Ndong, I., R. M. Becker, J. M. Haws, and M. N. Wegner. 1999. "Men's Reproductive Health: Defining, Designing and Delivering Services." *International Family Planning Perspectives* 25:S53–S55.

Nencel, L. 1996. "Pacharacas, Putas, and Chicas de su Casa: Labeling, Femininity, and Men's Sexual Selves in Lima, Peru." In *Machos, Mistresses, Madonnas: Contesting the Power of Latin American Gender Imagery*, ed. M. Melhuus and K. A. Stolen. New York: Verso.

Olayinka, B. A., L. Alexander, M. T. Mbizvo, and L. Gibney. 2000. "Generational Differences in Male Sexuality that May Affect Zimbabwean Women's Risk for Sexually Transmitted Diseases and HIV/AIDS." *East African Medical Journal* 77(2):93–97.

Panter-Brick, C., ed. 1998. *Biosocial Perspectives on Children*. Cambridge: Cambridge University Press.

Parker, R., R. M. Barbosa, and P. Aggleton, eds. 2000. "Introduction: Framing the Sexual Subject." In *Framing the Sexual Subject: The Politics of Gender, Sexuality, and Power*. Berkeley: University of California Press.

Paul, J. P., J. Catania, L. Pollack, and R. Stall. 2001. "Understanding Child-hood Sexual Abuse as a Predictor of Sexual Risk-Taking among Men Who Have Sex with Men: The Urban Men's Health Study." *Child Abuse and Neglect* 25(4):557–84.

Petchesky, R. P. 2000. "Sexual Rights: Inventing a Concept, Mapping an International Practice." In *Framing the Sexual Subject: The Politics of Gender, Sexuality, and Power,* ed. R. Parker, R. M. Barbosa, and P. Aggleton. Berkeley: University of California Press.

Pope, H. G., K. A. Phillips, and R. Olivardia. 2000. *The Adonis Complex: The Secret Crisis of Male Body Obsession.* New York: Free Press.

Potts, A. 2000. "'The essence of the hard on': Hegemonic Masculinity and the Cultural Construction of 'Erectile Dysfunction.'" *Men and Masculinities* 3:85–103.

Presser, H. B., and G. Sen. 2000. *Women's Empowerment and Demographic Processes: Moving Beyond Cairo.* Oxford: Oxford University Press.

Puddifoot, J. E., and M. P. Johnson 1997. "The Legitimacy of Grieving: The Partner's Experience at Miscarriage." *Social Science and Medicine* 45(6):837–45.

Pyne, H. H. 1994. "Reproductive Experiences and Needs of Thai Women: Where Has Development Taken Us?" In *Power and Decision: The Social Control of Reproduction,* ed. G. Sen and R. W. Snow. Boston: Harvard School of Public Health.

Rosaldo, M. Z. 1974. "Women, Culture, and Society: A Theoretical Overview." In *Women, Culture, and Society,* ed. M. Z. Rosaldo and L. Lamphere. Stanford: Sanford University Press.

Rubin, G. 1984. "Thinking Sex: Notes for a Radical Theory of the Politics of Sexuality." In *Purity and Danger: Exploring Female Sexuality,* ed. C. S. Vance. London: Routledge.

Sabo, D., and D. F. Gordon. 1995. "Rethinking Men's Health and Illness: The Relevance of Gender Studies." In *Men's Health and Illness: Gender, Power, and the Body,* vol. 8, ed. D. Sabo and D. F. Gordon. London: Sage.

Sargent, C. F. 1989. *Maternity, Medicine, and Power: Decisions in Urban Benin.* Berkeley: University of California Press.

Sargent, C. F., and C. Brettell, eds. 1996. *Gender and Health: An International Perspective.* Upper Saddle River, NJ: Prentice Hall.

Schneider, D. M. 1968. *American Kinship: A Cultural Account.* Englewood Cliffs, NJ: Prentice-Hall.

Schneider, P., and J. Schneider. 1995. "Coitus Interruptus and Family Respectability in Catholic Europe: A Sicilian Case Study." In *Conceiving the New World Order: The Global Politics of Reproduction,* ed. F. D. Ginsburg and R. Rapp. Berkeley: University of California Press.

Seidler, V. J. 1994. *Unreasonable Men: Masculinity and Social Theory.* London: Routledge.

Sellen, D. W., and R. Mace. 1997. "A Phylogenetic Analysis of the Relationship Between Fertility and Modes of Subsistence." *Current Anthropology* 38(5):878–89.

————. 1999. "A Phylogenetic Analysis of the Relationship between Sub-adult Mortality and Mode of Subsistence." *Journal of Biosocial Science* 31:1–16.

Smuts, B. B., and D. J. Gubernick. 1992. "Male-Infant Relationships in Nonhuman Primates: Paternal Investment or Mating Effort?" In *Father-Child Relations: Cultural and Biosocial Contexts*, ed. B. S. Hewlett. New York: Aldine de Gruyter.

Townsend, N. 2002. *The Package Deal: Marriage, Work, and Fatherhood in Men's Lives*. Philadelphia: Temple University Press.

Trevathan, W. R. 1996. "The Evolution of Bipedalism and Assisted Birth." *Medical Anthropology Quarterly* 10:287–89.

Tripp-Reimer, T., and S. E. Wilson. 1991. "Cross-Cultural Perspectives on Fatherhood." In *Fatherhood and Families in Cultural Context*, ed. F. W. Bozett and S. M. H. Hanson. New York: Springer.

Tyler, K. A. 2002. "Social and Emotional Outcomes of Childhood Sexual Abuse: A Review of Recent Literature." *Aggression and Violent Behavior* 7:567–89.

van Balen, F., and M. C. Inhorn. 2002. "Introduction—Interpreting Infertility: A View from the Social Sciences." In *Infertility around the Globe: New Thinking on Childlessness, Gender, and Reproductive Technologies*, ed. M. C. Inhorn and F. van Balen. Berkeley: University of California Press.

van Balen, F., and K. C. M. Trimbos-Kemper. 1994. "Factors Influencing the Well-Being of Long-Term Infertile Couples." *Journal of Psychosomatic Obstetrics and Gynecology* 15:57–164.

Vance, C. S. 1991. "Anthropology Rediscovers Sexuality: A Theoretical Comment." *Social Science and Medicine* 33(8):875–84.

Vlassoff, C., and L. Manderson. 1998. "Incorporating Gender in the Anthropology of Infectious Diseases." *Tropical Medicine and International Health* 3(12):1011–19.

Wang, Y. F. 2000. "Male Reproductive Health Research Needs and Research Agenda: Asian and Pacific Perspective." *International Journal of Andrology* 23(Suppl. 2):4–7.

Ward, V. M., J. T. Bertrand, and F. Puac. 1992. "Exploring Sociocultural Barriers to Family Planning among Mayans in Guatemala." *International Family Planning Perspectives* 18(2):59–65.

Webb, R. E., and J. C. Daniluk. 1999. "The End of the Line: Infertile Men's Experiences of Being Unable to Produce a Child." *Men and Masculinities* 2:6–25.

Windom, C. S., and J. B. Kuhns. 1996. "Childhood Victimization and Subsequent Risk for Promiscuity, Prostitution, and Teenage Pregnancy: A Prospective Study." *American Journal of Public Health* 86:1607–12.

Wingood, G. M., and R. J. DiClemente. 1998. "Gender-Related Correlates and Predictors of Consistent Condom Use among Young Adult African-American Women: A Prospective Analysis." *International Journal of STD and AIDS* 9(3):139–45.

Wood, J. W. 1994. "Maternal Nutrition and Reproduction: Why Demographers and Physiologists Disagree about a Fundamental Relationship." *Annals of the New York Academy of Science* 709:101–16.

Worthman, C. M. 1995. "Hormones, Sex, and Gender." *Annual Review of Anthropology* 24:593–616.

———. 1999. "Faster, Further, Higher: Biology and the Discourses on Human Sexuality." In *Culture, Biology, and Sexuality*, ed. A. Miracle and D. Suggs. Athens: University of Georgia Press.

Yanagisako, S. J., and C. L. Delaney, eds. 1995. *Naturalizing Power: Essays in Feminist Cultural Analysis*. New York: Routledge.

Zabin, L. S., G. R. Huggins, M. R. Emerson, and V. E. Cullins. 2000. "Partner Effects on a Woman's Intention to Conceive: 'Not with this partner.'" *Family Planning Perspectives* 32(1):39–45.

Zeidenstein, S., and K. Moore, eds. 1996. *Learning about Sexuality: A Practical Beginning*. New York: Population Council.

Chapter 4

MEN'S INFLUENCES ON WOMEN'S REPRODUCTIVE HEALTH: MEDICAL ANTHROPOLOGICAL PERSPECTIVES

Matthew R. Dudgeon and Marcia C. Inhorn

Since the mid-1990s, reproductive health has emerged as an organizational framework linking more traditional reproductive issues, such as family planning and maternal and child health, to a suite of additional concerns, including sexually transmitted infections (STIs), infertility, sexual dysfunction, and sexual violence. Several related factors precipitated this paradigm shift to reproductive health, including:

- the emphasis on reproductive and sexual rights by feminists in developing and developed countries (Corrêa and Reichmann 1994; Petchesky 2000);
- the denunciation of population control as a motivation for contraceptive research and distribution (Bandarage 1997; Dixon-Mueller 1993a);
- the need to address the HIV/AIDS pandemic and the increasing incidence of heterosexual transmission (Cates and Stone 1992; Dixon-Mueller 1993b; Mbizvo 1996; Parker, Barbosa, and Aggleton 2000); and
- the failure of family planning and maternal-child health programs to address complex reproductive health issues, such as sexuality (Cliquet and Thienpont 1995).

In developing frameworks for a new reproductive health paradigm, attention has been drawn to the absence of men from previous reproductive health initiatives and the need to incorporate men into any emerging programs (Collumbien and Hawkes 2000; Hawkes 1998; Mundigo 1998, 2000). Men are important actors who influence, both positively and negatively, both directly and indirectly, the reproductive health outcomes of women and children. The ongoing challenge to the reproductive health framework is how to characterize men's possible influences and to assess their impact on women's and children's health. The 1994 International Conference on Population and Development Programme of Action (ICPD) in Cairo, Egypt, explicitly calls for the inclusion of men in women's reproductive health through three avenues: the promotion of men's use of contraceptives through increased education and distribution; the involvement of men in roles supportive of women's sexual and reproductive decisions, especially contraception; and the encouragement of men's responsible sexual and reproductive practices to prevent and control STIs (Basu 1996; DeJong 2000). Feminists from developed and developing countries have extended the examination of men's involvement in reproductive health beyond these three domains by critiquing the patriarchal power structures in societies restricting women's autonomy and access to resources (Bandarage 1997). Such structural constraints range from asymmetries in pay and work opportunities, to legal systems that allow for domestic violence and rape (Boonstra et al. 2000; Pollard 1994) yet criminalize abortion (Silberschmidt and Rasch 2001), to the comparative lack of research on and development of male contraceptive technologies (Mundigo 1998).

Although the importance of these macrostructural relationships between men's and women's reproductive health is clear, perspectives for understanding these relationships are not. For example, the concept of patriarchy, men's systematic domination of key structural and ideological resources and positions, which is often institutionalized on multiple levels (e.g., legal, medical, political), does not fully explain differences in reproductive health outcomes. Yet, it is clear that patriarchal relations do affect women's reproductive health on a "macro" level. For example, women's reproductive health is affected by male policymakers, male health care administrators, and male service providers, who may perpetuate a dominant "male definition" of what is important and what is not without taking heed of women's perceptions and felt needs. However, as shown in the first part of this chapter, the reverse also may be true, when men's reproductive health needs are underemphasized in rights-oriented reproductive health policy discussions that explicitly privilege the rights of women.

On the "micro" level, men also affect women's reproductive health as partners of women and fathers of their children. As will be shown in the second part of this chapter, male partners' influences on women's reproductive health are complex, involving effects both direct and indirect, and both biological and social. Understanding male partners' effects on reproductive health, and particularly the range of meanings of reproductive behaviors and beliefs within particular social and cultural settings, represents an important avenue for research in medical anthropology. Because of its long empirical tradition in non-Western settings, as well as its qualitative research strategy of ethnography, the discipline of anthropology—and particularly the subdiscipline of medical anthropology—represents a prime field for discovery of local reproductive norms and practices, including how individuals living within communities define and experience their reproductive health and health problems. This focus on meaning and the lived experience of reproductive health within particular local, cultural contexts allows medical anthropology to inform reproductive health discussions based on findings from epidemiology, demography, and other sectors of international health, including population policy and family planning. Clearly, the cultural meanings of reproduction will have a significant impact on men's and women's understandings of their own reproductive health status and will influence their health care–seeking behavior. Thus, reproductive health policymakers have increasingly come to recognize the "value added" by qualitative health research when attempting to improve understandings of male involvement in reproductive health, as well as provide culturally appropriate interventions (Drennan 1998; Mbizvo 1996; Presser and Sen 2000).

This chapter presents medical anthropological perspectives and ethnographic research findings that contribute to the understanding of men's influence on women's reproductive health. In addition, the chapter points to major lacunae, where medical anthropological research is still developing. The chapter opens with a summary of current frameworks regarding men's and women's reproductive rights, critiquing the notion of "rights" from an explicitly anthropological perspective. As part of this discussion, the question of equality versus equity is critically addressed, with suggestions for approaches to incorporate men into reproductive health programs.

The chapter then turns to a number of specific examples of men's influences on women's reproductive health in the areas of contraception, abortion, STIs, pregnancy and childbirth, infertility, and

fetal harm. Although clearly not an exhaustive list, these examples
have been chosen in order to highlight both past and recent ethnographic research of medical anthropologists, some of them working
within international public health settings (Hahn 1999). In addition,
these examples illustrate how medical anthropology often "takes
over" where standard epidemiological and demographic research
"leaves off" (Nations 1986), by attempting to understand why men
and women behave the way they do in the realm of reproductive
relations. Thus, in each section, the contributions of medical anthropologists are distinguished from public health research cited. In the
concluding section, suggestions are provided for reproductive health
research that reaches men and leads to better reproductive health
outcomes for women.

Reproductive Rights: Equity, Equality, and Intervention

Post-Cairo, reproductive health is argued to be a basic human right
and, as such, is protected by existing international agreements on
human rights, including documents on the rights of women, children, and indigenous peoples (Cook and Dickens 1999, 2000; Cook,
Dickens, Wilson, and Scarrow 2001; Cottingham and Myntti 2002;
Petchesky 1998; Sen, George, and Ostlin 2002). However, the de-
lineation of rights and responsibilities in the area of reproductive
and sexual health proves to be a difficult task. Why? Presently, the
framework of reproductive rights depends heavily on the compliance of nation-states with the programmatic statements of the international conventions they have signed. However, it is often in
the traditional and marginalized communities in which anthropologists typically work where state laws have the least influence and
the state is least accountable. These communities, or some of their
members, may explicitly reject the concept of reproductive rights
as conflicting with local law or community norms. In addition,
the very concept of a "right" may be difficult for some members
of more marginal communities to understand and operationalize.
For example, in a cross-cultural study, Petchesky and Judd (1998)
found that many women understood their rights ad hoc in terms of
their desire to avoid conditions of suffering they had experienced in
the past. Furthermore, although the notion of reproductive rights
is usually conceived of in terms of individual persons, reproduction never involves single individuals and rarely involves only two
people. Instead, as many anthropologists cited in this chapter have

shown, reproduction often lies at the intersection of group interests, including families, households, kinship, ethnic, and religious
groups, states, and international organizations.

In discussions of the role of anthropology in reproductive health,
anthropology has heretofore been conceived of as a tool for investigating and explicating local perspectives on reproductive health
and rights in order to implement ideals of human rights (Population Council 2001). However, a critical medical anthropological perspective must question the exercise of power through reproductive
health rights as leveraged by international law. For example, the right
to contraceptive access is not necessarily met by the contraceptive
method mix available or promoted in many developing countries.

Beyond the rights debate, a second important distinction—and
one that is key to best providing reproductive health services for both
men and women—is that between reproductive health equality and
reproductive health equity (see Basu 1996; Blanc 2001; Petchesky
1998; Population Council 2001). "Equality" emphasizes egalitarian
reproductive health outcomes for all men and women, achieved ideally through equal or complementary services. Conversely, "equity"
refers to an approach that emphasizes justice in reproductive health
outcomes, achieved through services provided within the context
of existing and recognized differences in reproductive physiology as
well as inequalities in economic and social resources.

Because the concept of equity rests on subjective measures of
fairness and justice, international stakeholders, such as the World
Health Organization (WHO), have tended to endorse goals of equality as measured through more objective indicators, such as maternal mortality (Population Council 2001). Implicit in discussions of
equity is the realization that the reproductive and sexual needs of
women often are culturally subordinate to those of men and that
men locally have rights over women's reproduction and sexuality.
Thus, the achievement of equity could in many contexts require
privileging the reproductive rights of women over those of men.

In these discussions of equality versus equity, particular notions
of men's involvement in reproduction have been used to inform
frameworks for incorporating men. Men have traditionally been
portrayed, either explicitly or implicitly, as relatively unconcerned
and unknowledgeable about reproductive health. They have been
seen primarily as impregnators of women or as the cause of women's
poor reproductive health outcomes, through STI exposure, sexual
violence, or physical abuse. In addition, they have been regarded
(often rightly so) as formidable barriers to women's decision making
about fertility, contraceptive use, and health care utilization (Greene

2000). Indeed, some of these generalizations about men have been empirically demonstrated across cultures. Relative to women, men tend to have more sexual partners over their lives, are more likely to have multiple partners simultaneously, are more likely to pursue commercial sex, are more likely to have extra-partner sexual relations, and are more likely to commit an act of violence against women, adolescents, and other men. Men have the option to be absent at childbirth, tend to commit smaller percentages of their income to children and childcare, and contribute less time to direct childcare (Greene and Biddlecom 2000).

In examining some of these stereotypes in demographic research, Greene and Biddlecom (2000) show consistent exceptions to many of these generalizations. They find that

- men may be more, less, or equally informed about contraceptives than women;
- many men participate in birth control through male and coital-dependent methods;
- men's pronatalism varies, with average fertility preferences often differing little from women's and with wide variation between men from different regions;
- men's dominance in reproductive decision making varies and may vary over the reproductive life course of the couple;
- men may not prevent women from covertly using contraceptives; and
- men as well as women may have financial motives for sex, as children may legitimate partners' claims to one another's resources.

An important advance in characterizing men's involvement has been the more explicit theorization of the role of power in sexual and reproductive relationships. Blanc (2001) distinguishes between the power of individuals within a social group and their relative power within dyadic sexual and reproductive relationships. She argues that the difference between power to (i.e., power as positive possibility for oneself) and power over (i.e., power as negative and limiting of others) is of particular importance in these relationships.

Recent attempts to conceptualize reproductive health interventions based on these observations about power have led to two major frameworks for the incorporation of men into programs and services. Basu (1996) has described the first framework—one he finds in the programmatic statements of both the Cairo and Beijing conferences—as "Women's Rights and Men's Responsibilities." Namely, though both women and men have rights and responsibilities in the area of reproductive health, this framework differently addresses rights and responsibilities for men and women because of existing power differentials and the unequal distribution of resources between men and women. Extrapolating to the realm of reproductive health, women's and men's contributions to reproductive health are seen as unequal and their experiences of reproductive health as fundamentally different. Interventions following from this framework tend to focus on the reproductive health problems caused by men, along with approaches to empowering women. This framework focuses on the need for reproductive health equity rather than equality. Yet, as Basu points out, by focusing on equity versus equality, this framework may not achieve its goal; interventions excluding men may do less to achieve reproductive health equity than those including them.

Basu discusses explicitly the need for equality in addressing men's individual reproductive rights; even so, he does not address men's rights as they involve other individuals. Because reproduction always involves more than one individual with rights, the discussion of reproductive rights must address the coexisting reproductive rights of men and women in relationship to each other. This is particularly important for integrating men into this perspective, given that men often have culturally explicit and implicit rights to women's sexuality and reproduction.

Rather than only discussing men's responsibilities as partners, or their rights as individual reproductive actors, an anthropological perspective emphasizes men's rights regarding other reproductive participants, and how these rights—as derived from international treaties and conventions—may differ from locally defined notions of rights. To redirect the reproductive rights discussion in this way leads to numerous complex ethical questions. For example, do men have the right to withhold care or support from a pregnant mother? Is responsibility for care to be derived solely from genetic paternity, from consanguine or marital relations, or from some combination? Do men have the right to have multiple partners or children with multiple partners? Do they have the right to withhold information about their STI status? Do they have the right to play a part in the termination of pregnancy? These questions will have to be addressed in future reproductive rights discussions.

A second framework for including men in reproductive health, "Men as Partners" (Becker and Robinson 1998; Wegner, Landry, Wilkinson, and Tzanis 1998), emphasizes a client-based approach that seeks to provide sustainable reproductive health care for men without compromising (but hopefully improving) services for women. Such a perspective recognizes men's important contributions to reproductive health, as well as men's needs and attempts to reconcile conflicting reproductive goals within the context of reproductive partnerships, primarily married couples. The approach adheres to the three avenues for involvement issued at the ICPD, with services provided through screening, education, counseling, diagnosis, and treatment (Ndong, Becker, Haws, and Wegner 1999). Such an approach focuses on men as partners—that is, as members of a family, usually as husbands, with a significant locus of responsibility for reproduction. The framework therefore envisions male involvement in reproduction and addresses men's own bioreproductive and psychosexual needs.

However, given the explicit focus of this framework on the cooperation of men and women in reproductive decision making, this framework downplays the different reproductive and sexual strategies and goals that men and women may pursue separately, including outside of the marital union. Greene and Biddlecom (2000) have observed that, in this approach, the ideological assumption of heterosexual monogamy with fidelity associated with reproductive health actually becomes a programmatic goal. This perspective has been difficult to implement, as it requires a positive and more general definition of "partner." Moreover, it does not clearly answer whether or not a partner approach implies that services for men should be integrated or separate from those for women; this is a contentious issue that depends heavily on existing services as well as the kinds of services provided. The partner perspective also makes several implicit assumptions about men and reproductive health—namely, that educating men about men's and women's reproductive health needs will make men more sensitive and responsive to these needs, and that incorporating men into reproductive health programs will improve both men's and women's reproductive health outcomes. Such assumptions may not hold in all contexts.

Men's Influences on Women's Reproductive Health: Examples from Medical Anthropology

Difficulties in defining reproductive health, rights, and equity have become as apparent as men's involvement in reproductive health has increasingly been addressed on an international level. From an anthropological perspective, these difficulties arise in large part because of the significant variation—biological and cultural—in how different groups of men and women encounter, define, and experience reproductive health problems, as well as the significant variation in family and legal structures that, in part, produce these problems. A medical anthropological perspective emphasizes the diversity in local health needs and the importance of understanding this diversity in order to develop appropriate interventions. As noted earlier, medical anthropology has tended to describe cultural variations in health belief systems, emphasizing actors' own descriptions and experiences of reproductive health and illness within local cultural systems. Furthermore, a critical branch of medical anthropology examines how structures of inequality within and between social groups cause, perpetuate, and augment reproductive health problems (Farmer 1999). In the wake of the AIDS epidemic, numerous researchers have called for ongoing qualitative studies to understand not only the ways reproductive health problems are experienced by men and women on a local level, but also to understand the structural factors leading to poor reproductive health outcomes (e.g., Farmer, Connors, and Simmons 1996).

The remainder of this chapter examines medical anthropological research about men's influences on women's reproductive health, at the same time taking note of some of the specific areas where medical anthropology has failed to produce sufficient ethnographic findings. In each section, medical anthropological research is highlighted against a backdrop of groundbreaking empirical findings from public health and demography, the first disciplines to acknowledge the importance of male involvement in reproduction. As this review demonstrates, much of the medical anthropological research examines dyadic, heterosexual relationships between women and their male partners, explicitly focusing on men's involvement *from their own perspective*. However, at least some of this research remains cognizant of larger structural relationships, involving gender asymmetries and imbalances in economic and political power, affecting the interactions within the male–female reproductive dyad.

Men's Influence on Contraception

Contraceptive use and effectiveness depend directly on men's involvement. Of all the contraceptive options currently available to men, only one—vasectomy—is completely under male control. With the use of condoms and withdrawal, some degree of negotiation is involved, and cooperation is necessary for the method to be used effectively. The use of female-centered methods—such as oral contraceptives, injections, implants, intrauterine devices, spermicides, and barrier methods—such as the diaphragm or female condom, may be significantly influenced by male partners in that men may mediate the economic resources required to access these methods, or may indirectly sanction or directly prohibit women's use of these methods. Furthermore, the absence of a stable male partner may be one of the most important determinants of women's desire to avoid a pregnancy, especially young women and women with few resources.

Several anthropological studies examine how social organization and culture may influence contraceptive patterns and men's influences on them. For example, research from Africa, including Ghana (Ezeh 1993) and Nigeria (Bankole 1995), suggests that men may have significant influence over women's contraceptive decisions, while the converse may not be as true. Bankole (1995) reports that for the Nigerian Yoruba, an apparent "equality" in spousal desire for more children breaks down when the number of children is taken into consideration. Men's wishes for more children are more likely to be met when couples have few children, while women's wishes prevail with more surviving children in the family. Men's desires, however, affect most directly the first decade of a marriage and the first four children.

Anthropological perspectives also provide context for the results of contraceptive research. For example, in Kenya, where more than 90 percent of men approve of contraception, more than half of them believe women should be responsible for it. Furthermore, 37 percent of men approve of female rather than male sterilization (Were and Karanja 1994). Another study from Kenya (Dodoo 1993) notes the importance of lineage and descent, such that partners are tied more directly to their lineage groups than to each other. In this situation, bride wealth compensates a bride's family for her lost fertility, securing the rights to her children to her groom's lineage rather than to her own. In this context, men may be much more invested than women in the use and timing of contraception.

Bankole (1995) and Dodoo (1993) have suggested that estimates of unmet contraceptive need in sub-Saharan Africa may be invalid when derived from data collected only from women. In Zimbabwe, for example, men report making final decisions in contraceptive use, even while women are held responsible for obtaining contraceptives (Mbizvo and Adamchack 1991). These and a number of other studies demonstrate discordance within couples regarding contraceptive use (Becker 1999; Bongaarts and Bruce 1995; Casterline, Perez, and Biddlecom 1997; Casterline and Sinding 2000; Klijzing 2000; Ngom 1997; Wolff, Blanc, and Ssekamatte-Ssebuliba 2000; Yebei 2000).

Within such a context, how is "unmet need"—a concept problematized in the U.S. context (see Santelli et al. 2003)—to be elaborated and usefully employed? Men's intentions, as well as women's, play a part in achieved fertility and contraceptive use, especially in early childbearing. Bankole (1995) documents how Yoruba women of Nigeria are better able to negotiate future pregnancies and family size after they have successfully borne several children for their husbands and husbands' lineages. In effect, a woman's value depends on, and is confirmed by, her reproductive success. Bankole goes on to assert that "[w]hen a woman does not want a child, but her husband does, the birth of such a child cannot be regarded as unwanted" (318). From an anthropological perspective, such a view begins to address the potential for conflict between men's and women's reproductive goals.

Economic context and its relationship to other demographic factors undoubtedly contribute to a partner's influence. Throughout the world, women in poorer countries with lower levels of female education show the highest rates of unmet need (Potts 2000), while financial independence has been linked to women's consistent use of condoms (Soler et al. 2000). Recent reviews of qualitative and quantitative research suggest that, rather than a purely economic explanation, unmet need is conditioned by social opposition, lack of knowledge of contraceptives, and method-related problems and side effects (Casterline and Sinding 2000; Westoff 2001).

Rather than taking evidence of male influence on fertility and contraceptive behavior as prima facie evidence of (or against) unmet contraceptive need, some anthropologists have attempted to make sense of male preferences and reproductive behaviors within local cultural systems of sex and reproduction. For example, among Maya of Mexico and Guatemala, many indigenous men profess that women who are sexually aggressive or responsive cause anxiety that may interfere with their sexual enjoyment (Mendez-Dominguez 1998; Paul 1974; Ward, Bertrand, and Puac 1992). Such cases are not rare; in many parts of the world, male sexual pleasure appears to be dependent on passive female sexuality. Conversely, in some parts of the world, men's concerns about the ability of their wives to achieve sexual pleasure may preclude condom use. For example, Ali (2002) shows that one of the reasons Egyptian men do not use condoms is because of the belief they could not receive and were incapable of giving sexual pleasure. The rural and urban Egyptian men he interviewed insisted that women received heightened sexual pleasure when they felt the ejaculate passing into their bodies. This pleasure "was mixed with the gradual cooling down of female bodies from a hot state" (130). In the case of contraception, anthropological research demonstrates how difficult it is to assume the conditions under which men will or will not use contraception, their reasons for wanting or not wanting to use contraception, and their actual patterns of use relative to their ideas about use.

Men and Sexually Transmitted Infections

As shown above, male beliefs about women's sexual passivity and sexual pleasure may preclude the possibility for the negotiation of condom use or other contraceptives, which is extremely problematic in areas of the world where condoms are believed to be the best protection from HIV and other STIs. In such cases, the problem of "unmet need" for barrier contraceptives (and STI prevention) involves a direct conflict between the sexual needs and desires of men, the health and safety of women, and the goals of contraceptive service providers. More important, contraceptives are never "needed" when couples are attempting to conceive. For example, among infertile couples in some parts of the world, particularly sub-Saharan Africa, contraceptives, including condoms, are rarely used, leading to an increased risk for STIs, including HIV/AIDS (Boerma and Mgalla 2001).

Thus, men's sexual behaviors (including their use of barrier contraceptives) have major implications for the transmission of STIs, including bacterial, viral, and parasitic agents that can lead to acute and chronic conditions in men and women, as well as pregnancy-associated diseases affecting the well-being of offspring. Wasserheit (1992, 1994) has discussed how the physiological micro-environment, the behavioral interpersonal environment, and the sociocultural macro-environment all affect the epidemiology of STIs and other reproductive-tract infections. For example, a macro-environment of poverty will affect men's and women's decisions to participate in sex with multiple partners or to undertake commercial sex work, affecting their access to information, barrier contraceptives, and adequate health care.

From an anthropological perspective, the interaction of these environments must be investigated in local contexts, where no mechanically deterministic relationship exists, even though structural inequalities constrain choices and risks (Farmer 1992, 1999). A prime example is the high prevalence of HIV in both West and East Africa, which has influenced men to seek sex with virgins in an attempt to avoid exposure (see Silberschmidt and Rasch 2001; Smith

1999). Through unprotected sex, men (including HIV-positive men unaware of their sero status) may expose adolescent and even pre-pubescent girls to STIs, and may damage their immature vaginas.

Condoms (including the female condom) are the only effective contraceptives protecting against the transmission of most STIs for both women and men during penile–vaginal intercourse (Davis and Weller 1999). As men must cooperate in order for condoms to be used effectively during sex, much emphasis has been placed on condom use as men's contraception. Some feminist writers have seen the refusal to wear condoms as a sign of hegemonic, heterosexist masculinity (Patton 1994). Though asymmetries in the negotiation of condom use between men and women may depend heavily on hegemonic male prerogatives, great variation exists in men's acceptance of condoms and the meanings of that acceptance.

Anthropological research with young Australian men suggests that men can incorporate condom use as a healthy expression of heterosexual male identity and that condom use can be eroticized (Vitellone 2000). Men in Zimbabwe showed significant generational differences in number of partners and condom use, suggesting that male sexual behaviors may change over the course of a lifetime (Olayinka, Alexander, Mbizvo, and Gibney 2000). Being unmarried and duration of relationship were significant predictors for increased odds of condom use among U.S. women between 1988 and 1995, suggesting the need for a more complex understanding of male partner effects (Bankole, Darroch, and Singh 1999).

Taken together, such research suggests that no direct correspondence exists between condom use and gender equality. Men's condom use can be incorporated into very patriarchal socioeconomic systems, even without changes to those systems, depending on men's perceptions of their reproductive health needs and sexual pleasure. Moreover, condom use may be more or less associated with family planning in the context of high STI prevalence. Through anthropological research, the potential exists to elucidate the beliefs and structures shaping men's behaviors around the use of contraception for both STI and pregnancy prevention.

Men's Influence on Abortion

Even under the best conditions, abortion is a physically and emotionally difficult event. Its continued practice despite legal prohibitions in many parts of the world makes abortion dangerous and life threatening. Thus, abortion has social, psychological, and health consequences for both men and women, even though relatively little research has examined men's roles in women's abortion decisions and experiences (Adler 1992).

Abortion is perhaps the best example of the direct connection between laws and policies and poor reproductive health outcomes, and in most countries, men write, ratify, and enforce abortion law (see Cottingham and Myntti 2002). In Turkey, for example, abortion among married women is restricted to those with their husbands' permission, reflecting conservative interpretations of Islamic law (Gursoy 1996). Furthermore, men may directly affect women's decisions about abortion. They may provide or withhold economic and emotional support for an abortion or parenting, or they may actively or passively impose their own desires for or against an abortion. Men's influences also may be less direct and involve other areas of reproductive health; for example, in the United States, women with abuse histories are less likely to involve their partners in abortion decisions and have different reasons for seeking abortion than non-abused women (Glander, Moore, Michielutte, and Parsons 1998).

Given that the social acceptability and desirability of pregnancy and abortion may change with the age of parents, pregnancy at different stages in life may show variable patterns of partner influence. Among American teenagers presenting for antenatal care rather than abortion, women tend to report that their partners' support is important in their decision not to terminate the pregnancy (Henderson 1999).

Several anthropologists have taken abortion as a central theme in their study of reproduction (Carter 1995; Ginsburg 1989; McClain 1982; Scheper-Hughes 1993). Although many of these studies have focused on women's abortion decisions, access, and experiences, men's influences on abortion choices and outcomes also have been examined. For example, in her investigation of amniocentesis and abortion in New York City, Rapp found that partners' beliefs greatly influenced women's use or refusal of prenatal tests like amniocentesis (1999). She examines the use of prenatal diagnostic procedures that identified potential risks of undesirable pregnancy outcomes, or those for which no therapy is available and abortion is often recommended by medical practitioners. In addition to describing the distinct experiences of women and men in genetic counseling (often mediated by ethnicity and economic resources), Rapp shows how important men are in the decisions women make about bringing disabled children to term. Women who felt that their male partners would love and help raise a disabled child were less likely to undergo such tests, relying heavily on their partners' beliefs about the desirability of a disabled child.

Browner's work on reproduction (1979, 1986, 2000; also see Browner and Perdue 1988) has consistently explored how men influence their partners' reproductive decisions and options. Browner's path-breaking study (1979) of clandestine abortion in Cali, Colombia, reveals not only the high percentage of intentional abortions (an estimated one-third to one-half of pregnancies in Latin America), but also the important role men play in abortion-related decisions. Browner argues that men in Colombia strongly influence their partners' abortion decisions, as women abort children to avoid becoming single mothers. In instances in which women were told directly or perceived that their partners would abandon them, they sought abortions more frequently and with more resolve.

Similar to Rapp, Browner (2000) has examined the use of fetal testing, conducting interviews in the United States among Mexican-origin parents with high-risk pregnancies. She found that 50 percent of the women made fetal testing decisions independently of their partners, while 23.5 percent made decisions jointly with their partners, and that men made the decisions in the remaining cases. Structural factors, such as economic independence and the local health care system, affected women's decisions. However, Browner argues that these factors only become meaningful when interpreted through cultural processes. "Women incorporated the man if they were uncertain about his feelings about the pregnancy, and they wanted him involved in any decisions that could have long-term consequences for them both" (2000:81). Even when women are seen as solely responsible for decisions about testing and abortion, men are expected to play a supportive role. At the same time, Browner suggests that women are expected to shoulder the entire responsibility if something goes wrong with the pregnancy.

Men's Influence on Pregnancy and Childbirth

Unfortunately, the influence of men's intentions and practices on conception, pregnancy, and childbirth outcome have been little studied and are poorly understood within medical anthropology, even though pregnancy and childbirth have been studied by medical anthropologists in a variety of international contexts. In U.S.-based public health studies, male partners' intentions and desires have been shown as affecting the timing of a first pregnancy (Chalmers and Meyer 1996), women's prospective desire for becoming pregnant

(Lazarus 1997), feelings upon learning of pregnancy (Major, Cozza-relli, Testa, and Mueller 1992), and subsequent changes in women's evaluation of pregnancy wantedness, both during pregnancy and postpartum (Montgomery 1996). Understanding partner effects on intendedness of pregnancy is important in explaining such issues as desired family size, timing of first pregnancy, and women's com-pleted fertility (Santelli et al. 2003). Also in the U.S. context, Joyce, Kaestner, and Korenman (2000) show an association between the stability of women's pregnancy intendedness over time and partners' disagreement on the issue. Zabin, Huggins, Emerson, and Cullins (2000) found that women's desire to conceive is more closely re-lated to their evaluation of their particular relationship rather than to abstract notions of completed family size. Such research suggests that women often define pregnancy intention as influenced by their relationship to their partners and their partners' desires.

One of the most important areas of reproductive health affected by men is pregnancy care and outcome. Yet, men's participation in and influence on prenatal care is poorly understood from an anthropological perspective. Extrapolating from the early anthro-pological ethnographies of human birth, Kay (1982a) lists some "extrinsic" factors of pregnancy, such as food, sleep, and the visible body, that may affect birth outcome. In her path-breaking but now somewhat dated review, men are listed as one of the extrinsic fac-tors in pregnancy, with influences potentially leading to maternal and infant mortality.

Globally, there are as many as 600,000 maternal deaths each year, as well as a staggering burden of maternal morbidity (Khattab, Younis, and Zurayk 1999; Koblinsky 1995). Adequate prenatal care is consistently associated with the detection of pregnancy conditions such as hypertension and anemia and its lack with poor pregnancy outcomes such as low birth weight and preterm births (Fiscella 1995; Mustard and Roos 1994; Quick, Greenlick, and Roghmann 1981). Unfortunately, ethnographic information on prenatal care—its use and adequacy by women, as affected by their partners—is lacking in both developing and industrialized countries.

In the United States, one of the most consistent predictors of ad-equate prenatal care utilization is the mother's relationship with the father (Casper and Hogan 1990; D'Ascoli, Alexander, Petersen, and Kogan 1997; Gaudino, Jenkins, and Rochat 1999; Lia-Hoagberg et al. 1990; McCaw-Binns, La Grenade, and Ashley 1995; Oropesa, Lan-dale, Inkley, and Gorman 2000; Schaffer and Lia-Hoagberg 1997). However, research and interventions in the area of prenatal care, as well as other aspects of pregnancy outcome, consistently target women rather than men (Bloom, Tsui, Plotkin, and Bassett 2000; Carter 2002; Johansson et al. 1998; Wall 1998). This is due not only to the perceived need to channel resources to women during and after pregnancy, but also to the slowly changing perception that men are only tangentially involved in the mother-fetus health package (Gerein, Mayhew, and Lubben 2003). Thus, most epidemiological investigations rely on indicators such as marital status rather than on more qualitative analyses of the relationship of women with their partners. Furthermore, very little research, if any, has been conducted on the kinds of care men provide during pregnancy or the effects of such care on maternal reproductive health outcomes.

To date, anthropologists have primarily addressed men's influences on prenatal care in developing countries in only the broadest sense, examining how male-dominated biomedical services interact with existing pregnancy practices. For example, in discussing traditional midwifery in southern Oaxaca, Mexico, Sesia (1996) uses Jordan's concept of authoritative knowledge (see Jordan 1997) to argue that traditional midwives have maintained their position as primary sources of prenatal care because both male and female individuals in the community share midwives' medical knowledge. Conversely, physicians and other biomedical practitioners possess an authoritative knowledge base that is not evenly distributed or accessible by the community. Similarly, Sargent (1989) has argued that the encouragement of hospital-based birth by public health programs serving the Bariba of Benin has paradoxically limited women's reproductive choices by enhancing the power of male heads of households to make decisions about obstetric care. Among the Bariba, men's educational and occupational status affect women's prenatal and obstetric care choices because of the importance of emerging status distinctions within the community.

As the vast majority of maternal deaths occur during or within the first forty-eight hours after delivery, the management of obstetric emergencies has been one of the key points of intervention strategies in reducing maternal mortality. Frameworks for addressing obstetric emergencies refer to the "three delays": recognition of an emergency, decision to seek care, and transportation to care. Men potentially affect the outcome of an obstetric emergency at all of these levels as partners, relatives, neighbors, and service providers (Network 1992). Yet, few studies of any type directly investigate the actual roles men play during, or men's experiences of, obstetric emergencies. Information on men's involvement in obstetric emergencies usually comes from accounts provided by women after the event has occurred. Moreover, relatively few interventions have targeted men in obstetric decision making (Howard-Grabman, Seoane, and Davenport 1994). An exception may be western highland Guatemala, where training programs for midwives and other community health care providers have emphasized men as involved in the negotiation of decisions during obstetric emergencies (MotherCare 1996).

Unlike obstetric emergencies, preterm birth has proven resistant to intervention, with no predictive clinical markers, causing many clinicians to despair of lowering rates of preterm births below certain thresholds (Johnston, Williams, Hogue, and Mattison 2001). Rates of preterm birth continue to show marked stratification between developed and developing countries as well as between different socioeconomic and ethnic groups within developed countries, such as the United States (Rowley and Tosteson 1993). Although mechanisms of preterm birth are poorly understood, preterm delivery seems to be governed by two maternal physiological factors: a neuroendocrinological response sensitive to acute and chronic stressors and an immuno-inflammatory response sensitive to microbial infections (in the form of bacterial vaginosis) (Wadhwa et al. 2001). These physiological pathways suggest several plausible mechanisms for men's influences on preterm delivery. For one, men may prove to be a source of chronic stress for women, or, alternately, they may alleviate other sources of chronic stress. Such chronic stress, often experienced years before pregnancy, has been hypothesized to "set" maternal reproductive physiology for early delivery (Hogue, Hoffman, and Hatch 2001). Stress during pregnancy caused by men may also lead to premature delivery. Moreover, men may introduce infection into the vagina of a partner during pregnancy. Low birth weight is often an outcome of preterm birth but is also caused directly by insufficient caloric and micro-nutrient intake during pregnancy. Because men mediate women's access to economic resources in many parts of the world, women's nutritional status, especially during pregnancy, may depend heavily on male partners and relatives. Yet, direct epidemiological evidence for an effect of paternal factors on preterm or low birth weight deliveries has been inconclusive (Basso, Olsen, and Christensen 1999a, 1999b; Shea, Farrow, and Little 1997). Nonetheless, after birth, the father's involvement in caregiving has been associated with improved outcomes for preterm and low birth weight babies' cognitive development (Yogman, Kindlon, and Earls 1995).

Aside from the plausibility of men's influences, few anthropological studies have addressed men's relationships to their partners either prior to or after a preterm delivery, although some anthropologists have focused on the relationship between men's couvade symptoms (sympathetic pregnancy, which includes weight gain, indigestion, and nausea), men's involvement in pregnancy, and pregnancy outcomes (Conner and Denson 1990). Anthropological investigations of pregnancy and birth traditionally have focused on obstetric practices (Davis-Floyd 1992; Davis-Floyd and Sargent 1997a, 1997b; Kay 1982b), as well as women's birth experiences and care decisions (Sargent 1989). Although a recent emphasis on power differentials negotiated in obstetric care points to the role of men (Davis-Floyd and Sargent 1997a, 1997b), more qualitative research from an anthropological perspective is needed to include men as a major part of women's social environment in both pre- and postnatal health.

Men's Influences on Infertility

Worldwide, between 8 and 12 percent of couples suffer from infertility, or the inability to conceive a child at some point during their reproductive lives (Reproductive Health Outlook 2003). However, in some non-Western societies, especially those in the "infertility belt" of central and southern Africa, rates of infertility may be quite high, affecting as many as one-third of all couples attempting to conceive (Collet et al. 1988; Ericksen and Brunette 1996; Larsen 2000). In developing countries, many cases of infertility are due to infection, including sterilizing STIs men pass to their female partners. Unfortunately, in vitro fertilization (IVF), which was designed to overcome infection-induced tubal infertility, is often unavailable or unaffordable in non-Western settings (Inhorn 1994a, 2003a; Okonofua 1996). Thus, permanent childlessness may be the result of men's STIs.

A growing ethnographic literature demonstrates that women worldwide bear the major burden of infertility (Boerma and Mgalla 2001; Feldman-Savelsberg 1999; Greil, Leitko, and Porter 1988; Inhorn 1994b; Inhorn and van Balen 2002). This burden may include blame for the reproductive failing; emotional distress in the forms of anxiety, depression, frustration, grief, and fear (Greil 1997); marital duress, leading to abandonment, divorce, or polygamy; stigmatization and community ostracism; and, in many cases, bodily taxing, even life-threatening forms of medical intervention. For example, Inhorn (1994b, 2003b) has shown that poor urban Egyptian women are forced to seek infertility treatments, even in cases of proven male infertility, because they are blamed and stigmatized by the ensuing childlessness. In some cases, their quests for conception are truly iatrogenic when poorly trained, mostly male physicians utilize outdated technologies leading to reproductive tract damage (Inhorn 1994b, 1996).

Anthropologists have shown that infertility is a form of reproductive morbidity with profoundly gendered social consequences, which tend to be more grave in non-Western settings (Inhorn and van Balen 2002). In many non-Western societies, infertile women's suffering is exacerbated by strong pronatalist social norms that mandate motherhood. Yet, policymakers in these countries are often obsessed with curbing population growth rates, ignoring infertile women's suffering because of their "barrenness amid plenty."

Infertility, like most reproductive health issues, is usually conceptualized as a "woman's problem" in both indigenous systems of meaning and in global reproductive health policy discussions. However, the reality of infertility challenges this assertion because the biology of infertility does not reside solely or even largely in the female reproductive tract. The most comprehensive epidemiological study of infertility to date—a WHO-sponsored study of 5,800 infertile couples at thirty-three medical centers in twenty-two countries—found that men are the sole cause or a contributing factor to infertility in more than half of all couples around the globe (Cates, Farley, and Rowe 1985). The four primary types of male infertility are low sperm count (oligospermia), poor sperm motility (asthenospermia), abnormal sperm morphology (teratozoospermia), and complete absence of sperm in the ejaculate (azoospermia). The causes of these types of male infertility are largely idiopathic, or unknown (Irvine 1998). However, male infertility can be partly explained by exposure to reproductive toxicants, including those that are occupational, environmental, and behavioral in nature (Bentley 2000). For example, among infertile men in Mexico, smoking has been associated with lower sperm density, viability, and motility, and a higher percentage of abnormal sperm (Merino, Lira, and Martinez-Chequer 1998). Similarly, in Egypt and other urban areas of the Middle East, patterns of heavy male smoking, coupled with ambient lead pollution in the air, may be responsible for the significant rates of male infertility, including among men with severe reproductive impairments (Inhorn 2002, 2003b).

Increasingly in Egypt, as well as in many other parts of both the industrialized and developing worlds, a new reproductive technology called intracytoplasmic sperm injection (ICSI) has allowed otherwise hopelessly infertile men to father biological children. With ICSI, as long as a single viable spermatozoan can be retrieved from an infertile man's body—including through painful testicular biopsies or aspirations—it can be injected directly into an ovum under a high-powered microscope, thereby producing live offspring for men who would not have otherwise procreated. Although ICSI, as a variant of IVF, is being heralded as a revolution in the management of male infertility (Fishel, Dowell, and Thornton 2000), the bioethical dimensions of ICSI are being debated. In particular, men's serious genetic disorders, which may have prevented them from reproducing in the first place, may be passed on to offspring, sometimes in amplified form (Bittles and Matson 2000).

That such concerns over potential fetal harm are salient among couples using ICSI to overcome male infertility is apparent from anthropological studies in Egypt and Lebanon (Inhorn 2003a, 2003b). In Egypt, Inhorn found that the majority of infertile men choosing to avail themselves of ICSI nonetheless worried considerably about the health and "shape" of future children conceived from their "weak" (and sometimes morphologically deformed) sperm. In both Egypt and Lebanon, infertile men also feared that other men's "healthy" sperm might be intentionally or inadvertently "mixed" with their own, thereby producing illegitimate offspring (Sunni Islamic mandates prohibit third-party donation of sperm, eggs, and embryos) (Inhorn 2003a, 2003b). Furthermore, some men whose wives had grown too old to produce viable ova for the ICSI procedure were choosing to marry younger, more fertile women. The gender effects of ICSI were thus paradoxical, as a new reproductive technology designed to facilitate male procreation had created potentially precarious reproductive scenarios for the once-fertile wives of infertile Muslim men. As seen in the case of ICSI, infertile men's decisions to use new reproductive technologies may have major consequences for women's own reproductive and social well-being.

Men Causing Fetal Harm

The impact of occupational risk factors on reproductive health has been one area of research on men that predates the ICPD paradigm shift (Sever 1981; Sinclair 2000; Steeno and Pangkahila 1984). The majority of studies have focused on the effects of different occupational exposures on men's, rather than women's, fertility and reproductive well-being. However, much less research has been done on the effects of men's occupational, environmental, and lifestyle toxicant exposures on women's reproductive health and birth outcomes (Davis, Friedler, Mattison, and Morris 1992). Yet, birth defects are more often associated with paternal rather than maternal DNA

damage (Pollard 2000). With the increase in industrialization and
the proliferation of new chemical compounds that are potential endocrine disrupters, the magnitude and effects are likely to increase.
Theoretically, exposures that could transmit harm to a fetus might
damage the paternal germ line, the cells from which sperm cells are
produced. Paternal exposure to mutagens, in particular industrial
aromatic solvents, is highly associated with impaired semen quality
(De Celis et al. 2000; Tielemans et al. 1999), and may lead to adverse
pregnancy outcomes such as spontaneous abortion, congenital mal-
formation, and low birth-weight/preterm birth (Brinkworth, 2000;
Lindbohm 1995). Lifestyle choices such as smoking, drinking, and
drug use also may affect semen quality, but results are equivocal,
with little research directly connecting men's use of substances to
fetal harm.

In considering fetal harm in the United States, Daniels (1997,
1999) describes a complex web of relationships, including institutional and social ones, affecting reproductive health while still
emphasizing the importance of the individual as a locus of responsibility. Even given the limited conclusive evidence for transmission of fetal harm through occupational and environmental damage to paternal germ cells, Daniels argues that paternal exposures
profoundly influence fetal health. Moreover, Daniels examines perspectives on men and fetal harm as emblematic of broader attitudes
toward men's responsibility for social reproduction. "Crack babies"
are the children of "pregnant addicts" and "absent fathers"; these
are the terms framing discussion over fetal harm, such that men are
protected from responsibility while women (predominantly African
American women) are criminally prosecuted for fetal neglect and
abuse. "Debates over fetal risk are not so much about the prevention of fetal harm as they are about the social production of truth
about the nature of men's and women's relation to reproduction"
(1997:579). Daniels suggests that notions of masculinity denying
male health problems project vulnerabilities on to the bodies of
women. Sperm is thus either classified as damaged and incapable
of fertilization, or as unaffected and potent, while women's bodies
are characterized as highly vulnerable to occupational reproductive
risks (see Martin 1987). This all-or-nothing approach suggests that
abnormal or damaged sperm are incapable of causing fetal harm
such as birth defects.

Daniels argues that male vulnerability must be recognized and
suggests that targeting select groups of women (and men), such as
those who use crack cocaine, obscures the institutional and structural causes of fetal harm. Just as Daniels argues it is impossible to

separate responsibility for fetal harm along the lines of men/women or institutions/social structures, so too it is impossible to isolate who suffers from fetal harm. Men may "cause" fetal harm involuntarily through occupational exposures that affect their semen and at the same time suffer the feelings of compromised reproductive health if a pregnancy results in spontaneous abortion. Recent anthropological studies of pregnancy loss cross-culturally (Cecil 1996; Layne 2003) suggest that men are caught in a double bind: they feel the need to avoid showing emotion so they can support their partners through the physically difficult experience of pregnancy loss, at the same time experiencing similar emotions of the grief and loss experienced by their female partners. This is perhaps especially true as prenatal ultrasound imaging technologies have changed men's expectations of paternal bonding to unborn fetuses (Layne 1992, 1999; Morgan and Michaels 1999).

As Daniels argues, this area of reproductive health requires different definitions of rights and responsibilities for men and women based on their varying contributions to fetal harm. Anthropological research has the potential to describe different perceptions of rights and responsibilities depending on the actors involved in reproductive health—mother, father, and fetus. Rather than straightforward and constant agents, "mother," "father," and "fetus" are ideological concepts with reproductive health states dependent on their definition (Morgan and Michaels 1999). Because reproductive health depends on more than one individual, the idea that the individuals involved can be multiply defined—not just in terms of their rights and responsibilities, but also in terms of their identities and the boundaries between them—deeply affects how reproductive health may be achieved in any given setting.

Conclusion

This chapter has attempted to summarize some of the most important ways men affect the reproductive health of women. Such a summary might take the form of a "conceptual framework" of causes and effects, such as the various microbiotic vectors causing STIs or factors leading to contraceptive use or fetal harm. However, the anthropological perspectives and ethnographic examples elaborated in this chapter show how difficult such a summary would be. First, there are multiple and sometimes contradictory ways men can affect reproductive health problems. Therefore, much of the anthropological work discussed here attempts to trace the effects of men on women's reproductive health without systematizing or generalizing those effects. Few of the relationships between men's and women's reproductive health are universal, and even those that exhibit patterns (such as STIs and infertility) may not lend themselves to identical interventions in different contexts. Anthropology as a discipline is well situated to investigate which patterns of the relationship between men's and women's reproductive health are the most important in a given context and which are the most meaningful in terms of intervention.

The second issue centers on the importance of meaning. Reproductive health problems cannot be universally defined because they require the local elaboration of meaning within particular cultural contexts. The meaning of reproductive health events usually involves multiple individuals, be they sexual partners, kin, service providers, or larger social groups. Thus, what a particular reproductive health problem means depends on one's subject position—as an HIV-positive heterosexual man, a poor multiparous, middle-aged woman, or a teenage recipient of an abortion—as well as on what is defined as a reproductive health problem and by whom. The meanings of reproductive health states are important, not only in terms of effective treatment and intervention, but also because they involve the experiences of individuals as they negotiate healthy sexuality and reproduction.

The final issue involves the distinction between equality and equity in reproductive health services. In many cases, trying to distinguish between the two assumes an "outside" perspective that does not take into account the needs and desires of the men and women experiencing reproductive health problems. Men and women must be allowed to aid in the definition and prioritization of reproductive health problems. From both a medical anthropological and public health perspective, this requires informing men and women about these problems as they are defined by biomedicine, but also providing new tools, such as critical awareness of class, race, and gendered inequalities, for their description of these problems. It also requires allowing men and women to explain reproductive health problems from their own perspectives and to gauge the importance of these problems for their own sexual and reproductive well-being. Among different groups, at different times, different decisions may be made about equality versus equity of reproductive health services. Ultimately, these goals of egalitarian and equitable services can be pursued only when individuals and partners, men and women alike, can positively define their own experiences of sexual and reproductive health.

Acknowledgments

The original version of this chapter was published in *Social Science and Medicine* 59 (2004):1379–95. Copyright © 2004 by Elsevier Press. Reproduced with the permission of Elsevier Press.

References

Adler, N. E. 1992. "Unwanted Pregnancy and Abortion: Definitional and Research Issues." *Journal of Social Issues* 48(3):19–35.

Ali, K. A. 2002. *Planning the Family in Egypt: New Bodies, New Selves*. Austin: University of Texas Press.

Bandarage, A. 1997. *Women, Population and Global Crisis: A Political-Economic Analysis*. London, NJ: Zed.

Bankole, A. 1995. "Desired Fertility and Fertility Behavior among the Yoruba of Nigeria: A Study of Couple Preferences and Subsequent Fertility." *Population Studies* 49:317–28.

Bankole, A., J. E. Darroch, and S. Singh 1999. "Determinants of Trends in Condom Use in the United States, 1988–1995." *Family Planning Perspectives* 31(6):264–71.

Basso, O., J. Olsen, and K. Christensen. 1999a. "Low Birthweight and Prematurity in Relation to Paternal Factors: A Study of Recurrence." *International Journal of Epidemiology* 28(4):695–700.

———. 1999b. "Study of Environmental, Social, and Paternal Factors in Preterm Delivery Using Sibs and Half Sibs: A Population-Based Study in Denmark." *Journal of Epidemiology and Community Health* 53(1):20–23.

Basu, A. M. 1996. "The International Conference on Population and Development, Cairo, 1994. Is Its Plan of Action Important, Desirable and Feasible? ICPD: What about Men's Rights and Women's Responsibilities?" *Health Transition Review* 6:225–27.

Becker, S. 1999. "Measuring Unmet Need: Wives, Husbands, Or Couples?" *International Family Planning Perspectives* 25(4):172–80.

Becker, S., and J. C. Robinson. 1998. "Reproductive Health Care: Services Oriented to Couples." *International Journal of Gynecology and Obstetrics* 61(3):275–81.

Bentley, G. R. 2000. "Environmental Pollutants and Fertility." In *Infertility in the Modern World: Present and Future Prospects*, ed. G. R. Bentley and C. G. N. Mascie-Taylor. Cambridge: Cambridge University Press.

Bittles, A. H., and P. L. Matson. 2000. "Genetic Influences on Human Fertility." In *Infertility in the Modern World: Present and Future Prospects*, ed. G. R. Bentley and C. G. N. Mascie-Taylor. Cambridge: Cambridge University Press.

Blanc, A. K. 2001. "The Effect of Power in Sexual Relationships on Sexual and Reproductive Health: An Examination of the Evidence." *Studies in Family Planning* 32(3):189–213.

Bloom, S. S., A. O. Tsui, M. Plotkin, and S. Bassett. 2000. "What Husbands in Northern India Know about Reproductive Health: Correlates of

Knowledge about Pregnancy and Maternal and Sexual Health." *Journal of Biosocial Science* 32(2):237–51.

Boerma, J. T., and Z. Mgalla. 2001. *Women and Infertility in Sub-Saharan Africa: A Multi-Disciplinary Perspective.* Amsterdam: Royal Tropical Institute.

Bongaarts, J., and J. Bruce. 1995. "The Causes of Unmet Need for Contraception and the Social Content of Services." *Studies in Family Planning* 26(2):57–75.

Boonstra, H., V. Duran, V. Northington Gamble, P. Blumenthal, L. Dominguez, and C. Pies. 2000. "The 'Boom and Bust Phenomenon': The Hopes, Dreams, and Broken Promises of the Contraceptive Revolution." *Contraception* 61(1):9–25.

Brinkworth, M. H. 2000. "Paternal Transmission of Genetic Damage: Findings in Animals and Humans." *International Journal of Andrology* 23(3):123–35.

Browner, C. H. 1979. "Abortion Decision Making: Some Findings from Colombia." *Studies in Family Planning* 10(3):96–106.

———. 1986. "The Politics of Reproduction in a Mexican Village." *Signs* 11:710–24.

———. 2000. "Situating Women's Reproductive Activities." *American Anthropologist* 102(4):773–88.

Browner, C. H., and S. T. Perdue. 1988. "Women's Secrets: Bases for Reproductive and Social Autonomy in a Mexican Community." *American Ethnologist* 15:84–97.

Carter, A. T. 1995. "Agency and Fertility: For an Ethnography of Practice." In *Situating Fertility: Anthropology and Demographic Inquiry,* ed. S. Greenhalgh. Cambridge: Cambridge University Press.

Carter, M. 2002. "Husbands and Maternal Health Matters in Rural Guatemala: Wives' Reports on Spouses' Involvement in Pregnancy and Birth." *Social Science and Medicine* 55(3):437–50.

Casper, L. M., and D. P. Hogan. 1990. "Family Networks in Prenatal and Postnatal Health." *Social Biology* 37(1–2):84–101.

Casterline, J. B., A. E. Perez, and A. E. Biddlecom. 1997. "Factors Underlying Unmet Need for Family Planning in the Philippines." *Studies in Family Planning* 28(3):173–91.

Casterline, J. B., and S. W. Sinding. 2000. "Unmet Need for Family Planning in Developing Countries and Implications for Population Policy." *Population and Development Review* 26(4):691–723.

Cates, W., T. M. Farley, and P. J. Rowe. 1985. "Worldwide Patterns of Infertility: Is Africa Different?" *Lancet* 2(8455):596–98.

Cates, W., and K. M. Stone. 1992. "Family Planning, Sexually Transmitted Diseases and Contraceptive Choice: A Literature Update—Part I." *Family Planning Perspectives* 24(2):75–84.

Cecil, R., ed. 1996. *The Anthropology of Pregnancy Loss: Comparative Studies in Miscarriage, Stillbirth and Neonatal Death.* Oxford: Berg.

Chalmers, B., and D. Meyer. 1996. "What Men Say about Pregnancy, Birth and Parenthood." *Journal of Psychosomatic Obstetrics and Gynecology* 17(1):47–52.

Cliquet, R., and K. Thienpont. 1995. *Population and Development: A Message from the Cairo Conference*. Dordrecht, Netherlands: Kluwer.

Collet, M., J. Reniers, E. Frost, R. Gass, F. Yvert, A. Leclerc, C. Roth-Meyer, B. Ivanoff, and A. Meheus. 1988. "Infertility in Central Africa: Infection is the Cause." *International Journal of Gynecology and Obstetrics* 26(3):423–28.

Collumbien, M., and S. Hawkes. 2000. "Missing Men's Messages: Does the Reproductive Health Approach Respond to Men's Sexual Health Needs?" *Culture, Health and Sexuality* 2(2):135–50.

Conner, G. K., and V. Denson. 1990. "Expectant Fathers' Response to Pregnancy: Review of Literature and Implications for Research in High-Risk Pregnancy." *Journal of Perinatal and Neonatal Nursing* 4(2):33–42.

Cook, R. J., and B. M. Dickens. 1999. "Ethics, Justice and Women's Health." *International Journal of Gynecology and Obstetrics* 64(1):81–85.

———. 2000. Considerations for Formulating Reproductive Health Laws, Vol. WHO/RHR/00.1. Geneva: World Health Organization.

Cook, R. J., B. M. Dickens, O. A. F. Wilson, and S. E. Scarrow. 2001. *Advancing Safe Motherhood through Human Rights*. Geneva: World Health Organization.

Corrêa, S., and R. L. Reichmann. 1994. *Population and Reproductive Rights: Feminist Perspectives from the South*. London: Zed.

Cottingham, J., and C. Myntti. 2002. "Reproductive Health: Conceptual Mapping and Evidence." In *Engendering International Health: The Challenge of Equity*, ed. G. Sen, A. George, and P. Ostlin. Cambridge: MIT Press.

D'Ascoli, P. T., G. R. Alexander, D. J. Petersen, and M. D. Kogan. 1997. "Parental Factors Influencing Patterns of Prenatal Care Utilization." *Journal of Perinatology* 17(4):283.

Daniels, C. R. 1997. "Between Fathers and Fetuses: The Social Construction of Male Reproduction and the Politics of Fetal Harm." *Signs* 22(3):579–616.

———. 1999. "Fathers, Mothers, and Fetal Harm: Rethinking Gender Difference and Reproductive Responsibility." In *Fetal Subjects, Feminist Positions*, ed. L. M. Morgan, and M. W. Michaels. Philadelphia: University of Pennsylvania Press.

Davis, D. L., G. Friedler, D. Mattison, and R. Morris. 1992. "Male-Mediated Teratogenesis and other Reproductive Effects: Biologic and Epidemiologic Findings and a Plea for Clinical Research." *Reproductive Toxicology* 6(4):289–92.

Davis, K. R., and S. C. Weller. 1999. "The Effectiveness of Condoms in Reducing Heterosexual Transmission of HIV." *Family Planning Perspectives* 31(6):272–79.

Davis-Floyd, R. 1992. *Birth as an American Rite of Passage*. Berkeley: University of California Press.

Davis-Floyd, R., and C. Sargent, eds. 1997a. "Introduction: The Anthropology of Birth." In *Childbirth and Authoritative Knowledge: Cross-Cultural Perspectives*. Berkeley: University of California Press.

———. 1997b. *Childbirth and Authoritative Knowledge: Cross-Cultural Perspectives*. Berkeley: University of California Press.

De Celis, R., A. Feria-Velasco, M. Gonzalez-Unzaga, J. Torres-Calleja, and N. Pedron-Nuevo. 2000. "Semen Quality of Workers Occupationally Exposed to Hydrocarbons." *Fertility and Sterility* 73(2):221–28.

DeJong, J. 2000. "The Role and Limitations of the Cairo International Conference on Population and Development." *Social Science and Medicine* 51(6):941–53.

Dixon-Mueller, R. 1993a. *Population Policy and Women's Rights: Transforming Reproductive Choice*. Westport, CT: Praeger.

———. 1993b. "The Sexuality Connection in Reproductive Health." *Studies in Family Planning* 24(5):269–82.

Dodoo, F. N. 1993. "A Couple Analysis of Micro Level Supply/Demand Factors in Fertility Regulation." *Population Research and Policy Review* 12:93–101.

Drennan, M. 1998. *Reproductive Health: New Perspectives on Men's Participation*. Baltimore: Johns Hopkins School of Public Health, Population Information Program.

Ericksen, K., and T. Brunette. 1996. "Patterns and Predictors of Infertility among African Women: A Cross-National Survey of Twenty-Seven Nations." *Social Science and Medicine* 42(2):209–20.

Ezeh, A. C. 1993. "The Influence of Spouses over Each Other's Contraceptive Attitudes in Ghana." *Studies in Family Planning* 24(3):163–74.

Farmer, P. 1992. *AIDS and Accusation: Haiti and the Geography of Blame*. Berkeley: University of California Press.

———. 1999. *Infections and Inequalities: The Modern Plagues*. Berkeley: University of California Press.

Farmer, P., M. Connors, and J. Simmons, eds. 1996. *Women, Poverty, and AIDS: Sex, Drugs, and Structural Violence*. Monroe, ME: Common Courage Press.

Feldman-Savelsberg, P. 1999. *Plundered Kitchens, Empty Wombs: Threatened Reproduction and Identity in the Cameroon Grassfields*. Ann Arbor: University of Michigan Press.

Fiscella, K. 1995. "Does Prenatal Care Improve Birth Outcomes? A Critical Review." *Obstetrics and Gynecology* 85(3):468–79.

Fishel, S., K. Dowell, and S. Thornton. 2000. "Reproductive Possibilities for Infertile Couples: Present and Future." In *Infertility in the Modern World: Present and Future Prospects*, ed. G. R. Bentley and C. G. N. Mascie-Taylor. Cambridge: Cambridge University Press.

Gaudino Jr., J. A., B. Jenkins, and R. W. Rochat 1999. "No Fathers' Names: A Risk Factor for Infant Mortality in the State of Georgia, USA." *Social Science and Medicine* 48:253–65.

Gerein, N., S. Mayhew, and A. Lubben. 2003. "A Framework for a New Approach to Antenatal Care." *International Journal of Gynecology and Obstetrics* 80(2):175–82.

Ginsburg, F. D. 1989. *Contested Lives: The Abortion Debate in an American Community*. Berkeley: University of California Press.

Glander, S. S., M. L. Moore, R. Michielutte, and L. H. Parsons. 1998. "The Prevalence of Domestic Violence among Women Seeking Abortion." *Obstetrics and Gynecology* 91(6): 1002–6.

Greene, M. E. 2000. "Changing Women and Avoiding Men: Gender Stereotypes and Reproductive Health Programmes." *IDS Bulletin-Institute of Development Studies* 31(2):49–59.

Greene, M. E., and A. E. Biddlecom. 2000. "Absent and Problematic Men: Demographic Accounts of Male Reproductive Roles." *Demography* 26:81–115.

Greil, A. L. 1997. "Infertility and Psychological Distress: A Critical Review of the Literature." *Social Science and Medicine* 45(11):1679–704.

Greil, A. L., T. A. Leitko, and K. L. Porter. 1988. "Infertility: His and Hers." *Gender and Society* 2(2):172–99.

Gursoy, A. 1996. "Abortion in Turkey: A Matter of State, Family or Individual Decision." *Social Science and Medicine* 42(4):531–42.

Hahn, R. A. 1999. *Anthropology in Public Health: Bridging Differences in Culture and Society*. New York: Oxford University Press.

Hawkes, S. 1998. "Why Include Men? Establishing Sexual Health Clinics for Men in Rural Bangladesh." *Health Policy and Planning* 13(2):121–30.

Henderson, L. R. 1999. "A Survey of Teenage Pregnant Women and Their Male Partners in the Grampian Region." *British Journal of Family Planning* 25(3):90–92.

Hogue, C. J. R., S. Hoffman, and M. C. Hatch. 2001. "Stress and Preterm Delivery: A Conceptual Framework." *Paediatric and Perinatal Epidemiology* 15(Suppl. 2):30–40.

Howard-Grabman, L., G. Seoane, and C. A. Davenport. 1994. *The Warmi Project: A Participatory Approach to Improve Maternal and Neonatal Health*. Arlington, VA: MotherCare Project.

Inhorn, M. C. 1994a. "Interpreting Infertility: Medical Anthropological Perspectives—Introduction." *Social Science and Medicine* 39:459–61.

———. 1994b. *Quest for Conception: Gender, Infertility, and Egyptian Medical Traditions*. Philadelphia: University of Pennsylvania Press.

———. 1996. *Infertility and Patriarchy: The Cultural Politics of Gender and Family Life in Egypt*. Philadelphia: University of Pennsylvania Press.

———. 2002. "Sexuality, Masculinity, and Infertility in Egypt: Potent Troubles in Marital and Medical Encounters." *Journal of Men's Studies* 10(3):343–59.

———. 2003a. *Local Babies, Global Science: Gender, Religion, and In Vitro Fertilization in Egypt*. New York: Routledge.

———. 2003b. "'the worms are weak'": Male Infertility and Patriarchal Paradoxes in Egypt." *Men and Masculinities* 5(3):236–56.

Inhorn, M. C., and F. van Balen, eds. 2002. *Infertility around the Globe: New Thinking on Childlessness, Gender, and Reproductive Technologies*. Berkeley: University of California Press.

Irvine, D. S. 1998. "Epidemiology and Aetiology of Male Infertility." *Human Reproduction* 13(Suppl. 1):33–44.

Johansson, A., N. T. Nga, T. Q. Huy, D. Du Dat, and K. Holmgren. 1998. "Husbands' Involvement in Abortion in Vietnam." *Studies in Family Planning* 29(4):400–13.

Johnston Jr., R. B., M. A. Williams, C. J. Hogue, and D. R. Mattison. 2001. "Overview: New Perspectives on the Stubborn Challenge of Preterm Birth." *Paediatric and Perinatal Epidemiology* 15(Suppl. 2):3–6.

Jordan, B. 1997. "Authoritative Knowledge and its Construction." In *Childbirth and Authoritative Knowledge: Cross-Cultural Perspectives*, ed. R. E. Davis-Floyd and C. F. Sargent. Berkeley: University of California Press.

Joyce, T. J., R. Kaestner, and S. Korenman. 2000. "The Stability of Pregnancy Intentions and Pregnancy-Related Maternal Behaviors." *Maternal and Child Health Journal* 4(3):171–78.

Kay, M. A., ed. 1982a. "Writing an Ethnography of Birth." In *The Anthropology of Human Birth*. Philadelphia: F. A. Davis.

———. 1982b. *The Anthropology of Human Birth*. Philadelphia: F. A. Davis.

Khattab, H. A. S., N. Younis, and H. Zurayk. 1999. *Women, Reproduction, and Health in Rural Egypt: The Giza Study*. Cairo: American University in Cairo Press.

Klijzing, E. 2000. "Are There Unmet Family Planning Needs in Europe?" *Family Planning Perspectives* 32(2):74–81, 88.

Koblinsky, M. A. 1995. "Beyond Maternal Mortality—Magnitude, Interrelationship, and Consequences of Women's Health, Pregnancy-Related Complications and Nutritional Status on Pregnancy Outcomes." *International Journal of Gynecology and Obstetrics* 48(Suppl.):S21–S32.

Larsen, U. 2000. "Primary and Secondary Infertility in Sub-Saharan Africa." *International Journal of Epidemiology* 29(2):285–91.

Layne, L. L. 1992. "Of Fetuses and Angels: Fragmentation and Integration in Narratives of Pregnancy Loss." *Knowledge and Society* 9:29–58.

———, ed. 1999. *Transformative Motherhood: On Giving and Getting in a Consumer Culture*. New York: New York University Press.

———. 2003. *Motherhood Lost: A Feminist Account of Pregnancy Loss in America*. New York: Routledge.

Lazarus, E. 1997. "What Do Women Want? Issues of Choice, Control, and Class in American Pregnancy and Childbirth." In *Childbirth and Authoritative Knowledge: Cross-Cultural Perspectives*, ed. R. E. Davis-Floyd and C. F. Sargent. Berkeley: University of California Press.

Lia-Hoagberg, B., P. Rode, C. J. Skovholt, C. N. Oberg, C. Berg, S. Mullett, and T. Choi. 1990. "Barriers and Motivators to Prenatal Care among Low-Income Women." *Social Science and Medicine* 30(4):487–95.

Lindbohm, M. L. 1995. "Effects of Parental Exposure to Solvents on Pregnancy Outcome." *Journal of Occupational and Environmental Medicine* 37(8):908–14.

Major, B., C. Cozzarelli, M. Testa, and P. Mueller. 1992. "Male Partners, Appraisals of Undesired Pregnancy and Abortion: Implications for Women's Adjustment to Abortion." *Journal of Applied Social Psychology* 22(8):599–614.

Martin, E. 1987. *The Woman in the Body*. Boston: Beacon.

Mbizvo, M. T. 1996. "Reproductive and Sexual Health: A Research and Developmental Challenge." *Central African Journal of Medicine* 42(3):80–85.

Mbizvo, M. T., and D. J. Adamchack. 1991. "Family Planning Knowledge, Attitudes, and Practices of Men in Zimbabwe." *Studies in Family Planning* 22:31–38.

McCaw-Binns, A., J. La Grenade, and D. Ashley. 1995. "Underusers of Antenatal Care: A Comparison of Non-Attenders and Late Attenders for Antenatal Care, With Early Attenders." *Social Science and Medicine* 40(7):1003–12.

McClain, C. S. 1982. "Toward a Comparative Framework for the Study of Childbirth: A Review of the Literature." In *The Anthropology of Human Birth*, ed. M. A. Kay. Philadelphia: F. A. Davis.

Mendez-Dominguez, A. 1998. "The Sexuality of the Guatemalan Mam Indians and Its Changes with Urbanization." Paper presented at the conference "Men, Family Formation and Reproduction," Buenos Aires, 13–15 May.

Merino, G., S. C. Lira, and J. C. Martinez-Chequer. 1998. "Effects of Cigarette Smoking on Semen Characteristics of a Population in Mexico." *Archives of Andrology* 41(1):11–15.

Montgomery, M. R. 1996. "Comments on Men, Women, and Unintended Pregnancy." *Population and Development Review* 22:100–6.

Morgan, L. M., and M. W. Michaels, eds. 1999. *Fetal Subjects, Feminist Positions*. Philadelphia: University Of Pennsylvania Press.

MotherCare. 1996. *Guía Para Facilitadores De Comadronas: Educacíon Participativa*. Arlington, VA: MotherCare/John Snow.

Mundigo, A. I. 1998. "The Role of Men in Improving Reproductive Health: The Direction Research Should Take." In *Reproductive Health Research: The New Directions, Biennial Report 1996–1997*, ed. J. Khanna and P. F. A. Van Look. Geneva, Switzerland: WHO.

———. 2000. "Re-Conceptualizing the Role of Men in the Post-Cairo Era." *Culture, Health and Sexuality* 2(3):323–37.

Mustard, C. A., and N. P. Roos. 1994. "The Relationship of Prenatal Care and Pregnancy Complications to Birthweight in Winnipeg, Canada." *American Journal of Public Health* 84(9):1450–57.

Nations, M. K. 1986. "Epidemiological Research on Infectious Diseases: Quantitative Rigor or Rigormortis? Insights from Ethnomedicine." In *Anthropology and Epidemiology: Interdisciplinary Approaches to the Study of Health and Disease*, ed. C. R. Janes, R. Stall, and S. M. Gifford. Dordrecht: Reidel.

Ndong, I., R. M. Becker, J. M. Haws, and M. N. Wegner. 1999. "Men's Reproductive Health: Defining, Designing and Delivering Services." *International Family Planning Perspectives* 25:S53–S5.

Network, P. O. M. M. 1992. "Barriers to Treatment of Obstetric Emergencies in Rural Communities in West Africa." *Studies in Family Planning* 23(5):279–91.

Ngom, P. 1997. "Men's Unmet Need for Family Planning: Implications for African Fertility Transitions." *Studies in Family Planning* 28(3):192–202.

Okonofua, F. E. 1996. "The Case against New Reproductive Technologies in Developing Countries." *British Journal of Obstetrics and Gynecology* 103:957–62.

Olayinka, B. A., L. Alexander, M. T. Mbizvo, and L. Gibney. 2000. "Generational Differences in Male Sexuality That May Affect Zimbabwean Women's Risk for Sexually Transmitted Diseases and HIV/AIDS." *East African Medical Journal* 77(2):93–97.

Oropesa, R. S., N. S. Landale, M. Inkley, and B. K. Gorman. 2000. "Prenatal Care among Puerto Ricans on the United States Mainland." *Social Science and Medicine* 51(12):1723–39.

Parker, R., R. M. Barbosa, and P. Aggleton, eds. 2000. "Introduction: Framing the Sexual Subject." In *Framing the Sexual Subject: The Politics of Gender, Sexuality, and Power.* Berkeley: University of California Press.

Patton, C. 1994. *Last Served? Gendering the HIV Pandemic.* London: Taylor and Francis.

Paul, L. 1974. "The Mastery of Work and the Mystery of Sex in a Guatemalan Village." In *Women, Culture, and Society,* ed. M. Z. Rosaldo and L. Lamphere. Stanford: Stanford University Press.

Petchesky, R. P. 1998. "Introduction." In *Negotiating Reproductive Rights: Women's Perspectives across Countries and Cultures,* ed. R. P. Petchesky and K. Judd. London: Zed.

———. 2000. "Sexual Rights: Inventing a Concept, Mapping an International Practice." In *Framing the Sexual Subject: The Politics of Gender, Sexuality, and Power,* ed. R. Parker, R. M. Barbosa, and P. Aggleton. Berkeley: University of California Press.

Petchesky, R. P., and K. Judd, eds. 1998. *Negotiating Reproductive Rights: Women's Perspectives across Countries and Cultures.* London: Zed.

Pollard, I. 1994. *A Guide to Reproduction: Social Issues and Human Concerns.* Cambridge: Cambridge University Press.

———. 2000. "Substance Abuse and Parenthood: Biological Mechanisms, Bioethical Challenges." *Women and Health* 30(3):1–24.

Population Council. 2001. *Power in Sexual Relationships: An Opening Dialogue among Reproductive Health Professionals.* New York: Population Council.

Potts, A. 2000. "The Essence of the Hard On: Hegemonic Masculinity and the Cultural Construction of Erectile Dysfunction." *Men and Masculinities* 3(1):85–103.

Presser, H. B., and G. Sen. 2000. *Women's Empowerment and Demographic Processes: Moving beyond Cairo.* Oxford: Oxford University Press.

Quick, J. D., M. R. Greenlick, and K. J. Roghmann. 1981. "Prenatal Care and Pregnancy Outcome in an HMO and General Population: A Multivariate Cohort Analysis." *American Journal of Public Health* 71(4):381–90.

Rapp, R. 1999. *Testing Women, Testing the Fetus: The Social Impact of Amniocentesis in America.* New York: Routledge.

Reproductive Health Outlook. 2003. "Infertility: Overview and Lessons Learned." www.rho.org/html/infertilityoverview.

Rowley, D., and H. Tosteson, eds. 1993. "Racial Differences in Preterm Delivery: Developing a New Research Paradigm." *American Journal of Preventive Medicine* 9 (Special Issue, Suppl. 6):27–34.

Santelli, J., R. W. Rochat, K. Hatfield-Timajchy, B. C. Gilbert, K. M. Curtis, R. Cabral, J. S. Hirsch, and L. Schieve. 2003. "The Measurement and Meaning of Unintended Pregnancy." *Perspectives on Sexual and Reproductive Health* 35(2):94–101.

Sargent, C. F. 1989. *Maternity, Medicine, and Power: Decisions in Urban Benin.* Berkeley: University of California Press.

Schaffer, M. A., and B. Lia-Hoagberg. 1997. "Effects of Social Support on Prenatal Care and Health Behaviors of Low-Income Women." *Journal of Obstetric, Gynecologic and Neonatal Nursing* 26(4):433–40.

Scheper-Hughes, N. 1993. *Death without Weeping: The Violence of Everyday Life in Brazil.* Los Angeles: University of California Press.

Sen, G., A. George, and P. Ostlin. 2002. *Engendering International Health: The Challenge of Equity.* Cambridge: MIT Press.

Sesia, P. M. 1996. "'Women Come Here on Their Own When They Need to': Prenatal Care, Authoritative Knowledge, and Maternal Health in Oaxaca." *Medical Anthropology Quarterly* 10(2):121–40.

Sever, L. E. 1981. "Reproductive Hazards of the Workplace." *Journal of Occupational Medicine* 23(10):685–89.

Shea, K. M., A. Farrow, and R. Little. 1997. "An Investigation of the Effect of Paternal Occupation Group at Conception on Birth Weight and Gestational Age. ALSPAC Study Team of Pregnancy and Childhood." *American Journal of Industrial Medicine* 31(6):738–43.

Silberschmidt, M., and V. Rasch. 2001. "Adolescent Girls, Illegal Abortions and 'Sugar-Daddies' in Dar Es Salaam: Vulnerable Victims and Active Social Agents." *Social Science and Medicine* 52(12):1815–26.

Sinclair, S. 2000. "Male Infertility: Nutritional and Environmental Considerations." *Alternative Medicine Review* 5(1):28–38.

Smith, D. J. 1999. "Having People: Fertility, Family and Modernity in Igbo-Speaking Nigeria." PhD diss., Emory University, Atlanta.

Soler, H., D. Quadagno, D. F. Sly, K. S. Riehman, I. W. Eberstein, and D. F. Harrison. 2000. "Relationship Dynamics, Ethnicity and Condom Use among Low-Income Women." *Family Planning Perspectives* 32(2):82–88.

Steeno, O. P., and A. Pangkahila. 1984. "Occupational Influences on Male Fertility and Sexuality. I." *Andrologia* 16(1):5–22.

Tielemans, E., A. Burdof, E. R. Te Velde, R. F. A. Weber, R. J. Van Kooij, H. Veulemans, and D. J. J. Heederik. 1999. "Occupationally Related Exposures and Reduced Semen Quality: A Case-Control Study." *Fertility and Sterility* 71(4):690–96.

Vitellone, N. 2000. "Condoms and the Making of 'Testosterone Man': A Cultural Analysis of the Male Sex Drive in AIDS Research on Safer Heterosex." *Men and Masculinities* 3(2):152–67.

Wadhwa, P. D., J. H. Culhane, V. Rauh, S. S. Barve, V. Hogan, C. A. Sandman, C. J. Hobel, A. Chicz-Demet, C. Dunkel-Schetter, T. J. Garite, and L. Glynn. 2001. "Stress, Infection and Preterm Birth: A Biobehavioural Perspective." *Paediatric and Perinatal Epidemiology* 15(Suppl. 2):17–29.

Wall, L. L. 1998. "Dead Mothers and Injured Wives: The Social Context of Maternal Morbidity and Mortality among the Hausa of Northern Nigeria." *Studies in Family Planning* 29(4):341–59.

Ward, V. M., J. T. Bertrand, and F. Puac. 1992. "Exploring Sociocultural Barriers to Family Planning among Mayans in Guatemala." *International Family Planning Perspectives* 18(2):59–65.

Wasserheit, J. N. 1992. "Epidemiological Synergy: Interrelationships between Human Immunodeficiency Virus Infection and Other Sexually Transmitted Diseases." *Sexually Transmitted Diseases* 19:61–77.

———. 1994. "Effect of Changes in Human Ecology and Behavior on Patterns of Sexually Transmitted Diseases, including Human Immunodeficiency Virus Infection." *Proceedings of the National Academy of Sciences* 9(1):2430–35.

Wegner, M. N., E. Landry, D. Wilkinson, and J. Tzanis. 1998. "Men as Partners in Reproductive Health: From Issues to Action." *International Family Planning Perspectives* 24(1):38–42.

Were, E. O., and J. K. Karanja. 1994. "Attitudes of Males to Contraception in a Kenyan Rural Population." *East African Medical Journal* 71(2):106–9.

Westoff, C. F. 2001. "Unmet Need at the End of the Century." *DHS Comparative Reports* 1.

Wolff, B., A. K. Blanc, and J. Ssekamatte-Ssebuliba. 2000. "The Role of Couple Negotiation in Unmet Need for Contraception and the Decision to Stop Childbearing in Uganda." *Studies in Family Planning* 31(2):124–37.

Yebei, V. N. 2000. "Unmet Needs, Beliefs and Treatment Seeking for Infertility among Migrant Ghanaian Women in the Netherlands." *Reproductive Health Matters* 8(16):134–41.

Yogman, M. W., D. Kindlon, and F. Earls. 1995. "Father Involvement and Cognitive/Behavioral Outcomes of Preterm Infants." *Journal of the American Academy of Child and Adolescent Psychiatry* 34(1):58–66.

Zabin, L. S., G. R. Huggins, M. R. Emerson, and V. E. Cullins. 2000. "Partner Effects on a Woman's Intention to Conceive: 'Not with this partner.'" *Family Planning Perspectives* 32(1):39–45.

Part II.

FERTILITY AND FAMILY PLANNING

Chapter 5

MANHOOD AND MEANING IN THE MARKETING OF THE "MALE PILL"

Laury Oaks

The marketing of new technologies will have practical and symbolic implications for men's and women's sexual and reproductive health and reproductive responsibilities. Men's future contraceptive options are not merely a matter of scientific advancement. In addition, a range of important social, ethical, and health questions related to men's and women's lives must be faced regarding the potential marketing of new male contraceptives. These include two questions: How will advertising campaigns promoting new male contraceptives represent potential and ideal male pill users and their reproductive, sexual, and masculine identities and responsibilities? And how have scientists created their image of an ideal male pill user, and what are the implications of this vision for the future marketing of the drug and social understandings of men's and women's reproductive and sexual responsibility? To understand how the marketing of new male hormonal contraceptives may influence men's and women's control over their reproductive and sexual health, this chapter analyzes the significance of increased medicalization of the male body, and explores how new male contraceptive users and masculinity have been produced by reproductive scientists and in *Time*'s 1999 mock advertising campaign (Barovick, Hylton, Lofaro, Gray, Spitz, and Tartakovsky 1999).

Recent social science scholarship has explored why medical experts and reproductive rights advocates have undertheorized men's reproductive and sexual health (Daniels 1997, 1999, 2006; Dudgeon and Inhorn 2003, this volume; Gutmann 2007; Hirsch 2003; Loe 2004) and how reproductive technologies influence men's reproductive participation and their ideas about masculinity and fatherhood (Becker 2000; Browner 2000; Oudshoorn 2000, 2003; Schmidt and Moore 1998; Goldberg, Tjørnhøj-Thomsen, Inhorn, and Mosegaard this volume). At the same time, medical and advocacy attention to men's health has culminated in an international men's health movement that supports research and policy initiatives on a range of men's health issues, including the encouragement of "male involvement" in family planning (Baker 2001). The development of new male hormonal contraceptives optimistically suggests the possibility of a shift of the "contraceptive burden" from solely women to men or couples.

This chapter builds on Dutch feminist scholar of gender and technology Nellie Oudshoorn's path-breaking study of the technological development and social meanings around the male pill, in which she details how feminists, scientists, and the mass media have produced—at times collaborative and at other times contradictory—images of the male pill, its users, and women's "needs" (2000, 2003). My analysis complements Oudshoorn's by focusing on the medicalization of the male body and on a series of mock proposed advertising representations of the male pill. This component of the chapter is informed by social and cultural examinations that focus on the meaning of gender, sexuality, race/ethnicity, and other categories of analysis as seen in health campaigns (King 2006; Loe 2004; Patton 1996; Treichler 1999) and advertising campaigns (Bordo 1999; Goldman and Papson 1999).

I have cast a wide net in selecting English-language scholarship, health literature, and news reports in order to capture multiple representations of men's and women's reproductive responsibility and sexual agency in relation to contraception. Whether looking at scientific reports published in scholarly journals or the mock advertising of the male pill in the popular U.S. media, I read this material—which dated from the 1960s to the present—using a feminist framework that explores stated and implicit commentary on gendered expectations of men's and women's sexual and reproductive roles, needs, and risks, as well as how culture, race/ethnicity, and class influence representations of these dynamics.

Background: Inventing New Male Contraceptives

Together, European-based pharmaceutical companies Schering and Organon jointly predicted that a male hormonal contraceptive would become marketable in the United States and Europe by 2009 (Schering Aktiengesellschaft 2003).[1] What is popularly referred to as the male pill would likely consist of a hormonal implant and testosterone injection. The implant is designed to severely reduce or stop sperm production. Although the implant reduces the risk of "demasculinizing," side effects are likely to occur when only a hormone is given, such as impeded sexual function, reduced libido, acne, testicular shrinkage, and breast growth (Oudshoorn 2003:93–94). Achieving the contraceptive effect of the implant/injection takes from three to six months, and Schering Aktiengesellschaft (2003) reported that within this period, sperm levels fall to zero in 75 percent of men, revealing variation in the drug's action by individual. Another research focus is to inhibit egg fertilization (Schering Aktiengesellschaft 2003). The goal is an effective and acceptable reversible male contraceptive that will not cause unwanted sexual or health side effects. Oudshoorn argues that reproductive scientists' overwhelming attention to reducing side effects—in contrast to a relative lack of such high concern when the "female pill" and intrauterine device were first marketed—is related to a "cultural preoccupation with norms of masculinity that can best be summarized as 'no tinkering with male sexuality'" (2003:110).[2]

Despite this challenge, scientists and other advocates have urged such "tinkering" by working to develop new contraceptive devices for men. However, the Schering–Organon partnership has not carried through their research agenda, and male contraceptive advocates' attention has turned elsewhere, including to non-hormonal contraceptive research in India backed by Marksans Pharma (Stafford 2007). Schering–Organon's joint research ended in 2006, and in the following year, both ended their male contraceptive research and development programs. This was the result of changing business organization and strategy, the need for continued clinical trials, and the concern that sufficient numbers of men would not accept the implant/injection combination (Stafford 2007).

Scientists have sought to create a broader range of male contraceptive options for decades. In the 1960s, leaders in China and India called for new male contraceptives as the key missing component of population control programs (Oudshoorn 2000; 2003), and in 1976, the World Health Organization established a task force on male antifertility methods. The task force conducted clinical trials on new male contraceptives soon thereafter, sponsoring two studies involving sixteen centers in ten countries, with a total of 670 couples between 1980 and 1994.

Backing for the search for new male contraceptives was also voiced by feminists who were concerned not with population control, but also with assisting women in avoiding unwanted pregnancies. To support their research interests, scientists who advocated male contraceptive advances in the 1970s drew on the arguments of feminists who criticized the lack of attention to men's contraceptive development. Feminists identified the imbalance in scientific focus on controlling women's reproductive bodies as "sexist," in that it placed responsibility on women for reproduction and acceptance of contraceptive risk (Oudshoorn 2000, 2003).[3] In turn, scientists contended that new male contraceptives would contribute to "a shared responsibility in responsible parenthood" (Hermite et al. 1976, cited in Oudshoorn 2003:47). Nellie Oudshoorn, whose excellent 2003 book is the first on the male pill, argues that this contraceptive has the potential to meet feminists' demands on two levels, reducing women's contraceptive health risks and increasing male contraceptive responsibility. At the same time, a central contradiction for feminists exists: women may lose autonomy and the "right to control their fertility," while men gain their own reproductive control with the advent of new male contraceptives (Oudshoorn 2003:30).

The establishment of a link between the need for new male contraceptive technologies and the advocacy of gender equality and women's and men's shared reproductive and sexual health participation hinged on the 1994 UN International Conference on Population and Development (ICPD). The conference marked heightened visibility around official recognition of social justice and gender roles in relation to population and development. Due to the work of international women's health advocates and others (see Lane 1994; Sen, Germain, and Chen 1994), statements formulated before and during the ICPD—coupled with those at the 1995 Fourth World Conference on Women and NGO Forum in Beijing—reflected what is called a paradigm shift in population and development frameworks away from the crude thesis of population control toward reproductive and sexual health frameworks that directly address men and women in their decision making.

Facilitated by this shift and encouraged by the devastation of the global HIV/AIDS epidemic, health experts increasingly view men as an important audience for reproductive and sexual health messages. Peter Piot, the director of UNAIDS, has stated that men are "key to reducing HIV transmission" and have "the power to change the course of the AIDS epidemic" (quoted in Ringheim 2002:170). Indeed, the World AIDS Campaign in 2000 and 2001 was focused on men, in part to underscore that worldwide over 70 percent of HIV transmission is through heterosexual intercourse, and 5 to 10 percent is through sex between men. But, as I discuss below, there remains a gap between advocacy for male hormonal contraceptives and for men's increased participation in HIV prevention activities. In short, research scientists who support new male contraceptives represent the ideal male pill user as one who does not need to wear condoms because he is in a long-term, monogamous, and trusting relationship (Oudshoorn 2000). This assumption works against HIV/AIDS education, which insists that *all* sexually active men and women are at risk (Patton 1996), as well as scholars who demonstrate the inadequacies of assuming that a monogamous, trusting relationship is a sufficient health buffer (Sobo 1995; Woodsong and Koo 1999).

The invention of new male contraceptives has been informed by changing ideas about men's and women's contraceptive "needs" as well as their sexual and reproductive responsibilities. Shifts in attention to the male body are equally important in the history of the male pill. I have found that the sexual and reproductive health approach of scholars and activists provides a powerful basis for the analysis of the development and marketing of men's hormonal contraceptives and the increasing medicalization of the male sexual and reproductive body.

Medicalization of the Male Sexual and Reproductive Body

Pharmaceutical companies' fears of financial risk and an unquestioned "sexism" that places contraceptive responsibility primarily on women are two reasons why contraceptive development for men has been far slower than that for women (see Oudshoorn 2003). Another reason points to how the differences between male and female bodies justify this disparity. Scientists routinely label the male reproductive system as more complex than the female's. The research-based pharmaceutical company Schering Aktiengesellschaft has explained, "Unlike the task of preventing the development of a single egg cell per month, male contraception would involve finding a way to stop the production of 70 to 100 million sperm per day" (2001:41). Further, Schering noted that the average seventy-day period for spermatozoa to be formed and then released complicates the search for an effective and reversible male hormonal contraceptive. From this perspective, controlling and "disciplining" men's continuously reproductively able bodies is more difficult than that of women's (Daniels 1997, 1999, 2006; Martin 1991; Oudshoorn 1994, 2003).[4] Due to both scientific and popular fascination with the sperm-producing nature of the male reproductive body (see Moore this volume), the future marketing of a male hormonal contraceptive is poised to be a more celebrated accomplishment of scientific progress than the creation of the female pill in the 1960s.

An additional factor that has influenced male contraceptive research is related to the history of "illegitimacy" among scientists of
"applied" research on birth control (Clarke 1998; Oudshoorn 1994,
2003). The way that reproductive science has developed, and the
assignment of men's reproductive research as being of lesser import
within the field, is in part responsible for the imbalanced focus on
women's bodies. Yet the increased visibility of the medicalization of
men's sexual function has created a window of opportunity both
for enhanced male contraceptive research efforts and, potentially,
for the marketing of new male contraceptive products. The most
specific example of the successful medicalization of men's sexual
bodies—medicalization being the process through which phenomena become framed as medical problems best treated by medical experts (Riessman 1983; Zola 1972)—is the identification of "erectile
dysfunction" (ED) as a widespread medical disorder and the development and marketing of Viagra as its treatment (Loe 2001, 2004).
In the case of male contraception, the social problem that the medical discovery of a male pill will address is gender inequality around
responsibility for pregnancy prevention.

Viagra has been marketed primarily as a sexual, not a reproductive, fix. But Viagra has consequences for men's reproductive health
research. The record-breaking financial success of this "little blue
pill" has pushed the pharmaceutical company Pfizer and medical
professionals to legitimate the field of "andrology," the study of androgen, which might assist in understanding the male reproductive
body. Some pharmaceutical companies and medical experts are focusing on a medical diagnosis that goes beyond ED, called androgen
deficiency (Groopman 2002; Loe 2004). This expansion portends
not only the deepening medicalization of this condition, but also the
broadening of research and pharmaceutical markets targeting men.
The high visibility and financial success of the Viagra campaign may
pave the way for the promotion of male hormonal contraception:
men in the United States and elsewhere are being socialized to discuss sexual concerns with their doctors.[5]

Beyond the advertising hyperbole over ED products, the field of
men's health is gaining legitimacy. This is evidenced by men's health
advocates establishing the International Society for Men's Health in
2001 at the First World Congress on Men's Health in Vienna and
the 2001 launch of the *International Journal of Men's Health* (see
Baker 2001). In addition, international family planning advocates
aim to incorporate men's health into family planning programs and
bring men into family planning clinics (Oudshoorn 2003). Given
attempts to socialize men to broach sexual health topics with their
doctors, the huge financial success of ED drugs, and the work of the

international men's health movement to encourage men to consult health care professionals with greater frequency, I suggest that a generation of male hormonal contraceptive users is in the making.

However, the public health ideal vision of a future of ready routes for men to reach physicians for reproductive consultation, contraception prescriptions, and general health services may not become a reality. Male contraceptive researchers interviewed by Oudshoorn (2003) reported that when recruiting clinical trial participants in the early 1990s, they were met with a lack of cooperation from urologists and andrologists, most of whom in the reproductive field are interested in infertility; only general practitioners were willing to assist the researchers by putting up posters in their waiting rooms. I would expect the attitudes of even previously reticent health professionals to change when a male contraceptive technology is marketed due to doctors' recognition that a demand for new male contraceptives could attract new clients. However, optimism about the timely marketing of a male pill has been dampened given the lack of sustained research support by pharmaceutical companies. As one researcher pointedly insists, "The pharmaceutical industry is completely disconnected from the public and medical perceptions of need" regarding new male contraceptives (David Handelsman, quoted in Goodman 2008). Whether there is an eager and large population of future male pill consumers and doctors to prescribe the pill for them remains controversial.

Producing Male Hormonal Contraceptive Users through Media Advertising

The heightened medicalization of the male sexual and reproductive body suggests that, in the context of some Northern countries, new male contraceptives may have an institutional home within the health care system. Further needed are willing consumers. An important dimension of the creation of male hormonal contraceptive users will be media advertising. Indeed, researchers consciously have cultivated media attention, primarily through press releases, interviews, and newspaper stories, to recruit clinical trial participants, disseminate research findings, and influence public opinion about new male hormonal contraceptives (Oudshoorn 2000, 2003).

Capitalizing on the important role of the media in pharmaceutical marketing, *Time* (Barovick et al. 1999) solicited mock advertisements from selected advertising agencies following April 1999 reports on breakthroughs in male oral contraception in a British study of twenty-three men. *Time* playfully suggested that full knowledge about the pill's side effects (potentially affecting libido, sexual function, acne, and testicle and breast size) created a problem: "To overcome this marketing dilemma, we asked the fertile minds at various ad agencies to think up some potent campaigns" (1999). Revealing women's health advocates' interest in such developments, a Center for Reproductive Law & Policy newsletter (1999) featured three of the eight ads.[6] I analyze these three ads in depth before turning to examine the others. The ads provide commentaries on gender roles, masculinity, and the male body. The construction of the future male pill user is figured differently in the ads, suggesting that potential consumers are more diverse than reproductive scientists envision.

In the first image, a pack of pills takes the place of a condom in a man's wallet.

Figure 5.1. Advertisement for the male pill. GSD&M Advertising. Used with permission.

The announcement that "The male pill is here" suggests men can do away with their former, perhaps disliked, standby method, and that they have been waiting for an alternative. The second image portrays a young, slight, white man dressed in party attire and smiling widely: "Don't worry, ladies, I'm on the pill."

The avuncular or paternal presence of a taller man wearing a suit on the left, his arm draped proudly, perhaps protectively, around the young man's shoulder, suggests a coming of age event. The awkward, and plural, "ladies" as the subject of the young man's assuring statement might suggest that this uninitiated man has yet to learn an appropriate "pick-up line," but he knows declaring his contraceptive responsibility is sure to appeal to women. Directly in line with this ad, University of Washington reproductive scientist John Amory reports that male participants of an implant contraceptive acted out the assumption that a man's contraceptive responsibility is attractive and a conversation piece: "The guys were proud of their implants. They were conversation starters at cocktail parties. They would have a woman feel their arm" (Associated Press 2004).

These ads suggest that preparation for sexual encounters with multiple women are part of men's experiences and that "sex as

Figure 5.2. Advertisement for the male pill. Bill Heater, Heater Advertising, Boston. Used with permission.

recreation" is socially acceptable. This is notable given that reproductive scientists have identified men who engage in "casual sex"
as "nonusers" of the male pill. Scientists have done so in response
to global concerns about men preventing sexually transmitted infections (STIs) (see Oudshoorn 2003). They do not advocate male
pill use for men who appear at greater risk for STIs, following the
assumption that a man will not simultaneously use the male pill
and a condom. In fact, neither ad addresses HIV/AIDS and other
STI risks as what I would term a "sexual responsibility" issue, one
that ideally ought to accompany reproductive responsibility. One
place men who might use the pill are advised to "double contracept" is in a 1997 *Men's Health* magazine news clip noting that researchers aimed to have a male pill submitted to the FDA by 1999.
"Perhaps by then," the magazine quips, playing on the decades
since the arrival of the female pill and lyrics from the Prince song
"1999," "you'll be able to party like it's 1969 (as long as you wear a
condom)" ("Sex & Health Malegrams" 1997:40). The parenthetical
statement highlights a change in what constitutes sexual liberation
in an AIDS-threatened world.

   The third advertisement announces, "The sex drive of a 30-year-
old. The sperm count of a 130-year-old," pointing out that sex drive
and sperm count are not correlated.

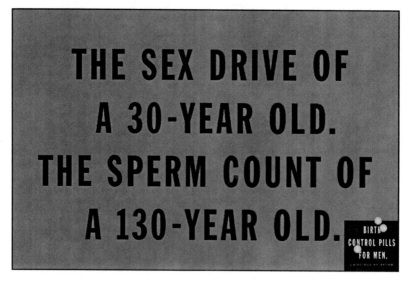

Figure 5.3. Advertisement for the male pill. Frank Haggerty Art Director/
Dan Roettger copywriter. Used with permission.

Thus, male contraception should not interfere with a significant measure of manliness. When I showed this image to college-age women in a reproductive politics class, students were quick to point out that in their experience, a thirty-year-old's sex drive would not appeal to college-age men because men are thought to "peak" sexually in their teens. In contrast to the previous ad, this one is marketed to men (and women) who are over thirty. But this is not surprising given that reproductive health professionals predict that new hormonal methods "will most likely be used by mature men in stable relationships" (McGee 1999), and a pioneering male contraceptive researcher warns, "You have to give it to a monogamous couple that know and understand and trust each other" (Alvin Paulsen, quoted in Oudshoorn 2000).

Such considerations suggest that a male pill will need to appeal not only to men, but also to couples, carrying the assumption that "understanding and trust" are central components of monogamous relationships, and imply that HIV/STI prevention is not an issue in monogamous relationships (see Oudshoorn 2003). However, research on health risk-taking reveals that for many, trusting one's sexual partner often constitutes a health risk (Sobo 1995; Woodsong and Koo 1999), and Oudshoorn (2003) argues that a significant amount of the mass media attention paid to the male pill has focused on the issue of trust or, more aptly, mistrust, of men by women. Trust works at varied levels in relation to this ad. The ad seeks to gain male trust that the pill will not influence libido and is in line with the construction of an "ideal" male pill user who is more mature, at age thirty or over, and has a sexual partner who trusts his reproductive and sexual responsibility.

The content of the mock ads that were carried by *Time* (Barovick 1999) but not featured by the Center for Reproductive Law & Policy attempt to persuade the potential male consumer through humor and by borrowing stock advertising strategies. Given the extreme importance of product names for attracting consumers, it is notable that only two ads featured names, "Sperminol" and "SpermX."[7] The Sperminol user is portrayed as a child-averse couch potato who desires uninterrupted leisure time, as the ad reads, "Nothing ruins televised golf like a baby that can't shut its yapper." The SpermX ad uses a stereotypical image of the muscular torso of a man modeling underwear and traces lines from the genital area to the tag line "Under new management." This suggests a shift from a state of nature—lifelong sperm production—to that of technological control and is a play on the scientific language for birth control as "fertility management" (Ringheim 1996:80).

Two ads feature split panels and images of what the male pill might look like. The first, stressing that some men would prefer a pill over vasectomy and that the pill is not only a woman's product, shows a scalpel on one side, and a small, round pill and the text "Easier to swallow: the pill—FOR MEN" on the other. The second ad features, on one side, the text "TAKING THE *MEN* OUT OF *SEMEN*," and on the other, the text "Birth Control for Men" with an image of an oblong, large, vitamin-sized pill. The only ad alluding to male consumers' potential fears of adverse sexual side effects states, "Outfit your little swimmers in a real snazzy pair of cement shoes." It carries an illustration of three upward-swimming sperm and the bottom line of "The birth control pill for men." Intriguing here is the heads-up image of the sperm, symbolizing that erection is not impaired by pill use. Further, the ad suggests that the mechanism of the pill is inadequate sperm motility. The designers perhaps considered this image as being less threatening to men and masculinity than that of a lack of sperm, which may imply lack of sexual function.

This playful advertising competition reveals that messages announcing the male pill comment on several dimensions of men's inclinations regarding contraceptives, including dislike of other methods and fear of children's impact on one's lifestyle. Some carry information about the side effects (or lack thereof) of the medication, while others educate the viewer about the mechanisms of the technology. That the mock ads cover this range of subjects points to the complexities of new male contraceptive marketing. It also reveals some pitfalls. Notably, *Time* introduced this call for mock advertising as based in a need to address the pill/patch combination, following press releases on a clinical trial using this method; however, none of the ads include an indication that a testosterone patch is needed, overly simplifying what is entailed in opting for this birth control method. Further, the ad implying that the pill works by impairing sperm motility misrepresents the medication's mechanism (which will be the severe reduction or stopping of sperm production). In short, when pharmaceutical companies offer a new male contraceptive, it will be interesting to see how the media and advertisers highlight particular images of masculinity and sexuality while educating the public about the contraceptive and cultivating willing consumers.

Male contraceptive marketing campaigns will not only sell a product; they will also challenge or reinforce normative constructions of gendered sexuality. The mock ads suggest that the male pill will maintain or enhance a man's youthful sex drive, virility, heterosexual attractiveness, and ability to control the timing of fatherhood. Notably, the ads do little to question this type of sexualized masculinity. Lacking are images of what Oudshoorn (2000) labels the "Caring Man," who is motivated to use male contraception by assuming the burden of responsibility from his long-term partner and who has a trusting, monogamous sexual relationship with her (and thus has no need to use condoms for STI prevention). Oudshoorn (2000, 2003) provides evidence from interviews with reproductive scientists that they see ideal new male hormonal contraceptive users as Caring Men. This is scientists' dominant construction of future male pill users.

It is important to point out that even in the case of these Caring Men who seek to take on primary contraceptive responsibility, radical gender role change is not a foregone conclusion. For example, echoing what American feminist sociologist Arlie Hochschild (2003) found regarding men's attitudes toward housework and childcare in the United States, some men framed their participation as "helping" their wives. One male clinical trial participant of a group of twenty-eight men and their partners in Britain admitted, "Quite honestly, I never would have volunteered if my wife hadn't complained. My motto is: 'If it isn't broken, don't fix it'. . . . We [men] know they [women] have problems sometimes. Why would we want to share in that?" (Ringheim 1996:86). Hochschild's theory of the "stalled revolution" in the redistribution of the gendered division of labor in the home suggests that as long as men "help" women with their responsibilities instead of "take on" responsibilities as their own— whether in the social reproduction of the home or biological reproduction—will be equality elusive.

It seems logical that Caring Men would be ideal targets for recruiting successful clinical trial participants, as allowing only men in monogamous relationships with women interested in male hormonal contraception creates greater opportunity for surveillance and data gathering. For example, data on whether a woman would become pregnant when her partner was on the pill was important in determining the effectiveness of male hormonal contraception, which theoretically, ethically, and likely practically would be more easily tracked in a clinical trial participant's monogamous female partner than his numerous partners. What is less understandable from a pharmaceutical marketing perspective is why reproductive scientists state repeatedly in interviews and press releases that the Caring Man is the primary target user (see Oudshoorn 2000, 2003). This effectively limits the types of men to whom the pill would be marketed and links to a "conservative" view of sexual relationships (long-term, between one man and one woman). An expanded vision of the intended market would lead to greater financial rewards.

Despite reproductive scientists' emphasis on the Caring Man, none of the mock ads feature a type of masculinity associated with this male type. This points to how the portrayal of caring male sexuality presents a challenge to understandings of gender relationships and masculinity around sexuality and reproduction that draw on the cultural construction of "hegemonic masculinity," a type of masculinity elevated beyond other forms of masculinity and all constructions of femininity (Connell 1995; also see Oudshoorn 2000, 2003). In my analysis, the mock dimension of the *Time* ad competition invites a creative outpouring of messages that play with, or mock, stereotypes of masculinity. The competition was framed as one in which advertisers were to appeal to men who might be concerned about potential "demasculinizing" side effects of male contraception, which could explain the ads' emphasis on hegemonic masculine characteristics based on virility, sexual performance, youth, attractiveness, and control.

At the same time, the ads shy away from mocking the Caring Man, one who within the hegemonic masculinity framework could be easily portrayed as lacking masculinity by taking on the stereotypically woman's job of responsibility for pregnancy prevention. The mock nature of the ad campaign may not fully explain the lack of attention paid to the Caring Man. Oudshoorn (2003) demonstrates that following a 1996 World Health Organization press release on advances in clinical trials of the male pill, popular media coverage in the Netherlands and the UK also failed to represent the Caring Man created by reproductive scientists. In short, "the story of the 'Caring Man' obviously did not fit into the journalists' favorite tales of the future" (Oudshoorn 2003:208).

The question of how manhood, as defined by sexuality and reproduction, will be influenced by new male hormonal contraceptives exists both at the levels of the physiological (the "masculine" parts of male bodies) and the representational (ideologies around masculine sexuality). According to Oudshoorn, the meanings of new male contraception have yet to unfold: "New male contraceptives may enable men to perform masculinities that include responsibility and care. As happened to women with the female pill, the male pill may discipline men as reliable contraceptive users. Whether this will happen or not lies ultimately in the hands of its users" (2003:241). I would underscore that the meaning of masculinity in relation to contraceptive use will not be created only by men who use the male pill, but also by the women having sexual relationships with these men. Furthermore, I believe that male hormonal contraceptive advertising campaigns will be crucial influences in how male contraceptive users are represented and which men—and couples—opt for this new technology.

Conclusion: Global Politics, Empowerment, and the Marketing of New Male Contraceptives

The mock men's pill advertisements in *Time* (Barovick et al. 1999), qualitative assessments of British men's and women's acceptance of a new method (Ringheim 1996), and Schering–Organon's original aim (abandoned in 2007) to enter European and U.S. markets suggest that when new male contraceptives are marketed in Northern countries, it will be through a consumer-choice strategy that may avert protests. The popular media and health experts often portray consumer options as "advances" in technologies. But critical attention must be paid to whether and how such contraceptives are marketed to specific groups—especially those categorized by race/ethnicity and income—and how the concept of "choice" operates across them (see Solinger 2001).[8]

Taking these concerns into account, the narrative of the development of new male contraceptives is intriguing. Although the 1987 Male Task Force explicitly stated the objective of developing male contraceptives applicable to developing countries, the target of new male technologies has expanded to include Northern countries at the demand of feminists (Oudshoorn 2003). Thus, in Oudshoorn's analysis, two categories of potential male contraceptive users were created: those in the South who were responsible heads of household and wanted to limit family size, and those in the North who, as "New Men," would seek to share with their sexual partners the health risks of contraception and family responsibilities (2003). Whereas the governments in Southern countries explicitly encouraged the development of new male contraceptives as part of family planning efforts, Northern governments did not. The imbalance hinges on the difference between figuring the contraceptive user as a population target or a consumer. Most remarkable is that in a reversal of the 1987 objective, the pharmaceutical partnership that was leading new hormonal male contraceptives stated that the technology was being "developed for the European and American markets" (Schering Aktiengesellshaft 2003). This could represent a strategy to gain investors and consumers by "choice" before expanding to other markets and should not be seen as a sign that new male contraceptives would be limited only to Northern countries.

The future marketing of male hormonal contraceptives presents challenges that speak to the meaning of empowerment for men, women, and couples in relation to reproductive and sexual health. In the North, it is likely that male contraceptives will be marketed primarily as representing choice among methods and as offering women's liberation from the contraceptive burden, relying on and appropriating feminist discourses. Although I have yet to see strong evidence of it, male contraception campaigns might also promote an empowering men's rights message, emphasizing the potential for sexually active men to be liberated from unwanted paternity and the social and legal responsibilities of fatherhood. This discourse, to a large extent, has been preempted by reproductive scientists' consistent focus on new male contraceptive candidates who are in long-term, "trusting" relationships and who, hypothetically, would not have these concerns motivating their contraceptive use.

Although the pharmaceutical company Schering Aktiengesellschaft has contended that "male contraceptives will pave the way for equality in birth control" (2001), it is clear that this optimism overlooks the complexities involved in gender equality and power. In their discussion of gender equality, feminists and international health activists Sonia Corrêa and Rosalind Petchesky-Pollack (1994) point to the lack (in most cultures) of social, economic, or educational incentives to increase men's involvement in childcare, as well as the existence of cultural norms that define women's social status within the bounds of heterosexual, monogamous relationships. New male contraception, they assert, will not "help to realize women's social rights nor gender equality until these larger issues are also addressed" (117). A male pill is not sufficient for a second "contraceptive revolution" that will alter the imbalance between women's and men's reproductive and sexual responsibilities. It would, however, present new possibilities and might motivate public and media scrutiny of stereotypes around expectations of men and women in the context of sexuality and reproduction.

Acknowledgments

An early version of this chapter was delivered at the 2001 American Anthropological Association Annual Meetings on the panel "Men, Reproduction, and Reproductive Health: Embodied Subjects, Powerful Gatekeepers, or Unwelcome Partners?" I thank Jennifer Hirsch for organizing the session. Thanks are also due to Barbara Herr Harthorn, Jessica Jerome, Alena Marie, Meika Loe, Jo Murphy-Lawless, and

Doug English for their suggestions. Alena Marie, Meika Loe, Anna Lulejian, and Vanessa Sorgman provided invaluable research assistance. I sincerely thank the editors of this collection for their perseverance and Alissa Surges for her organizational skills.

Notes

1. Schering announced its collaboration with Organon in November 2002, stating that the male hormonal contraceptive would likely be marketed in five to seven years (Schering Anktiengesellschaft 2002).
2. For analyses of the development and marketing of female contraceptives, see Hartmann 1995; Barroso and Corrêa 1995; Clarke 1998; Marks 2001; and Takeshita 2004.
3. Feminists since the late 1960s have advocated new male contraceptive development as the result of medical and ethical dissatisfaction with women's contraceptive technologies, especially the pill (Oudshoorn 2000; 2003). Feminist positions have varied. For example, Elaine Lissner of the Boston Women's Health Book Collective runs the Male Contraceptive Information Project, calling for increased research attention to and information on nonhormonal male contraceptives (Lissner 1994, Male Contraception Information Project 2009). Taking a different perspective, members of the International Women's Health Coalition planning conference before the 1994 ICPD contended that "[f]emale-controlled methods that provide both contraception and protection from sexually transmitted diseases, including HIV, should receive highest priority in contraceptive research and development" (quoted in Clarke 1998:203; also see Fathalla 1994).
4. Some reproductive scientists have criticized the representation of the male body as significantly more complex than the female's (Schwartz 1976).
5. As evidence of attempts to create a Viagra-savvy patient, pharmaceutical company Pfizer provides advice to men on how to approach a doctor about ED (www.viagra.com/consumer/getStarted/tipsForTalking.asp). That tips for specific conversation openers refer to Pfizer's Viagra advertising campaigns indicate that the company sees advertising as a crucial tool in persuading patients to try their product.
6. The Center for Reproductive Law & Policy was renamed the Center for Reproductive Rights in January 2004.
7. In my reading, Sperminol connotes household germ and bacteria cleaner Lysol, while SpermX mimics household glass cleaner Windex. Whether such associations are intended is unknown, but the possible links suggest market names resonating with those in the category of products targeting women consumers, as well as the symbolic nature of the male pill as a cleanser of the male reproductive system.
8. A 1996 study found greater success in suppressing sperm production among Asian than non-Asian men (World Health Organization 1996).

This finding is disconcerting in that it points to the possibility that new male contraceptives will be proven "more effective" among men of color than among white men. The "dark-skinned body," as feminist legal scholar Dorothy Roberts (1997) argues regarding women, may be the more controllable body, and male hormonal contraceptives may more easily become part of population-control policies in some countries than others. Although researchers pose the finding that hormonal contraceptives act differently in the bodies of men grouped by race as a scientific problem (see Anderson et al. 2002), it must be understood in the context of political and cultural contests over the meaning of men's reproduction and sexuality.

References

Anderson, R. A., Z. M. van der Spuy, O. A. Dada, S. K. Tregoning, P. M. Zinn, O. A. Adeniji, T. A. Fakoya, K. B. Smith, and D. T. Baird. 2002. "Investigation of Hormonal Male Contraception in African Men: Suppression of Spermatogenesis by Oral Desogestrel with Depot Testosterone." *Human Reproduction* 17(11):2869–77.

Associated Press. 2004. "Making the Male Birth Control Pill." April 19. http://www.cbsnews.com/stories/2004/04/19/health/main612637.shtml.

Baker, Peter. 2001. "The International Men's Health Movement." *British Journal of Medicine* 323(7320):1014.

Barroso, Carmen, and Sonia Corrêa. 1995. "Public Servants, Professionals, and Feminists: The Politics of Contraceptive Research in Brazil." In *Conceiving the New World Order: The Global Politics of Reproduction*, ed. Faye D. Ginsburg and Rayna Rapp. Berkeley: University of California Press.

Barovick, Harriet, Hilary Hylton, Lina Lofaro, Tam Gray, David Spitz, and Flora Tartakovsky. 1999. "If Men Took the Pill. . . ." *Time*, 10 May, 23.

Becker, Gay. 2000. *Elusive Embryo: How Men and Women Approach New Reproductive Technologies*. Berkeley: University of California Press.

Bordo, Susan. 1999. *The Male Body: A New Look at Men in Public and Private*. New York: Farrar, Straus and Giroux.

Browner, Carole. 2000. "Situating Women's Reproductive Activities." *American Anthropologist* 102(4):773–88.

Center for Reproductive Law & Policy. 1999. "At a Glance." *Reproductive Freedom News*, June (back cover).

Clarke, Adele E. 1998. *Disciplining Reproduction: Modernity, American Life Sciences, and "The Problems of Sex."* Berkeley: University of California Press.

Connell, R. W. 1995. *Masculinities*. Cambridge: Polity Press.

Corrêa, Sonia, and Rosalind Petchesky. 1994. "Reproductive and Sexual Rights: A Feminist Perspective." In *Population Policies Reconsidered: Health, Empowerment, and Rights*, ed. Gita Sen, Adrienne Germain, and Lincoln Chen. Boston: Harvard University Press.

Daniels, Cynthia. 1997. "Between Fathers and Fetuses: The Social Construction of Male Reproduction and the Politics of Fetal Harm." *Signs* 22(3):579–615.

———. 1999. "Fathers, Mothers, and Fetal Harm: Rethinking Gender Difference and Reproductive Responsibility." In *Fetal Subjects, Feminist Positions*, ed. Lynn M. Morgan and Meredith W. Michaels. Philadelphia: University of Pennsylvania Press.

———. 2006. *Exposing Men: The Science and Politics of Male Reproduction*. New York: Oxford University Press.

Dudgeon, Matthew R., and Marcia C. Inhorn. 2003. "Gender, Masculinity, and Reproduction: Anthropological Perspectives." *International Journal of Men's Health* 2(1):31–56.

Fathalla, Mahoud F. 1994. "Fertility Control Technology: A Women-Centered Approach to Research." In *Population Policies Reconsidered: Health, Empowerment, and Rights*, ed. Gita Sen, Adrienne Germain, and Lincoln Chen. Boston: Harvard University Press.

Goldman, Robert, and Stephen Papson. 1999. *Nike Culture: The Sign of the Swoosh*. Thousand Oaks, CA: Sage.

Goodman, Adam. 2008. "The Long Wait for Male Birth Control." *Time*, August 3. www.time.com/time/health/article/0,8599,1829107,00.html.

Groopman, Jerome. 2002. "Hormones for Men: Is Male Menopause a Question of Medicine or of Marketing?" *New Yorker*, July 29, 34–8.

Gutmann, Matthew. 2007. Fixing Men: Sex, Birth Control, and AIDS in Mexico. Berkeley: University of California Press.

Hartmann, Betsy. 1995. *Reproductive Rights and Wrongs: The Global Politics of Population Control and Contraceptive Choice*, rev. ed. Boston: South End Press.

Hirsch, Jennifer S. 2003. *A Courtship after Marriage: Sexuality and Love in Mexican Transnational Families*. Berkeley: University of California Press.

Hochschild, Arlie Russell. 2003. *The Second Shift*. New York: Penguin.

International Women's Health Coalition. 2001. www.iwhc.org.

King, Samantha. 2006. Pink Ribbons, Inc.: Breast Cancer and the Politics of Philanthropy. Minneapolis: University of Minnesota Press.

Lane, Sandra D. 1994. "From Population Control to Reproductive Health: An Emerging Health Policy." *Social Science and Medicine* 39(9):1303–14.

Lissner, Elaine A. 1994. "Frontiers in Nonhormonal Male Contraception: A Call for Research." http://gumption.org/mcip/paper.htm.

Loe, Meika. 2001. "Fixing Broken Masculinity: Viagra as a Technology for the Production of Gender and Sexuality." *Sexuality & Culture* 5(3):97–105.

———. 2004. *The Rise of Viagra: How the Little Blue Pill Changed Sex in America*. New York: New York University Press.

Male Contraception Information Project. 2009. "What We Do." www.new-malecontraception.org/.

Marks, Lara. 2001. *Sexual Chemistry: A History of the Contraceptive Pill*. New Haven: Yale University Press.

Martin, Emily. 1991. "The Egg and the Sperm: How Science Has Constructed a Romance Based on Stereotypical Male-Female Roles." *Signs* 16(3):485–501.

McGee, Michael. 1999. "Preparing for New Male Contraceptives." *Recent Sexuality Education Resources* 4(2). www.plannedparenthood.org/library/edup_1099.html.

Oudshoorn, Nellie. 1994. *Beyond the Natural Body: An Archeology of Sex Hormones.* London: Routledge.

———. 2000. "Imagined Men: Representations of Masculinities in Discourses on Male Contraceptive Technology." In *Bodies of Technology: Women's Involvement with Reproductive Medicine,* ed. Ann Rudinow Saetnan, Nelly Oudshoorn, and Marta Kirejczyk. Columbus: Ohio State University Press.

———. 2003. *The Male Pill: A Biography of a Technology in the Making.* Durham: Duke University Press.

Patton, Cindy. 1996. *Fatal Advice: How Safe-Sex Education Went Wrong.* Durham: Duke University Press.

Pfizer, Inc. 2003. Tips for Talking to Your Doctor. www.viagra.com/consumer/getStarted/tipsForTalking.asp.

Riessman, Catherine Kohler. 1983. "Women and Medicalization: A New Perspective." *Social Policy* 14(1):3018.

Ringheim, Karin. 1995. "Evidence for the Acceptability of an Injectible Hormonal Method for Men." *International Family Planning Perspectives* 21(2):75–78.

———. 1996. "Whither Methods for Men? Emerging Gender Issues in Contraception." *Reproductive Health Matters* 4(7):79–89.

———. 2002. "When the Client Is Male: Client-Provider Interaction from a Gender Perspective." *International Family Planning Perspectives* 28(3):170–76.

Roberts, Dorothy. 1997. *Killing the Black Body: Race, Reproduction, and the Meaning of Liberty.* New York: Pantheon Books.

Schering Anktiengesellschaft. 2001. "The Emancipation of Parenthood: Male Contraceptives Will Pave the Way for Equality in Birth Control." www.livingbridges.com/html/en/index.html.

———. 2002. "Schering AG and Organon Join Forces in Male Contraception." Press Release Corporate Communication of Schering AG, Berlin, Germany, 21 November.

———. 2003. "Male Fertility Control." http://schering.de/html/en/30_rd/areas/andro/fertcontr.html.

Schmidt, Matthew, and Lisa Jean Moore. 1998. "Constructing a 'Good Catch,' Picking a Winner: The Development of Technosemen and the Deconstruction of the Monolithic Male." In *Cyborg Babies: From Techno-Sex to Techno-Tots,* ed. Robbie Davis-Floyd and Joseph Dumit. New York: Routledge.

Schwartz, Neena B. 1976. "Comment on Bremner and de Kretser's 'Contraceptives for Males.'" *Signs* 2(1):247–48.

Sen, Gita, Adrienne Germain, and Lincoln Chen, eds. 1994. *Population Policies Reconsidered: Health, Empowerment, and Rights.* Boston: Harvard University Press.

"Sex & Health Malegrams: Coming to a Bedroom Near You." 1997. *Men's Health Magazine,* April, 40.

Sobo, Elisa J. 1995. *Choosing Unsafe Sex: AIDS-Risk Denial among Disadvantaged Women.* Philadelphia: University of Pennsylvania Press.

Solinger, Rickie. 2001. *Beggars and Choosers: How the Politics of Choice Shapes Adoption, Abortion, and Welfare in the United States.* New York: Hill and Wang.

Stafford, Ned. 2007. "Big Pharma Not Interested in 'Male Pill.' June 22. http://www.rsc.org/chemistryworld/News/2007/June/22060701.asp.

Takeshita, Chikako. 2004. "Negotiating Acceptability of the IUD: Contraceptive Technology, Women's Bodies, and Reproductive Politics." PhD diss., Virginia Polytechnic Institute and State University, Blacksburg.

Treichler, Paula A. 1999. *How to Have Theory in an Epidemic: Cultural Chronicles of AIDS.* Durham: Duke University Press.

World Health Organization Task Force on Methods for the Regulation of Male Fertility. 1996. "Contraceptive Efficacy of Testosterone-Induced Azoospermia or Oligozoospermia in Normal Men." *Fertility and Sterility* 65(4):21–29.

Woodsong, Cynthia, and Helen P. Koo. 1999. "Two Good Reasons: Women's and Men's Perspectives on Dual Contraceptive Use." *Social Science & Medicine* 49(5):567–80.

Zola, Irving. 1972. "Medicine as an Institution of Social Control." *Sociological Review* 20(4):487–504.

Chapter 6

REPRODUCTIVE PARADOXES IN VIETNAM: MASCULINITY, CONTRACEPTION, AND ABORTION IN VIETNAM

Nguyen Thi Thuy Hanh

Vietnam has one of the highest abortion rates in the world, with an annual number of eighty-three induced abortions per one thousand women (Goodkind 1994). In most other countries, high abortion rates tend to be associated with low rates of contraceptive use; thus, it seems surprising that Vietnam's high abortion rate is associated with a very high contraceptive prevalence rate. In 2002, 79 percent of all married women reported using some type of contraception (National Committee of Population, Family and Children [NCPFC] 2003). How can we account for the apparent paradox that large numbers of abortions seem to coexist with widespread contraceptive use?

In this chapter, I argue that in order to account for this paradox, we need to examine the role of men in relation to pregnancy prevention and abortion. We also need to consider how the norms of masculinity and femininity are promoted through the National Family Planning Program (NFPP). In 1988, the Vietnamese government, through its vigorous Information-Education-Communication Program and a system of financial and other sanctions for couples exceeding the two-child limit (Gammeltoft 1999; Johansson, Nga, et al. 1998; Zhang and Locke 2002), introduced its policy aimed at curbing the population growth rate in the country. In May 2003, the policy was replaced by a population policy, which acknowledged the fundamental reproductive health recommendations contained in the Program and Actions of International Conference on Population and Development, held in Cairo, Egypt, in 1994 (Family Care International 1994), by giving couples the right to freely choose the number of children in their family. However, the normative changes from the preceding years seem to remain. Since the 1980s, a cultural change has taken place in Vietnam, and it is now nearly unthinkable for many couples to have more than two children unless they "only" have two daughters.[1] A small family, or one following the previous policy, is considered the symbol of "a happy family" or the "new culture family," and most couples, especially those in urban areas, now strive to limit the size of their families.[2]

Birth control has been one of the state's major priorities in its national development. In the past two decades, the NFPP's vigorous propaganda has been the driving force behind changing attitudes about and perceptions of contraception. As the program has focused on women and has mobilized women's roles in contraception, family planning has become a part of daily life and the concern of families, mass organizations, government offices, and society in general. As a result, most Vietnamese women are actively involved in family planning, but this gendered unbalance in reproductive responsibility is questioned. In problematizing if and why men do not take reproductive responsibility, Matthew Gutmann (this volume) points to the role of states, international organizations, and agencies in creating a "female contraceptive culture" in family planning. The NFPP has overwhelmingly catered to women by educating them in family planning and encouraging them to use contraception, mainly intrauterine devices (IUDs).

Although family planning services and a variety of contraceptive methods have been made available to those in urban and rural areas, male contraceptives, such as condoms and vasectomy, have hardly been used. According to the 2002 Vietnamese Demographic and Health Survey (VNDHS), 38 percent of married women used IUDs, 6 percent of men used condoms, and 1 percent of men had a vasectomy. In addition, 14 percent relied on the withdrawal method and 8 percent on the safe period method.[3] The IUD has been and is the most common form of contraception, as it is available and free at all Vietnamese public health facilities (Gammeltoft 1999; Johansson, Lap, et al. 1998; Zhang and Locke 2002). The staff at health facilities often recommend modern contraceptive methods, such as birth control pills or tubal ligation for women, and condoms or vasectomies for men, and attempt to discourage both from using "traditional" or "natural" methods without other modern methods (Johansson, Lap, et al. 1998).[4] Regardless, many couples prefer the natural methods to the modern ones (AVSC International 1999; NCPFC 2003).[5]

Although abortion has been legal in Vietnam since 1954, this service has been predominantly provided for married women. During the late 1980s, the majority of abortion services were available at public health facilities. After the introduction of the NFPP in 1988, abortions have been performed for a reasonable price in most public hospitals as well as in some private clinics.[6] The legalization of abortion in Vietnam has been considered to be one of the policies increasing women's rights and promoting their involvement in family planning (Bélanger and Khuat 1999; Zhang and Locke 2002). Abortion is also considered to be one of the methods used to reduce the fertility rate and is seen as an expansion of family planning (Johansson, Lap, et al. 1998).

Given the apparently limited male involvement in pregnancy prevention and abortion in Vietnam (Johansson, Nga, et al. 1998) and in the world at large (Carter 2002; Gutmann this volume), it is surprising that so few studies have explored the social and cultural mechanisms behind male involvement in reproduction, men's role in reproductive health, and how perceptions of masculinity influence women's reproductive health. Although family planning is considered vitally important by men and women, both sexes tend to perceive the prevention of pregnancy as a female responsibility.

In this chapter, I demonstrate that high abortion rates in Vietnam are partly a consequence of men's reluctance to participate actively in the prevention of pregnancies despite their intentions to have no more than two children. This is shown with regard to what hinders men from using contraceptive methods and involvement in abortion decision making when pregnancy is not desired. In addition, I analyze gender dynamics, intimate relationships, and how dominant ideas of sexuality, masculinity, and gender create for men opportunities and obstacles in actively taking responsibility for the prevention and termination of unwanted pregnancy. Analytically, the chapter combines a practice-oriented approach that recognizes men's own agency and intentionality, and a more structurally oriented approach, which includes historical and political forces in the analysis.

Research Methods

This study was conducted in 2001 at the family planning department of the Gynecology and Obstetrics Hospital of Hanoi. The aim was to investigate men's role in induced abortion in Vietnam, with regard to their involvement in contraceptive choices, the abortion decision-making process, and post-abortion care.

Twelve men and ten women were interviewed in depth, in both semi-structured and conversational interviews; men and women were interviewed separately, and participant observation was used. All the women interviewed had recently had an abortion or were preparing for one; all the men were partners of women who had undergone an abortion or were preparing for one. Most interviews were conducted in the hospital, before the abortion procedure, and a few interviews were conducted at home, after the abortion. All respondents were volunteers and signed an informed consent agreement. Informal conversations with department staff were conducted to learn about hospital regulations, techniques, and the circumstances leading to induced abortion.

In Vietnam, the access to and use of contraception differs widely among married and unmarried couples, as sex outside marriage is generally not considered socially legitimate (Bélanger and Khuat 1999; Gammeltoft 1999). Even though my original data included married and unmarried couples, this chapter focuses solely on married couples, because the rate of abortions among married women has increased in recent years, along with the number of married men involved in the decision process (Johansson, Nga, et al. 1998; NCPFC 2003).

Because the main results of the study were based on urban couples seeking pregnancy termination at a high-quality hospital, this study does not represent Vietnamese men in general. It is assumed that urban and rural men have different ideas of masculinity in relation to sexuality and birth control, as well as different roles, positions, and power in the family, all of which influence family planning and abortion decisions.

Gender Roles and Masculinity in a Vietnamese Context

Gender Roles

In 1986, the Renovation (*Đổi mới*) and its accompanying economic reforms were launched, and the transition was made from central planning to a market economy with a socialist orientation. Major reforms included an open-door policy and corporate law to encourage foreign investors and exchange goods with international companies. The government also enacted new agricultural and financial laws, implemented development programs to reduce human poverty, and invested in the improvement of the environment, health, education, and communication (National Centre for Social Sciences and Humanities 2001), leading to increased wealth and changes in social relations (Population Council 1998).

Vietnamese, especially those of the younger generations, have been eager to reap the benefits of this renovation and to accept new lifestyles with the "modern" norms and values imported from Western culture. Though there is a drive to adapt to modern norms, there is also a need to follow "traditional" morals and values (Gammeltoft 1999; Khuat 1998). Although opinions and attitudes about sex are expressed more boldly than before (Population Council 1998), traditional gender perceptions and Confucian values persist and influence society (Que et al. 1999). Consequently, gender, sexuality, masculinity, and femininity are constructed with traditional and modern norms and values (Gammeltoft 2002; Tran et al. 1999). In addition, the feudal perceptions of women's chastity inside or outside marriage are highly valued (Gammeltoft 2002; Zhang and Locke 2002).

Sexuality, contraception, pregnancy, and abortion are aspects of reproductive health related to gender roles, masculinity, and femininity, and have been influenced by sociocultural, political, and economic changes (Tran et al. 1999). Vietnam's turbulent history has influenced the changes and transitions in the history of gender relations, and has been influenced by feudal Confucian ideology, French colonization, the war with the United States, a socialist Vietnam with a central planning economy, and the Renovation (Gammeltoft 1999; Santillan et al. 2002).

In feudal and precolonial Vietnam, Confucianism was the dominant cultural ideology shaping the perception of gender and moral norms in society and the family. Sexual relations before and outside marriage were considered immoral and depraved (Khuat 1998). In addition, the Three Submissions (*tam tòng*) of Confucianism dictate that a woman first owes obedience to her father, then, after marriage, to her husband, and after her husband's death, to her oldest son (Tran et al. 1999; Santillan et al. 2002). Men in the precolonial era held absolute power over their families, while women could not make decisions about their own lives, bodies, or children. In addition, sons were regarded as continuing the family line and were highly valued (Tran et al. 1999; Santillan et al. 2002; Zhang and Locke 2002).

However, French colonization, which began in the late nineteenth century, introduced the concepts of freedom, equal rights, and democracy, mainly to the urban areas. Arranged marriages began to be criticized, and romantic love was encouraged. In the 1920s and 1930s, gender equality and women's rights were vehemently argued (although among only some classes) (Gammeltoft 1999; Khuat 1998; Zhang and Locke 2002).

After the 1954 victory at Dien Bien Phu, French colonization ended. Thus began, in the North, the period of socialist construction, and in the South, the war with the United States (1954–75). The government created policies and legislation related to gender issues in order to improve human rights, especially those for women, resulting in significant changes in women's status in the family, even further emphasized by the Marriage and Family Law (1959, revised 1986). The law forbids married men from having extra spouses, and grants women rights equal to men in regard to property inheritance and the custody of children (Gammeltoft 1999; Tran et al. 1999; Zhang and Locke 2002).

During the war with the United States, both Confucian and socialist traditions were much more explicit about women's roles and responsibilities than men's. Men were responsible for protecting the country, while women maintained production and provided assistance to the soldiers (Zhang and Locke 2002). All were encouraged to contribute their efforts to the construction and defense of the nation. Individualism and romance were criticized, and working and fighting were praised (Khuat 1998). As Gammeltoft writes, "A slogan that was often used in the 1960s and 1970s to characterize the ideal socialist woman [was] 'Good at national tasks, good at household tasks'" (1999:176–7). In addition, the chastity and faithfulness of women were highly valued in order to preserve the honor of their families and men, particularly those who were soldiers. Women were now considered to be the key element for the change from a feudal to a cultural society, and their image was "faithful, heroic, and resourceful" (Gammeltoft 2001:265).

During the war and before the Renovation, premarital sexual relations and extramarital affairs were considered criminal and immoral. As Khuat writes, "If discovered, people would be severely punished and, as a result, they could never recover their social standing and dignity in the eyes of others" (1998:23). However, men who had been discovered were still able to get married or keep their families, whereas women had no chance of finding good husbands (although they could marry widowers or become second wives) (Khuat 1998). After the war, men returned home, and with their wives, contributed their efforts toward creating a "wealthy and happy family," and carried out their reproductive roles of sexuality and fertility.

Masculinity and Family Life

Each society shapes its own features of masculine and feminine values and gender norms (Scalway 2001). Masculinity in Vietnam is often associated with bravery, physical and psychological strength, independence, and sexual activity (Family and Society 2004). Men prove their masculinity through their sexual capacity and virility, and in Vietnam, as elsewhere, the notion of masculinity is not separate from sexuality (Scalway 2001).

Being married and having a family are important Vietnamese social norms desired by both men and women. Following marital and family law and cultural norms, married men have responsibilities to their wives and children (Tran et al. 1999). Moreover, the open-door policy created after the Renovation has provided more opportunity than before to improve lifestyles, and the image of the small, modern family became the goal of most couples (Gammeltoft 2001; Johansson, Nga, et al. 1998). Men's ideal role is to have a good career and be the breadwinner, while women are responsible for domestic work and the happiness of their families (Gammeltoft 1999). "In the eyes of most women, besides the physiological difference, the greatest difference between women and men is women's higher sense of responsibility for their family. Men are generally known to be much more carefree and relaxed than women" (Gammeltoft 2001:273).

Men and Birth Control

Toan (a pseudonym) is a forty-two-year-old army officer whose wife has had four abortions. The first abortion was induced when their daughter was nine months old; they thought pregnancy could be avoided because she was breastfeeding. After the abortion, their contraceptive choice was a combination of the withdrawal and safe-period methods. After their second child was born, his wife had an IUD inserted, but a year later, feeling uncomfortable with it, she had it removed. Since that time Toan has actively become involved in family planning, as he does not want his wife to use birth control pills, which he believes are harmful to her health.

> My wife intended to use pills once before, but worrying about side effects, we really did not want to take them. Additionally, we were afraid of not remembering to take them every day. It would break family planning. So, thinking again and again, the best solution was to apply my own methods—the traditional methods.

Toan and his wife decided to practice contraception by combining withdrawal, safe period, and condoms. He only used condoms on rare occasions, when he felt he could not withdraw before ejaculation. During his wife's safe period, they practiced sex without condoms or withdrawal. When I asked why he did not regularly use condoms, he said, "No man wants to use condoms. For the most part, it reduces sexual pleasure. Furthermore, if our children saw condoms by chance, it would be hard to explain to them."

In the four years after his wife's IUD had been removed, she had three induced abortions. However, the couple did not change their contraceptive practices. Rather, after each abortion, they added some days to the unsafe period. After her last abortion, she underwent an operation for an ectopic pregnancy, and the doctor suggested a tubal ligation. She wanted Toan to have the final say, and as he agreed, they no longer have to worry about contraceptives.

"Family planning is the female's task"

In Vietnam, contraception, being pregnant, giving birth, and childrearing are considered to be a woman's "natural function" (*thiên chức*); in other words, women are born to become wives and mothers, whereas men are born to become husbands and fathers (Tran et al. 1999). The husbands and wives in my study seemed to consider sexuality and contraception as being women's natural role. As a forty-year-old man said,

> Almost all husbands seem to consider that use of contraceptive methods is a woman's responsibility. They expect their partners to practice contraception. Men always hold their wives responsible for contraception. Almost all Asian men say that this is the female's task.

Many of the men I interviewed believed they had the right to sex, and that their wives had to fulfill their sexual needs and assume all contraception responsibilities. By taking these responsibilities, women reaffirm their traditional roles for the family's well-being and sacrifice themselves for the welfare of others in the family (Gammeltoft 2001; Khuat 1998). According to Gammeltoft, "Fertility control is often perceived as a burden and as a burden which women—due to their childbearing capacities—have to bear" (2001:274). One man commented on men's lack of reproductive responsibility:

> In my opinion, there are many irresponsible men. They don't want to share the contraceptive burden with their wives. If women have husbands like that, it is better for them to apply their own female methods, and try to protect themselves.

Contraceptive choices did not vary much among the married couples. Female methods, mainly the IUD, were almost all couples' first choice. Although men and women could easily get support from family planning services, methods for women were regarded by both men and women as the most convenient and effective. If women could not use the IUD for health reasons, couples resorted to other common female methods such as the birth control pill or the safe period of a woman's menstrual cycle. However, none of the men wanted their wives to take birth control pills for fear of side effects (both immediate and long term) and the difficulty of remembering to take the pills every day. Part of the men's reasons for using "traditional methods" was a concern for their wives' health, and thus most men preferred the safe-period method. Regardless, both men and women thought the preparation for sexual practice was a woman's task. As a forty-year-old man responded when asked if he or his wife were responsible for contraception,

> We are men, so we cannot care about the "small things" like buying condoms or remembering her safe days. My wife always has to prepare for this. She either counts for the safe days or reminds me to apply the withdrawal method. If not, she can go to buy condoms.

Women are therefore voluntarily involved in family planning and try to carry on reproductive tasks without the help of men. Most of the women interviewed said they fulfilled their marital responsibilities by preparing for sex or by not requiring their husbands to use contraception. A thirty-six-year-old woman said,

> Many nights during my unsafe period, I did not plan to practice sex, but my husband had high sexual needs. So when he demanded, I had to please him. I asked him to use contraception—withdrawal or condoms, but I did not really try to force him. Sex is something sensitive in marital life, so if I refused to have sex with him or forced him to practice contraception, I would feel sorry for him. He had no fear of unwanted pregnancy, but if an unintended pregnancy occurred, I could not say it was his mistake. I agree that he should take initiative when having sex, but I need to be responsible for remembering my safe period or preparing condoms. He cannot remember to do that.

A thirty-six-year-old woman explained how she had failed in using birth control:

> Sometimes I think my unwanted pregnancy is my husband's mistake. But in fact I feel bad, because I think this is my responsibility. I did not carefully prepare for each sexual practice, so I got pregnant. My husband always shifts the responsibility of buying condoms to me, but I rarely buy them.

Husbands and Contraceptive Choices

As mentioned earlier, IUD use in Vietnam is rather high in comparison to other contraceptive methods. Most of the women undergoing an abortion had not used the IUD, mainly due to health problems. Almost all the men did not like using condoms and tried to avoid them, as they were inconvenient and reduced sexual pleasure. As Toan said,

> There are really two problems. One is being shy about buying condoms. If I go to the drug store to buy condoms, people may think I go with prostitutes. When people see that someone is keeping a condom, they think that this person is a wanton, or it has something to do with lust. If a man has a condom in his pocket, other people will think that he is not a good man. In addition, I feel uncomfortable because we have to prepare them when having sex, and it reduces men's sexual pleasure. This is contrary to nature.

Moreover, the use of condoms was associated with extramarital sex and protection from sexually transmitted infections (STIs). Men believed they only needed to be concerned about avoiding pregnancy because they could not contract an STI from their wives. A thirty-eight-year-old man said, "Married couples don't need to use a condom. I know that my wife does not have any STIs, and of course, we aren't infected with HIV/AIDS." In contrast, when I asked which contraceptive method men used when they had sex with women outside marriage, all of the men spontaneously responded that they had to use condoms to avoid STIs. As one man said, "Only mad-men don't use condoms when they have sex outside marriage! Men have to protect themselves!" Men can choose other effective modern male methods such as vasectomy, but all respondents feared this method, which they considered "opposite to nature," and would prevent them from having more children. As Toan said,

> In general, all men fear male sterilization. It is opposite with nature, it is like a man is emasculated as eunuchs in the past. Where do sperm go if I have a vasectomy? If we [men] did that, we would lose our masculinity. We would become feminine. Some people have said that men who have been sterilized start having mental problems afterwards. So it is better for men not to use this method.

Men explained the reluctance to be sterilized as a fear of losing masculinity. Thus, many men found that it was preferable to use the withdrawal method, which is considered "natural" despite its ineffectiveness.

Many of the men believed that sexuality is a natural function of human life and people should not act against nature.[7] Some studies on contraception show that men prefer to use withdrawal (some-times in combination with safe periods) because they consider these methods not to cause health problems; they are user controlled, low cost, private, and do not require outside assistant or intervention (AVSC International 1999; Gammeltoft 1999; NCPFC 2003). This may partly explain why the use of condoms and undergoing vasec-tomy are used less often than other male methods.

Although male respondents wanted to be involved in pregnancy prevention, they were reluctant to take responsibility for contracep-tion. Men expressed that they had tried to share this responsibility with women but voiced their difficulty in putting this responsibility into practice. Many studies in Vietnam and other countries have found that, due to various reasons, men do not like using available contraception. However, they want to prevent pregnancies in order to keep their families smaller and do not want their wives to use potentially harmful contraceptive methods.[8]

In summary, use of birth control is not only influenced by the NFPP, but also by the ideas of masculinity, sexuality, and cultural norms about gender roles in the Vietnamese family. First, birth control is considered to be a woman's task, an idea shaped both by the state discourse addressing the involvement of women while ignoring that of men, and by dominant ideas about domestic and reproduction issues being the woman's domain. Second, men are afraid that taking responsibility for contraception will lessen or take away their masculinity. Finally, limited contraceptive choices for men do not allow them to fulfill their responsibility while al-lowing them to be "real men." Conversely, though men wanted to be real men by taking care of their families and limiting family size, the use of male contraception seemed to conflict with real male sexuality.

Making the Decision to Have an Abortion

"We have enough children"

Almost all the couples in this study cited that the main reason for choosing an abortion was that they already had two children. For these couples, the decision to have an abortion was rather quick, as they felt there was no other option. As a thirty-eight-year old man said,

> I have two children already. I have never thought about having one more child, therefore we easily and quickly decided to have an abor-tion. We always take the initiative to solve the problem ourselves.

> When my wife's menstrual period is five to seven days late, we go to the hospital to "solve the problem."

Even though men did not want their wives to undergo an abortion for fear it might be harmful to their health, abortion was the dominant norm. As a thirty-eight-year-old man said,

> It is quite simple with us. We [decided when] we had our second child. Of course, I don't want this [abortion] to occur. But we are sure that we don't want to have more children. I know that induced abortion will affect a woman's health, but when my wife got pregnant, we had to make the decision to terminate it. So we made the decision right after recognizing my wife's pregnancy.

For couples with two children, it was easy to decide to have an abortion. "Each family should have two children" or "Two children are enough for each married couple" are slogans commonly used in official rhetoric, and have become an objective for many families. The couples' decisions seemed to be fairly uncomplicated, as the NFPP seems to have made the decision for them. In these cases, men and women had equal roles in the decision-making process, which seemed to follow a formula: two children + unwanted pregnancy = induced abortion.

Furthermore, the attitudes about and perceptions of birth control have been influenced by the official regulations and norms of the state, which urges people to limit the number of children to make space for "a small and happy family" (Johansson, Lap, et al. 1998; NCPFC 2003). The two-child family norm is pervasive, almost an obligation, and family planning is seen as necessary to the wealth and development of Vietnam (Gammeltoft 2001; Zhang and Locke 2002).

"We didn't prepare to be pregnant with a male fetus"

If couples had fewer than two children, the decision-making process was more difficult, took longer, and abortion was induced later in the pregnancy. Most couples with one child wanted to terminate an unwanted pregnancy to keep the desired "child spacing." A woman with one daughter had an abortion because she had not carried out the preparations required to have a son (i.e., a special diet and having intercourse at a certain time). When asked about this issue, her husband replied,

> With couples who have a high level of education like we do, the desire to have a son is still great. Each of my brothers has two daughters, so their hope is to have a son. Moreover, there is a lot of information

about "giving birth to the baby of the desired sex," and if my wife got pregnant [without planning], the chance to have a son is only fifty percent. Besides, my wife had some abortions during the time we had to build the house, because it would have been too hard for her to give birth. That is why we have to have the abortion, even though my family is in good economic condition.

Some of the men interviewed said that having a son proved their masculinity and fulfilled their responsibilities to their forefathers. A man with two sons said, "I have to thank my wife, because she gave birth to two sons for me. I am proud of this, because my wife helped me to prove my masculinity and complete my responsibility with my father's family."

Although not many mentioned that the reason for their abortion was due to the "wrong sex of the fetus," some studies show that in Vietnam having a son is important, creating pressure for couples, especially women in rural areas (Bélanger 2002; Zhang and Locke 2002). Therefore, many couples opt for sex-selective abortions of a female fetus (Bélanger 2002).

"We want our children to have the best living conditions and education"

Even though all couples mentioned their economic status, this was not the major reason for an abortion. Couples wanted a better future, comfortable lives, and a high level of education for their children. A twenty-eight-year-old man said,

> My wife wanted to keep the unborn child, but I think that if we had children while we were in difficult economic conditions and could not afford to have them, they would become unhappy. So we had a long and stressful time before we could make the decision.

A forty-year-old man said,

> I've never intended to have three children, even if I have two daughters, because besides the state encouraging each couple to have two children, I have to consider the financial situation of the family. It is not simple for a couple to have one more child. I am a man, I am the "pillar" of my family, so I have to be able to afford to give my children everything from the time they are born to the time they become adults, both food and education.

Vietnamese, mostly those in the urban areas, prefer the nuclear-family model, in which members try to improve their living conditions and educational level, and enjoy their lives with "one or two children" (Duong 2004; Johansson, Nga, et al. 1998). If the husband cannot provide for his wife and children, he will be seen as "talentless" and "less masculine." Some of the men said that many children living under poor living conditions may contribute to their families' unhappiness. The men I talked with explicitly expressed their fulfillment of being a "real man" in the family rather than their concern about the ethical issue of abortion.[9]

"I am male, so I am not able to give birth"

Many of the women went to the hospital to have an abortion as a regular gynecological occurrence. A few of them had not discussed their abortions with their husbands; rather, they informed them of their pregnancies and arranged a time for their abortions. Men seemed to have less power than women in making this decision. As a thirty-eight-year-old man said,

> I am male, so I am not able to give birth even though I want the child, am I? The fetus is inside my wife's body, not inside mine. So, of course if she doesn't want to keep the child I have to agree with her to have an abortion, because if I don't agree she can go without me. But if she does that, it means she doesn't respect me, and I feel that I have lost my honor and that I am powerless in my own family.

Firestine's 1995 study on male involvement in abortion in the West discusses whether or not abortion is only a woman's right. Though a woman wishes to control her own body, Firestine questions if the body of the child inside her and its father should be disregarded, and for this reason, the author defends men's right to be actively involved in the abortion. However, even though men *do* want a voice in the decision-making process, it may be difficult for them to prevent an abortion.

In summary, men in different situations had different reasons for an abortion and different roles in the decision-making process. In general, the cultural ideal of a small family was the main motivation behind most abortions. The couples in this study decided on abortion because their own hopes and desires for their family life were congruent with state goals for building civilized families within a modern society. Men's other reasons for abortion were male sex selection, family economic status, and roles in the family and of masculinity. When coping with an unwanted pregnancy, most couples tried to find the best solution for their families. They adopted an ambivalent attitude when trying to decide between abortion and responsibilities toward family and children. In the decision-making process, men might have a role equal to their wives, and couples could easily have the same view about induced abortion. However, some women had abortions without their husbands' consent, a decision that made men feel powerless and unhappy about what they perceived as their wives' disrespect toward them.

Conclusion

This chapter shows how men's and women's places in the reproductive sphere in Vietnam are strongly influenced by official norms regarding family planning, childbearing, and dominant gender norms. In some ways, men have a strong influence over decisions about birth control and abortion. Even though individual men did not want to expose their wives to the stressful and potentially harmful experience of abortion, it was difficult for Vietnamese men to take responsibility for the prevention and termination of unwanted pregnancy.

The results of the study show the social forces shaping ideas of masculinity and men's identities as men, creating the dynamic to pull them toward active or passive involvement in birth control and terminating unwanted pregnancy. Among the previously mentioned social forces, the main difficulty is the strong social norms that associate femininity with the domestic sphere, including childbearing and pregnancy prevention, while associating masculinity with the public sphere and the "larger" affairs beyond the family and the household. Although family planning is important for men in that it can contribute to their small, modern, and economically healthier families, birth control is a task that helps women fulfill their responsibilities to the family. This occurs not only because of the focus of family planning being placed on women, but also because of the ideas that domestic and family issues are the women's domain. Therefore, women actively participate in the creation and reproduction of ideas of masculinity. In addition, the different levels of men's involvement in the decision to have an abortion relate to men's status in the family and the social norms of their familial role. Men are actively or passively involved in decisions about induced abortion, depending on their economic power in their families and the family's ideas about masculine roles.

It is clear that sex, contraception, pregnancy, and abortion are reproductive issues that need to involve both men and women. But as men have the right to gain pleasure from sexual activities, they are limited in taking responsibility for contraception and the termination of unwanted outcomes. Despite the fact that men think positively about reproductive health and try to avoid any harm to their wives, their practice is still not active enough. As in many countries, the gap between Vietnamese men's perception and behavior on reproduction is the result of cultural norms and values about men's and women's familial roles, policies on reproductive health and contraception, bias toward women, and lack of motivation and contraceptive methods for men that hinder them from actively controlling their contraceptive practices (Dudgeon and Inhorn 2004). Thus, men's contraception and their involvement in contraception and abortion will not likely change because men learn more about contraception or because they have a high level of education. Rather, a willingness to share reproductive responsibility is needed.

The change of perceptions and attitude on masculine roles in reproductive health, especially on contraception, in the historical and cultural Vietnamese context will take a long time and require the involvement of the state as well as that of international organizations and other agencies concerned with reproductive health. The success of women's family planning and their roles in the family may predict the success of the promotion of men's equal participation in family planning. New forms of contraception will present men with new possibilities and choices to be effectively involved in birth control (Oaks this volume). When men support women's reproductive needs and desires, they will fulfill their own sexual and reproductive needs and desires.

Acknowledgments

I owe my most sincere thanks to the editors of this book for inviting me to participate in this collection and their valuable comments on my chapter. I wish to express my appreciation to DANIDA, through ENRECA, for financial support, and the Department of International Health, Faculty of Public Health, University, where I researched my master's thesis, which served as the Copenhagen basis for this chapter. I am most deeply indebted to my adviser Tine Gammeltoft at the Institute of Anthropology, Copenhagen University, who provided me with continual encouragement, advice, support, and sharing of her insight of reproductive health in Vietnam, both academically and personally. My thanks to Margrethe Silberschmidt and Hanne Mogensen, both of Copenhagen University, who assisted me with their great enthusiasm and valuable comments in an earlier version of this chapter. I am grateful to the Faculty of Public Health, Hanoi Medical University, where I work, for their help and encouragement. I also owe my thanks to Nguyen Huy Bao, Director of the Obstetrical and Gynecological Hospital of Hanoi, and the staff in the family planning department for their support during my fieldwork. We also wish to thank the women and men who participated in the research.

Notes

1. According to the results of a study on son preference in a rural village in North Vietnam, couples undergo sex-selective abortions of female fetuses and neglect their daughters in order to obtain the goal of a small-size family (Bélanger 2002:321).
2. Johansson writes that, "During the 1970s and early 1980s, the government in the North carried out campaigns for creating the 'new culture family,' emphasizing the importance of the family in rearing a new generation of revolutionary citizens. Whereas women's virtues as loyal, hardworking wives, mothers, and citizens were praised, the 'new culture family' campaigns criticized men for resisting gender equality and their wives' participation in public life" (1998:3).
3. Safe period is a contraceptive method in which sexual intercourse is restricted to the beginning and end of the menstrual cycle. It is calculated on the length of the menstrual cycle or by relying on the change of body temperature that occurs at ovulation. The method's reliability depends on uniform, regular periods, and its failure rate is higher than that of other modern methods. According to the VNDHS 2003, half of all pregnancy terminations were performed on women who had used the traditional methods of withdrawal or safe period.
4. Some studies show that the withdrawal method is not effective. For example, half of all induced abortions in Turkey are due to failure of the withdrawal method (AVSC International 1999).
5. According to the 2003 VNDHS, 38 percent of married women have used the withdrawal method, and 23 percent have used periodic abstinence.
6. The cost of a first-trimester abortion is 100,000 VND (US$6.50). Procedures performed from eight to fifteen weeks are by means of dilation and curettage (D&C) and cost 200,000 VND (US$13). Between sixteen to twenty-two weeks gestation, the principal method is the modified Kovac's procedure or medicine (Cytotex), which costs 1,000,000 VND (US$65).
7. As Johansson writes, "The traditional Vietnamese cosmology was based on Yin and Yang, the female and the male principle, conceived of as two primordial forces from which everything else in the universe was created. A proper balance between Yin and Yang was essential to maintain harmony and good health" (1998:20).
8. Studies in Vietnam were conducted by the Population Council (1997), Ngoc Bao Vu (1997), and Gammeltoft and Thang (1999). Studies in Kenya or Tanzania were conducted by Silberschmidt (1999) and Silberschmidt and Rasch (2001). Dudgeon and Inhorn (2004) summarize research on reproductive health with an anthropological perspective.

9. Although most respondents had thought about the ethical issue of abortion, they felt that because the fetuses were aborted early and were not yet human, they did not see abortion as killing a human being; thus they did not violate moral norms.

References

AVSC International and Reproductive Heath Alliance Europe. 1999. "Male Contraception: Planning for the Future." Paper presented at a symposium held 12–13 May, 1999, London, England.

Bélanger, D. 2002. "Son Preference in a Rural Village in North Vietnam." *Study in Family Planning* 33(4):321–34.

Bélanger, D., and Khuat Thu Hong. 1999. "Single Women's Experiences of Sexual Relationships and Abortion in Hanoi, Vietnam." *Reproductive Health Matters* 7(14):71–82.

Carter, M. 2002. "Husbands and Maternal Health Matters in Rural Guatemala: Wives' Reports on Their Spouses' Involvement in Pregnancy and Birth." *Social Science & Medicine* 55:437–50.

Center for Population Studies and Information, Copenhagen University. 2000. Bibliography for the Research on Reproductive Health in Vietnam since the ICPD in Cairo, 1994.

Dudgeon, M.R., and M. C. Inhorn. 2004. "Men's Influences on Women's Reproductive Health: Medical Anthropological Perspectives." *Social Science & Medicine* 59:1379–95.

Duong, Boi Ngoc. 2004. "Nhung kinh nghiem quy bau" [The value experiences]. *Bao Lao dong* 193, 11 July.

Family and Society. 2004. "The Virtues of a Real Man." www4.tintucvietnam.com/News/printView.aspx.

Family Care International. 1994. Action for the 21st Century: Reproductive Health and Rights for All. Summary Report of Recommended Action on Reproductive Health and Rights of the Cairo ICPD Program of Action, September 1994.

Firestine. 1995. "Men Have Rights in Abortion." http://homepages.go.com/prolifeman/authors/bucknellian3251995.htm.

Gammeltoft, Tine. 1999. *Women's Bodies, Women's Worries: Health and Family Planning in a Vietnam Rural Community*. Richmond, VA: Curzon.

———. 2001. "'Faithful, heroic, resourceful': Changing Images of Women in Vietnam." In *Vietnam Society in Transition: The Daily Politics of Reform and Change*, ed. John Kleinen. Amsterdam: Het Spinhuis.

———. 2002. *The Irony of Sexual Agency: Premarital Sex in Urban Northern Vietnam. Gender, Household, State: Đổi mới (the Renovation) in Vietnam*. Ithaca: Southeast Asia Program, Cornell University.

Gammeltoft, Tine, and Thang Nguyen Minh. 1999. *Tinh yeu cua chung em khong gioi han* [Our love has no limits: An anthropological study of premarital abortion in Hanoi]. Hanoi: Nha xuat ban Thanh nien.

Goodkind, Daniel. 1994. "Abortion in Vietnam: Measurements, Puzzles, and Concerns." *Study in Family Planning* 25(6):342–52.

Johansson, Annika. 1998. *Dreams and Dilemmas: Women and Family Planning in Rural Vietnam*. Ph.D. diss., Stockholm: Department of Public Health Sciences, Karolinska Institute.

Johansson, Annika, Nguyen Thu Nga, Tran Quang Huy, Doan Du Dat, Kristina Holmgren. 1998. "Husbands' Involvement in Abortion in Vietnam." *Study in Family Planning* 29(4):1–14.

Johansson, Annika, Nguyen The Lap, Hoang Thi Hoa, Vinod K. Diwan, and Bo Eriksson. 1998. "Population Policy, Son Preference and the Use of IUDs in North Vietnam." *Reproductive Health Matters* 6(11):69–76.

Khuat, Thu Hong. 1998. "Study on Sexuality in Vietnam: The Known and Unknown Issues." Regional Working Papers No. 11. Population Council.

National Centre for Social Sciences and Humanities. 2001. "National Development Report in Vietnam—*Doi moi* and Human Development in Vietnam." Hanoi: National Political Publishing House.

National Committee of Population Family and Children (NCPFC). 2003. Demographic and Health Survey. Annual Report.

Population Council. 1997. "Men's Attitudes toward Family Planning: A Pilot Study in Two Communes of Northern Vietnam." Research Report No. 8.

———. 1998. "Vietnamese Youth Reproductive Health Needs in the Đổi mới Era: Challenges and Opportunities." Report. POPLINE Document Number 143663.

Santillan, Diana, Sidney Schuler, Hoang Tu Anh, Tran Hung Minh, Bui Thanh Mai. 2002. "Limited Equality: Contradictory Ideas about Gender and the Implications for Reproductive Health in Rural Vietnam." *Journal of Health Management* 4(2):251–67.

Scalway, Thomas. 2001. "Young Men and HIV: Culture, Poverty and Sexual Risk." http://panos.org.uk/aids/young_men_HIV_TXT.htm.

Silberschmidt, Magrethe. 1999. *Women Forget that Men are Masters: Gender Antagonism and Socioeconomic Change in Kisii District, Kenya*. Stockholm: Nordic Africa Institute, Uppsala and Almquist & Wiksell International.

Silberschmidt, Magrethe, and Vibeke Rasch. 2001. "Adolescent Girls, Illegal Abortion and 'Sugar-daddies' in Dar es Salaam: Vulnerable Victims and Active Social Agents." *Social Science & Medicine* 52:181–86.

Tran, Thi Que, Vu Ngoc Uyen, and Nguyen Thi Bang. 1999. *Gender Basic Concepts and Gender Issues in Vietnam*. Hanoi: Statistical Publishing House.

Vu, Ngoc Bao. 1997. "Psycho-Social and Cultural Factors Affecting Modern Contraceptive Practice among Women Seeking Pregnancy Termination in Hanoi, Vietnam." MA thesis, Mahidol University, Thailand.

Zhang, H. X., and C. Locke. 2002. "Contextualising Reproductive Rights Challenge: The Vietnam Situation." *Women's Studies International Forum* 25(4):443–53.

Chapter 7

REPRODUCTIVE POLITICS IN SOUTHWEST CHINA: DECONSTRUCTING A MINORITY MALE-DOMINATED PERSPECTIVE ON REPRODUCTION

Aura Yen

Soon after the establishment of the Chinese Communist Party (CCP), in 1950, an ethnic-identification project was conducted, which identified fifty-five ethnic minorities. These minority groups make up 8 percent of the Chinese population and have impoverished status, restricted access to education, and minimal prospects for upward mobility (Mackerras 2003). Geographically, the western provinces are home to 80 percent of ethnic minority groups; most of the smaller groups are distributed throughout southwest China.

Across China, the CCP directs state integration and modernization toward ethnic minorities, and state policies continuously impact their lives. Drawing on the ethnic identification project's delineations and categorizations of ethnicity, the state has instigated its socialist transformation and modernization of minority areas. The CCP has influenced minority people's reproductive lives through social mobilization and laws, including those related to marriage, family planning, and maternal and infant health care. The rhetoric of eugenics, of improving the quality of the population, and wealth prevail in family planning slogans, while state-prescribed marital and reproductive practices focus on population regulation.

Although the government upholds a sense of national identity and homogenizes its population through a series of public policies and social reforms, ethnic minorities can reject state transformation. For example, ethnic minorities in China's southwest have been able to resist state policies and social reforms because of their geographic remoteness, autonomy from the center of state power, and history of ethnic relations. Minority leaders directed rebellions against rulers throughout the Mongolian conquest and the Qing reforms of the minority chieftainship (Guo 2000:1). According to French ethnographer Inez de Beauclair (1986), the Miao and Kam people in the mountainous regions of southeast Guizhou only submitted to Chinese rule as late as the eighteenth century.

This chapter examines one such minority setting—Shan village, located in Guizhou, southwest China—where resistance to state control over reproduction is deliberately packaged.[1] Male village leaders lead strategies of duplicity to resist the state's attempts to transform the marital and reproductive practices of ethnic minorities. Instead of directly resisting or challenging the rationale of this policy, they manipulate political resources to promote Shan village as a family planning model by propagating the Shan myth.[2]

According to the myth of Shan village, village women manage birth control by means of traditional cultural practices and ethnomedicine, thereby ensuring that 98 percent of village households produce one son and one daughter each. Figure 7.1 shows Shan village leaders gathering around a large stone and worshipping their ancestors. Painted in Mandarin on the front door of the communal house is the family planning slogan "Value the Ecological Environment, Implement Family Planning." This illustration reinforces the political and religious authority of village leaders: while male leaders give voice to population and reproductive matters, they co-opt women's reproduction to construct a myth that echoes political slogans and propaganda.

Because Shan's apparently outstanding achievement is in alignment with China's current family planning policy, the media and official staff have responded enthusiastically. However, according to some of the village women I interviewed, Shan villagers do not have contraceptive medicine, nor are they able to control the sex of fetuses. Instead, abortion and infanticide limit the number of births, with infanticide also utilized for the purpose of gender selection.

This chapter identifies the interplay between the state and (male) village leaders and shows how this negotiated relationship ultimately affects village women's reproductive health. First, I examine state discourse and how it seeks to shape ethnic minority reproductive

Figure 7.1. Sketch of a meeting of village elders by a local artist. Used with permission.

practices. Next, I demonstrate how male village leaders mediate differential power relations in the local society and how they respond to state power. Finally, I present village women's narratives about their reproductive matters and some of the effects local reproductive politics have had on women's health. By considering the characteristics of China's reproductive politics—namely, concealment, duplicity, and collusion—I conclude that male leaders' control over village reproduction damages women's agency and negatively impacts women's reproduction health.

Theoretical Approach and Method

In this study, women's health is linked to local and state power, and feminist anthropology is utilized to explore gender, social, and political influences on Shan women's health. My ethnographic findings are analyzed through the politics of reproduction. By comparing some of the village leaders' accounts to the Shan women's, I deconstruct the model-village myth and expose the various unofficial practices undertaken. Because this study is concerned with how dominant discourses mediate and regulate reproduction, male control over village reproduction is exposed, and Shan women's accounts of their social, reproductive, and health experiences show the effects local reproductive politics have had on their reproductive health.

Feminist anthropologists examine the social and constructed nature of reproductive strategies and practices. They draw out the meanings and experiences of gender, maternity, reproduction, and modernity, as well as the possible effects on women's lives and health. In a review of the development of the anthropology of reproduction, Ginsburg and Rapp (1995) show that the field developed from a cross-cultural comparison of human reproduction and related practices, with a consideration of reproduction in terms of stratified social relations. With the global spread of Western medicine, the implementation of development programs, and the development of women's movements, research suggests that politics of reproduction emerge as diverse aspects of the institutional and social control impacting reproductive lives (Ginsburg and Rapp 1991, 1995; Greenhalgh 1994; Handwerker 1990; Kligman 1998). In addition to exploring the different agencies and social hierarchies to which women are subjected, researchers are interested in how women interact with husbands, elders, social institutions, and the state. Greenhalgh's investigations (1993, 1994, 2003) into the peasantized one-child policy and unplanned persons in China and Kligman's (1998) work on reproductive deceptions in Romania shed light on the complexities of formal and informal relations between states and their citizens in the arena of reproduction. An examination of women's reproductive issues as seen through the lens of politics and economics is necessary in understanding that women's subordination has originated from the politics of reproduction.

British social economist Naila Kabeer (1994) notes the importance of reversing the hierarchy of knowledge and power in development, and suggests considering it in terms of transforming both the social relations of knowledge production and the type of knowledge produced. To do so, feminist theorist Chandra Talpade Mohanty (1991) requires us to ask the fundamental questions of how, where, and by whom knowledge is produced and what counts as knowledge. German feminist Chris Weedon (1992) seeks to transform the power structure and practices that determine how discourses are produced and disseminated. Her work stresses difference in social power, subjectivity, and discourse, and examines social power relations from the perspective of the social and institutional context in which texts are located. This approach exposes hidden and silenced meanings within texts, and looks for openings from which meanings can be changed. This study adopts a similar analytical approach to the population-control myth constructed by males.

Discourses are informed by power and personal interests, and they play a foundational role in shaping different subjectivities (Weedon 1992). This study breaks down the illusions inherent in the political propaganda regarding Shan village and gains access to the underside in order to understand women's needs and health from the perspective of their social realities, everyday practices, and lived experiences. I draw on discourse analysis to analyze the representations, power manipulation, political practices, and subjectivities emerging from this village. Shan women's narratives and reproductive histories enable me to expose many of their reproductive health issues.

In order to gain a basic understanding of the village, I conducted household visits, consulted registers, and recorded birth, mortality rates, and the like. I did encounter difficulties in collecting basic data about the village and mainly relied on prolonged participant observation over a period of almost twelve months. It was not until after I had visited the households of twenty-one village and team cadre families and had several communications with village leaders that I learned that the latter were intent on keeping their distance. The village cadres had warned the villagers not to divulge too much, advising them to keep silent if they had no ready answers. At first, most villagers were afraid the government would punish them for participating in my research, and they concealed their kinship, age, childbearing status, and reproductive practices. Unregistered people who should not have been in the household hid during my visits, and information I was given appeared suspiciously homogenous and in accordance with the village myth. In addition, the village secretary and leaders were unwilling to show me their household register, and I was unable to obtain birth and mortality data from the county's family planning bureau. For these reasons, not enough data can be provided here to accurately reflect the varying economic, health, and education levels in Shan.

However, three months after my arrival, I was more fluent in the village language. I also had observed daily life and activities, rituals, and important social events in which kinship and social relations were reaffirmed, and I often asked shamans to name the family members and kinship relations participating in the rituals. This seemed preferable to directly asking the family and potentially arousing a defensive stance. Active listening and observation became my primary tools. While the villagers were speaking, I recorded my observations in field notes with their prior permission. My academic training had led me to pay attention to Shan women's health issues, and unstructured interviews enabled me to become familiar with culture and uncover women's social realities, reproductive experiences, and health problems. I learned to respect the privacy of villagers who felt unsafe talking to me, and I came to respect the village's culture, history, and ethnic identity. I visited those who disseminate village information to outsiders—village elders, cadres, health workers, and elites. My database information for discourse analysis included local gazettes, social investigation reports (1963), local and national newspapers (1987–2004), academic articles (1991, 2001), and official investigation reports from the local government's family planning bureau (2000).[3]

Eventually, I was permitted to join the village women's social gatherings and become involved in their activities. After initial reluctance, some of the married women and couples befriended me and introduced me to their natal families, children, and peers. Based on my friendship with these informants and some shamans, I learned about sex/gender and belief systems, both of which were crucial to understanding hierarchical power relations in Shan, as well as their perceptions and interpretations regarding reproduction and reproductive health. Being able to joke about sexuality with the village women marked a turning point in my fieldwork, as it narrowed the gap caused by differences in ethnicity, class, and status. Some women shared their stories and experiences and became key informants in terms of data collection. However, I cannot claim to represent all their voices, as I gained information only from a few groups of women. Ambiguity and deception were evident in their narratives because they were influenced by dominant discourses.

Shan Village

Shan village is located in eastern Guizhou Province, in southwest China, and is in a valley surrounded by mountains, some of which are 2,300 feet high. Shan has approximately 160 households and a population of over 730 people, with most of them belonging to the same minority group. There are five patrilineal descent groups, and intra-village marriage is practiced because of the distance from relatives in far-off villages. Therefore, villagers depend on their own resources, lineages, and social and kinship networks. Lineage in Shan village is in accordance with patrilineal and patrilocal principles. A husband does not reside with his wife's natal family. Sons possess irrigated and non-irrigated rice fields, wooded land, a house, and a granary; in turn, they provide their aging parents with food and are responsible for their burials. Daughters have a "Daughter's Field," a cotton field, and a vegetable garden, and inherit silver, cloth, and skills from their mothers. Because daughters marry within the village, they are expected to attend to their parents' health and well-being, and provide them with clothing. If an older person has no descendants, the lineage chooses one of the closest patrilineal kin to inherit the person's property and take care of him or her in later life.

State Discourse and Representations: Minority Reproduction

In response to China's excessively large population, the post-Mao government has utilized reproductive issues to construct China's modernity, regulating reproduction to support the state project of socioeconomic development and nation building (Anagnost 1995; Greenhalgh 2001b). Through education and labor, the state has raised women's status by increasing their participation in socialist construction, thus encouraging women to delay marriage, have fewer births, and space children appropriately (Greenhalgh 2001b). By curtailing births, the state is seen as liberating women from the feudalism and patriarchy that previously oppressed them (Anagnost 1997; Greenhalgh 2001a; Wang 1999). Moreover, the post-Mao government has defined birth planning as a macroeconomic issue and claimed a collectivist perspective on reproduction (Population Council 1996). To control population quantity as well as "quality," officials advocate "late marriage, late childbearing, few births, quality births [*wanhun, wanyu, shaosheng, yousheng*]" (Greenhalgh 2003). In the name of modern nation-state building, as well as women's liberation, the Chinese government exercises institutionalized control over women's reproduction throughout China.

In the process of transforming minority social practices, the state placed the customs of the Han majority as superior to those of the ethnic minorities. Striking cultural differences between the Han and ethnic minorities are perhaps most noticeable in the areas of sexuality, marriage, and reproduction. Yan Ruxian, a Chinese specialist on minority marriage and families, reveals the pretensions of the state agenda and the ideologies aimed at transforming minority practices (1989). Although she acknowledges that ethnic minorities have practiced a diversity of forms of marriage and family, such as arranged marriage, visiting (walking) marriage, early marriage, and polygyny, she argues that their marital practices and reproduction modes should be reformed to meet the policies of population control and modernization. The government believes that late marriage, late births, and fewer and more eugenic births are the proper methods to ensure a modern, scientific, and civilized way of life. From this perspective, the state justifies the modernization of ethnic minorities while asserting the cultural superiority of the Han (Diamant 2000; Diamond 1995; Gladney 1994; Harrell 1995).

Current family planning regulations in Guizhou Province permit a minority couple to have two children, born four years apart.[4] Three months after giving birth to her first child, the woman must have an intrauterine device (IUD) inserted. After producing two children, one member of the couple is forced to be sterilized. When the state encountered enormous difficulties in implementing family policy in rural villages, it utilized Shan's reproductive myth. As a result, in the 1980s Shan became exempt from check-ups by the local family planning agency, and in the 1990s it was cited as a family planning model. Furthermore, Shan villagers are exempt from forced sterilization.

While the state directs the discourse of population control, some Chinese academics produce works supporting the submission of ethnic minorities to state reproductive policies. Several commentators have noted that minority elites have enabled the cause of modernization, and they note minority agency in socialist development by reporting how distinctive marital practices, family education, and customary laws have enabled these groups to practice population control. Some claim that a number of minority villages have actually championed the state's family planning policy. However, as Litzinger (2000) points out, we must consider who lauds such birth control practices, as well as the discursive context of supportive texts and the purposes of their reports. In his analysis of alternative modernities in the Dayaoshan, Guangxi Province, Litzinger maintains that the local ethnic subjects—party cadres and Yao elites—intentionally promote their unique cultural practices to appear germane to the project of socialist modernization in reform-era China.

This strategy enables these ethnic subjects to move beyond the troublesome history of Maoist socialist reforms as well as the hegemony of class. Yao scholar Liu (1984) contends that the voluntary family planning customs of the Chashan Yao are linked directly to economic considerations, marital practices, inheritance principles, family education, and the customary laws of the *Shipai* (stone tablet) system. She concludes that the long and excellent tradition of birth control among the Chashan Yao results from the "fruits [*Jiejing*] of a labouring people's wisdom [*Yaomin laodong zhihui*]," which anticipated the state's family planning policy and even foresaw socialist modernization (Litzinger 2000:219). From Litzinger's perspective, Liu's construction of the Chashan Yao as exemplars of family planning and birth regulation occurred when the local government was speeding up its family planning program in conjunction with the introduction of the Civilized Village Campaign. In effect, Liu has carved out a new narrative space for the Chashan Yao and contributed to the discourse of ethnic reproductive practices in the context of socialist modernization.

In the final analysis, minority elite's reports of traditional methods of birth control accommodate family planning objectives while laying claim to the contribution of ethnic culture to contemporary socialist development. Such rhetoric applies to the Shan village leaders.

Male Village Leaders' Control of Reproduction: The Sex/Gender System

Shan women confront both state and male control over reproduction. The village power hierarchy dominates the social values of Shan, and influences the sex/gender system and decisions regarding marriage and reproduction. It is clear that the leaders, who are upper-caste senior males, establish socially and culturally constructed relations in order to prioritize the development of their families and the interest of the upper caste.

Shan's three major caste divisions—upper, middle, and lower—are determined by hereditary ranking as well as personhood. Heredity links to family background, whereas personhood relates to a family's association with clean/unclean and human/demon spirits. The "unclean" and "demon" group, as well as latecomers with foreign surnames, belong to the lower caste, while those with "clean" and "good" human spirits are seen as being superior in politics and marriage.

Although a young man or woman is free to choose his or her sexual partner, this does not mean the sexual partner will become a marriage partner. In most cases, the elders of upper-caste families arrange their children's marriages and make decisions regarding premarital pregnancy; that is, whether a couple will marry or if an abortion will be induced. Patrilateral cross-cousin marriage, preferred by upper-caste families, results in affine alliances, and facilitates the concentration of human resources and political influence. However, many lower-caste families permit their children to select their marital partners through the process of courting. These rigid class distinctions determine village marriages and reproductive decisions, thereby continuing the established social order.

Marital status does not prevent men or women from courting. Prior to the Chinese government's enactment of the marriage law in 1950, upper-caste married men were known to practice polygyny. The elders arranged primary marriage partners and preferred that their children married close relatives, but upper caste married men were at liberty to choose second and third wives. Married men continue to visit young women at the music hall and participate in social activities, just as when they were single. However, they must stop visiting the music hall when their own children are allowed to marry, as parents should not impede the rights of the next generation from procreating (Heritier 1995).

Newly married women are allowed to accept the advances of young men who are not their husbands. However, this ceases once they become pregnant with their husbands' children, as the woman is recognized as being linked to a patrilineal family. Married women without children may choose to remarry, elope, or decline the invitation of the husband's family. For example, one woman, L, was already married but accepted M's courting. L decided to withdraw from her marriage in order to marry M, and L's previous husband was paid 8.8 Chinese ounces of silver.

The cultural practices of courting and the relics of polygyny indicate that male sexuality is privileged. Even though monogamy became the norm after the marriage law was implemented, married upper-caste men with children continue to visit young women. Girls in their teens easily fall in love with upper-caste married men because they are high ranking, good singers, or wealthy. Free courtship and polygyny seriously impact women's status and health. Married men cannot marry their young lovers, but should the woman be pregnant, she can ask the man to pay for her abortion. Because the result of polygyny can be teenage pregnancy and abortion, the behaviors of male partners can have a direct effect on female sexual health and reproductive decisions regarding abortion.

While married men are flirting with young girls, their wives are left with time-consuming housework and childcare. Men are permitted to make extramarital sexual advances as long as they maintain their marriages, as this behavior is not seen as threatening their marriages, and wives do not see it as conjugal infidelity. In a study of the White Hmong, in Northern Thailand, Tapp notes, "Adultery can only take place where a married woman is involved, since polygyny and premarital sex are permissible" (1989:26). A woman can have sexual relationships with others, but if she has a child with someone other than her husband, she will be divorced, and the pregnancy will be aborted.

Power hierarchies in Shan shape and influence women's reproductive decisions. Village leaders represent the interests of the upper caste and dominate the village hierarchy; their interests and control over sexuality and reproduction are acted out through the village's sex/gender system. In addition, through construction of the village myth, the leaders mediate state reproduction policies.

Local Mediators and Myth Construction

Greenhalgh (1993, 1994, 2003) notes the pivotal role of the village cadres in manipulating the local politics of reproduction in rural China. As Shan village leaders are the local power holders, the state relies on their cooperation in implementing policies and realizing policy targets. The politics of reproduction in Shan highlight the clash of interests between the state and local village leaders, who represent the interests of the upper caste.

Despite the numerous political movements and administrative changes in the village, the traditional community leaders—the village elders—have retained their dominance over village life. When the CCP penetrated minority areas in the 1950s, a new political power—the cadres—infiltrated Shan. The elders successfully integrated the party cadres into the top of the village hierarchy via marriage and political dealings, and this new political breed forms part of the village leaders' group. Theoretically, cadres are responsible for communicating government mandates, but in reality they work with the village elders to respond to state policies. Once cadres became village leaders, the interests of the ruling class were no longer challenged.

Prior to the establishment of the CCP government, upper-caste men in Shan married young, took more than one wife, and produced large families. Their privileged status was influenced by state social reforms and minority population policy, but has not changed completely. According to the marriage law, the legal age for a woman to marry is twenty and for a man twenty-three; polygyny is forbidden. The Shan myth has allowed Shan leaders to retain their privileged status in politics, marriage, and reproduction.

Village leaders fluent in Mandarin manage family planning at the village level. Most village women are illiterate and unable to speak Mandarin; therefore, they cannot participate in negotiations and state their health needs. Under the circumstances, village leaders are pivotal negotiators in state reproductive policies, and are familiar with the conditions needed to conceal unofficial practices and retain their reproductive myth. Mother Ting[5] told me that as early as the late 1970s, the first and second village secretaries, along with the village head (1973–85), reported the village's mythical practice of birth control. In view of this reproductive myth and the fact that in 1989, four village elders were working as core cadres in the township government, the latter granted villagers the preferential condition of not having to undergo sterilization. Consequently, village men no longer had to be sterilized after having two children.

Shan upper-caste men claimed their fertility control was derived from historical experience and cultural practices, as well as ethnomedicine such as herbs. When, in the Qing Dynasty, the village ancestors settled on what they thought would be their permanent land, their proliferation caused conflicts with nearby villages, as well as poverty. Upon uprooting to what is now Shan, their previous home became the graveyard, and the village elders implemented fertility regulation. Customary law required every family to obey the elders' decisions; violating the law resulted in the confiscation of the violator's cattle or pigs. One elder, Grandfather Qin, reported that whenever they worshiped their ancestors, the elders restated the customary law, and anyone violating customary law was punished by divine justice. Because this ritual was thought to cause misfortune to offenders, they vowed not do it again.

According to the principles of geomancy, village leaders explained that the village was a ship among the mountains—if overpopulated, the ship would explode. The practice of fertility control has been a subject of songs and translated into Mandarin. One song includes the lyrics "People can breed more, but the land cannot. If another son is raised, he will not have the share of the field. If another daughter is reared, she will not have the share of silver. And no one would marry either a man or a woman without property." Grandfather Qin was the commune leader and a sorcerer familiar with ritual texts and classical Chinese poems. He probably composed these songs and provided Chinese translations, as he had considerable political knowledge and experience. He explained why the village tradition is to have only one son and one daughter: "If the villagers have two sons, the fields will be divided into two shares. A rich household has twenty acres. If the couple has two sons, each son has ten acres. They will become a middle-peasant household. If a middle-peasant household has two sons, they become poor peasants, and no one would marry poor peasants, since they barely support their family. By considering the future of their offspring, the villagers decided to have two children, a son and a daughter, and no more." He also explained that having a son for every household means having enough land and food and a comfortable life. This resonates strongly with a family planning policy slogan supporting the cause of modernization: "Few births generate faster growing wealth: the way to comfortable living."

This position contrasts sharply with findings from my fieldwork. According to data from the 1880s through 1950, at least ten families had more than three sons. After 1950, upper-caste families, especially cadre families, had two sons and two daughters. Lower-caste families normally had two to three children of both genders. The villagers told me that in the past, the rich had produced more sons to inherit their large properties, and hired help for farming, household chores, and childcare. Several villagers stated that only the families of the rich were able to have more sons, who are successful in finding wives, whereas the sons of poor families encounter difficulties. It seems that the current privilege of the rich in terms of reproduction stems from their status and kinship as cadres who underreport excess births.

Although the village leaders stress the importance of traditional knowledge and ethnomedicine in choosing gender and contraception, village women maintain they do not have this knowledge. As Grandfather Qin said, "Most women have the knowledge to judge the sex of the baby. If they know the sex of the baby is not the one they want, the women have an induced abortion within three to six months." Grandfather Gi, a sorcerer, revealed their contraceptive methods to me in front of his silent wife.[6] During the dates close to and after menses, the couple would not have intercourse.[7] Women are capable of differentiating the male fetus from the female fetus, according to how the woman walks when she is three months pregnant. If the sex of the fetus is not preferred, herbs are taken to change the gender or an abortion is induced. Grandfather Gi added that Grandfather Qin is the person who knows the herbs.

In summary, male leaders suggested that prior to the family planning policy, villagers regulated fertility control through customary law, and practiced it according to cultural traditions and ethnomedicine. Village women and a few village leaders knew how to limit births and choose the preferred gender at birth. The villagers have thus been seen as resolving overpopulation.

Political Manipulation in Reproductive Deceptions

The construction of the Shan reproductive myth is based on the leaders' political participation in reproductive deceptions. These organized deceptions involve men at different levels of power: village leaders, local officials, and elites at prefectural and provincial institutions. As a Chinese scholar informed me, village leaders discarded household registers compiled through the 1960s, and did not recommence the registers until the 1980s. They claim the previous data has been lost and show outsiders the registers that have been constructed. Although it is difficult to ascertain when the 1960s data was discarded, my suspicion is that it was around the time the myth was constructed. After transcribing parts of the 1980s registers and comparing the data with the genealogies I had constructed, I found that the household registers, including birth dates, family members, and population statistics, tell of zero-population growth from 1950 until 1990.

Village leaders communicate with the minority elites at the provincial and prefectural levels. As Mackerras (1994) points out, the government has been planning since 1950 to train political, vocational, and technical cadres from different ethnic nationalities for the purpose of undertaking social transformation. This means that a few minority elites were promoted to political positions in provincial and prefectural institutions; those who entered politics utilized their control of institutional and academic resources to facilitate Shan's fame. Two previous village heads (who served from 1977 to 1985 and from 1998 to 2000, respectively) and a sorcerer visited a a retired chairman of the CCP's representative committee in Guiyang. One of his reports states that Shan villagers were stringent in conducting punishment if someone had not followed family planning, and that if the couple had a second violation, they were expelled from the village. However, this report is clearly untrue, as those families were neither punished nor expelled. On the contrary, their reputations were left unscathed, and some even worked as village cadres and leaders.

In a popular piece of ethnography reworked into the political propaganda for this village, Wu, one of the few village elites working in the county center, modifies Shan's cultural practices to cater to state policies on eugenic births and late childbearing. He claims that because of cultural practices of courtship and marriage, village women marry around eighteen or nineteen but do not have their first child until around the age of twenty-two. The couple does not live together until the woman becomes pregnant. Instead, after the wedding, young wives live with their natal families but help their husbands' families during busy seasons and stay at their husbands' homes during festivals. This marital practice utilizes sexual abstinence as a check on population growth. Wu also reports that two lineages of women know the prescriptions and methods of contraception, depicting Shan as abandoned by modern civilization or as a relic of an earlier one. When Shan village became famous, Wu was promoted from county government to a prefectural institution.

During my fieldwork, six reporters visited the village and were introduced to and accompanied by male local officials, elites, and village leaders who spoke Mandarin. Photographs were taken of the female herbalist, families with a son and a daughter, and young people in traditional clothing. Most mass-media reports originate after a meeting between village leaders and elites. Not having any prior knowledge of Shan, the journalists romanticized the village, a misrepresentation that occurs repeatedly.

Initially, the county government did not agree with a 1987 local newspaper article about Shan's myth. In addition, local people knew that the villagers reached their family planning targets by means of infanticide, information reported in a 1992 newspaper article.[8] Nevertheless, local officials soon realized that the myth allowed them to gain funding from higher administrative units and commercial interests in tourism. Once Shan had been established as a family planning model, high-level government officials allocated more funds and brought visitors to this poor minority area. Thus, a shift occurred: local officials began to assist in propagating the Shan myth. Funds were allocated to build a road connecting Shan to the county. From 2002 to 2003, villagers were required to work on the road because the county government had intended to develop Shan as a tourist site to show ethnic minority characteristics and exemplary family planning. The villagers felt the road was built for outsiders, and the more open Shan village becomes, the more talk there is of traditional practices.

Eventually, village leaders, elites, cadres, and local officials colluded to undertake organized deceptions. Father Deng, a cadre, commented that as soon as outsiders or higher-level officials entered the village, local officials immediately notified village leaders. While in the village, I heard the party secretary or the village head announce that women who were pregnant or carried babies on their backs should not be seen. In the opinion of Mother Deng, local officials and the family planning station have financially benefited from the myth, while villagers have maintained good reputations and avoided sterilization. Some maintained that village cadres have also benefited.

Village Women's Reproductive Matters

The picture of Shan's reproductive lives as presented by village leaders, elites, and the mass media is inconsistent with the reality of village women, who told me of infanticide, abortion, and child mortality. Because these issues contradict the reproductive myth, women silently bear induced abortions and reproductive illnesses. By representing the differences between the dominant discourse and women's accounts of reproductive matters, I highlight the reproductive issues identified by village women. Following are the four main divergences between the dominant discourse and women's narratives.

The key divergence is infanticide. Some women over the age of seventy revealed that village women have not taken ethnomedicine for contraception, but instead have depended on infanticide by suffocating the baby with the placenta. In a pragmatic sense, the need to restrict births is due to women's high participation in agricultural production and the difficulties of bearing children in a short period of time. Infanticide is also used to kill unhealthy children, twins, and those with disabilities. Women do not consider infanticide a sin. Mother So, who is from a lower-caste family, said, "As a mother, I had to kill it because I would have had bad fate. It did not have a good fate, either. If I had wanted it, others would have criticized me for having excess births."

The second difference between the dominant discourse and women's experience is that infanticide is the only method that has been used to choose gender at birth. Because villagers seldom marry outside the village, they pay close attention to the balance of gender. While conducting my fieldwork, a twenty-five-year-old woman gave birth to a female infant. Her mother told me that her son-in-law's family had killed the infant because the baby was a second daughter. According to village women, they give birth at home, squatting while their husbands hold them and older female relatives assist in delivery. The husband also participates in childbirth by practicing infanticide, which is both emotionally and physically difficult for the woman. However, if the husband is not present, the woman must perform it herself.

The third difference is abortion. Male leaders and elites stress that the female herbalists own the knowledge of contraception and how to identify or choose gender. However, as Mother Po said, "Female herbalists were made up. Those women only knew how to abort unwanted pregnancy. If they were real herbalists, why were so many women sick with reproductive illness?" In other words, village women only know which herbs induce abortion.[9] The construction of female herbalists and the role of ethnomedicine were distorted specifically for the purposes of constructing the reproductive myth. Abortion is used to eliminate pregnancies resulting from different spiritual or caste unities and illegitimate births, except when the man insists on marrying the pregnant woman. Unmarried women may also induce abortion because China's family planning program does not allow them to use contraceptives. Married women also induce abortion if their contraception fails.

Last, sexual and reproductive practices that encourage early marriage and early childbearing exist, albeit covertly. According to some women's narratives, parents arranged their marriages when they were thirteen or fourteen, and some girls married at fifteen or sixteen. Most of them, however, were married before the age of nineteen. According to Mother Shan, newly married couples were warned not to get pregnant immediately after the wedding, as the village head had told local officials that the custom of entering the husband's home resembled a Han Chinese engagement. Thus, cultural customs went underground to avoid being transformed by the state. Village women reported that that after the wedding, the new wife is invited to dinner with her husband's family and when festivals are celebrated. The husband's family might then ask the daughter-in-law to stay the night with the husband, a practice that gives the woman a degree of power in that she can decide whether to stay.

Although the Shan population-control myth as constructed by male village leaders highlights how Shan consciously limits births, village women did not necessarily desire fewer children. Many knew that even if they bore many children, some of the children would die from disease or infanticide. Some regretted having had only one son if their other son had died young. In the village, around twenty older people lived alone. Having witnessed her father's lonely life, Mother Min doubted that past villagers had wanted fewer children. After their daughters married, older people had to depend on themselves until they could no longer work. Had they raised more children, they would have had more assistance, as well as visitors.

Effects of Reproductive Politics on Village Women's Health

When Mother So's IUD—the only contraceptive provided by the local family planning station—caused heavy bleeding, the family planning health worker removed it and instructed her to use ethnomedicine for contraception. She was also warned not to become pregnant, but she did. Although Mother So did not think it was good for her health, she had taken herbs to induce abortion twice before and practiced infanticide once. This time she did not induce abortion, nor could she afford to have one performed; instead, she and her husband intended to practice infanticide. When her abdomen grew noticeably large, she spent most of her time in a shed outside the village to avoid gossip. In order to perpetuate the myth, the cadres had concealed her previous pregnancies. However, when the village accountant informed her that the family planning workers were arriving the next day, she knew that to avoid punishment she would have to immediately induce abortion.

As village women are influenced by leaders' representations and the dominant discourse, some degree of ambiguity and deceit permeated their narratives in order to avoid political scrutiny and social risk. Reproductive deceptions perpetuated by the leaders prevent a full understanding of women's reproductive health problems and gender issues, such as teenage abortion, abortion due to contraceptive failure, sex selection, and infanticide. As their health needs and problems are not addressed, they lack the necessary resources to resolve these issues.

Despite the presence of a family planning program, sex-selected infanticide persists. To some extent, women with IUDs benefit from modern contraceptives in that they avoid unwanted pregnancies. Because they seldom marry outside the village, they want healthy children of both genders, which directs their reproductive decision to commit sex-selected infanticide. As village leaders control the dominant discourse, women's agency and health issues are not addressed. Although local officials, elites, and village leaders are beneficiaries of the reproductive myth, village women are sacrificed for local reproductive politics.

Conclusion

Shan village leaders uphold the reproductive myth of Shan village as a model village for family planning but, in fact, adversely affect village women's reproductive health. By representing the interests of the upper caste and dominating the village hierarchy, their control over reproduction is reflected in their sex/gender system and manipulation of the local politics of reproduction.

Free courtship and polygyny have had a serious impact on women's health. The elders of upper-caste families normally require the abortion of premarital pregnancies, as they cross the boundaries of caste and personhood. As teenage pregnancy cannot be resolved by marriage, women must confront the potential health risks of abortion. Hierarchical relations in the sex/gender system justify gender and social inequality, but also contribute to a lack of attention to women's health problems. Such neglect results in forced or poorly performed abortions and reproductive illnesses, which affect women's status. As Shan village women are constrained by the social hierarchy, women's agency is limited by internalized social norms and gender roles.

In some ways, the reproductive deceptions perpetuated by the Shan village leaders have enabled a decrease in the state's surveillance, management, and restrictions of fertility. The Shan myth and unofficial practices enable upper-caste families to sustain their practices of early marriage, early births, and larger families, and the village leaders to undermine family planning policy and unofficially maintain a degree of autonomy over reproduction.

Village women's narratives revealed they did not have access to many modern contraceptive methods, nor were they able to control the sex of fetuses, as the myth claimed. Instead, abortion and infanticide are practiced to limit the number of births and to select sex. Furthermore, the narratives suggest that the low number of children in the population is the result of high infant and child mortality. Because of women's living conditions, gender roles, the gendered division of labor, and social hierarchies, they experience menstrual disorders, amenorrhea, vaginal infection, miscarriages, stillbirths, and premature births. These reproductive experiences have greatly affected their health, which is ignored to perpetuate the Shan myth. Namely, it is difficult to systematize women's health issues in the face of misrepresentation. In summary, the reproductive politics of Shan village in southwest China show how male dominance may be deleterious to women's reproductive health.

Notes

1. In order to protect the villagers from social or political harassment or recriminations from having spoken with me, the village and the particular minority group to which the villagers belong are not identified here, and all names are pseudonyms.
2. I label the dominant official story of Shan village as a "myth" of population control, as it is constructed by political propaganda and not the realities of the villagers' lives.
3. These references are not included because the titles refer to the village name.
4. At the request of the state, during the 1980s all minority autonomous regional governments passed family planning regulations to attain population-control targets (Mackerras 1994:234). The penalty for

"unapproved" births is 600 Chinese yuan (US$72.50). Since July 1998, those working in official institutions have conformed to the one-child policy. Since 2000, farmers whose first child is a daughter are permitted a second child but must pay 500 Chinese yuan (US$60.41) for the birth certificate, an amount few minority peasants can afford.

5. The villagers follow a system known as teknonymy. When their first child is born, both parents lose their birth names, and their names become the firstborn child's. For example, if the newborn is named Yu, its parents become Father Yu and Mother Yu, and the grandparents are Grandmother Yu and Grandfather Yu. Since a couple does not have formal kinship terminology until they have a child, teknonymy allows the couple to connect socially and ensure their social status. Single men or women, such as the seventy-two-year-old bachelor Yao, keep the names they were given at birth, implying that in failing to produce a new generation, their social status is thusly marked.

6. Because only village leaders and men can attend public meetings, they influence women's viewpoints. Village women refrained from expressing their opinions while their husbands, particularly those who were village leaders, spoke with me. In later interviews, I spoke with women when their husbands were not present.

7. Although leaders say that villagers would not have intercourse around the time of a woman's menses in order to prevent pregnancy, this is not an indication of villagers' true knowledge of conception or practices.

8. These references cannot be included because they name the village.

9. To induce abortion, Shan women cut the root of *Hang Gam Ku* to the length of a middle finger, around which they tie a thread, inserting the root into the vagina. In the meantime, they boil three herbs in water and ingest the medicine. According to Mother So, the root was in her body for twelve hours before abortion occurred. During the abortion process, women tremble with cold, and the overall symptoms are similar to those for malaria. Most village girls are familiar with this procedure—some induce abortion and others go to the health clinic in the county center.

References

Anagnost, Ann. 1995. "A Surfeit of Bodies: Population and the Rationality of the State in Post-Mao China." In *Conceiving the New World Order: The Global Politics of Reproduction*, ed. F. Ginsburg and R. Rapp. Berkeley: University of California Press.

———. 1997. *National Past-times: Narrative, Representation, and Power in Modern China*. Durham: Duke University Press.

de Beauclair, Inez. 1986. *Ethnographic Studies: The Collected Papers of Inez De Beauclair*. Taipei: Southern Materials Centre.

Diamant, Neil J. 2000. *Revolutionizing the Family: Politics, Love, and Divorce in Urban and Rural China, 1949–1968*. Berkeley: University of California Press.

Diamond, Norma. 1995. "Defining the Miao: Ming, Qing, and Contemporary Views." In *Cultural Encounters on China's Ethnic Frontiers*, ed. S. Harrell. Seattle: University of Washington Press.

Ginsburg, Faye, and Rayna Rapp. 1991. "The Politics of Reproduction." *Annual Review of Anthropology* 20:311–43.

———, eds. 1995. *Conceiving the New World Order: The Global Politics of Reproduction*. Berkeley: University of California Press.

Gladney, Dru. 1994. "Representing Nationality in China: Reconfiguring Majority/Minority Identities." *Journal of Asian Studies* 53(1):92–123.

Guo, Xaolin. 2000. "The Research of Ethnicity: Reverse Impact of PRC Minority Policies." Paper presented at the conference "Ethnicity, Politics and Cross-Border Cultures in Southwest China: Past and Present," Lund University, 25–28 May.

Greenhalgh, Susan. 1993. "The Peasantization of the One-Child Policy in Shannxi." In *Chinese Families in the Post-Mao Era*, ed. D. Davis and S. Harrell. Berkeley: University of California Press.

———. 1994. "Controlling Births and Bodies in Village China." *American Ethnologist* 221(1):3–30.

———. 2001a. "Fresh Winds in Beijing: Chinese Feminists Speak out on the One-Child Policy and Women's Lives." *Signs* 26(3):847–76.

———. 2001b. "Managing 'the missing girls' in Chinese Population Discourse." In *Cultural Perspectives on Reproductive Health*, ed. C. M. Obermeyer. Oxford: Oxford University Press.

———. 2003. "Planned Births, Unplanned Persons: 'Population' in the Making of Chinese Modernity." *Signs* 30(2):196–215.

Handwerker, Penn W., ed. 1990. *Birth and Power: Social Changes and the Politics of Reproduction*. Cambridge: Cambridge University Press.

Harrell, Stevan, ed. 1995. *Cultural Encounters on China's Ethnic Frontiers*. Seattle: University of Washington Press.

Heritier, F. 1995. "Sterility, Aridity, Drought." In *The Meaning of Illness*, ed. M. Augé and C. Herzlich. Luxemburg: Harwood Academic.

Kabeer, Naila. 1994. *Reversed Realities: Gender Hierarchies in Development Thought*. London and New York: Verso.

Kligman, Gail. 1998. *The Politics of Duplicity: Controlling Reproduction in Ceausescu's Romania*. Berkeley: University of California Press.

Litzinger, Ralph A. 2000. *Other Chinas: the Yao and the Politics of National Belonging*. Durham: Duke University Press.

Liu, Yulian. 1984. "Liang zhong shengchan de lilun'gei wo de qishi'—luolun Chashan, Hualan, Ao Yao de shengyu wenti" [What I have learned from the "theory of the two modes of production"—A brief account of the problem of reproduction among the Chanshan, Hualan, and Ao Yao]. Unpublished manuscript.

Mackerras, Colin. 1994. *China's Minorities: Integration and Modernization in the Twentieth Century*. Hong Kong and New York: Oxford University Press.

———. 2003. *China's Ethnic Minorities and Globalisation*. London and New York: Routledge.

Mohanty, Chandra Talpade. 1991. "Under Western Eyes: Feminist Scholarship and Colonial Discourses." In *Third World Women and the Politics of*

Feminism, ed. C. T. Mohanty, A. Russo, and L. Torres. Bloomington: Indiana University Press.

Population Council. 1996. "Chinese Government White Paper on Family Planning." *Population and Development Review* 22(2):385–93.

Tapp, Nicholas. 1989. *Sovereignty and Rebellion: The White Hmong of Northern Thailand*. Singapore, Oxford, and New York: Oxford University Press.

Wang, Zheng. 1999. *Women in the Chinese Enlightenment: Oral and Textual Histories*. Berkeley: University of California Press.

Weedon, Chris. 1992. *Feminist Practice and Poststructuralist Theory*. Cambridge: Blackwell.

Yan Ruxian. 1989. "Marriage, Family and Social Progress of China's Minority Nationalities." In *Special Issue on Ethnicity & Ethnic Groups in China*, ed. N. Tapp and C. Chiao. Hong Kong: Chinese University of Hong Kong.

Zhao, Zongwei. 1995. "Deliberate Birth Control Under a High-Fertility Regime: Reproductive Behavior in China before 1970." *Population and Development Review* 23(4):729–68.

Part III.

Infertility and Assisted Reproduction

Chapter 8

THE SEX IN THE SPERM:
MALE INFERTILITY AND ITS
CHALLENGES TO MASCULINITY IN
AN ISRAELI-JEWISH CONTEXT

Helene Goldberg

"The woman suffers more in a physical way. The man suffers in a different way. It is really torture: you have to put your sperm in a cup," insisted an infertile man sitting in the hospital waiting room while his wife's follicles were being measured next door. What was unusual about this American-born man was that he volunteered a conversation about his own infertility as I passed, and soon after we were engaged in deep dialogue. It was late summer 2002, and I had come to Jerusalem to learn about men's experiences with their infertility.

A central area of focus over the past few decades in the social sciences has been women's experiences with infertility and its treatment (see Inhorn 1994; Inhorn and van Balen 2002; Kahn 2000; Ragoné 1999; Teman 2001, 2003; introduction to this volume). Meanwhile, a great imbalance exists when comparing the number of studies on male and female infertility (Carmeli and Birenbaum-Carmeli 1994; Tjørnhøj-Thomsen 1999), indicating that until recently male infertility has not been studied comprehensively.

Sperm donation and sperm banking have especially caught the attention of social scientists (Becker 2002; Birenbaum-Carmeli, Carmeli, and Yavetz 2000; Carmeli and Birenbaum-Carmeli 2000;

Nachtigall et al. 1997; Schmidt and Moore 1998). Even though an increasing number of studies are addressing various other aspects of male infertility (e.g., Carmeli and Birenbaum-Carmeli 1994; Goldberg 2004; Inhorn 2003, 2004, this volume; Lloyd 1996; Tjørnhøj-Thomsen 1999, this volume), it would take a radical shift of focus among scholars to balance these with studies of women and infertility. The lack of attention to male infertility also exists within the medical arena, where there is an absence of knowledge of andrology and male infertility. Options for infertile men are limited (Birenbaum-Carmeli, Carmeli, and Casper 1995; Tjørnhøj-Thomsen 1999) and in some cases even harmful (Inhorn this volume).[1]

In the context of my larger project, I hoped that by focusing on male infertility in Israel, I could contribute to expanding the ethnographic body of research on the anthropology of reproduction by directing our focus to the unheard men of the infertility experience. I imagined it would be possible to pinpoint such men in a clinical setting, and that is how I set out to conduct fieldwork in Israel.

Infertility is a public concern in Israel. The country has the world's highest numbers of fertility clinics (Carmeli and Birenbaum-Carmeli 2000; Kahn 2000) and the world's greatest use of fertility treatments per capita.[2] Fertility clinics are heavily subsidized by national health insurance, and their use is unlimited for all Israeli citizens regardless of socioeconomic standing until the birth of a minimum of two children (Kahn 2000:2).[3] It is well asserted that reproduction is encouraged in Israel and often related to the state's interest in surviving as a Jewish state (Kanaaneh 2002; Yuval-Davis 1982), persecution of Jews in the past (Goldberg 2006; Kahn 2000; Teman 2006), the central importance of children to Jewish life, and the demand in Jewish law "to be fruitful and multiply" (Carmeli and Birenbaum-Carmeli 2000; Ivry 2001; Kahn 2000; Sered 2000; Weiss 2002).

Central to the nationhood and family in Israel are the symbols of nature and blood, which expand beyond the nuclear family into a collective (Carmeli and Birenbaum-Carmeli 2000). According to Jewish law and a dominant understanding, the mother is seen as passing on the Jewish identity of a child. Linage is passed through the father, and the nation-family is imagined to originate with Abraham and his seed: as I have argued elsewhere, the nation-family can be seen as a nation created by sperm (Goldberg 2006).

In his seminal work on American kinship, anthropologist David Schneider (1980) argues that key symbols to the family are sexual intercourse, nature, blood, and marriage. In addition, an important aspect of kinship and family is gender (Collier and Yanagisako 1987). That gender, notions of blood or genetics, conjugality, intercourse, and nature are also central symbols to Israeli kinship and reproduction was apparent when examining the treatment of male infertility (see also Goldberg 2006, forthcoming). As British anthropologist Marilyn Strathern (1992) has noted, assisted reproductive technologies (ARTs) tend to challenge traditional understandings and make them explicit when demanding their renegotiations, offering a window to study kinship and reproduction. In this chapter, I examine how ARTs challenge notions of masculinity, as well as make them explicit, and how masculinity is associated with sexual reproduction and the image of sperm.

I was inspired to focus on Israel by American anthropologist Susan Kahn's (2000) groundbreaking study of single Israeli-Jewish women's use of sperm from anonymous donors. Kahn refers to the understanding of Jewishness as stemming from the mother, the state's interest in reproducing Jews, and the importance of motherhood to illuminate why single female Jewish reproduction is possible. Her focus on this pocket of Israeli society could leave the reader with the impression that men are unimportant to Israeli-Jewish reproduction. However, as Israeli sociologists Yoram Carmeli and Daphna Birenbaum-Carmeli point out, an extreme secrecy surrounds sperm donation to Israeli couples in order to uphold the image of the natural family (Birenbaum-Carmeli, Carmeli, and Yavetz 2000; Carmeli and Birenbaum-Carmeli 2000). Furthermore, Israeli legislation of gestational surrogacy, the only legal type of surrogacy in Israel, holds that married couples using sperm from the husband (and the egg from the wife or a third donor) are solely allowed to use surrogacy (Teman 2001). These are a few of the many indications that male partners are understood as central to Israeli-Jewish reproduction and kinship. In general, public attention and debates surround the use of ARTs, as well as issues such as women's access to treatment, surrogacy, and prenatal testing (Ivry 2004; Kahn 2000; Teman 2001, 2003). In contrast, there seems to be little public focus on male infertility.

As I entered Israeli clinics, I found that men had not only been missing from writings and debates about infertility, but that they were often also missing in the clinics. When they were present, they often seemed to be in the background, and I had difficulties locating men to interview, a topic I address later. I had come with the desire to learn about men's experiences but very often found that all that was left of the men in the clinic was their sperm. Sperm as an iconic signifier became central to my research, and rather than exploring the male experience, my study became one of analyzing the social construction of male infertility and the image of sperm.

Studies of male infertility tend to agree that it goes hand in hand with a taboo, which can be explained by the close conceptual connection between masculinity and sexual reproduction (Goldberg 2004; Inhorn 2004; Tjørnhøj-Thomsen this volume). Notions of roots and patrilineal descent, associations made between sperm and authentic fatherhood, and the wish to have one's genetic child were important reasons why the couples, men, and even medical staff would insist on treatments using infertile sperm rather than the alternatives. In this chapter, I do not explore how male infertility is interpreted as a threat to linage and fatherhood (Goldberg forthcoming); instead, I explore how masculine ideals of militarism, body type, and sexual ability are embodied in the sperm. The intention is to zoom in on the taboo of male infertility and offer reasons why it is so difficult to "put sperm in the cup." More specific, the aim is to explore how masculinity is articulated and challenged through the visualization and manipulation of sperm in the infertility setting in the Israeli-Jewish context. I start by introducing the field and some of the methodological challenges that introduced me to a central aspect of male infertility: the image of the infertile sperm. Next, I explore how ideals of masculinity are attached to sperm and challenged by infertility. Finally, I show how an equation between reproduction and sexual intercourse is made explicit and renegotiated when new actors are involved.

Finding Sperm: The Male Fertility Complex

My fieldwork is based on participant observation in fertility clinics in Jerusalem and the Jerusalem area between September 2002 and February 2003. My interviewee list includes four men with male-factor problems, five couples in treatment because of male infertility, four female patients, two social workers, an infertility support-group counselor, four biologists, four doctors from various fertility clinics, two rabbis, two Ministry of Health employees, and a female religious supervisor (*masgicha*) working at the in vitro fertilization (IVF) clinic.[4] Interviews lasted from fifteen minutes to five hours and were recorded and transcribed verbatim.[5] Approximately half the participants were interviewed on several occasions. Furthermore, participant observation in the clinics led to many daily conversations with patients, doctors, biologists, nurses, and others. The majority of patients in the clinics were Jewish, both secular and religious, as were all of the staff, and among them were immigrants from all over the world. In addition, I analyzed and interpreted newspapers, popular images, and debates in the Israeli media that pertained to the project.

Irvine (1998) notes that male infertility primarily involves low sperm count (oligospermia), poor semen motility (asthenospermia), defective sperm morphology (teratospermia), or no sperm in the ejaculate (azoospermia). A dilemma of male infertility is that it manifests itself inside the woman's body by the woman not becoming pregnant. Until then, it is hidden in the testicles of men, as anthropologist Marcia Inhorn argues (2003, 2004). In fact, it is hidden in the sperm and only visualized by medical technology.

If sperm quality is lower than normal, different methods for assisting fertilization exist, depending on the problem. In the clinics where I conducted my fieldwork, the most common three treatment forms were intrauterine insemination (IUI), IVF, and intracytoplasmic sperm injection (ICSI). Before each of these procedures, the woman's body is treated with hormones, and on the day of the procedure, the man gives a sperm sample. During both IVF and ICSI procedures, the woman's follicles are surgically removed.[6] By injection of a single sperm cell into the ovum, ICSI has been a revolutionary method since the 1990s, allowing men with low sperm quality to become genetic fathers.

Sociologist Judith Lorber argues that when it comes to male infertility, healthy women submit themselves to lengthy treatments to conceive a child while the man "in most cases only has to produce sperm on demand" (1992:169). Treatment of male infertility does involve more than producing sperm, and producing sperm is often more stressful than acknowledged (see Goldberg forthcoming; Tjørnhøj-Thomsen this volume). This is especially true in a Jewish religious setting, where masturbation, as the *masgicha* argued, is "against everything men ever learned" stemming from religious prohibitions against wasting sperm (see Goldberg 2004; Kahn 2002).

I began my fieldwork in a Jerusalem state hospital's IVF clinic, where I was allowed to participate in operations, fertility lab work, consultations, scanning, and staff meetings. The staff was exceptionally open and included me in their daily routines. After a few days in the clinic, I began to wonder if I had come to the wrong place, as fewer men than women came. To my surprise, I soon realized that this particular IVF clinic was known throughout the country as being especially dedicated to the treatment of male infertility. In fact, the clinic should have been known as an ICSI clinic—over 80 percent of the lab fertilizations done with ICSI—often because of a low sperm count or poor sperm quality. Furthermore, the clinic specialized in fine-needle extraction of sperm from testicles, a technique used when no sperm or no functional sperm exists in the ejaculate, followed by ICSI. Wives often came alone to the clinic for the routine checkups and consultations, but even when accompanied by their partners, the men often seemed to stay in the background.

After a month at this clinic, I moved to a sperm bank, following my research plan that had been approved by the IVF clinic's director. I imagined that the sperm bank would make it easier to find men with fertility problems. However, I ran into my first barrier when the director gently but firmly told me I was not allowed to interview patients who came to receive sperm donation. He argued that I had to "concentrate only on IVF," insisting sperm donation was too private. Surprised by this, especially after the openness of the IVF clinic, I asked for and was granted permission to interview the sperm bank staff. However, scheduling appointments with biologists from the sperm banks turned out to be more challenging than scheduling appointments with famous rabbis or doctors. By the end of my stay, however, I was able to interview three different female lab workers from two different sperm banks and even spend some time observing in each of the sperm banks.

In contrast, there were no barriers to interviewing women being treated at the clinics. There were plenty of female patients to talk to, and they often volunteered conversations. One day, I asked a doctor if I could be present during an ovum pick-up, and in a jocular manner he answered, "Yes, and you can bring all your friends!" My different experiences when approaching rooms in the clinical setting gave me the impression that those treating women were more "public," while those focusing on men's bodies, or rather their sperm, were more "private." This is paradoxical in that they were all located within the public sphere of a hospital and should have been equally accessible. The easy access gained to those areas treating women suggests that female infertility was seen as less problematic than male infertility. Somehow, male infertility demanded more secrecy and privacy.

My difficulties in gaining access to sperm banks and finding men to interview made me search for yet another location that would deal more explicitly with male infertility. Thus, it was a happy day when I reached my new location, a clinic with its name proudly displayed on the exterior wall: "The Male Fertility Complex." As I entered the complex, I was struck by the photographs of gigantic sperm cells that decorated the waiting room walls, the lab, and the consultation room. Enlarged 12,000 times or more, the pictures showed the shape and the deformation of the sperm in detail. In contrast, the walls of the IVF and regular fertility clinics I had visited had been decorated with baby pictures.[7] As I entered the Male Fertility Complex, it became clear that male infertility is not only about the challenge to father genetic children. As illustrated by the exhibited photographs of deformed sperm, male infertility is about having infertile sperm and is accompanied by associations having little to do with childlessness per se.

Unlike the hospital clinic, where gynecologists reigned, this clinic was led by biologists specializing in spermatology research. The clinic conducted advanced semen analysis and chose sperm for ICSI under a special microscope. The staff was enthusiastic about my research, feeling their work and male infertility were in the shadow of infertility gynecologists focusing mostly on the woman's body. However, once I started interviewing patients in the clinic, I again ran into problems. When interviewing the first man, a lab worker came and sent him from the room to fill out forms and told me not to conduct interviews without the lab manager present. She involved the lab manager, who offered to "[T]ake out three cases from the file and tell you everything, if you want, instead of you asking them everything. It will be like you are talking with them."

Every time I approached my target or lifted my gaze beyond the sperm, something happened. If this had happened only once, I could have seen these barriers as coincidental or as internal power struggles. However, the fact that I was repeatedly stopped when attempting to approach infertile men suggests more was at stake. The clinical staff can be seen as gatekeepers contributing to the continued hiding of male infertility (see Carmeli and Birenbaum-Carmeli 2000).

Staff assumed that male patients would be too embarrassed to talk, but the clinical focus on sperm rather than on men and the staff's gatekeeping practices emerged as part of the anthropological inquiry. Male patients noticed staff's readiness to protect them from the stigma of infertility. A man who had just found out that he had a fertility problem told me about his first encounter with a clinic.

> So I am calling there and talking to the woman [the secretary], and apart from all the coverage and insurance aspects, she was explaining to me all kinds of stuff, and she says, "Listen, you should know that you shouldn't feel ashamed. You know, I see in here that fifty percent of the problems are the men, because of men." I never met her and she was like giving me reassurance that I am okay, not to worry and stuff like that. That is nice.

After the director of the Male Fertility Complex became involved, I was finally allowed to interview patients and couples, who had much to say. Several of them had never told others about their fertility problem, and they enjoyed the chance to talk (Goldberg 2004). In the context of male infertility, it was an advantage to be a stranger committed to confidentiality (Inhorn 2004), and it is possible that the staff, more than the patients, suffered from a "male fertility complex." The stigma of male infertility was brought into the clinics, affecting staffs' maneuvering. The sensitivity surrounding the manipulation and visualization of infertile sperm brought with it some problematic associations that made it easier to conduct research when focusing on sperm than on infertile men.

Masculine Sperm: Militarism, Image of Body and Self, and Sexual Performance

Gender studies in Israel have highlighted how Israeli ideas of gender are constructed around military men and reproductive women (Klein 1999; Teman 2006). Anthropological studies in Israel tend to focus on female reproduction and motherhood (Kahn 2000; Sered 2000; Teman 2001, 2003), as well as masculinity and militarism (Ben-Ari 1998; Klein 1999; Sasson-Levi 2002; Weiss 2002), the latter being reemphasized by the ongoing conflict. One could argue that these studies unwittingly reinforce the Israeli gender ideas, as representations of gender are culturally specific. American anthropologist Emily Martin convincingly shows that ideas about conception, egg, and sperm are based on cultural stereotypes (1991). These ideas shape scientific descriptions in American medical and biological texts, where ova are depicted as feminine, passive gametes waiting to be conquered by a winning, active, and aggressive sperm cell. Even scientific texts based on newer research, which shows that conception is based on interplay between the female and male reproductive systems, draws on gender stereotypes and values.

In the Israeli context, gender-specific metaphors are also used to describe reproduction and gametes. In Israel, where masculinity is often connected to militarism, it is not surprising to find that reproduction and sperm cells are often imagined and described through military rhetoric. Sperm may be described as soldiers on a mission or as "platoons of soldier sperm" (Ivry 2001, this volume). The connection between soldiers and sperm was made very explicit in the heated local debate about the possibility of opening a sperm bank for soldiers of the Israeli Defense Forces. A newspaper article debating the issue (Sinai 2002) carried an illustration of a jar of animated sperm cells wearing military helmets and hats, an image epitomizing the cultural ideal of "real men" having military sperm.

Figure 8.1. "Young womb wanted to establish Jewish family in the Land of Israel." Illustration by Gila Kaplan featured in *Ha'aretz*, 4 November 2002. Used with permission.

These military images were also invoked in the context of male infertility, when the director of the Male Fertility Complex told me that sperm cells are the most unique cells in the human body. He applauded infertile sperm, arguing it can recognize its own problem, self-destruct, and outsmart the egg. As he put it,

> The sperm can destroy himself like a missile—he can destroy his nucleus if there is some defect in it. When it reaches the zona pelucida [the "cell shell" of the egg], it will destroy itself. The machinery will still run [it will still be swimming although the nucleus is dead]. The egg lost because it allowed for this sperm to come in.

In general, the medical staff I encountered spoke of sperm with admiration, even when infertile. Interestingly, in the above quote, the infertile sperm is not seen as a failure but as hypermasculine. In this account, sperm has a masculine role, not by fertilizing the egg but by using "empty promises" of fertilization to fool its way into penetrating the egg. Furthermore, sperm is self-destructive, commits suicide upon fulfilling its mission, and has an "honorable Kamikaze death" (see Moore this volume). Finally, even an infertile sperm cell is smarter than an egg! In addition, the wall of a Jerusalem sperm bank had a drawing of a few gigantic, evil-looking sperm cells surrounding a much smaller, chubby egg with long eyelashes. Besides the reversal of size of sperm and egg, the irony was of course that the image of sperm cells as aggressors survives even in a sperm bank. These images show how gendered notions of masculinity affect the Israeli imaginations of sperm working their way into the clinic.

Wondering how masculine images of sperm affect infertile men's self-image, I asked medical staffers if they thought that men made a connection between masculinity and sperm production. The director of the Male Fertility Complex immediately responded that "I am a sergeant in the army, and the army is a masculine place. In my unit, they think there is a connection, that the strong males are fertile." He continued by explaining that he himself believed in a connection between masculinity and sperm production. "In the general population I think there is, but not here [among his patients]. Men who are more masculine also produce more testosterone, which affects the semen production." This biologist argued that masculinity and sperm production is connected in general; however, his patients differed from the general population, being both infertile and masculine. He defined masculine men as "strong, dominant in a social way, the leader, the strong leader, who makes decisions . . . quite risky decisions."

However, this biologist was among the minority, as other medical staff rejected any connection between masculinity and sperm count. Yet, that they made such a connection was revealed in their descriptions, interpretations of patients' reactions, actions, and explanations. Rebecca, the director of a sperm bank, noted,

> One of my donors is very thin [implicitly considered not to be masculine]. I say this only to you. He has a beautiful, beautiful sperm count. I don't look at someone and think that he has a good or a bad sperm count. Some of the men who come here look like Goliath. They are tall and big, and they have problems. You can't tell.

Rebecca expresses a difference between what she would have expected based on first impressions and what is actually the case: some of the men she would have expected to have a high sperm count have a low one, and vice versa. She concludes that one cannot tell simply by looking at the men; thus, it is wrong to connect masculinity to sperm count. However, her surprise that her thin donor had a "beautiful" sperm count shows she was making a connection between sperm quality and body type. A doctor at the IVF clinic argued that the popular connection between sperm count and masculinity caused a few men to first refuse undergoing a sperm test, "which will show them in another light." He added, "It is a huge blow to the male ego. If he is not producing sperm, his self-image is injured." Therefore, although medical staff say they do not link masculinity to sperm quality, some of them may make a connection.

Several staff members believed they could tell from the way a couple walks in if it is the man or the woman who has the fertility problem. Social worker Perah, who counseled and conducted group sessions for infertile women and couples, said,

> I don't know enough to diagnose the sperm, but when a couple comes to my clinic I can tell if it is a male or a female problem. The body language, without any talking. It is very difficult to translate body language to language, but first of all, the men who come to my clinic come because the woman took him. He comes like a prisoner. He looks as if he is feeling guilty, but he won't talk about it almost ever. He looks like a person that comes to the electric chair.

Some medical staff echoed that men with poor sperm quality can be spotted by their body language. Rebecca, from the sperm bank, said,

> If they have a problem you can see it on them. She [the wife] only wants to get pregnant. If you look at the man you see a very hard situation. The body language, their eyes. Sometimes they just put the glass [the sperm sample] here and flee. Some don't come at all. The wife comes. Or he will say, "Oh, my wife's doctor wanted this. I am sure I am all right." It is not their doctor who sent them but the wife's. They think they are all right. It is very hard for them that something is wrong with them. It is a long, long way for them. For them to accept that something is really, really wrong with their sperm.

These statements illustrate that some staff interpret men's reactions to the clinical visualization of their infertility as affecting their self-image and behavior. In fact, the information received after the sperm test not only becomes central for the man's and couple's understanding of the fertility problem and their chances of having a genetic child, but according to the staff and the men and women with whom I spoke, it also affects the man's self-image. Ben, who was a sergeant in the army and was dressed in his uniform, told me it had been very hard for his ego at first, a statement echoed by every man I interviewed. Jonathan, who already had two children, one of whom was the result of treatment, explained, "It took me a while also to get out of being depressed, of saying, 'Oh, I am not macho, I am not a man.'" However, after learning that other men have fertility problems, he learned to separate his self-image and sperm quality. David, who had lived in the United States for several years but had returned home to do the testing for free, reflected on his test results.

> I am looking at my semen test results; okay, that is life, nobody is perfect. I assume that if you are totally infertile, if you don't have sperm that is like. . . . There is a huge gray zone, and I guess what I am doing is, there are a lot of channels to comfort your ego. By looking at this parameter, my sperm count is very high, but my morphology is very low, or vice versa. There are still things there to compensate, and maybe it helps also, it helps technically because it serves fertility. If there is a certain amount of fertile sperm out there, it can work. But it also helps with yourself; I think it helps in a way.

David's reaction to the test results brings up two issues. First, he wishes to have a child, and despite his poor sperm morphology, having a child through treatment is still an option. Second, he is trying to "comfort" himself, or his "ego." He comforts himself by arguing that the results could have been worse, he could have had no sperm, been azoospermic; instead, only his morphology is low, while his count is high.

In other words, sperm quality is measured on a scale from better to worse, and the patient's own interpretation of the test results may differ from situation to situation. In some cases, having a few infertile sperm cells was of major importance. In the Male Fertility Complex, the staff agreed that the worst situation for a man, and for them as staff, was having to tell men they were azoospermic. However, on several occasions, they had seen male patients who had come to them after years of being told they had no sperm, but their advanced microscope had been able to locate a few sperm cells. When they would show these men their sperm under the microscope, the men would always cry. The director said,

> The men feel so bad if they don't have sperm. They will be so happy to know that they have sperm, even if none of them are motile. When I tell them they have sperm, they are crying. Sometimes they hug me. They speak about [sperm] donation, and he feels miserable. I spoke to a man who was told he was azoospermic. I told him to bring me a slide of his testis. I put it on my electro-microscope and showed him

where the sperm were. I told him, "You are not azoospermic." He was holding me and kissing me.

Judging from these accounts, male infertility is an embodied condition involving more than sperm production (Lorber 1992). In some situations, having sperm is more important than whether it can be used for fertilization and result in genetic fatherhood. Having sperm, even infertile sperm, becomes of major importance and a central masculine confirmation; to use David's words, it comforts your ego.

Another reason why having sperm, preferably fertile sperm, is of crucial importance is that it is popularly connected to sexual performance. In many cultural settings, the concept of masculinity or manhood is tied to ideas about sexuality (Goldberg 2004; Gutmann this volume; Inhorn 2004; Shokeid 1974; Tjørnhøj-Thomsen 1999). One doctor said,

> Just look in the Bible, in the literature . . . any important man is fat and rich, has many wives and many children. It is a symbol of success in many, many cultures. [Having] many children makes you a man. And as long as you have an erection, as long as you can have intercourse, you cannot be infertile, impossible. If you have no children, you can blame it on your wife. It took a long time to separate intercourse, erection and intercourse, and fertility and, even today, in many places in the world it is unaccepted, unaccepted that [a] man is responsible for being infertile. In the new, modern Western world, it is accepted, you know you need a man, a sperm and an egg to have a child, and you can have very good sexual lives for many years, until you find that you have no sperm.

Even in the modern Western world, where "we know better," ideas about the inability to have intercourse are evoked when it comes to male infertility. In Tjørnhøj-Thomsen's study, this is exemplified when a friend of an infertile man suggests, "Just send her to me, mate" (this volume).[8] According to these ideas, an infertile man must be a bad lover or unable to perform sexually. Michal told me that her husband Jonathan, whose sperm quality was the main reason for their fertility problem, felt like less of a man because he could not easily get her pregnant. When I asked her why, she quoted her husband, who kept repeating, "I have lost as a husband and as a lover." In other words, his knowledge of his poor sperm quality influenced his perception of his sexual performance and role as a husband, even though they could have intercourse and already had children.

The taboo of male infertility and the silence surrounding it, as compared to female infertility, may best be understood by the conceptual connection to failed penile function, or impotency. This connection was repeatedly made outside the clinic. When I presented my fieldwork about male infertility to locals, as well as those in international forums, people were convinced this was a study about men with impotency. For example, a female Danish-Israeli academic reacted to my project by explaining in detail about a new product against impotency that she had seen advertised on local television. Sarah, a nurse at the IVF clinic, explained that the conceptual connection to impotency motivates women to conceal their husbands' infertility:

> If it is the man who has the problem, the woman will pretend it is hers to others. And they will think it is her fault. A woman will say it is her who has the guilt if it is the husband's. But no man will say, "It is my problem" if it is the wife's problem. If men have a problem with the sperm, all will think that it is impotence. But it is not!

Several studies from different cultural settings indicate that women often willingly take the blame for male infertility, pretending they are the ones with the problem, because male infertility seems more stigmatized than female (Carmeli and Birenbaum-Carmeli 1994; Inhorn 2004; Tjørnhøj-Thomsen 1999).

In summary, having fertile sperm goes hand in hand with understandings of masculinity. Emily Martin (1991) argues that gender stereotypes are used to construct images of "masculine" sperm. In the context of male infertility, masculine ideals affect how people see themselves and others. The reverse side of the images of masculine sperm is that poor sperm quality and infertile sperm are associated with failed masculinity. Yet, in the context of male infertility, staff and patients may set new parameters of how to define masculinity, although they do not disassociate masculinity from sperm quality and production.

Sperm and Intercourse: Sexless Reproduction in the Clinic?

"The Talmud says, 'There are three partners in the creation of man: God, his father, and his mother.' Today, we can add the fourth partner: the doctor." This quotation, by former president of Israel Yitzhak Navon, is prominently displayed on the cover of a pamphlet distributed to Israeli IVF clinics by the infertility-support organization Children of My Heart. The quotation also raises the final issue to be addressed in this chapter: how to define the role of new actors, sperm donors, and medical staff, when reproduction takes place in the clinic as a result of male infertility.

Schneider (1980) claims that the relationship between husband and wife is a conjugal one, that each partner is given the right to the other's sexual act. The sexual act is proper between husband and wife and expresses erotic love between the two and children are products of this love (38–39, 43). As discussed above, virility, potency, and erection emerge as some of the central aspects of masculinity associated with sperm. In the use of ARTs in Israel, aside from the ultra-Orthodox Jewish contexts, where for religious reasons physical intercourse is often a prerequisite to fertility treatment (Goldberg 2004), children are no longer conceived through a conjugal sexual relationship between husband and wife. Categorically speaking, the husband can be seen as being replaced by a donor or doctor.

Sperm donation for a couple is concealed in Israel, because sperm donation poses a challenge to fatherhood and the natural family central to Israeli kinship (Carmeli and Birenbaum-Carmeli 2000; Goldberg forthcoming). In the informed consent a couple must sign to receive sperm donation, it is suggested that the husband's sperm is mixed with the donor's.[9] Besides the challenge to fatherhood, a more subtle concern when considering a sperm donation revolves around another issue: discomfort with the idea of another man's sperm entering the woman's body. A central concern to rabbis when debating the use of sperm donation is the question of whether the use of sperm donation to a married woman is adultery (Gold 1988; Goldberg 2004; Kahn 2000, 2002).[10] Adultery is one of a number of concerns when considering sperm donation, a concern that also arises in the West (Edwards 1993; Tjørnhøj-Thomsen 1999) and that especially highlights the conceptual connection made between sperm, intercourse, and masculinity.

The concern over adultery was brought up by the director of an infertility-support organization who told me about a call from an angry man. The man had consented to a sperm donation but wanted a guarantee that the same donor's sperm would be used if the couple wanted a second child, a guarantee the doctor was unable to make.[11] The husband had complained, "So now my wife is sleeping with an entire football team." One donor had been acceptable, but the idea of multiple donors' sperm had given the man associations of the wife sleeping around. Only one of the men I interviewed, Adam, who was azoospermic, used adultery as one reason among others for why he would not consider sperm donation: "You don't like to share your wife." The problem in these situations is that sperm is seen as a sexual substance inseparable from the man who produced it and from intercourse with him.[12]

Besides sperm donors, the clinical staff can also be seen as new actors in reproduction and as taking over the "man's job" (Tjørnhøj-Thomsen 1999:149–50). Carmeli and Birenbaum-Carmeli (1994) describe a situation in an Israeli clinic where a husband was not allowed to be present while his wife was being artificially inseminated with his own sperm. The doctor kept the husband from the room, arguing it would be too painful for him to witness his wife being "impregnated by another man," even though the husband's own sperm was being used (669). This doctor's behavior implies that not just the sperm but the act of "using it" has sexual connotations.

I asked other doctors' opinions regarding this doctor's argument. In general, they did not agree with him and some rejected it outright. The director of the IVF clinic was emphatic: "It is nonsense. We are just technicians. We are not impregnating anybody's wife!" Sometimes the medical staff would similarly diminish their role, insisting they had no influence or control and were not God but only technicians helping fertilization on its way. This self-positioning as helping with a couple's conception is echoed by "reproductive assistants" in several other studies (Franklin 1997; Teman 2006; Tjørnhøj-Thomsen 1999). Ironically, in more casual conversations, staff members often took more credit and responsibility for fertilization. Some staff called children conceived from their treatment their "children," and doctors were at times referred to as God. A director of a sperm bank called her lab "my kingdom," indirectly referring to herself as Creator.

Paradoxically, given the insistence on only being helpers in a couple's reproduction, several among the medical staff described it as very problematic that they were interfering with "the most intimate situation between husband and wife." To involve husbands in the process, one doctor would invite them to press the syringe used for IUI. Anthropologist Corrine Hayden (1995) refers to similar practices in lesbian partnerships, where the partner who is not choosing to gestate the child inseminates the other woman, to take part in the reproduction. Another doctor encouraged husbands to be present during IUI to show them it was just a medical routine and to assure them nothing "improper" had taken place between the wife and the doctor.

> If the woman would like to have her husband there, he will see that what is done is just a technical approach to help: that is all! Then he will not have any suspicions. . . . Look, what he [the doctor] is doing is very simple; he puts in a speculum, injects, that is all. And then covers

her and goes away and we [the couple] stay together. The couple leave, they can go back home together, quiet where nobody interferes in the intimacy of the relationship. They can have sex together. What was done in the clinic is just technical, a technical issue, that is all. It is there in the vagina but technical, a technical issue.

Although this doctor, contrary to the doctor in Carmeli and Birenbaum-Carmeli's study (1994), allows husbands to witness insemination to avert suspicion, it later turned out that he also drew a line, just in a different place.

For instance, you know today, think about the ultrasound, the vagina ultrasound. There, for instance, I prefer that the husband would stay outside! Because you take the monitor, it is like a penis, you insert it into the vagina, and you move it here and there, it is like eh, and the imaginations so, so, so wild that they connect having. . . . Here it is important, I would say, "Stay outside!" It is your decision [the doctor's], take it for her! Fortunately enough, the girls are the technicians. Women technicians, not men, the majority are women except for the physicians who are doing it. I am sure it is a problem, I am sure.

In some situations, the sexual connotations could be downplayed by, for example, including the husband to prevent "any suspicions." In other situations, however, the connotations appeared to the doctor to be too severe, as in the above example, where the doctor feared the husband would connect vaginal ultrasound with sexual intercourse. In these situations, the husband should stay outside, because it would be too problematic for the doctor to keep the role as a technician, conducting a "technical issue" against the husband's potential "wild imaginations."

A final, religiously motivated way of circumventing sexual connotations was introduced by the director of the Male Fertility Complex, who referred to himself as modern Orthodox. Part of his job was to choose the "right" sperm cells for ICSI under his microscope. I asked him what he thought about the situation in Carmeli and Birenbaum-Carmeli's study, where the doctor refused to let the husband witness the insemination of his wife. The director immediately responded, "There is a connection. I was worried about this, that a man is not to fertilize his wife. I asked a big rabbi to get the ok to be a messenger."[13] He explained this religious role as appropriate to the situation because "[y]our ego doesn't exist, you are exercising someone else's will." In practice, he would ask religious male patients if he could be their messenger before selecting their sperm, and after a bit of reflection they would understand what he meant. He did not ask the secular men because he was convinced they would look at him like he was "crazy." By being a messenger and acting on someone else's behalf, he could overcome the (sexual) connotation.

Although the physical act of intercourse is not taking place in the clinic, the conception of intercourse is not left at the door. The conception of intercourse enters the clinic and affects the thinking and maneuvering of ARTs. Using the lens of male infertility, it appears nearly impossible to overwrite the sexual connotations of intimate body parts, fluids, and reproduction itself. Central to notions of masculinity is the ability to reproduce sexually, and the infertile man's role in reproduction is challenged both as genitor and as impregnator. To counter the notion of replacement by a donor or a doctor, the role of the new reproductive actors is carefully negotiated according to the situation, to overcome the dilemmas they present: donor sperm may be mixed with the husband's, donation may be outright rejected, the new agents may act as helpers, and husbands may be included or excluded.

Conclusion: Why Putting Sperm in the Cup Is a Challenge to Masculinity

The empirical silence surrounding male infertility seems to have been reinforced by the unbalanced gendered emphasis on women's infertility in medicine, anthropology, and other disciplines. In my ethnographic pursuit of the hidden world of male infertility, I learned much about the associations made with infertile sperm and less about men's personal experience. This chapter explores why "putting sperm in the cup" is a challenge to masculinity and why male infertility is surrounded by silence. This chapter shows that sperm carries notions of ideal masculinity, such as militarism, body image, and sexual capability, ideals challenged by the clinical visualization of the infertile sperm. This visualization and the presence of new reproductive actors make explicit that infertile men are not to have children via intercourse. In other words, male infertility is a major challenge to masculinity, which staff and patients must renegotiate in the clinical setting. Though the clinical setting leaves room for redefinition of masculinity, this seems to be done within a frame where masculinity as a starting point is connected to sperm.

In conclusion, sex is imagined to be embodied in sperm in three ways: in terms of gender, or that a man is made by the ownership of sperm; men are virile, and their sperm is plentiful and fertile; and reproduction is triggered by intercourse where the man's sperm is transferred to the woman's body. All these ideas are made explicit, challenged, and renegotiated by male infertility and the visualization and manipulation of sperm in the clinic. In short, male infertility and the image of infertile sperm challenge ideal masculinity by presenting notions of failed masculinity and manhood. Thus, the conceptual links evoked by the infertile sperm can be used to interpret the silence of male infertility.

Acknowledgments

First, I want to thank the men, women, and medical staff who shared their time, opinion, and experiences with me while I was in Israel. I also want to thank Elly Teman for lengthy discussions while I was in the field and for valuable advice in writing this chapter. Thanks to Tine Tjørnhøj-Thomsen for unlimited support and encouragement throughout this project, and for debates and suggestions in writing this chapter. Also, I thank Maruska la Cour Mosegaard and Marcia Inhorn for their helpful suggestions on how to restructure this chapter. Finally, thanks to Dansk-Israelsk Studiefond for financial support to conduct this research.

Notes

1. Birenbaum-Carmeli, Carmeli, and Casper (1995) suggest that men are discriminated against in fertility treatment, as disproportionate interest and funding in medical research has been aimed at female fertility problems, making it harder to solve male infertility.
2. Between 1995 and 2001, treatment increased by 100 percent. In 2003, 3,400 treatments were given per one million citizens in Israel as compared to 600 in France, 500 in Britain, and 300 in the United States (Wagner 2003).
3. Fertility treatment is subsidized until the woman reaches the age of 45. Recently it was proposed that the state should pay for only one child. However, many women protested and the bill was not passed (Wagner 2003).
4. A *masgicha* is a religious woman specifically trained to supervise every step of the fertility treatment of religious Jews. She supervises the work in the lab to ensure that no mistakes take place and the treatment does not break religious law (see Kahn 2000, 2002).
5. Fieldwork was conducted in English and in very basic Hebrew. Interviews were conducted exclusively in English. All names used in this chapter are pseudonyms.
6. In IUI, sperm is injected into the woman's uterus. In IVF, the ovum and sperm are placed together in a lab test tube. After two to three days, fertilized eggs, or embryos, are transferred to the woman's uterus. In ICSI, a single sperm cell is injected directly into the surgically removed ova, and

upon fertilization the embryos are transferred to the women's uterus. For details on treatment, see Berger, Goldstein, and Fuerst 2001.

7. According to personal conversations with Michal Nachman, who wrote her dissertation on ovum donation in Israel, clinics for egg donation decorate their walls with baby pictures. In one of the ovum donation clinics in which Nachman conducted fieldwork, there was a poster of a baby popping out of a chicken egg (2002:2).

8. To use one of many personal anecdotes regarding how sexual conduct rather than sperm quality is linked to reproduction, a Danish relative who is in his seventies recently insisted that men can have children whenever they want, no matter how old they get, as long as "they can get it up." With Viagra, he continued, even "men who can't get it up can have as many children as they want, at any age."

9. Michal Ricter translated this document from Hebrew to English (28 October, 2002).

10. This is one of the many rabbinical concerns regarding sperm donation and related to religious law. The concern over sperm donation is often related to the quote "Thou shall not implant thy seed into thy neighbor's wife" (Leviticus 18:20; also see Gold 1988:109 and Kahn 2000:96).

11. Some couples who accepted sperm donation liked to be reassured that the same donor would be used in the future so that the children would be genetic siblings. In both of the sperm banks I visited, staff members insisted they try to accommodate this wish.

12. This popular association between intercourse and sperm donation was brought up by a female friend who lives with her same-sex partner. She is in the process of undergoing IUI to have a child, whom she plans to coparent with her partner as well as a male friend who is the donor. She explained that she did not want her partner's brother to be the sperm donor because "I do not want to have high-technological intercourse with my brother-in-law."

13. A messenger usually exercises the will of God. This rhetoric of referring to oneself as a messenger of God or of the nation is common in Israeli society, as evidenced in the military, where soldiers see themselves as messengers of the nation, and in the context of surrogacy, where surrogates call themselves messengers helping God give the couple a child (Teman 2006).

References

Becker, Gay. 2002. "Deciding Whether to Tell Children about Donor Insemination: An Unresolved Question in the United States." In *Reproduction around the Globe: New Thinking on Childlessness, Gender and Reproductive Technologies*, ed. Marcia Inhorn and Frank van Balen. Berkeley: University of California Press.

Ben-Ari, Eyal. 1998. *Mastering Soldiers: Conflict, Emotions and the Enemy in an Israeli Military Unit*. Oxford: Berghahn Books.

Berger, Gary, with Marc Goldstein and Mark Fuerst. 2001. *The Couple's Guide to Fertility*, 3rd ed. New York: Broadway Books.

Birenbaum-Carmeli, Daphna, with Yoram S. Carmeli and Robert F. Casper. 1995. "Discrimination against Men in Infertility Treatment." *Journal of Reproductive Medicine* 40(8):590–94.

Birenbaum-Carmeli, Daphna, with Yoram S. Carmeli and Haim Yavetz. 2000. "Secrecy among Israeli Recipients of Donor Insemination." *Politics and the Life Sciences* 19(1):69–76.

Carmeli, Yoram S., and Daphna Birenbaum-Carmeli. 1994. "The Predicament of Masculinity: Towards Understanding the Male's Experience of Infertility Treatments." *Sex Roles* 30(9/10):663–77.

———. 2000. "Ritualizing the 'Natural Family': Secrecy in Israeli Donor Insemination." *Science as Culture* 9(3):301–24.

Collier, Jane Fishburne, and Sylvia Junko Yanagisako, eds. 1987. *Gender and Kinship: Essays Towards a Unified Analysis*. Stanford: Stanford University Press.

Edwards, Jeanette. 1993. "Explicit Connections: Ethnographic Enquiry in North-West England." In *Technologies of Procreation: Kinship in the Age of Assisted Conception*, ed. Jeanette Edwards, Sarah Franklin, Eric Hirsch, Frances Price, and Marilyn Strathern. Manchester: Manchester University Press.

Franklin, Sarah. 1997. *Embodied Progress: A Cultural Account of Assisted Conception*. London and New York: Routledge.

Gold, Michael. 1988. *And Hanna Wept*. Philadelphia, New York, and Jerusalem: Jewish Publication Society.

Goldberg, Helene. 2004. "The Man in the Sperm: A Study of Male Infertility in Israel." MA thesis, Institute of Anthropology, University of Copenhagen.

———. 2006. "Kampen for overlevelse: demografisk bevidsthed og forestillinger om forbundethed i den israelske-jødiske familie." *Tidsskriftet Antropologi* 50:13–30.

———. Forthcoming. "The Secret of the Sperm: Male Infertility in an Israeli-Jewish Context." In *Kin, Gene, Community: Reproductive Technology among Jewish Israelis*, ed. Daphna Birenbaum-Carmeli and Yoram S. Carmeli. Oxford: Berghahn Books.

Hayden, Corrine P. 1995. "Gender, Genetics, and Generation: Reformulating Biology in Lesbian Kinship." *Cultural Anthropology* 10(1):41–63.

Inhorn, Marcia. 1994. *Quest for Conception: Gender, Infertility, and Egyptian Medical Traditions*. Philadelphia: University of Pennsylvania Press.

———. 2003. "'The worms are weak': Male Infertility and Patriarchal Paradoxes in Egypt." *Men and Masculinities* 5(3):236–56.

———. 2004. "Middle Eastern Masculinities in the Age of New Reproductive Technologies: Male Infertility and Stigma in Egypt and Lebanon." *Medical Anthropology Quarterly* 18(2):162–82.

Inhorn, Marcia, and Frank van Balen, eds. 2002. *Infertility around the Globe: New Thinking on Childlessness, Gender, and Reproductive Technologies*. Berkley: University of California Press.

Irvine D. S. 1998. "Epidemiology and Aetiology of Male Infertility." *Human Reproduction* 13(suppl. 1):33–44.

Ivry, Tsipy. 2001. "Pregnancy as Gambling, Pregnancy as Body Building: Prenatal Care in Comparative Perspective." Paper presented at the Lafer Center Conference on "Gender, Health and the Body: Changing Relations," Hebrew University of Jerusalem.

———. 2004. "Pregnant with Meaning: Conceptions of Pregnancy in Japan and Israel." PhD diss., Hebrew University, Jerusalem.

Kahn, Susan Martha. 2000. *Reproducing Jews: A Cultural Account of Assisted Conception in Israel*. Durham: Duke University Press.

———. 2002. "Rabbis and Reproduction: The Users of New Reproductive Technologies among Ultraorthodox Jews in Israel." In *Reproduction around the Globe: New Thinking on Childlessness, Gender and Reproductive Technologies*, eds. Marcia Inhorn and Frank van Balen. Berkeley: University of California Press.

Kanaaneh, Rhoda A. 2002. *Birthing the Nation: Strategies of Palestinian Women in Israel*. Berkeley: University of California Press.

Klein, Uta. 1999. "The Contribution of Military and Military Discourse to the Construction of Masculinity in Society." Paper presented at the seminar "Men and the Violence against Women," Strasbourg, France.

Lloyd, Mike. 1996. "Condemned to be Meaningful: Non-Response in Studies of Men and Infertility." *Sociology of Health and Illness* 18(4):433–54.

Lorber, Judith. 1992. "Choice, Gift or Patriarchal Bargain? Women's Consent to In Vitro Fertilization in Male Infertility." In *Feminist Perspectives in Medical Ethics*, ed. Helen B. Holmes and Laura M. Purdy. Bloomington: University of Indiana Press.

Martin, Emily. 1991. "The Egg and the Sperm: How Science Has Constructed a Romance Based on Stereotypical Male-Female Roles." *Signs* 16(3):485–501.

Nachman, Michal. 2002. "Border Traffic: Ova Donation and the Reproduction of Life and Death in Israel." Paper presented at the Annual Meetings of the American Anthropological Association. New Orleans, Louisiana.

Nachtigall, R. D., J. M. Tschann, S. S. Quiroga, L. Pitcher, and G. Becker. 1997. "Stigma, Disclosure, and Family Functioning among Parents of Children Conceived through Donor Insemination." *Fertile Sterile* 68(1):83–89.

Ragoné, Helena. 1999. "The Gift of Life: Surrogate Motherhood, Gamete Donation and Constructions of Altruism." In *Transformative Motherhood: On Giving and Getting in a Consumer Culture*, ed. Linda L. Layne. New York: New York University Press.

Sasson-Levy, Orna. 2002. "Constructing Identities at the Margins: Masculinity and Citizenship in the Israeli Army." *Sociological Quarterly* 43(3):357–83.

Schmidt, Matthew, and Lisa Jean Moore. 1998. "Constructing a 'Good Catch,' Picking a Winner: The Development of Technosemen and the Deconstruction of the Monolithic Male." In *Cyborg Babies: From Techno-Sex to Techno-Tots*, ed. Robbie Davis-Floyd and Joseph Dumit. New York: Routledge.

Schneider, David M. 1980. *American Kinship: A Cultural Account*, 2nd ed. Chicago and London: University of Chicago Press.

Sered, Susan. 2000. *What Makes Women Sick: Maternity, Modesty and Militarism in Israeli Society*. Hanover and London: Brandeis University Press.

Shokeid, Moshe, ed. 1974. "The Emergency of Supernatural Explanations for Male Barrenness among Moroccan Immigrants." In *The Predicament of Homecoming: Cultural and Social Life of North African Immigrants in Israel*, ed. Shlomo Dreshen and Moshe Shokeid. Ithaca and London: Cornell University Press.

Sinai, Ruth. 2002. "Fertility Science Outstrips ils Ethical Bonds." *Ha'aretz*, November 4.

Strathern, Marilyn. 1992. *After Nature: English Kinship in the Late Twentieth Century*. Cambridge: Cambridge University Press.

Teman, Elly. 2001. "Technological Fragmentation and Women's Empowerment: Surrogate Motherhood in Israel." *Women's Studies Quarterly* 31 (3/4):11–34.

———. 2003. "The Medicalization of 'Nature' in the 'Artificial Body': Surrogate Motherhood in Israel." *Medical Anthropology Quarterly* 17(1):78–98.

———. 2006. "Birthing a Mother: The Mythology of Surrogate Motherhood in Israel." PhD diss., Hebrew University, Jerusalem.

Tjørnhøj-Thomsen, Tine. 1999. "Tilblivelseshistorier. Barnløshed, slægtskab og forplantningsteknologi i Danmark." PhD diss., Institute of Anthropology, University of Copenhagen.

Wagner, Matti. 2003. "Fertility Treatment Funding to Continue." Jerusalem Post, 4 November.

Weiss, Meira. 2002. *The Chosen Body: The Politics of the Body in Israeli Society*. Stanford: Stanford University Press.

Yuval-Davis, Nira. 1982. *Israeli Women and Men: Divisions Behind the Unity*. London: Change International Reports.

Chapter 9

"It's a bit unmanly in a way": Men and Infertility in Denmark

Tine Tjørnhøj-Thomsen

Low sperm count and poor semen quality seem to be an increasing problem for young Danish men compared to those in other European countries (Carlsen, Swan, Petersen, and Skakkebæk 2005; Jørgensen et al. 2001). There is every indication that an increasing number of men will be confronted with the problems of infertility. When I asked a man how he felt when he found out his sperm quality was very poor and that he would likely never father a biological child, he responded, "It's a bit unmanly in a way."

In this chapter I investigate what feeling "unmanly in a way" means and how male infertility affects notions of masculinity and fatherhood in a Danish context. I address these questions through an examination of men's thoughts, experiences, and feelings in relation to their wished-for fatherhood, their infertility and childlessness, and assisted reproductive technologies (ARTs) in Denmark.[1] There have been only a few qualitative studies of this field in Denmark (e.g., Koch 1989; Schmidt 1996). Research on the implications of infertility and on new reproductive technologies has generated considerable interest, especially in Western societies. However, men's experience of male infertility and childlessness as a health and a social problem is understudied on a global level (Inhorn 2004; Inhorn and van Balen 2002). As Mary-Claire Mason points out, "Men are shadowy figures when it come to matters of fertility" (1993:1).

Infertility has primarily been considered a female problem, and women have been expected to be more socially and emotionally burdened than men by involuntary childlessness. Because medical tests and treatments mostly have been directed toward women, their experiences have been the central object of popular, scholarly, and scientific attention. As I demonstrate in this chapter, these conditions have resulted in implications for the way men talk and feel about their own infertility.

In order to understand the implications of male infertility and childlessness in general and male infertility in particular, I will rely on kinship theory. Recent anthropological studies of infertility, new reproductive technologies (including ARTs) (Edwards et al. 1993; Franklin 1997; Franklin and Ragoné 1998; Goldberg 2004; Layne 1999; Strathern 1992a, 1992b, 1995; Tjørnhøj-Thomsen 1999, 2003a, 2005), lesbian kinship (Hayden 1995; Weston 1991, 1995, 1997), adoption (Howell 2001; Modell 1994), and divorce (Simpson 1994, 1997) have been accompanied by a revival and retheorizing of kinship within the anthropological discipline (e.g., Bouquet 1993; Carsten 2000; Franklin and McKinnon 2001; Peletz 1995; Schneider 1984). This body of new anthropological kinship studies constitutes an important theoretical and analytical anchor for the analysis and discussions presented in this chapter.

British anthropologist Marilyn Strathern writes that infertility and procreative technologies "make us think again about what we take for granted, what we look for in family life [and] how we regard the relationships between parents and children" (1993b:140). In addition, American anthropologist Marcia Inhorn points out that infertility provides "a convenient lens through which fertility-related beliefs and behaviors can be explored" (1994:23). Likewise, I argue that male infertility and men's encounters with ARTs provide a lens through which notions of masculinity, kinship, and sexuality can be explored.

I also argue that masculinity—which refers here to the thoughts of and practices connected with being a man—is constituted relationally and contextually. As is shown throughout the chapter, notions of masculinity surface when men think of their sperm count and the reproductive and bodily impairment that a low sperm count is thought to indicate. Notions of masculinity can be read from their partners', family members', and friends' reactions, from responses to their infertility and childlessness, and from their own attempts to come to terms with infertility, reproductive technology, and a form of fatherhood that may not involve the wished-for genetic connection to their children. Notions of masculinity also emerge from the ways men think of themselves as fathers-to-be and as part of a family; thus they incorporate notions of kinship and relatedness. By referring, for example, to their childhood and old age, the men in this study bring up the significance of generation and time, and by referring to their partners, the men highlight the issues of gender and conjugality.[2] Thus, the men themselves draw the contours of the different relational and social contexts that must be taken into account in analyzing and conceptualizing their lives and identities as men.

I first present my methodology, followed by an overall framework for understanding the individual, social, and cultural implications of infertility and childlessness. I then discuss gendered aspects of infertility and childlessness, and focus on men's thoughts and feelings about their procreative life by comparing them with the corresponding thoughts and feelings described by women. The chapter ends with a focus on men's reactions and responses to finding out they have poor-quality sperm and are infertile.

Methodology

The chapter builds on research conducted in Denmark between 1995 and 1998 (Tjørnhøj-Thomsen 1999). Initially I was interested in discovering what happens when medicine and ARTs intervene in people's lives, by examining their narratives and preconceived notions of kinship and relatedness. The overall aim was partly to give an ethnographic account of a specific reality that remains virtually undescribed elsewhere, and partly to arrive, through this insight, at a more broadly applicable theory of the relationship between technology and notions of kinship and gender.

When I embarked on my fieldwork in 1995, the political, public, and ethical debates on ARTs was just beginning. For the first time, Denmark was due to pass a comprehensive package of legislation in the field, and "involuntary childlessness" and "artificial insemination" were hot topics in the media. The debate centered, among other things, on the limits that should be imposed on ARTs and its practitioners and consumers. The fact that my research coincided with this public debate influenced my project (for details, see Tjørnhøj-Thomsen 2003b, 2004).

A considerable amount of my fieldwork was spent with three local groups of the National Association for the Involuntarily Childless in Denmark (NAICD).[3] In these local groups, infertile men and women (most often heterosexual couples) with different backgrounds and infertility problems regularly met to support each other by exchanging stories, knowledge, and their experiences of being infertile and undergoing treatment. Taking part in their meetings over a period of two years provided me with the opportunity to gain insight into their contemplations, decisions, hopes, and distress, and to understand how infertility and its treatment affected their lives. I also learned about their considerations in contemplating alternative ways of having children, such as donor sperm, in vitro fertilization (IVF), or intracytoplasmic sperm injection (ICSI), as well as adoption. Adoption was considered an alternative to ARTs and was often brought up in conversation after an unsuccessful treatment, although the majority of my informants attempted to have their "own" (biological) child.

My fieldwork also included in-depth interviews with twenty-two childless couples. Each couple was interviewed twice over a six-month period in their home. Interviewing both partners at the same time allowed for a particular conjugal or relational subtext to the interview, as the couple's relationship impacted the conversation to a greater or lesser degree (Hirsch 1993). This method created a special dialogue about childlessness and revealed the couples' mutual disagreements, compromises, and their different—gendered—experiences. A striking characteristic of these discussions was each couple's straightforwardness. It surprised me that they were willing to give a stranger access to such private aspects of their lives. Paradoxically, my being a stranger was what gave me access to this intimate space. I was often told that it was nice to talk to "a stranger," and that they had brought up many subjects not previously discussed with anyone else.[4] However, by no means were they always in agreement as to which private spaces they wished to share with a stranger: occasionally, one partner would discuss a topic the other did not want mentioned.

In addition to visiting a number of clinics under the auspices of the NAICD, I carried out shorter periods of fieldwork at two public fertility clinics, where several of the childless couples I had come to know were receiving treatment. The insights gained into the worlds of childless people and the clinics prompted me to pursue other lines and sites of empirical investigation. Consequently, I turned my attention to the public debate being articulated within the childless community and the clinics, as well as in my own everyday life, and started to participate in adoption courses, political meetings, and conferences on ethics and medical issues.

From the association meetings and the "conjugal sub-text" (Hirsch 1993:71) of the interviews, it became evident that gender is a difference that "makes a difference" in the context of infertility and childlessness. It was also evident that although men and women differ in their thoughts and feelings about their own infertility and childlessness, they share common interests and concerns that deserve investigation. Thus, even though this chapter focuses on men's experiences of infertility and childlessness, I also include female partners' perspectives in order to contextualize men's experiences.

Infertility, Coming into Being, and Kinship

In comparison to other Western countries, Denmark has the largest proportion of ART use among women in the fertile age groups (Nygren and Nyboe Andersen 2002). Increasingly, couples are seeking to overcome infertility issues with the assistance of medical technology. Infertility can be defined as the inability to become or to "make another" pregnant (Lundström 1998). It is first recognized when a couple wants and tries to have a child, and when the social implications of infertility become visible (Koch 1989). If a couple has tried to conceive for about one to two years, they are often classified as "infertile" or "involuntarily childless."

There are many reasons for childlessness. In Denmark, damaged fallopian tubes are the most common female factor, often caused by abdominal infections (Nyboe Andersen, Horness, and Ziebe 1996:36), while the most common male factor is reduced or poor sperm quality. In the Danish medical professional literature, the various reasons for infertility are typically classified into three groups, depending to some extent on whether the cause is traced to the man's or woman's body. One-third of cases can be attributed to female factors and one-third to male factors, while the remaining third is "unexplained" (Lundström 1998; Nyboe Andersen et al. 1996). However, this tripartite division is not always meaningful, because the reason initially given as the cause for the couple's childlessness may be altered when new knowledge is obtained through further investigation and treatment attempts, as well as doctor's various interpretations of them.

Couples in my study reported that the infertile partner often felt inferior, guilty, and anxious about the sustainability of the conjugal relationship, feelings that were directed toward the other partner, as well as the fertile partner's family (Tjørnhøj-Thomsen 1999:107). To infertile men, this sense of guilt is often reinforced by the fact that few effective (body-intervening) treatments are available to them. Many of my male informants were frustrated about not being able to take their equal, or bodily, share in the treatments. The woman's body is at the center of fertility treatment, even when she is not the infertile partner. In Denmark, as in other countries, andrology—the study of disease in the male reproductive organs and thus the male counterpart to the well-established medical field of gynecology (Lundström 1998)—has not been officially recognized as a branch of medicine. Because of that, it has failed to attract younger researchers and potential "knowledge-creators" to the same degree as those found in gynecology, which has had consequences for the range of treatments offered to men and for the way men think about and deal with their infertility (see Birenbaum-Carmeli, Carmeli, and Casper 1995). A fertility expert I interviewed told me that at his clinic they had also "started pulling off the pants of men," a remark that illustrates this gender bias but also signals Denmark's growing interest in andrology and men's reproductive lives. Nevertheless, some couples in my study found they had to take the initiative themselves by insisting on having the "whole" man, and not just his sperm, properly checked.

The individual, cultural, and social implications of infertility, childlessness, and reproductive technology must be understood in relation to historically and culturally conditioned notions of kinship (Strathern 1992a, 1992b, 1993a, 1993b). British anthropologist Marilyn Strathern writes that in Euro-American culture, "kinship affords a context in which people readily conceptualise the *relational* dimension of their lives" (1993a:6). Compared with other social relationships, kinship designates social relationships and forms of relatedness of a very specific nature. Strathern points out that what distinguishes kinship relations from other social relationships is that they "are thought to have their foundation and rationale in the very conditions of coming into being, the procreation and nurture of human beings, and thus in the facts of life" (ibid.).

Euro-American notions of kinship are anchored in what might be called a culturally specific and hegemonic story of coming into being. Stories of coming into being are what parents tell their children when children ask how they came into the world. These stories are culturally specific narratives about how individuals or persons come into being, which actors and contributors (whether animate or inanimate) are involved, and how they contribute. Stories of coming into being also tell how those involved are connected, show the significance of this connectedness, and describe the actual context and conditions of reproduction (Delaney 1991; Franklin 1992, 1997; Tjørnhøj-Thomsen 2003a; Yanagisako and Delaney 1995).

In Denmark, as in other Western societies, the dominant story of coming into being gives a high cultural and symbolic priority to biological procreation.[5] This knowledge about the biological and bodily processes involved in procreation imbue kinship relations with a particular symbolic meaning as lasting relationships that generate special feelings and notions of relatedness (see Schneider 1980; Strathern 1992a, 1992b). The same story informs certain "ideologies of authenticity" (Weston 1995). To my informants, having their *own* child was also a question of being or becoming "real"—a real man, a real woman, and a real family. Such concepts of authenticity are closely associated with being both genetically and bodily related to a common child. This again depends on the capacity of bodies, individually and together, to function both as actors in, and contributors to, this special story of coming into being. This story is also concerned with gender identity, as the cultural construction of what is female or male draws on knowledge about men's and women's specific, complementary, and asymmetrical roles in procreation and the cultural meanings attributed to them. The hegemonic story of becoming and the notions of kinship and gender built into it are challenged by infertility and ARTs. In the following section, I examine what this meant for the men and women in my study.

Infertility and Sociality

The individual and social implications of infertility must first be understood in relation to the confusion and uncertainty it creates in individual lives (Becker 1994). This confusion begins with the body, whose inability to procreate also threatens the individual's sense of self and expectations of a particular life trajectory. In the Danish context, infertility gives rise to a feeling of having been cheated, not only by the body and by nature, but also by the widespread belief that procreation and children—like other conditions of postmodern life—should be a matter of individual control, choice, and responsible timing (Lundin 1997; Wirtberg 1992). Many of my informants put emphasis on education, work security (a topic that particularly concerned women), and stable social and economic circumstances as a precondition for bringing children into the world, or as they stated, "being ready" for children.

When the hoped-for children fail to arrive, this creates a disruption in the life that the Danish would-be parents had imagined living, as well as a loss of control and a disorientation of each individual's identity. Many felt they could not progress in life (see Franklin 1997) but were living in a limbo "with the pause button on," as one woman said. Infertility throws into disarray the careful timing and planning that precedes most Danish couples' decision to have children; it threatens their expectation of a life with children and a certain culturally informed notion of progression. All of this creates a sense of uncertainty about the future and posterity, a break in their biography and genealogy, and disorientation in each individual's sense of identity (Tjørnhøj-Thomsen 2005:76). One of the many questions my informants asked was, "Who will I be, then, if I won't be a parent?" These men and women also looked back on their lives in an attempt to explain this incomprehensible turn of events and to answer questions like "Why me/us?" and "Why now?" just as they tried to find possible solutions to their childlessness and thus an acceptable life story and identity for themselves.

The experience of being childless and undergoing treatment was often described in terms of being split between culturally conditioned constructions of time. One man told me, "You quickly become old when you're childless. Everyone around you is having children, and the children grow bigger and the clock goes on ticking." Others felt they were not considered to be adults because they had not made the transition into parenthood. At the same time, many childless couples started to live in a hypothetical "what-if" state in which, without consciously meaning to, they began to arrange their lives in accordance with the hoped-for pregnancy.

But there is more at stake, in the sense of the temporal and generational dimensions of kinship and the individual's particular life project. In general, children are conceived not only in relation to a notion of the future, but also in relation to the past. Several of my informants pointed out that having children and a family would give them the chance to reexperience, repeat, and in certain cases revise their own childhood experiences and how their own parents had raised them. Many also had difficulty imagining themselves becoming old alongside their partners if they did not have children. Thus, children are not only the product of a particular consolidated conjugal relationship between partners (see Edwards 1993), but are also expected to bring an extra dimension of community and permanence to that particular relationship. In Denmark, infertility and childlessness often give rise to speculation about the couple's future and challenge modern notions of conjugalness (Gillis 1996)

Both men and women expressed the idea that through children they can recreate parts of themselves (see Strathern 1992a) and reproduce both their own and their partner's characteristics. The longing for self-reproduction, for "one's own" child, emerged from the meaning given to "resemblance," a notion most people encounter in the familiar discussions of which family members physically or mentally resemble another. Such discussions should be seen as

a symbolic confirmation of the family as a genetic community between the deceased and the living relatives in the genealogy.

The infertile and childless men and women in my study felt prevented from taking part in the daily relationship with children, from
being a family and creating a home. Likewise, they felt excluded
from the specific rituals and social communities that the ability to
have children and a family life engenders and to which it gives access
(Tjørnhøj-Thomsen 2005:78). Celebrating Christmas is one example
of a social, kinship, and family event where the couple's childlessness and feelings of exclusion were pronounced, because children
take leading parts and seem to be the epicenter of social and family
interest and attention. These exclusions also had consequences in
terms of lack of competence, self-perception, and identity.

Seen from the perspective of infertility and childlessness, the ability to have children gives access to social communities and identities in time and space. To have children is to become part of society,
genealogy, and history. It also highlights how kinship relations are
integrated in, and connected to, other forms of social community.
However, all my informants reported entering a period of reflection
and reformulation, where cultural values relating to coming into being, kinship, and procreation, values usually taken for granted, had
to be revised and reformulated (see Edwards 1993).

The Centrality of Gender

During my fieldwork, notions of gender were being played out in
public debates and private dialogues about infertility and ARTs.
They appeared as a distinguishing mechanism, associating women
with, for example, the realm of feelings, openness, responsibility for
the family's well-being, and interest in the issue of procreation. For
instance, when artificial insemination was being debated publicly
and politically in Denmark between 1995 and 1997, gender was a
prominent theme in expressing the outside world's attitude toward
involuntary childlessness and reproductive technology. In what follows, I refer especially to the debates preceding the adoption of the
"Law on Artificial Insemination," passed in 1997.

One issue that emerged from these debates was whether fertility
treatment should be unavailable to women over the age of forty;
other issues included artificially conceived children and the parental
abilities of older first-time parents. What caused the greatest com-
motion, however, was the minister of health's proposal that fertility
treatment should be unavailable to men over the age of forty-five.

Those against this proposal pointed out that, unlike the quality of women's eggs, men's sperm did not deteriorate with age. In this sense, an older mother appeared more "unnatural" than an older father. Several older fathers of small children reported via the media that their advanced age made them feel more mature and ready for fatherhood than when they were younger (Tjørnhøj-Thomsen 1999:76). Thus, gender and age became interwoven in the question of maternal and paternal abilities.

During my interviews, the childless men and women in my study referred constantly to gender as a difference that makes a difference. They referred to gender when emphasizing, structuring, and giving meaning to specific experiences and practices. In doing so, they gave expression to cultural notions about gender differences, the essence of the two genders, gendered experience, and the realities of fertility treatment (see Becker 2000). They compared men's and women's experience of, and response to, infertility, childlessness, and reproductive technology, and generalized about gender differences in this regard. Moreover, they reproduced and challenged gendered stereotypes.

During the interviews and the NAICD meetings I attended, notions of gender came to the forefront in reflections about "openness." A widespread notion prevailed that it is good to be "open" about infertility and childlessness. Openness, or "talking about it," particularly with others in the same situation, was seen as a form of psychological relief. There was general agreement that it was a relief to overcome one's inhibitions, meet others, and talk about it, thereby breaking out of the loneliness and isolation childlessness can bring. One man described the advantage of openness as "It may sound strange, but it can be comforting to know that there are other people who feel the same." Moreover, silence and secretiveness on the issue were seen as being damaging to social relationships, especially those with family and friends (Tjørnhøj-Thomsen 2004).[6] Many also felt a sense of relief in eventually telling their families about their special situation, not least because family members—especially the potential grandparents—tended to ask them about having children.

However, openness was selective in various ways. Childless men and women were not open to the same extent with all their friends and acquaintances, nor did they discuss all aspects of their infertility and treatment with them. In discussions about the importance of openness, it was recognized that many found it difficult to practice in reality and that the preoccupation with openness indicates that infertility is experienced as private and intimate. However, it is interesting to note that men and women had very different approaches to openness. Both men and women expressed the view that with their friends and colleagues, men are more closed about their infertility and childlessness. They "don't expose themselves, as women do," and are more "shy." There was also a tendency to be more silent about men's infertility than women's. The vast majority of the infertile men I talked to had told close colleagues or friends about their problem, although the topic had not become a recurring one.

These indications of gender differences in communicative styles do not mean that men are incapable of expressing their feelings. Rather, it means they do not have the same "tradition" as women of discussing such matters and do not feel the same need to talk about the personal and emotional aspects of their infertility and childlessness (Swedin 1996). It could also mean that they speak about such matters in a different kind of language than women do (see Schmidt 1996). Men may have difficulty in finding the right words to talk about their reproductive functions, even when attempting to discuss the subject with other men. One infertile man related how he and his colleagues had discussed a TV program about the decline in sperm quality. He found it particularly interesting that one of his colleagues was unable to say the word "sperm" (in Danish, *sæd*). "He couldn't say 'sperm.' It was so funny. He couldn't say it but referred to 'those tadpoles' instead. Every time he came to the word[s] sperm or sperm quality, he stopped short."

Gendered Childlessness, Gendered Parenthood

There are historic and cultural reasons why men have not had the occasion to talk about and compare notes on their reproductive experiences, and have not built up a tradition of doing so. In general, men have not developed the special "communities of experience" women have created—and continue to reproduce among their friends and colleagues—around their reproductive lives, pregnancies, births, and infant care. Unlike their male partners, the childless women in my study seemed to be faced with female communities from which they felt painfully excluded, such as those celebrating the virtues of motherhood. This sense of exclusion was manifested in feelings of not being heard or understood by the people around them and not being able to take part in their discussions and receive social acknowledgment. As discussed earlier, having children is not simply a question of becoming parents and creating families, but of access to wider social communities that presuppose and transcend the family.

Men did not experience these feelings of exclusion to the same degree. I suggest that this is because they do not have or are only beginning to develop these communities based on the exchange of procreative experiences. In everyday life, they are not confronted with their childlessness to the same degree as women. To a greater extent than women, men can separate infertility and childlessness from their social and working lives and their relationships with other men. As some informants said, they are better able than women to "bury themselves in their work" and thus establish what Wirtberg defines as "pain-free zones" for themselves (1992).

While the childless women in Denmark were constantly forced to think about how they could combine their reproductive lives (fertility treatment and their hoped-for motherhood) with their paid work, men seldom brought up this issue. Moreover, the majority of men did not allow themselves to be as emotionally provoked as women by encounters with pregnant women, prams, and small children. As one man said, "It would be nice to have children, but it's not like I have to stop and swallow a lump in my throat every time I see a pregnant woman." Nor did they report that childlessness affected them in the same way (see Schmidt 1996). They "take one thing at a time" or "take things as they come." Often they expressed that "It's worse of course for my wife" or "It's worse for women."

By focusing on their partner's privation and suffering, men confirmed and emphasized the cultural meanings of motherhood for women's lives and identity, while their own loss and meanings of fatherhood were pushed into the background. Thus, the men in my study also reproduced their own marginalization from the reproductive domain. This by no means suggests that these men were unaffected by their infertility or childlessness. Precisely because they were in a situation where they would have liked to have had children but could not immediately do so, they paid attention to other people's parenthood and other men's fatherhood. As one man said,

> The last two years, every single time a person rode by on a bike I'd find myself looking to see whether there was a child carrier on the bike. That's really something I seem to focus on: well I'll be damned, he actually has a kid, and I wonder how old he is. I wonder what he does and what he's like. Imagine. He's actually a father.

This quote shows that infertile and childless men are to a growing extent confronted with their childlessness, as fathers have become more visible in everyday life and in advertisements. These striking representations of young fathers with their children, and their fellowship with other fathers, suggest other dimensions of manhood and new emerging masculinities (Olsen 1999), in which infertile and childless men could not immediately partake.

Although Danish men and women shared notions and expectations about becoming parents, they also attached different expectations to parenthood and family life. Men's pictures of themselves as parents and fathers were directed toward play, leisure time, outdoor activities, and rough-and-tumble play with slightly older children. Unlike women, men saw play as an important part of their life with children. One man said, "The chance you have to play with children, that's something I'm looking forward to." Women placed greater emphasis on having the chance to experience pregnancy, birth, and breastfeeding. Some men said that very small children (and hence, other people's small children) didn't mean much to them, but all the men emphasized that, just as they would accompany their partners to fertility tests and treatments, they would participate in the pregnancy, birth, and care of the infant. Indeed, some felt better prepared than men without fertility issues, because they "have been through so much" with their partners in connection to fertility treatment. They regarded themselves as more knowledgeable, experienced, and supportive than other men, and better prepared for the drama of the birth.

Some men spoke of their longing to "come home to children," and the desire for children was sometimes verbalized as the desire "to have a family and create a home." One man said, "Both of us wanted to get a house with a garden with a view to have a proper home and family." He thus associated the idea of home with family but also made a distinction between house and home. Seen from this perspective, it is children who make a "house" into a "home" (see Carsten 1997; Schneider 1980). The same man was open about another source of concern: "Just as you can be lonely as a single, so you can be lonely in a twosome," formulating his longing for children and his feeling that something was missing from his relationship with his partner.

Home is where the family is expected to manifest a particularly intimate, exclusive, and close relationship and to engage in the types of activities defining family life (Bourdieu 1996). In speaking of "coming home," the man quoted above saw himself as the family member who does not *stay* at home but *returns* there after work. This reflects a gendered division of labor, which persists in Denmark, even though it was more evident earlier in the twentieth century, when the man as the main breadwinner was physically separated from the home by his work outside, and the home and children were the woman's main domain (Rosenbeck 1987).

The longings of Danish childless men reflected a notion of fatherhood combining elements from both "traditional" and "modern" concepts of the father. To some extent, men portrayed themselves as the main breadwinners and, as such, located outside the domain of home. In general, women were expected to be taking parental leave if the couple's desire for children was fulfilled. But men took it for granted that they would be involved in many of the preparations and rituals connected with pregnancy and birth, and expected they would take part in and devote time each day to caring for the children and being with the family. Several of my informants emphasized that their practice of fatherhood would be different from that of their own fathers. Thus, there were clear signals that Danish men wanted a different kind of parenthood from that shown not only by their fathers but also by their partners—one that will not simply be a copy or adaptation of motherhood.

Gendered Fertility Treatment

When it came to acknowledging and doing something about their childlessness, the women in my study were the ones who took the initiative to find out about doctors, study waiting lists, check out the different treatment options available, and investigate alternative forms of treatment. It was the women who took the initiative to get in touch with other childless couples (via NAICD) and the anthropologist, and it was also the women who spoke most often and asked most questions during the consultation with the doctor (Mason 1993; Schmidt 1996). "The woman is the car—the man is the trailer" was how one childless woman described the division of reproductive labor. As women often emphasized when comparing their reproductive work with that of men, women are the ones who "expose their bodies" to fertility treatment, a process many of them found both physically and psychologically grueling. Regardless of which partner is infertile, the fertility treatment must succeed, if at all, in the female partner's body. The female body, then, attracts a lot of attention in terms of responsibility for a successful outcome.

In a Danish context, both medical personnel and the women involved put great emphasis on the need for the man to be present for the treatment so that he could support his partner and they could be "in it together." The couple made a lot of efforts to coordinate their respective working and leisure times with the various investigations and treatments. This is one of many reasons why fertility treatment is so stressful. By far, the majority of men in my study put great weight on being present, even when it was not actually required (as it is, for example, when they had to produce the necessary sperm at the clinic). As one man said, "After all, it's my child too." Many men felt awkward and sidelined at the clinic, where the focus is on the woman's body. They were worried about whether they would be capable of producing sperm, which at certain clinics must take place through masturbation performed in a small room specifically arranged for that purpose, and where they were required to achieve ejaculation "on command" without the intimacy and bodily context of ordinary sexuality. Men also felt anxiety about whether the quality and amount of their sperm would be sufficient, as it often varies greatly from day to day; their ability to produce sperm of both sufficient quantity and quality was important for their self-confidence.

Men also found it difficult to know the best ways to support and comfort their partners, where they should be, and what they should do or say. As one man said,

> but that thing about having to go and deliver a sperm sample and put it in a cupboard so they can have a look at it. It was like that was my part in the whole thing. And I think that was really weird. Also the fact that my job of becoming a father was, so to speak, taken over by the doctors. Everything that happens takes place between the doctors and my wife. In that sense, I'm kept out of it, but in fact I don't really think I feel bad about that. I just think it's very different from what it would be like if there wasn't any problem about us our having children.

At certain clinics, active efforts were made to counteract men's sense of being sidelined, by allowing them to use the remote control to a monitor that televised one channel of scans of the woman's ovaries gradually being emptied of eggs, and another channel that showed the laboratory's enlargement of the eggs that have been removed. Such visualizing technologies somehow incorporated men into the process of coming into being.

Sperm and Masculinity

It is a shock when the body does not function as assumed. When a person is infertile, the body, its organs, and its products emerge from their normal obscurity as the objects of a subject (Becker 1994; Leder 1990), and become the focus of an almost painful degree of attention. In the course of fertility treatment, the body's organs and products become visible and are the objects of evaluation through means such as ultrasound scans and microscopy. This visibility also generates new stories and narratives about the body and the self.

In Denmark, poor or insufficient sperm quality is a frequent reason for male infertility. In the first instance, men's infertility is investigated through a sperm analysis, in which the lab technician records the number of sperm cells per milliliter of fluid and their mobility, swimming capacity, and appearance. In the laboratory, sperm is only a procreative substance, and sperm quality is a measure (though neither definitive nor even particularly good one) of a man's chance of becoming a father. But for the men involved, sperm is also a sexual substance closely bound up with the sexual act, with the specific role of the man in the story of coming into being, and with male sexuality.

The information that a man has poor-quality sperm—that is, too few sperm cells, or cells that are slow or deformed—inevitably poses a sharp contrast to how sperm is portrayed in Danish children's books and in medical literature, where sperm cells are presented as "numerous," "fast," "active," and "competitive." The lucky winner of the race, the fertilizing sperm, is sometimes shown as wearing a hat and a flower in his buttonhole and carrying a cane, like a real gentleman. In her humorous article, "The Egg and the Sperm," Emily Martin (1991) shows how notions about gender and gender stereotypes are manifested in scientific accounts of fertilization and the nature of sex cells, and how sperm cells—as compared with eggs—are described with adjectives laden with masculinity. Seen from this perspective, there is not much masculinity in poor-quality sperm.

As a rule, men in my study reacted skeptically to the information they had poor-quality sperm. Common statements were, "That can't be true" or "There must have been a mistake." Often, the desire to receive an explanation for infertility gave rise to soul searching and anger about the body or a former behavior or way of life. In an attempt to find an explanation for their infertility, several men speculated whether it was due to their own mother's lifestyle or her use of medical drugs during pregnancy. This subject attracted a good deal of attention in the Danish media, which emphasized women's procreative responsibility, arguing that her lifestyle before and during pregnancy are decisive for her child's life chances.

As mentioned above, to be identified as the infertile partner gives rise to feelings of guilt. Many men felt guilty toward their partner because, even in cases of male infertility, treatment is focused on the woman's body. One man said,

> I've never had any mishaps, so you tend to think that having children is just like everything else, it's just something you do. So it's a

> bit unmanly in a way. I know very well that's rubbish, but even so I
> can't help thinking that I can't do the things I want without dragging
> a whole lot of other people into it. . . . There is a kind of hidden taboo
> around the fact that you're not fully functional as a man, but I have to
> say I felt this most at the beginning. Now I've come to terms with it.

The knowledge that they had poor-quality sperm affected men's
feelings of masculinity, not just in relation to their sexual life, but
also because it restricted their scope as individuals and led them into
an unwished-for dependence on others. In this situation, many men
became painfully aware of the gender asymmetry in the interest
medical research shows in women's as opposed to men's procreative
capacities, and the greater knowledge about female reproduction,
a bias reflected in the availability of treatments. As one man put
it, "As a man you get to know that your sperm quality is reduced.
And that's the end of the story. They don't offer any treatment, they
don't offer you anything." The lack of available treatments for men
increased their feelings of guilt toward their partners.

Although the distinction between sexuality and procreation has
long been culturally accepted—indeed virtually required—in Western society, they are inseparable when it comes to the emotional
handling of infertility. What provokes infertile men's sense of being
unmanly is that male infertility is culturally associated with impotence, loss of virility, and the notion that infertile men are sexually
dysfunctional (Inhorn 2004; also see Goldberg this volume). On the
common-sense level, most people would reject this association, like
the man quoted above who said, "I know very well that's rubbish,
but . . ." As the "but" indicates, common sense does not mean that
their feelings about infertility are not based on this association.

The special situation in which men find themselves leads them
to reflect on and to contest or redefine such cultural models. One
man told, to general amusement, that even though his sperm quality was extremely poor, the sperm still came out with great force,
meaning, of course, that his low-quality sperm had nothing to do
with his sexual life and capacities. Women, too, registered the special relationship between sperm quality, sexuality, and masculinity.
One woman told how she and her partner had avoided telling a
brother-in-law about her husband's poor sperm quality. A previous
remark from the brother-in-law that "he only had to jump on his
wife once, and that was it" led the couple to expect, as the woman
put it, "he would take it to mean my husband wasn't a real man,
and all that stuff." Another woman felt that it was "lucky" for her to
be the infertile partner.

> It's got something to do with it being worse for the man. Role play, that's what it is! There's the idea that after all it's the man that's the provider, I don't know, it's so ingrained. It's as if . . . a man can't lose a limb . . . as if the man has to be intact.

This statement draws an analogy between infertility and an outer, more spectacular handicap that the speaker assumes is worse for a man because, among other things, it imposes a limitation on his physical capacities and role as provider. This view reflects the idea that men—to a greater extent than women—have to be physically "well functioning," "independent" and "able to provide," as if these aspects are implicitly associated with their procreative capacities and sexuality. There are interesting parallels between the "dilemmas of identity" experienced by men suddenly struck by chronic illness or invalidity and those articulated by infertile men and their partners (Charmaz 1995).

Some partners of infertile men gave the impression that the cause of the couple's childlessness lies within their own bodies. They did not want to expose their partners to ridicule and took it upon themselves to protect the men from remarks like "dishwater in the syringe" or "Just send her along to me, mate." In summary, though childlessness was described as being worse for women, infertility was judged as being worse for men.

The Importance of a Biological Child

Although men's chances of having a biological child depend on sperm quality, ICSI has made it possible for men with very poor sperm quality to achieve that. In ICSI, a laboratory technician or biologist selects one of the normal sperm cells and uses a fine needle to inject the sperm directly into the egg. If sperm quality is too poor for this form of treatment, or if the woman does not want to subject herself to the stress involved, the couple may decide to use a sperm donor or to adopt.

Infertile men's statements about using a donor provided good insight as to why it was so difficult for them to accept the use of a donor. The men made explicit those aspects of kinship and fatherhood taken for granted, and showed the complex relationship among kinship, sexuality, and reproduction. In my study, men's initial objection to using a donor revolved around their relationship with their partner and the involvement of a third party in their story of coming into being. Although some men remarked on how the doctor has taken over the job, what bothered them was not so much the doctor's role, but the thought of a strange man's sperm in their partner's body and their own exclusion from the story of coming into being. The sperm donor's contribution was thus associated with a sexual relationship with the partner or with infidelity (Goldberg this volume). Another objection regarded the partners' asymmetrical relationship to the child. Some men and their partners preferred straightforward adoption to the use of a donor, because adoption means the couple would be related to the child on an "equal" footing. The donor was seen as creating an unequal (genetic) connection to the child and as creating an imbalance in the partners' relationship. A third objection to using a donor was the father's relationship with the child. As one man said, "For then the child wouldn't be a part of me. It's as simple as that." A genetic relationship was inevitably associated with kinship and thus with the feelings, obligations, and durability a genetic bond is almost automatically assumed to carry. The prospect of not being genetically connected to the child created insecurity about the possibility of child–parent bonding, as well as the long-term consequences for their relationship if the child were to know about the donation.

The majority of couples intended to tell the child about how he or she was conceived, but had concerns about when and how to inform the child and what the consequences would be. One man expressed his objection to donor sperm:

> So, donor sperm is completely out of the question, it isn't even an option. I couldn't reconcile myself to that. I've given many hours of thought to it. Adoption may be worth discussing, but I'd rather not [go in for it]. What's so enormously difficult with all this is that when I say no, that puts an end to the discussion. And I think that's incredibly egoistic with regard to my partner, who would like to go for it. I couldn't manage ever coming to terms with myself if it was a halfway thing. That would be the worst thing that could happen. It would have catastrophic consequences if I suddenly found out that I couldn't love the child we had had.

This man's statement makes clear that for infertile men, becoming a father also affects their relationship with their partner.[7]

There are indications, however, that despite some men's initial opposition, they would eventually accept the use of donor sperm. Men often felt they could not deny their partner the chance to experience pregnancy and birth because "that is one of the supreme experiences for a woman." Some took the view that in using a donor, rather than adopting a child, the couple would have the mutual chance to care for an unborn child by following their own standards and ideas of responsible behavior during pregnancy. As one man said, "It's also important for us men to follow our wife's pregnancies and births, and make sure that they get the chance to have that experience." When this man's partner became pregnant with donor sperm, he often played Elvis Presley for her pregnant belly. He did what is required of an expectant father (see Han this volume). Because he cannot be genetically connected to the child, he saw a particular advantage in the new expectations for fathers that were promoted in the 1960s, and according to Gillis, "attempted to reconstruct rites of fatherhood that will give symbolic recognition to the expectant father and make him part of the birthing process" (1996:200). Although this applies to all potential fathers, this conception of fatherhood gives some infertile men special resources for (re)defining their own role as fathers.

As expressed above, coming to terms with using donor sperm demands a redefinition of cultural values, not least in order to ensure, despite infertility, continuity in a person's own life story and identity. Some men in my study were able to accept the use of a donor by "emptying" the genetic connection of associations with sexuality, kinship, and inheritance. Their strategy was to distinguish the donor's contribution from notions of the donor as a person (rival) and a parent. In terms of what "stamps" the child, the genetic aspects of fatherhood were played down in favor of the social relatedness created through everyday interaction. The "real" father was redefined: instead of being rooted in genetic connectedness, he became rooted in the relatedness established through care, intimacy, and the child's upbringing (Becker 2000). In the process, these men also sought to redefine ideas about authenticity based on genetic connectedness and origins. One man who had accepted the use of donor sperm said, "I will always be the child's real father," just as he repeatedly stressed that what was at issue was "stamping" the child. After numerous failed attempts at the clinic to inseminate his wife with his own sperm, this man had arrived at the position of "I don't care whether I have my own child. I would just like to be a family."

Conclusion: Infertility and Authenticity

The suffering and longings of infertile men and women must be understood in relation to the disorder that infertility creates in their bodies and in their expectations of a particular life story and identity, one drawing on historically and culturally conditioned notions of kinship and gender. When hoped-for children fail to arrive as expected, this produces a sense of life disruption and social exclusion. Infertility highlights that having children and being parents gives access to social communities and identities in time and space, and that family life and kinship relations are part of and connected to other forms of social communities.

In this chapter, I have shown how gender is a difference that makes a difference in the Danish context of infertility, childlessness, and ARTs. Notions of gender were played out and highlighted in public debates and private dialogues. The infertile and childless men and women in my study referred to gender as a way of marking and giving meaning to specific experiences and practices. In the process, cultural notions about the nature of gender, and therefore of specifically masculine features, were brought to light and challenged or reinforced. Examples include notions of women as open, emotional, and especially concerned with the well-being of the family, and of men as emotionally closed, silent, and lacking in initiative concerning their reproductive lives.

Both men and women expressed the view that men were handling childlessness more easily than their partners. This difference is apparently due to the fact that in everyday life and social interaction men are not—and do not let themselves be—affected by their childlessness to the same degree as women. This again reflects a gender-specific division of reproductive labor and concerns that persists in Denmark and is displayed in notions of motherhood and fatherhood and in the social responses and attentiveness to infertility and childlessness.

The longings of childless people also reflect different expectations of and emphases on motherhood versus fatherhood. It was evident that men and women attached different gendered expectations to their wished-for parenthood and family life. For instance, men's pictures of themselves as fathers included play with their children, while women seldom related these activities to their wished-for motherhood. The notions of relatedness embedded in the expectations of fatherhood embrace masculine features and are very different from those embedded in the expectations of motherhood.

But it is not only the differences between the sexes that are at stake. When men ponder and relate their infertility and childlessness, they refer to their own childhoods and relationships with their partners, parents, siblings, colleagues, friends, and other men. Though there is no doubt that gender makes a difference, it is a difference that is mediated and at times overshadowed by other more relevant differences. In any case, notions of masculinity develop through men's relationship with other men.

In Denmark, as in other Euro-American contexts, notions of kin-ship and gender are connected to a culturally specific story of coming into being, in which bodily and biological processes play a promi-nent symbolic role, not least as a source of ideas about authenticity. Becoming what is understood as a "real" man and a "real" father depends on the body's capacity to be an actor in and a contributor to this particular story. These criteria of authenticity become especially evident when seen from the perspective of infertile men. Male infer-tility is culturally associated with impotence, loss of virility, and sexu-al dysfunction. In order to insist on being manly, infertile men sought to oppose this closely interwoven cultural association among fertility, sexuality, and masculinity, which is also linked to ideas about men as physically independent and as providers. They also had to combat the cultural association between genetic and real fatherhood, and in-sist on other sources of authenticity. This was accomplished by stress-ing and upgrading the social aspects of fatherhood, such as the care and intimacy relating to the upbringing of children.

Acknowledgments

I want to thank the men and women who told me their stories and shared their experiences with me. Thanks to Helene Goldberg, Mar-uska La Cour Mosegaard, and Marcia Inhorn for their support and suggestions in writing this chapter.

Notes

1. Although the concepts of "infertility" and "involuntary childlessness" are often used interchangeably, it is important to distinguish them. In many cases, a couple's involuntary childlessness is caused by the in-fertility of one of the partners, which means that as a rule the term "infertility" refers to an individual (even though the couple may also be infertile without either partner being infertile). The involuntarily childless people who contributed to my study were all heterosexual couples. I use "childless" here for infertile and involuntarily childless people. This term does not include those who have chosen not to have children.
2. "Conjugality" denotes the special form of relatedness existing between partners in a marriage or a marriage-like relationship.
3. The association was founded in 1990 and is countrywide, drawing to-gether a community of people based on their common interests and experiences. It consists of county-based groups whose active mem-bers meet regularly for various activities such as lectures (e.g., about

alternative treatments, psychological problems, and adoption) and visits to clinics. The almost two-year period I spent with couples in the
association coincided with what could be conceptualized as a "liminal"
period in their lives, and was therefore associated with great uncertainty, vulnerability, and suffering. However, it was also a time of intense
reflection. Indeed, Turner describes this phase as a "phase of reflection"
where the ritual subjects are forced to make explicit, redefine, and re-
formulate values hitherto taken for granted (1967:107). For childless
people, this may mean reformulating the values associated with being
able to have one's own, biological children, and redefining kinship to
move away from the focus on genetic connectedness toward a new
focus on caring and intimacy. Because of this intense process of redefining values and making them explicit, the specific time I shared with
childless couples allowed me to develop a rich and varied ethnography
concerning different aspects of relatedness.

4. Daly and Dienhart (1998) draw on George Simmel to understand this
    apparent paradox. Simmel points out that the stranger, by virtue of his
    or her presumed "objectivity," is often met with the most "astonishing
    revelations and admissions which constitute a kind of confession of
    everything the person systematically conceals from his or her near and
    dear" (Simmel 1998:97; author's translation). As Simmel writes, the
    stranger is "free" and "mobile" and therefore not entangled in local and
    family "fixations" (ibid.).

5. The dominant meanings attributed to biology and genetic connect-
    edness in our society are not universally shared, just as knowledge
    about coming into being, and its interpretation, has changed over time.
    Whereas today we emphasize the equal genetic contribution of both fa-
    ther and mother, and the duo genetic theory of reproduction, a mono-
    genetic theory of reproduction prevailed in Europe and the United
    States until the mid-twentieth century: monogenetic in the sense that
    only the man was held to contribute to genesis.

6. A parallel may be drawn here to Michel Foucault's notion of the "con-
    fessing society." Foucault (1980) describes how the "confession"—a
    verbal admission of one's thoughts and actions—has come to play an
    important role in many forms of human relationships in Western so-
    ciety. The confession is always played out in a particular (power) rela-
    tionship between the person confessing and the person who punishes
    or forgives, and it is accompanied by feelings of liberation and relief.

7. My study did not include couples who had used a donor egg. In Den-
    mark, there are very few egg donations, because among other things,
    only women undergoing IVF are legally permitted to donate eggs.

References

Becker, Gay. 1994. "Metaphors in Disrupted Lives: Infertility and Cultural
    Constructions Continuity." *Medical Anthropology Quarterly* 8(4):456–71.

————. 2000. *The Elusive Embryo: How Women and Men Approach New Reproductive Technologies*. Berkeley: University of California Press.

Birenbaum-Carmeli, Daphna, Yoram S. Carmeli, and R. F. Casper. 1995. "Discrimination against Men in Infertility Treatment." *Journal of Reproductive Medicine* 40(8):590–94.

Bourdieu, Pierre. 1996. "On the Family as a Realized Category." *Theory, Culture & Society* 13(3):19–26.

Bouquet, Mary. 1993. *Reclaiming English Kinship: Portuguese Refractions of British Kinship Theory*. Manchester: Manchester University Press.

Carlsen, Elisabeth, Shanna H. Swan, Jørgen Holm Petersen, and Niels E. Skakkebæk. 2005. "Longitudinal Changes in Semen Parameters in Young Danish Men from the Copenhagen Area." *Human Reproduction* 20(4):942–49.

Carsten, Janet. 1997. *The Heat of the Hearth: The Process of Kinship in a Malay Fishing Community*. Oxford: Clarendon.

————, ed. 2000. "Introduction: Cultures of Relatedness." *Cultures of Relatedness*. Cambridge: Cambridge University Press.

Charmaz, Kathy. 1995. "Identity Dilemmas of Chronically Ill Men." In *Men's Health and Illness: Gender Power and the Body*, ed. Donald Sabo and Davis Gordon Frederick. London: Sage.

Daly, Kerry, and Anna Dienhart. 1998. "Navigating the Family Domain: Qualitative Field Dilemmas." In *Doing Ethnographic Research: Fieldwork Settings*, ed. Scott Grills. Thousand Oaks, CA: Sage.

Delaney, Carol. 1991. *The Seed and the Soil: Gender and Cosmology in Turkish Village Society*. Berkeley: University of California Press.

Edwards, Jeanette. 1993. "Explicit Connections: Ethnographic Enquiry in North-West England." In *Technologies of Procreation: Kinship in the Age of Assisted Conception*, ed. Jeanette Edwards, Sarah Franklin, Eric Hirsch, Frances Price, and Marilyn Strathern. Manchester: Manchester University Press.

Edwards, Jeanette, Sarah Franklin, Eric Hirsch, Frances Price, and Marilyn Strathern, eds. 1993. *Technologies of Procreation: Kinship in the Age of Assisted Conception*. Manchester: Manchester University Press.

Foucault, Michel. 1980. *The History of Sexuality: An Introduction*, vol. 1. New York: Vintage Books.

Franklin, Sarah. 1992. "Making Sense of Missed Conceptions: Anthropological Perspectives of Unexplained Infertility." In *Changing Human Reproduction: Social Science Perspectives*, ed. Meg Stacey. London: Sage

————. 1997. *Embodied Progress: A Cultural Account of Assisted Conception*. London and New York: Routledge.

Franklin, Sarah, and Susan McKinnon, eds. 2001. *Relative Values: Reconfiguring Kinship Studies*. Durham: Duke University Press.

Franklin, Sarah, and Helena Ragoné, eds. 1998. *Reproducing Reproduction. Kinship, Power and Technological Innovation*. Philadelphia: University of Pennsylvania Press.

Gillis, John. 1996. *A World of Their Own Making: Myth, Ritual and the Quest of Family Values*. New York: Basic Book.

Hayden, Corinne P. 1995. "Gender, Genetics and Generation: Reformulating Biology in Lesbian Kinship." *Cultural Anthropology* 10(1):1–14.

Hirsch, Eric. 1993. "Negotiated Limits: Interviews in South-East England." In *Technologies of Procreation: Kinship in the Age of Assisted Conception*, ed. Jeanette Edwards, Sarah Franklin, Eric Hirsch, Frances Price and Marilyn Strathern. Manchester: Manchester University Press.

Howell, Signe. 2001. "Self-Conscious Kinship: Some Contest Values in Norwegian Transnational Adoption." In *Relative Values: Reconfiguring Kinship Studies*, ed. Sarah Franklin and Susan McKinnon. Durham: Duke University Press.

Inhorn, Marcia. 1994. *Quest for Conception: Gender, Infertility, and Egyptian Medical Traditions*. Philadelphia: University of Pennsylvania Press.

———. 2004. "Middle Eastern Masculinities in the Age of New Reproductive Technologies: Male Infertility and Stigma in Egypt and Lebanon." *Medical Anthropology Quarterly* 18(2):162–82.

Inhorn, Marcia, and Frank van Balen, eds. 2002. *Infertility around the Globe: New Thinking on Childlessness, Gender, and Reproductive Technologies*. Berkeley: University of California Press.

Jørgensen, Niels, et al. 2001. "Regional Differences in Semen Quality in Europe." *Human Reproduction* 16(5):1012–19.

Koch, Lene. 1989. *Ønskebørn. Kvinder & Reagensglasbefrugtning*. Charlottenlund: Rosinante.

Layne, Linda L., ed. 1999. *Transformative Motherhood: On Giving and Getting in a Consumer Culture*. New York: New York University Press.

Leder, Drew. 1990. *The Absent Body*. Chicago: University of Chicago Press.

Lundin, Susanne. 1997. *Guldägget. Föräldraskap i Biomedicines Tid*. Lund: Historiska Media.

Lundström, Peter. 1998. *Politikens bog om Barnløshed*. Copenhagen: Politikens Forlag.

Mason, Mary-Claire. 1993. *Male Infertility: Men Talking*. New York: Routledge.

Martin, Emily. 1991. "The Egg and the Sperm: How Science Has Constructed a Romance Based on Stereotypical Male-Female Roles." *Signs* 16(3):485–501.

Modell, Judith S. 1994. *Kinship with Strangers: Adoption and Interpretations of Kinship in American Culture*. Berkeley: University of California Press.

Nyboe, Andersen, Anders, Peter Horness, and Søren Ziebe. 1996. *Klar Besked om Barnløshed*. Copenhagen: Aschehough Dansk Forlag A/S.

Nygren, Karl G., and Anders Nyboe Andersen. 2002. "Assisted Reproductive Technology in Europe: Results Generated from European Registers by ESHRE." *Human Reproduction* 17(12):3260–74.

Olsen, Bente Marianne. 1999. *Nye fædre på orlov. En analyse af de kønsmæssige aspekter ved forældreorlovsordninger*. PhD diss., Institute of Sociology, Copenhagen.

Peletz, Michael. 1995. "Kinship Studies in Late Twentieth-Century Anthropology." *Annual Review of Anthropology* 24:343–72.

Rosenbeck, Bente. 1987. *Kvindekøn: Den moderne kvindeligheds historie 1880–1980*. Copenhagen: Gyldendal.

Schmidt, Lone. 1996. *Psykosociale Konsekvenser af Infertilitet og Behandling.* PhD diss., Copenhagen: FADLs Forlag.

Schneider, David M. 1980. *American Kinship: A Cultural Account.* Chicago: University of Chicago Press.

———. 1984. *The Critique of Kinship.* Ann Arbor: University of Michigan Press.

Simmel, George. 1998. *Hvordan er samfundet muligt? Udvalgte sociologiske skrifter.* Copenhagen: Gyldendal.

Simpson, Robert. 1994. "Bringing the 'Unclear' Family into Focus: Divorce and Re-Marriage in Contemporary Britain." *Man* 29(4):831–51.

———. 1997. Representations and the Re-Presentation of Family: An Analysis of Divorce Narratives. In *After Writing Culture: Epistemology and Praxis in Contemporary Anthropology,* ed. Allison James, Jenny Hockey, and Andrew Dawson. London: Routledge.

Strathern, Marilyn. 1992a. *After Nature: English Kinship in the Late Twentieth Century.* Cambridge: Cambridge University Press:.

———. 1992b. *Reproducing the Future: Anthropology, Kinship and the New Reproductive Technologies.* Manchester: Manchester University Press.

———. 1993a. "Introduction: 'A Question of Context.'" In *Technologies of Procreation: Kinship in the Age of Assisted Conception,* ed. Jeanette Edwards, Sarah Franklin, Eric Hirsch, Frances Price, and Marilyn Strathern. Manchester: Manchester University Press.

———. 1993b. "Regulation, Substitution and Possibility." In *Technologies of Procreation: Kinship in the Age of Assisted Conception,* ed. Jeanette Edwards, Sarah Franklin, Eric Hirsch, Frances Price, and Marilyn Strathern. Manchester: Manchester University Press.

———. 1995. "Displacing Knowledge: Technology and the Consequences for Kinship." In *Conceiving the New World Order: The Global Politics of Reproduction,* ed. Faye D.Ginsburg and Rayna Rapp. Berkeley: University of California Press.

Swedin, Göran. 1996. "Modern Swedish Fatherhood: The Challenges and the Opportunities." *Reproductive Health Matters* 4(7):25–33.

Tjørnhøj-Thomsen, Tine. 1999. *Tilblivelseshistorier. Barnløshed, slægtskab og forplantningsteknologi i Danmark.* PhD diss., Institute of Anthropology, Copenhagen.

———. 2002. "Fra forældreskab til barnløshed." *Kvinder, Køn & Forskning* 11(1):5–18.

———. 2003a. "Childlessness, Procreative Technologies and the Creation of New Mythologies." *FOLK,* 45:33–59.

———. 2003b. "Samværet: Tilblivelser i tid og rum." In *Ind i verden: En grundbog i antropologisk metode,* ed. Kirsten Hastrup. Copenhagen: Hans Reitzels Forlag.

———. 2004. "Slægtskab: Tilblivelse, forbundethed og fællesskab." In *Viden om verden: En grundbog i antropologisk analyse,* ed. Kirsten Hastrup. Copenhagen: Hans Reitzels Forlag.

———. 2005. "Close Encounters with Infertility and Procreative Technology." In *Managing Uncertainty. Ethnographic Studies of Illness, Risk and the*

Struggle for Control, ed. Vibeke Steffen, Richard Jenkins, and Hanne Jessen. Copenhagen: Museum Tusculanum Press.

Turner, Victor. 1967. *The Forest of Symbols*. Ithaca: Cornell University Press.

Weston, Kath. 1991. *Families We Choose: Lesbians, Gays, Kinship*. New York: Columbia University Press.

———. 1995. "Forever Is a Long Time: Romancing the Real in Gay Kinship Ideologies." In *Naturalizing Power: Essays in Feminist Cultural Analysis*, ed. Sylvia Yanagisako and Carol Delaney. London: Routledge.

———. 1997. "The Virtual Anthropologist." In *Anthropological Locations: Boundaries and Grounds of a Field Science*, ed. Akhil Gupta and James Ferguson. Berkeley: University of California Press.

Wirtberg, Ingegerd. 1992. *His and Hers Childlessness*. Stockholm: Department of Psychiatry and Psychology, Karolinska Instiutet.

Yanagisako, Sylvia, and Carol Delaney. 1995. "Naturalizing Power." In *Naturalizing Power: Essays in Feminist Cultural Analysis*, ed. Sylvia Yanagisako and Carol Delaney. London: Routledge.

———, eds. 1995. *Naturalizing Power: Essays in Feminist Cultural Analysis*. London: Routledge.

Chapter 10

MALE GENITAL CUTTING: MASCULINITY, REPRODUCTION, AND MALE INFERTILITY SURGERIES IN EGYPT AND LEBANON

Marcia C. Inhorn

For nearly two decades, female genital cutting (aka female circumcision, female genital mutilation, female genital surgery) has been a topic of global reproductive health and human rights activism. It began with a Western feminist campaign to eradicate this practice and evolved into a more culturally nuanced, indigenous activism seen in many African and Middle Eastern countries where the procedure continues to be practiced. The controversies surrounding the Western-spearheaded campaign to eliminate female genital cutting from the globe have evoked, on the one hand, images of child abuse and torture and neocolonial visions of culturally disrespectful Eurocentric paternalism (or maternalism, as the case may be) on the other hand. Perhaps no other female reproductive health topic has elicited such global outrage, as shown by American medical anthropologist Ellen Gruenbaum in *The Female Circumcision Controversy: An Anthropological Perspective* (2001), which offers a deeply sensitive and highly nuanced account of both sides of the debate from the author's standpoint as a long-term ethnographer of Sudan.

What is missing in the global outcry over genital cutting is an acknowledgment that males around the world are also having their genitals cut, beginning in infancy and ending in late adulthood. Worldwide, male circumcision rates are estimated to be between 25 and 40 percent (Circlist 2004). In the Muslim world, Israel, and the United States, circumcision rates are much higher (between 75 and 100 percent), with males routinely circumcised shortly after birth or in early childhood, either because of religious mandates (in the Jewish and Islamic worlds) or because of hygienic and accompanying aesthetic preferences and rationales. The American Academy of Pediatrics considers male circumcision to be an elective surgery, with no compelling medical benefits that warrant it as a routine procedure for newborns. Nevertheless, the majority of parents still circumcise their sons at birth or in the first week of life, with an estimated 1.2 million newborn males circumcised in the United States annually at a cost of between $150 and $270 million (American Academy of Pediatrics 1999). Although male circumcision is clearly accompanied by pain and discomfort, especially in the absence of effective local anesthesia, and is usually practiced on children who have no say in the matter or power to prevent the surgery from taking place, male circumcision has not evoked a similar global response. Presumably, this is because male circumcision has different sexual implications than female circumcision. To wit, one of the reasons female circumcision has evoked such a visceral response among Western feminists is that it challenges Eurocentric notions of female orgasm and women's ability to achieve sexual pleasure (Lane and Rubinstein 1996; Parker 1995). The same is not true for male circumcision; though it, too, may affect sexual pleasure, it is usually not linked to the inhibition of male orgasm, hence the lack of comparable prioritization as a global health issue. In other words, when it comes to cutting young genitals, there is a striking lack of comparability in global reactions to male versus female versions of the procedure.

Furthermore, males continue to undergo genital cutting well into adulthood, for purposes very much related to their reproductive futures. Globally, many men undergo vasectomy, or surgical sterilization, as a permanent form of birth control. Vasectomy rates in China and the United States are 10 and 14 percent, respectively, but even in semirural, conservative regions of Oaxaca, Mexico, some men are choosing vasectomy as a way to share the contraceptive burden and reproductive "suffering" of their wives, as shown by anthropologist Matthew Gutmann (2007). In addition, vasectomy in Oaxaca is viewed by some men in Gutmann's study as a way to enhance pregnancy-free extramarital affairs. Either way, the use of vasectomy in Oaxaca serves as a form of male participation in contraception, one of the goals being promoted after the International Conference on

Population and Development (ICPD), hosted in Cairo, Egypt, more than a decade ago (Dudgeon and Inhorn this volume).

Sharing the reproductive suffering of wives through male genital cutting may manifest itself differently in different parts of the world, including Cairo. In the Middle East, many men are willing to undergo painful male genital cutting to *enhance*, rather than inhibit, male fertility. Specifically, a little-known surgery called "varicocelectomy" is promoted by Middle Eastern urological surgeons as a way to maximize fertility in subfertile men as well as men whose wives are infertile. Varicoceles are varicose-type dilations of the scrotal veins that drain the testes that occur in about 15 percent of all men. Supposedly, if left untreated, they lead to a progressive decline in semen quality, which may be related to male infertility. Thus, urological surgeons have promoted varicocelectomies as a way to improve semen quality, even in the absence of well-designed studies to prove their efficacy in helping to achieve pregnancy (Kamischke and Nieschlag 1998).

Furthermore, in the Middle Eastern region, some urologists convince fertile men that they, too, should undergo varicocelectomy in order to prevent the possibility that a small, subclinical varicocele will lead to future male infertility problems. Men in the Middle East who are otherwise unlikely candidates for genital surgery end up agreeing with urologists to put their testicles "on the line" (in this case, the operating table) in order to stave off future reproductive problems and to share in their wives "quests for conception" (Inhorn 1994). Although varicocelectomies are part of an often-futile quest for enhanced reproductive fitness, the eagerness of some entrepreneunal Middle Eastern urologists to perform these surgeries, as well as the willingness of many men to undergo them, bespeaks the importance of fertility as a major component of Middle Eastern masculinity and marriage.

This chapter explores the relationship of varicocelectomy and other related forms of genital cutting to social norms of masculinity in the Middle East. The chapter begins by examining the considerable controversy over varicocelectomy that has emerged within the Western biomedical community. Despite a vociferous debate over the efficacy of this surgery and the introduction of new, improved techniques to overcome male infertility, varicocelectomy continues to be practiced widely in the Middle East, in part because of patient demand. But why do men want varicocelectomy? And what do they have to say about their experiences? The chapter's focus shifts from biomedical discourse on varicocelectomy to patient discourse among men who have undergone the surgery. Although most men

seem to experience postoperative "buyer's remorse," their motivations for undergoing varicocelectomy are powerful. On the one
hand, they can demonstrate their commitment to marriage—in a
region of the world where marriage is highly valued (Inhorn 1994).
The very marks of varicocelectomy left on a man's body symbolize
this shared suffering. On the other hand, varicocelectomy holds the
promise of increased fertility in a region of the world where fertility and manhood are closely related. Indeed, varicocelectomy cannot be understood without examining Middle Eastern masculinity,
which in turn, requires contextualization within the wider sphere
of Middle Eastern gender studies, the final topic of this chapter. The
ultimate goal of this chapter is to reveal why a little-known but
biomedically controversial urological surgery is so popular in the
Middle East. To answer this question, I begin with my 1988 journey
to the region.

Situating Male Genital Cutting: Research
Settings, Methods, and Prevalence Rates

The importance of male genital cutting in the Middle East became
apparent to me in the first weeks of my doctoral research in Alexandria, Egypt, in the fall of 1988. An Egyptian physician who agreed
to review a semistructured reproductive history interview guide I
had constructed laughed when he read my naive questions about
vasectomy. I had assumed that some Egyptian men might choose
vasectomy as a form of contraception and that some might become
secondarily infertile due to a previous vasectomy. But according to
this physician, "No Egyptian man agrees to a vasectomy." On the
contrary, he told me, men in Egypt have surgeries to *promote* their
fertility. Over time this statement was repeated to me by other Middle Eastern physicians and women I interviewed. The study that
I conducted in Alexandria included 190 married Egyptian women
(Inhorn 1994), 100 of whom were infertile and 90 of whom were
fertile. None of their husbands used vasectomy as a form of permanent contraception, because, as their wives told me, Egyptian men's
ongoing ability to produce offspring is perceived by them to be crucial to their masculinity.

When I returned to Cairo in 1996, to conduct a study of in vitro
fertilization (IVF) among infertile Egyptian couples, I discovered
that fertility-enhancing surgeries were indeed being conducted on
infertile Egyptian men. Among the sixty-six middle- to upper-class
couples I interviewed in two Cairo-based IVF clinics, 70 percent

were presenting for IVF primarily because of male infertility problems, and 17 percent of the men in the study had undergone a varicocelectomy to supposedly overcome their infertility problems (Inhorn 2003). Some had undergone this surgery twice, due to failure of a previous repair or a recurrence of the varicocele. In at least one case, the surgery itself caused the iatrogenic outcome of obstructive azoospermia, or lack of any sperm in the ejaculate due to a blockage of the epididymis.

The high prevalence of both male infertility and varicocelectomy in Egypt piqued my curiosity. Thus, I resolved to undertake a study of male infertility and its treatment in the Middle East, in the midst of the massive globalization of new reproductive technologies in this part of the world (Inhorn 2003). In January 2003, I embarked on an eight-month study of Middle Eastern masculinities in the age of new reproductive technologies in Beirut, Lebanon (Inhorn 2004a). I was fortunate to gain ethnographic access to two of the busiest and most successful IVF clinics in central Beirut (Inhorn 2004b). Between these two clinics, I was able to recruit 220 Lebanese, Syrian, and Lebanese-Palestinian men into my study; 120 of them were infertile cases (i.e., based on spermogram results and World Health Organization definitions of male infertility), and 100 were fertile controls (i.e., the husbands of infertile women whose spermogram results showed them to have normal sperm parameters). This epidemiological case-control design also served important ethnographic purposes; it allowed me to understand the experiences and perspectives of infertile men as well as men who were *not* infertile but who were experiencing childless marriages.

I collected a large amount of data during the eight-month study period in Beirut. This included 220 complete eight-page reproductive history/epidemiological questionnaires, which I administered verbally to each man in the study; 1,200 pages of qualitative interview transcripts, generated from open-ended interviews with all of the men in the study and some of their wives; more than 200 pages of interview transcripts generated from open-ended interviews with six IVF physicians, two embryologists, and one IVF unit head nurse; 550 pages of field notes, based on participant observation and informal interviews and conversations with staff and patients at the two IVF clinics; and more than 200 blood samples, which were frozen in the Beirut IVF laboratories and then hand-carried by me via airplane to the United States for purposes of toxic metal analysis.

This chapter is based primarily on reproductive history and ethnographic data from a 2003 Lebanese study. As I was to discover,

55 of the 121 infertile men in the Lebanese study—exactly 45 percent—had undergone varicocelectomies. Four of these men had undergone the operation twice and one man a staggering three times!
Twenty-two of these men (18 percent) had had both testicles ma-
nipulated in the surgery; sometimes they showed me the incision
scars in both their right and left inguinal areas. Five men suffered
from serious complications, including formation of a hydrocele (i.e.,
"bag of water" forming around the testis), which required second
surgeries. The vast majority of the infertile men who had undergone varicocelectomy noted, with defeat and anger, that the varicocelectomy was not successful, leading to no improvement in their
low sperm counts. Furthermore, three of the infertile men in the
study had had varicocelectomy surgeries to supposedly overcome
azoospermia—a complete absence of sperm in the ejaculate that is
clearly *not* caused by a varicocele. Ultimately, all of the azoospermic
men in the study (12 out of 120, or 10 percent) ended up undergoing testicular aspirations or biopsies, another form of male genital
cutting in which sperm are drawn out directly from the testicles. In
total, 64 of the 120 infertile controls in the study—53 percent—had
undergone one or more genital surgeries as part of the male infertility treatment quest.

These high figures among infertile men may seem less surprising
than the data from fertile men in Lebanon. Stunningly, eighteen of
the 100 fertile controls (18 percent) in the study had also undergone
varicocelectomy, in six cases before marriage. According to these
men, physicians had convinced them that small varicoceles detected
on routine exams could lead to future male fertility impairments;
thus, they became convinced of the need for surgery. Among the
rest of the fertile men who had undergone a varicocelectomy following marriage, it constituted the male contribution to the infertility treatment quest. Ultimately, three of the fertile men suffered
complications from varicocelectomies, including hydroceles neces-
sitating additional surgery. However, these men were fortunate in
that repeat genital surgeries did not impair their fertility.

The high percentage of varicocelectomy surgeries among both infertile and fertile men in Lebanon might make sense if varicocelectomies could truly improve low sperm counts or prevent low sperm
counts from developing. However, the efficacy of varicocelectomy
as a therapeutic and preventive surgery remains seriously in doubt.
In the next section, I briefly review the Western biomedical debate
surrounding varicocelectomy, contrasting it with the other forms of
male genital cutting performed on infertile men as part of assisted
reproduction. Special attention is paid to Lebanese IVF physicians'

and embryologists' critical discourse on varicocelectomy and their explanations for why the surgery continues to be practiced in such great numbers in Lebanon.

Biomedical Discourses of Male Genital Cutting

The Varicocelectomy Controversy

Varicoceles are varicose veins in the scrotum, which can make the scrotum feel like it contains a "bag of worms." Varicoceles may be large or small, with the small ones detectable only by an advanced technology such as ultrasound. About 15 percent of all men have varicoceles; however, 21 to 41 percent of men with deterioration of the spermogram (i.e., infertile men) present with a varicocele (Takihara, Sakatoku, and Cockett 1991). In the largest varicocele prevalence study to date, undertaken among 9,034 male partners of couples consulting for infertility, the World Health Organization (WHO) (1992) determined that 25 percent of the men with sperm defects had varicoceles, as opposed to only 12 percent of the men with normal spermograms. Thus, the WHO study concluded that varicoceles are clearly associated with a deterioration of testicular function and subfertility, although not in all males. Furthermore, the causal pathophysiology, or why varicocelectomies lead to subfertility, remains unclear. Four causal mechanisms—disorders of thermoregulation, endocrine anomalies, biochemical anomalies, and hemodynamic anomalies—have been proposed (Audebert 2004), with the most commonly cited reason being elevated intrascrotal temperature, which is damaging to sperm production (Irvine 1998).

Although there is a substantial body of evidence suggesting that varicoceles cause progressive testicular damage, considerable controversy exists in the biomedical community over whether the correction of a varicocele through varicocelectomy actually improves fertility and pregnancy outcomes. Many urological surgeons, including in the Western countries (Goldstein 1995; Laven et al. 1992; Madgar et al. 1995), support varicocelectomy as a means of tying off damaged veins and restoring sperm production. In the United States, varicocelectomies remain popular and are advertised on clinic websites.

What is a varicocelectomy? First, it does not constitute a direct form of testicular cutting, although the testicles are physically handled in the operation. Namely, a small incision is made in the lower abdomen on the side of the affected testicle. The affected testicle is "delivered" (much like a baby is delivered through cesarean section) through the incision so that the surgeon can examine the testicle and its circulatory system. Offending veins are "ligated" (tied off, as in tubal ligation), and the testicle is returned to the scrotum. With the advent of microsurgical techniques (using a surgical magnifying microscope), the surgeon can find and preserve the tiny testicular artery that brings blood to the testes, and also identify and preserve the lymphatic system, eliminating the risk of hydrocele. Thus, microsurgery helps to avoid the three most common complications of varicocelectomy—hydrocele, testicular artery injury, and varicocele recurrence. Furthermore, these newer microsurgical techniques have allowed the surgery to be done on an outpatient basis. In the United States, for example, about 30,000 men undergo varicocelectomy annually, the vast majority of them sent home on the same day with pain medication (Virginia Mason Medical Center 2004).

Although urological surgeons are eager to promote varicocelectomy as a safe, simple, outpatient procedure that reestablishes proper testicular blood flow, hence improving male fertility through enhanced sperm production, the reproductive medicine community is less sanguine about the procedure. As pointed out in a review of male infertility diagnosis and treatment methods called "Do We Treat the Male or His Gamete?" Belgian reproductive medical specialist Devroey and colleagues (1998) argue that no peer-reviewed data based on well-designed clinical studies are available to demonstrate the benefit of varicocelectomy in overcoming male infertility. Thus, they conclude that "conventional therapies," including varicocelectomy, are "empirical and ineffective" in the treatment of male infertility (183). In the same issue of *Human Reproduction*, German reproductive medical specialists Kamischke and Nieschlag published a review of "Conventional Treatments of Male Infertility in the Age of Evidence-Based Andrology" (1998). As they pointed out, evidence-based medicine demands "high-quality, properly designed, truly randomized, placebo-controlled" studies, which have "pregnancy as the main outcome measure" (67). With varicocelectomy, "the purported improvement of male fertility has hardly been assessed by controlled clinical trials aiming to appraise pregnancy rates" (68). In a properly randomized, controlled, prospective trial, which compared a varicocelectomy treatment group with a control group that received clinical infertility counseling over a twelve-month period, no significant differences in the cumulative pregnancy rate of the two groups were found (Nieschlag, Hertile, Fischedick, and Behre. 1995). Thus, Kamischke and Nieschlag concluded that "intervention can no longer be recommended," because "it remains questionable whether interventive treatment is superior to no treatment or to counseling in terms of fertility" (1998:69).

In the years since the first major critiques of varicocelectomy were published, the evidence against it has mounted. According to a WHO–sponsored report (Vayena, Rowe, and Griffin 2001), varico-celectomies are no longer warranted in treatment of male infertility. Specifically, a meta-analysis of randomized controlled studies has failed to show "any benefit of this approach" in the 23 percent of infertile men presenting with a varicocele (Tournaye 2001). Indeed, "less than twenty percent of men with reproductive failure have po-tentially treatable conditions for which a rational or proven effective treatment is available" (Tournaye 2001:83).

The Introduction of ICSI

Instead of surgical treatment on the male genital tract to overcome male infertility, most evidence points to treatments that manipulate the male gamete—namely, the spermatozoon. In Belgium in 1992, intracytoplasmic sperm injection (ICSI) was introduced for this pur-pose. A variant of IVF, ICSI requires only a single viable spermatozo-oan, which is injected directly into an oocyte by means of a micro-manipulator on a high-powered microscope. ICSI essentially "forces" fertilization to occur, even with very low sperm counts and poor sperm motility. It has proven "highly efficient in cases of severe male infertility that would otherwise be untreatable" (Tournaye 2001:84).

Even in cases of azoospermia, where no spermatozoa are found in the ejaculate, sperm can be removed directly from the testi-cles for use in the ICSI procedure (Devroey et al. 1998). Testicular sperm can be retrieved by different techniques, including testicu-lar sperm extraction, which refers to an open excisional testicu-lar biopsy; testicular sperm aspiration, which refers to methods by which testicular sperm are aspirated from the testicles; and fine-needle aspiration, in which thin-gauge needles are used to aspirate sperm from the testicles. These techniques are performed under either general or local anesthesia. As a form of testicular "needle-work," they are usually accompanied by significant pain and dis-comfort.[1] However, for azoospermic men, ICSI with testicular ex-traction of sperm represents the only hope for producing biological offspring. In other words, ICSI has brought with it a new form of male genital cutting, but one that has proven remarkably effective in the production of offspring among azoospermic men who would otherwise be permanently sterile.

Since the early 1990s ICSI, with and without testicular cutting, has been used extensively around the world to produce offspring for infertile males. A cumulative live birth rate of 60 percent has been reported after five cycles of ICSI in patients under thirty-eight using it as their first line of treatment (Osmanagaoglu et al. 1999). Moreover, fertilization failures are rare (2.8 percent) in men who produce sperm in their ejaculate (Tournaye 2001). Thus, ICSI is now the preferred method for overcoming male infertility in assisted reproduction centers around the world, including in the Middle East.

The Middle East boasts a booming private industry in assisted reproduction (Inhorn 2003). Egypt, for example, hosts fifty IVF centers for a population of seventy million and tiny Lebanon, with its three to five million inhabitants (depending on which estimate is used), boasts approximately fifteen IVF centers, one of the highest per capita rates in the world. In both Egypt and Lebanon, ICSI is routinely used in cases of male infertility, following its introduction in Egypt in 1994. Thus, ICSI has enabled thousands of infertile Arab men to become biological fathers (Inhorn 2003).

Views of Varicocelectomy from IVF Clinicians

Given the success of ICSI in the region, the question remains as to why so many varicocelectomies continue to be performed on Middle Eastern men. This is a question I posed in interviews with six Lebanese IVF physicians, as well as two embryologists and an IVF nurse. Their responses to the varicocelectomy question were telling. The doctor with perhaps the most to say about varicocelectomy explained it this way:

> You know, varicocelectomy, it's probably one of the most common surgeries done here. I don't know why. Basically, there is a big difference in the concept of the effect of varicocele on the semen parameters between urologists and infertility specialists. It's very common, whenever a urologist is checking a man and finding a small varicocele without even sometimes checking his semen analysis, [that] he will do a varicocelectomy. And you know, sometimes the effect is worse on the sperm later on. So, definitely, there should be strict indications to do these varicocelectomies.
>
> I know at least in the army here, they do a checkup for everybody. Everyone who wants to join the army, they do check up for this varicocele in the genital exam. And everyone who has a varicocele

is subject to varicocelectomy. So, imagine—it is said in the literature [that] fifteen percent of men have an anatomic varicocele. So if everybody has varicocelectomy, all the patients that have been coming from the army or are related to the military, they have a high incidence of varicocelectomy. And most of them ended up having oligospermia [low sperm count]. To start with, it was a little bit low, [but] it ended up very severe oligo.

Another IVF physician explained that Lebanese urologists need to believe in the efficacy of varicocelectomy in order to claim competence and expertise in the world of infertility:

I think many urologists still feel that varicocele remains a major problem. And some even believe that if the semen parameters are normal and you allow it [varicocele] to remain, it may actually affect the semen parameters. But actually, the trend has changed, [as of] some fifteen years ago, ten years ago. I would say more in Europe than in the US. There was a urology conference [in a Beirut suburb] some four years ago, and some European urologists were brought in here to stress the fact that varicocelectomy should not be done indiscriminately. And then, after a whole day of conference, they had an interactive button on each table so that everyone could share his or her view. So then they asked several questions to see if there has been a change in the views of the people present. When they reached the question of varicocelectomy, they gave a case and they said, "Do you think a varicocelectomy should be done?" And 90 percent responded "yes."

When I asked this physician if Lebanese urologists want to do varicocelectomies as a lucrative form of surgery, he replied, "The main reason is money." He added, "Some still hold it to be the only contribution urologists can have toward the fertility problem." Another Lebanese IVF physician, who had given a presentation at the Beirut conference, said,

It's really difficult to convince urologists of the evidence that [varicocelectomy] has no role in improving the pregnancy rate. Actually, I gave a talk in a urology meeting four years ago here in Beirut. It was a regional meeting, and so I gave a talk about varicoceles, and I think that everybody hated me in that room.

When I asked whether it was because they perceived him to be taking away their income, he remarked,

I think most of them, they do it for the money. It's really very easy to convince somebody with a mild defect of the spermogram or oligospermia [i.e., low sperm count] that he has an indication [for varicocelectomy].

These themes were repeated in virtually every interview with Lebanese physicians and embryologists. First, they described varicocelectomies as unwarranted but stressed that the majority of infertile Lebanese men and many fertile men with small varicoceles still undergo them. Second, they criticized urologists in Lebanon for performing varicocelectomies with great abandon. They said urologists need to perform varicocelectomies if they are to attract infertile patients and make money off this large patient population. Third, they stressed that it is easy to convince a vulnerable infertile man that a varicocelectomy will be the solution to his infertility problem. Infertile men are, in effect, an "easy sell," as most of them would do anything to overcome this difficult and emasculating condition. Finally, because infertility is a threat to masculinity, even fertile men may be convinced by urologists to undergo a varicocelectomy, believing that their future fertility is at stake.

These issues were emphasized in an informal conversation I had with three embryologists, all at the same IVF clinic. They explained to me that each of them had a brother who had undergone a varicocelectomy. In one case, the brother had an excellent sperm count—140 million before and after the surgery—so the varicocelectomy was clearly unwarranted. But a urologist had convinced him that this might help his wife to become pregnant. It did not; after two years of marriage, his wife was still not pregnant. In another case, the brother had a "borderline" sperm count of 35 million—still well above the WHO definition of 20 million as a low sperm count. A urologist convinced him to undergo a varicocelectomy, which did nothing to change the sperm count or to overcome pain with sexual intercourse, which was likely due to his childhood circumcision. In the third case, the embryologist had argued with his brother *not* to have the varicocelectomy, telling him that it was a useless operation. But his brother was convinced by the urologist's advice and went ahead with the varicocelectomy anyway—again, for naught. When I asked the embryologists why all three of their educated brothers had undertaken unnecessary varicocelectomies, they attributed it to physician avarice. Varicocelectomies are money-making ventures for urologists, who can charge US$1,000 for their services (in an economy where the average physician has a monthly salary of US$2,000) plus generate substantial income for a hospital and business for its operating room.[2] Unlike in the United States, varicocelectomies in Lebanon are performed in the hospital (but not necessarily with an advanced surgical microscope), with additional hospital charges and operating-room fees accruing to the patient. Given that monthly household incomes in Lebanon are well below US$1,000, the surgery is a significant sacrifice for Lebanese families to make.

One of the three embryologists described the varicocelectomy situation in Lebanon as a kind of urological "abuse" of men, especially infertile ones who are under significant social pressure to impregnate their wives.

> I think [the men in this clinic] were kind of abused by the urologist. You know, I think any man, [he] goes to be checked. They tell him, "You know, you could have a varicocele," or something. I think they [urologists] abuse it just for doing operations on patients. Because mostly before and after the operation, the sperm doesn't change quality. In some cases, it might be effective, but not in all of them. I know a lot of people who had the operation and the sperm stayed the same. [And] that's not counting sometimes that it gets worse. Some of them [urologists], they abuse this kind of operation. You know, there are several grades in the varicocele. Sometimes it's Grade I or Grade II; these don't need to be operated. If it's a Grade III or Grade IV, these need an operation. So the urologists, they start doing the operations at Grade I. Anything they see, they just want to make the operation.

When I asked this embryologist whether Lebanese urologists might reconsider shifting from doing varicocelectomies to vasectomies in order to offer useful surgical skills, he remarked,

> Well, there is a difference in the population in the thinking between the Eastern countries and the Western countries. Here, it's very important for men to have children. It's very important—this is like the goal of their life almost. In England, they can live without children, without any problem. But here, there is social stress and family stress that keeps on pressuring people to have children. Men just have to have kids in order to continue to be a real man. This is the popular thinking.

In short, vasectomies cannot become a popular surgery in Lebanon, because they eliminate fertility potential. On the contrary, varicocelectomies offer men the hope of improved fertility and the easy production of offspring, which, according to this embryologist, are "like the goal of their life." Thus, it could be argued that Lebanese urologists are simply offering a lucrative service that men want in order to fulfill their social and ego needs. But the question remains, what do men want? Why do men agree to undergo varicocelectomy, and what do they have to say about their experiences? These questions are explored in the next section.

Men's Experiences of Male Genital Cutting

Buyer's Remorse

For the many men in this study, varicocelectomy stood out as their only experience of hospitalization and surgery. Most men were proud of their good health, and many commented that they rarely, if ever, visited a physician. Yet, nearly half of the infertile men and nearly one-fifth of the fertile men had undergone a varicocelectomy operation, including several who had undergone the surgery before marriage or more than once. Most had consented to the surgery, because a doctor they trusted had recommended it as a way to improve their sperm count or, in the case of fertile men, to preserve their future fertility. Most were stoic about the surgery, saying it was not too painful and that they had recovered without complications. They could always indicate whether the operation had been performed on one or both testicles, based on recalling in which side(s) of the lower abdomen the incisions had been made. Some men stood to show me their incisions without embarrassment, much as they showed me their gunshot and shrapnel wounds from living through the Lebanese civil war.

But stoicism gave way to anger and remorse among a significant number of men in the study. The critique of varicocelectomy by Lebanese infertility specialists also emerged in interviews with men, including those who had experienced complications from the operation; those who had experienced no improvement in their semen parameters or whose sperm counts had worsened following the operation; and those who believed they had been duped into a varicocelectomy by physicians. The angry and/or remorseful men, who saw themselves as having undertaken an unnecessary operation at the hands of an unscrupulous and greedy urologist, were the majority. Only a handful of men felt that they (or, more accurately, their sperm counts) had benefited from the surgery. A few examples are illustrative of the overwhelmingly critical discourse of men who had undergone a varicocelectomy, only to find themselves in a Lebanese IVF clinic facing ongoing infertility problems.

One Lebanese man, who resided permanently in West Africa, returned to Lebanon after his brief first marriage to a cousin broke up.[3] Seeking a solution to his infertility, he underwent a varicocelectomy in 1997 with, in his words, "no improvement." In his view, "The doctors here are all liars. I didn't even have it [a varicocele], but I did it because the doctor told me to."

Another man whose first wife divorced him because of his infertility problems described the varicocelectomies he undertook twice, once within each marriage:

In 1985, I did my first varicocelectomy, then two times, in the first marriage and the second marriage. Maybe this operation was a mistake. They did something wrong in the second operation and my testicle became swollen on the right—very swollen for two months. I went to a doctor and he said that there were five ccs of water on the right, and on the left, two ccs of water in the testicle. He did another operation to drain the testicles. And in this last operation, they told me it killed the cells. There was an infection, and they had to drain it.

When I asked him why he had been willing to undergo two varicocelectomies, he said,

In Lebanon twenty-five years ago, anyone who has a problem having children, they directly tell him to do a varicocelectomy. The doctors here, they say you have to do it. But before the operation, my percentage [of sperm motility] was high, and after the operation, it decreased. It was futile.

Another man described a varicocelectomy he had undertaken before marriage:

I didn't have any serious varicocele problem, but I used to follow doctors' advice. I did it just so the doctor would be working. These doctors do the operation for materialistic purposes. Only one doctor told me to do it. I did a Doppler [ultrasound] at [a hospital in Southern Lebanon], and they said there is no varicocele. But this one doctor said, "Your testicle is small; you need this varicocelectomy." So I did it.

This man was one of several in the study who had been imprisoned during the Lebanese civil war. In this man's case, his testicular problems stemmed from genital beatings he sustained while a prisoner in Southern Lebanon and a series of testicular operations he undertook after his release. For him, the varicocelectomy represented a final genital operation in a series of agonizing genital events, which he described in graphic detail.

Another man, also wrongfully imprisoned during the Israeli invasion of Southern Lebanon in 1982, described the complications of his varicocelectomy seventeen years later:

The operation was a failure. It caused complications. I had water retention in the testicles, and they were swollen for two years, and the swelling was increasing. There was a "bag of water," and I did another surgery to remove the water. So the [sperm] count [before the operation] was twenty-two to twenty-three million and the motility stayed seventy percent. But after the surgery to remove the water—this was in 2002—there were no sperms. After the operation, it went to zero.

I took a course of medications [which he names] after the operation. After the medicines, the count increased from 100,000 to 1 million.

When I asked him if the operation was a mistake, he responded,

Of course the varicocelectomy was a mistake. A doctor was recommended to me [in a Southern Lebanese city]. He was a professor there—or at least they considered him a professor. Maybe he deceives the people. At first, this doctor told me, "Maybe this operation will succeed or maybe not. There's a six to seven percent chance of complications." I was among the six to seven percent. I was pushed to do this operation by the doctor, because he gave me some sort of hope. He said, "Fifty percent of men who do a varicocelectomy have pregnant wives." That's why, in the end, I did the varicocelectomy.

Hopes of Impregnation

This hope remark is telling. Varicocelectomies "give men hope" that they will be able to impregnate their wives in a society where marital fertility is very important. Men in Lebanon, as well as in other Middle Eastern societies, feel compelled by societal norms to father children. Thus, varicocelectomy continues to be touted as the means to achieve this goal. Several men in this study said that they were convinced to do a varicocelectomy based on the examples of other men whose inability to impregnate their wives had been overcome following the surgery.

Such was the case of a Lebanese man living in West Africa who returned to Lebanon in 1988 to undertake a varicocelectomy after he was unable to impregnate his wife of three years. As he explained, "I didn't want to do the operation, but I saw several possibilities. And I was really lost about what solution to take." As in the other cases cited above, the varicocelectomy did not help him. Eventually, pressured by his family members to "see his child," he undertook a brief polygynous marriage to a second wife, who bore a daughter in 2001.[4] He kept the marriage and the child secret from his wife, stating, "I'm very loyal. I've been married for seventeen years, and I've had no other women except this one woman. This is because I love my wife."

Another fertile man explained that he did a varicocelectomy "for his wife" of nine years, given that she had already suffered through a miscarriage, two ectopic pregnancies, and the stillbirth of IVF twins.

They told me there is a varicocele, but it doesn't affect [my fertility]. Yet, I did the operation, about four to five years ago. My wife thought that maybe by doing the operation, maybe things would improve.

> She wanted me to do it, because she got scared that [the varicocele] might lead to further problems. Even though the doctor said it wasn't necessary, because I got my wife pregnant the first year of our marriage, I did it for her.

Many men in this study, both fertile and infertile, spoke lovingly of their wives and emphasized that they would never divorce them or take a second wife. They viewed the quest for conception as a mutual endeavor, and they had come with their wives to IVF centers, often after several years of marriage, in order to try another way of conceiving a child. Both fertile and infertile men often felt sorry for the physical risks their wives had had to take as part of infertility treatment, particularly with repeated IVF or ICSI cycles. They expressed concern over the long-term risks of the powerful hormones women were required to take to stimulate their ovaries and over the various "operations" (i.e., retrieval of ova and transfer of embryos) performed on women under general anesthesia as part of an IVF or ICSI cycle.

It was clear to the men in this study that women suffer when undergoing infertility therapies. On the one hand, varicocelectomies represent these men's good-faith efforts to share the physical risks and suffering of infertility experienced by their wives. On the other hand, they contribute to men's own masculine desires to produce highly valued offspring. In social terms, varicocelectomies are undertaken for two main reasons: to bolster marriage through shared suffering and to bolster masculinity through fertility. Varicocelectomy scars, which are proudly revealed by some men, represent a kind of bodily marking, symbolizing male responsibility for reproduction and men's investment in their marriages and commitment to fatherhood.[5] Both socially and symbolically, varicocelectomies reveal a great deal about gender and marital relations in Lebanon and elsewhere in the Middle East where these operations are widely performed. For this reason, they need to be theorized in gendered terms.

Theorizing Male Genital Cutting in Middle Eastern Gender Studies

Middle Eastern Masculinities

I would argue that Middle Eastern varicocelectomy practices, as well as other forms of male genital cutting described in this chapter, cannot be understood without reference to Middle Eastern masculinity as it is being theorized in Middle Eastern studies. Namely, a repeating theme in the small but growing literature on Middle Eastern masculinities is one of homosocial competition among men in the realms of virility and fertility, which are typically conflated (Ali 1996, 2000; Lindisfarne 1994; Ouzgane 1997). According to Ouzgane, a scholar of contemporary Arabic literature, virility emerges as "the essence of Arab masculinity" (1997:3) in the novels of some of the region's most eminent writers, with men in these stories both distinguishing themselves, and being distinguished from other men, through the fathering of children and especially sons. Men living in pronatalist Middle Eastern communities are expected to have children, as reflected in the relatively high marriage and fertility rates across the region (Population Reference Bureau 2004).

Furthermore, on a social-structural level, Middle Eastern men achieve social power in the classic patriarchal, patrilineal, patrilocal, endogamous extended family (Eickelman 1998; Joseph 1993, 1994, 2000; Kandiyoti 1988; Moghadam 1993) through the birth of children, especially sons, who will perpetuate patrilineal structures (Delaney 1991; Inhorn 1996; Obermeyer 1999; Ouzgane 1997). In this region of the world, which "with some truth, is still regarded as one of the seats of patriarchy" (Ghoussoub and Sinclair-Webb 2000:8), men who do not become family "patriarchs" through physical and social reproduction may be deemed "weak" and ineffective (Lindisfarne 1994). Moreover, they may be encouraged to take additional wives in order to contribute to the patrilineage and to "prove" their masculine virility and fertility (Inhorn 1996).

If this is the case—as much of the theoretical, empirical, and contemporary popular literature from this region suggests—then the experience of infertility or subfertility for a Middle Eastern man can only be imagined as an extremely threatening and emasculating condition (Inhorn 2004a), one that needs to be overcome by any means, including varicocelectomy. The widespread acceptance of varicocelectomy as a fertility-enhancing surgery in the Middle East bespeaks a world in which the performance of masculinity is homosocially competitive and men work hard to sustain their public images as powerful, virile patriarchs. Men living within such an environment will likely "do what they can"—even if it means resorting to a varicocelectomy—in order to impregnate their childless wives. With impregnation, they prove their manhood and perpetuate the patrilineage through the production of offspring. Thus, in Foucauldian terms (1977), varicocelectomies are one of the ways male reproductive bodies are disciplined to meet Middle Eastern societal demands of virility, fertility, and patriarchal continuity.

Furthermore, men must achieve these patriarchal goals within the confines of marriage, because in the Muslim world, marriage is considered a moral and legal mandate and adultery a major sin (Inhorn 2003; Serour 1996). Indeed, marriage is a highly valued and normatively upheld institution throughout the Middle East. Islam extols the virtues of marriage, regarding it as *Sunna*, or the way of the Prophet Muhammad. Among Middle Eastern Christian populations, including those living in Lebanon and Egypt, marriage is similarly revered, and divorce is either difficult or impossible to obtain. Thus, Middle Easterners are among the "most married" people in the world (Omran and Roudi 1993), with well over 90 percent of adults marrying at least once in a lifetime. This is a region of the world where long-term marital commitments accompanied by love are highly valued, despite Western stereotypes of widespread marital polygamy and divorce.[6]

Conjugal Connectivity

Marriages in the Middle East are definitely evolving toward a companionate ideal, or what I have termed in my own work as "conjugal connectivity" (Inhorn 1996). In *Infertility and Patriarchy: The Cultural Politics of Gender and Family Life in Egypt*, I draw upon Lebanese-American anthropologist Suad Joseph's (1993, 1994, 1999) provocative work on "patriarchal connectivity" in the Middle East—or the ways patriarchy operates through both male domination and deeply enmeshed, loving commitments between Arab patriarchs and their family members. As argued by Joseph (1993, 1994, 1999, 2004), "intimate selving" in Arab families involves expectations of patriarchal connectivity, whereby men assume patriarchal power in the family not only with advancing age and authority but through the explicit production of offspring, whom they love and nurture as well as dominate and control.

Moving beyond Joseph's focus on the Arab family to the Arab couple, I suggest that the loving commitments of patriarchal connectivity also operate in the marital sphere. In my earlier work on Egypt (Inhorn 1994, 1996, 2003), I have demonstrated that both men and women, including poor men and women, are negotiating new kinds of marital relationships based on loving connectivity, which is experienced and expected in families of origin but has heretofore been unexpected and unexamined in the conjugal unit. That conjugal connectivity is operative among couples experiencing infertility problems in both Egypt and Lebanon attests to shifting marital praxis and the importance of love, mutual respect, and the sharing of life's problems even in the absence of desired children.

Despite widespread expectations within the Middle East that infertile marriages are bound to fail—with men necessarily blaming
women for the infertility and divorcing them if they do not produce children, especially sons—such expectations may represent
indigenous stereotypes. I would argue that the success of so many
infertile marriages in the Middle East bespeaks the strengthening
of conjugal connectivity at the expense of patriarchy, which—as
confirmed by other Middle Eastern feminist theorists (Moghadam
2004)—is being undermined.

That patriarchy is shifting in favor of conjugal connectivity and
more egalitarian gender dynamics are also suggested by research on
men and reproduction in Lebanon. In a 2002 article "Challenging
the Stereotypes," American medical anthropologist Cynthia Myntti
and a team of Lebanese researchers explore the use of withdrawal
(*coitus interruptus*) as a form of male-controlled contraception. Instead of the stereotype of the "dominant Mediterranean male" who
controls reproductive decision making, Myntti and her colleagues
found that men and women were mutually negotiating and agreeing to withdrawal as a form of contraception, in recognition of the
need to limit childbearing and to spare the wife's health and future
fertility. In other words, Lebanese men were taking responsibility
for contraception out of concern for their wives, in what could be
described as a shared commitment toward mutually agreed upon
reproductive goals and sexual pleasure.

Based on my research in Lebanon and Egypt, the same sort of
dynamics are operative within the framework of infertile marriages.
Despite a Middle Eastern social complex of classic patriarchy, competitive masculinity, and high fertility rates, men who find themselves
having reproductive difficulties within marriage are often willing to
contribute in the ways they can to facilitate mutually agreed upon
reproductive goals. Men desire children with the wives they love.
Thus, when reproduction is delayed, men within the Middle East
are often willing to participate in the embodied aspects of infertility treatment—ranging from semen collection to surgery—whether
or not they actually have a male infertility problem. For men who
are infertile, varicocelectomy is but one of the therapeutic strategies
they are willing to undertake in order to enhance their reproductive
potential (Inhorn 2003, 2004a). Yet, even among men who are *fertile*, undertaking a varicocelectomy—to purportedly increase sperm
count and prevent any future demise in sperm parameters—is one
way men can share their wives' suffering and participate in the treatment quest. Indeed, varicocelectomy can be thought of as a measure
that a "good" husband takes to prove his loving connectivity to his

infertile wife. Ultimately, Middle Eastern men's willingness to undertake varicocelectomies, even when medically unnecessary, bespeaks the deep feelings of love, loyalty, and commitment that many fertile men feel toward their long-suffering infertile wives.

Unseating Stereotypes about Men and Reproduction

The willingness of Middle Eastern men to have their genital areas cut open for such reasons may come as a surprise, especially given Western stereotypes of Middle Eastern men as inherently violent, fanatical, and unloving. Clearly, "tropes of male terrorism" need to be unseated for the Middle East, much as *machismo* for Latin America (Gutmann 1996, 2003). Furthermore, a strong feminist argument that has been put forward regarding men and reproduction requires serious challenge. Namely, Western feminist scholars such as Judith Lorber (1989) and Irma van der Ploeg (1995) have claimed in their work that men participate little in the unpleasant embodiment of infertility treatment, even when they are the infertile partner. Lorber uses the term "patriarchal bargain" (following Turkish feminist scholar Deniz Kandiyoti) to describe the ways in which women married to infertile men must consent to treatment on their own bodies in order to resolve the cultural pressure on women to become mothers. Van der Ploeg takes this argument one step further by suggesting that men's bodies "by contrast, seem to remain relatively stable and untouched, even when . . . male pathologies are at issue" (1995:461).

As I have demonstrated in this chapter, this earlier feminist argument about the "unscathed" infertile male body is both untrue and inherently dated. In addition to varicocelectomies, which have been performed on male bodies for decades, the newest reproductive technologies require, in some cases, painful genital penetration in the form of testicular biopsies and aspirations. Men who are azoospermic are routinely subjected to genital cutting on diagnostic and therapeutic levels.[7] For azoospermic men in the Middle East, testicular aspirations and/or biopsies may represent the third in a series of genital cutting procedures, beginning with male circumcision in childhood, proceeding to varicocelectomy following marriage, and ending in testicular aspiration and/or biopsy as the "last resort" in assisted conception. Thus, in the Middle East, many infertile men share painful "body histories" with their wives (Inhorn 2003), a fact that has been little discussed or recognized by feminist scholars, infertility scholars, or the public health experts concerned with men and reproductive health.

Male genital cutting to enhance or restore fertility—even when these invasive procedures are pointless and potentially damaging—is an underappreciated aspect of male reproductive health that deserves further global scrutiny. Male genital cutting involves surgeries performed for many reasons, including physician avarice, masculinity expectations within patriarchal regimes, and husbands' desires to share the burdens of reproduction with beloved wives. Male genital cutting in all of its forms is a topic requiring serious and sustained attention, much as female genital cutting has been highlighted in global public health advocacy. The importance of male genital cutting is a timely topic for the twenty-first century, not only in the Middle East but in the rest of the world, including the United States, where male genital cutting practices continue unabated. If we care so much about women's genitals, then we must also care about men's genitals and begin to question the various reasons why male genital cutting is performed so widely around the globe.

Acknowledgments

I want to express my gratitude to the numerous men in Egypt and Lebanon who spoke to me about their infertility and reproductive lives. The IVF physicians, nurses, and staff members who helped me recruit male patients into this study deserve great credit—Antoine Abu Musa, Johnny Awwad, Abbass Fakih, Michael H. Fakih, Walid Ghutmi, Najwa Hammoud, Antoine Hannoun, Azhar Ismail, Da'ad Lakkis, Zaher Nassar, Gamal Serour, Khaled Sakhel, Hanady Shrara, Mohamed Yehia, Salah Zaki, and Tony Zreik. I also want to thank my primary research assistants Mary Ghanem (in Lebanon) and Tayseer Salem (in Egypt), as well as Huda Zurayk and Rima Afifi, who cordially provided me with institutional affiliations in the American University of Beirut Faculty of Health Sciences. I am grateful to Beth Talbot and Nina Kohli-Laven for research assistance on this chapter, as well as to Matthew Gutmann for sharing his new work on vasectomy in Mexico. This research was generously supported by the National Science Foundation and the U.S. Department of Education Fulbright-Hays Program.

Notes

1. The multiple testicular penetrations often required to extract sperm from the testicles are exquisitely painful; that is why the procedure is always performed under either local or general anesthesia. In one of the clinics in which I worked, testicular aspirations were routinely being performed under general anesthesia. In the other clinic, testicular

biopsies were performed under local anesthesia in a clinical consultation room off the main IVF clinic waiting area. Azoospermic men who were taken into these rooms for the purposes of testicular biopsy often emerged walking slowly with their legs spread. I once tried to interview one of these men, with his encouragement, following his testicular biopsy. But his pain and discomfort became overwhelming, and his urologist recommended that he return to the clinical consultation room to lie down. Occasionally, men were required to undergo these painful biopsies when "performance anxiety" prevented them from producing a necessary semen sample at the time of IVF ova retrieval.

2. I questioned all of the men in my study about their monthly income levels. Most Lebanese men made US$1,000 or less a month, resulting in annual incomes of less than US$12,000. Physicians' salaries were usually higher. According to Lebanese public health professor Kassem Kassak and colleagues (n.d.), average physician incomes in Lebanon are approximately US$2,000 a month.

3. For more than a century, the Lebanese have migrated abroad from their small country, seeking new homes and fortunes in Africa, Latin America and the Caribbean, and the Western countries. A significant number of Southern Lebanese Shi'a have migrated to the countries of West Africa, including Senegal, Sierra Leone, and Côte d'Ivoire, where fortunes have been made in diamond mining and other forms of entrepreneurship. This outmigration was intensified during the fifteen-year Lebanese civil war (1975–1990). Today, many of these West African Lebanese return to Lebanon for vacations or to find marital partners. In addition, "medical migration" to Lebanon is very common, given migrants' greater confidence in Lebanese medical institutions than in West African ones. Similar "ex-patriotism" can be found among Egyptian medical migrants returning to Egypt from the Arab Gulf (Inhorn 2003).

4. This was a unique case of polygyny, which was rare in this study population. In this case, the man spoke by cell phone with his young daughter every day but did not see her or her mother in order to protect his wife's feelings. Nonetheless, he was hoping to find a way to bring the daughter into his marital home, the chances of which he believed were better if his wife could have a child of her own. Although this man did not question the paternity of his daughter and assumed that he was fertile, his semen analysis revealed an extremely low sperm count and poor motility, or what in medical terms is known as "severe oligoasthenospermia."

5. I am grateful to my coeditors for pointing out the potential symbolic associations of varicocelectomy.

6. Divorce rates in the Middle East are estimated to be about 25 percent, half the rate recorded in the United States (Fluehr-Lobban 1990). Furthermore, across the region, polygyny rates are only 3 to 4 percent (Omran and Roudi 1993).

7. Azoospermia, probably due to microdeletions on the Y chromosome, is more frequent in the Middle East than in the West. IVF physicians speculate that it may be due to consanguineous marriage practices (i.e., family and village endogamy).

References

Ali, Kamran Asdar. 1996. "Notes on Rethinking Masculinities: An Egyptian Case." In *Learning about Sexuality: A Practical Beginning*, ed. S. Zeidenstein and Kirsten Moore. New York: Population Council.

———. 2000. "Making 'Responsible' Men: Planning the Family in Egypt." In *Fertility and the Male Life-Cycle in the Era of Fertility Decline*, ed. Caroline Bledsoe, Susanna Lerner, and Jane I. Guyer. Oxford: Oxford University Press.

American Academy of Pediatrics. 1999. "Circumcision Policy Statement." *Pediatrics* 103:686–93.

Audebert, Alain. 2004. "Varicocele and Male Hypofertility—Current Data." www.gyneweb.fr.

Circlist. 2004. "Worldwide Male Circumcision Rates." www.cirlist.com/rites/rates.html.

Delaney, Carol. 1991. *The Seed and the Soil: Gender and Cosmology in Turkish Village Society*. Berkeley: University of California Press.

Devroey, P., M. Vandervorst, P. Nagy, and A. Van Steirteghem. 1998. "Do We Treat the Male or His Gamete?" *Human Reproduction* 13(Suppl. 1):178–85.

Eickelman, Dale F. 1998. *The Middle East and Central Asia: An Anthropological Approach*, 3rd ed. Upper Saddle River, NJ: Prentice Hall.

Fluehr-Lobban, Carolyn. 1990. *Modern Egypt and its Heritage*. Pittsburgh: Carnegie Museum of Natural History.

Foucault, Michel. 1977. *Discipline & Punish: The Birth of the Prison*. Trans. Alan Sheridan. New York: Vintage Books.

Ghoussoub, Mai, and Emma Sinclair-Webb, eds. 2000. *Imagined Masculinities: Male Identity and Culture in the Modern Middle East*. London: Saqi Books.

Goldstein, M. 1995. *Surgery of Male Infertility*. Philadelphia: W. B. Saunders.

Gruenbaum, Ellen. 2001. *The Female Circumcision Controversy: An Anthropological Perspective*. Philadelphia: University of Pennsylvania Press.

Gutmann, Matthew. 1996. *The Meanings of Macho: Being a Man in Mexico City*. Berkeley: University of California Press.

———, ed. 2003. *Changing Men and Masculinities in Latin America*. Durham: Duke University Press.

———. 2005. "Scoring Men: Vasectomies and the Totemic Illusion of Male Sexuality in Oaxaca." *Culture, Medicine, and Psychiatry* 29(1):79–101.

———. 2007. *Fixing Men: Sex, Birth Control, and AIDS in Mexico*. Berkeley: University of California Press.

Inhorn, Marcia C. 1994. *Quest for Conception: Gender, Infertility, and Egyptian Medical Traditions*. Philadelphia: University of Pennsylvania Press.

———. 1996. *Infertility and Patriarchy: The Cultural Politics of Gender and Family Life in Egypt*. Philadelphia: University of Pennsylvania Press.

———. 2003. *Local Babies, Global Science: Gender, Religion, and In Vitro Fertilization in Egypt*. New York: Routledge.

———. 2004a. "Middle Eastern Masculinities in the Age of New Reproductive Technologies: Male Infertility and Stigma in Egypt and Lebanon." *Medical Anthropology Quarterly* 18:34–53.

———. 2004b. "Privacy, Privatization, and the Politics of Patronage: Ethnographic Challenges to Penetrating the Secret World of Middle Eastern, Hospital-based In Vitro Fertilization." *Social Science & Medicine* 59:2095–108.

Irvine, D. S. 1998. "Epidemiology and Aetiology of Male Infertility." *Human Reproduction* 13 (Suppl. 1):33–44.

Joseph, Suad. 1993. "Connectivity and Patriarchy among Urban Working-Class Arab Families in Lebanon." *Ethos* 21:452–84.

———. 1994. "Brother/Sister Relationships: Connectivity, Love, and Power in the Reproduction of Patriarchy in Lebanon." *American Ethnologist* 21:50–73.

———, ed. 1999. *Intimate Selving in Arab Families: Gender, Self, and Identity.* Syracuse, NY: Syracuse University Press.

———, ed. 2000. *Gender and Citizenship in the Middle East.* Syracuse, NY: Syracuse University Press.

———. 2004. "Conceiving Family Relationships in Post-War Lebanon." *Journal of Comparative Family Studies* 35:271–93.

Kamischke, A., and E. Neischlag. 1998. "Conventional Treatments of Male Infertility in the Age of Evidence-based Andrology." *Human Reproduction* 13 (Suppl. 1):62–75.

Kandiyoti, Deniz. 1988. "Bargaining with Patriarchy." *Gender and Society* 2:274–90.

Kassak, K. M., H. Ghomrawi, A. M. A. Osseiran, and H. Kobeissi. n.d. "The Providers of Health Services in Lebanon: I. A Survey of Physicians." Unpublished manuscript.

Lane, Sandra D., and Robert A. Rubinstein. 1996. "Judging the Other: Responding to Traditional Female Genital Surgeries." *Hastings Center Report* (May–June):31–40.

Laven, J. S., L. C. Haans, W. P. Mali, et al. 1992. "Effects of Varicocele Treatment in Adolescents: A Randomized Study." *Fertility & Sterility* 58:756–62.

Lindisfarne, Nancy. 1994. "Variant Masculinities, Variant Virginities: Rethinking 'Honour and Shame.'" In *Dislocating Masculinity: Comparative Ethnographies,* ed. Andrea Cornwall and Nancy Lindisfarne. London: Routledge.

Lorber, Judith. 1989. "Choice, Gift, or Patriarchal Bargain? Women's Consent to In Vitro Fertilization in Male Infertility." *Hypatia* 4:23–36.

Madgar, I., R. Weissenberg, B. Lunenfield, et al. 1995. "Controlled Trial of High Spermatic Vein Ligation for Varicocele in Infertile Men." *Fertility & Sterility* 63:120–24.

Moghadam, Valentine M. 1993. *Modernizing Women: Gender and Social Change in the Middle East.* Boulder: Lynne Rienner.

———. 2004. "Patriarchy in Transition: Women and the Changing Family in the Middle East." *Journal of Comparative Family Studies* 35:137–62.

Myntti, Cynthia, Abir Ballan, Omar Dewachi, Faysal El-Kak, and Mary E. Deeb. 2002. "Challenging the Stereotypes: Men, Withdrawal, and Reproductive Health in Lebanon." *Contraception* 65:165–70.

Nieschlag, E., L. Hertile, A. Fischedick, and H. M. Behre. 1995. "Treatment of Varicocele: Counseling as Effective as Occlusion of the Vena Spermatica." *Human Reproduction* 10:347–53.

Obermeyer, Carla Makhlouf. 1999. "Fairness and Fertility: The Meaning of Son Preference in Morocco." In *Dynamics of Values in Fertility Change*, ed. Richard Leete. Oxford: Oxford University Press.

Omran, Abdel Rahim, and Farzaneh Roudi. 1993. "The Middle East Population Puzzle." *Population Bulletin* 48:1–40.

Osmanagaoglu, K., et al. 1999. "Cumulative Delivery Rates after ICSI: A Five-Year Follow-up of 498 Patients." *Human Reproduction* 14:2651–55.

Ouzgane, Lahoucine. 1997. "Masculinity as Virility in Tahar Ben Jelloun's Fiction." *Journal of Violence, Mimesis, and Culture* 4:1–13.

Parker, Melissa. 1995. "Rethinking Female Circumcision." *Africa* 65:506–23.

Population Reference Bureau. 2004. *World Population Data Sheet: Demographic Data and Estimates for the Countries and Regions of the World.* Washington, DC: Population Reference Bureau.

Serour, Gamal I. 1996. "Bioethics in Reproductive Health: A Muslim's Perspective." *Middle East Fertility Society Journal* 1:30–35.

Takihara, H., J. Sakatoku, and A. T. K. Cockett. 1991. "The Pathophysiology of Varicocele in Male Infertility." *Fertility & Sterility* 55:861–68.

Tournaye, Herman. 2001. "Gamete Source and Manipulation." In *Current Practices and Controversies in Assisted Reproduction*, ed. Effy Vayena, Patrick J. Rowe, and P. David Griffin. Geneva: World Health Organization.

Van der Ploeg, Irma. 1995. "Hermaphrodite Patients: In Vitro Fertilization and the Transformation of Male Infertility." *Science, Technology, & Human Values* 20:460–81.

Vayena, Effy, Patrick J. Rowe, and P. David Griffin, eds. 2001. *Current Practices and Controversies in Assisted Reproduction.* Geneva: World Health Organization.

Virginia Mason Medical Center. 2004. "Varicocele Repair of Varicocelectomy." www.vmmc.org/dbFertility/sec1596.htm.

World Health Organization. 1992. "The Influence of Varicocele on Parameters of Fertility in a Large Group of Men Presenting to Infertility Clinics." *Fertility & Sterility* 57:1289–93.

Part IV.

CHILDBIRTH AND FATHERHOOD

Chapter 11

"WE ARE PREGNANT": ISRAELI MEN AND THE PARADOXES OF SHARING

Tsipy Ivry

Introduction: Bringing Male Perspectives to the Fore

The front cover of a 1998 Hebrew textbook on gynecology and obstetrics depicts the triad of a pregnant woman, her male partner, and
her gynecologist (Schenker and Elchalal 1998). The pregnant patient is in the center of the photograph, lying on a hospital bed while
both her partner and the gynecologist gaze at her face. Whereas a
firm gaze and physical contact are established between the smiling
woman and the smiling gynecologist, who has both his hands on her
belly, neither of them has established any contact with the woman's
male partner, who is standing behind the bed, as if a politically correct addition to the scene. This picture might call for a critical deconstruction of the idealized representation of doctor–patient relations (the calm and smiling pregnant woman literally in the hands
of her gynecologist), a well-treated relationship in the anthropology
of reproduction. In this chapter, I would like to shift the focus to the
male partner. His gaze is clearly focused on the pregnant woman
lying on the hospital bed. How does she look from his perspective?
What kind of role is he expected to take in the process of pregnancy
and birth? And what are the implications of his attempts to share
this experience with his partner in the way pregnancy is negotiated

between medical staff, female partners, and male partners? Utilizing data gathered in birth education classes in Israel, I attempt to approach these questions from a Jewish-Israeli context and add a culturally situated account of men's involvement in pregnancy to the anthropology of reproduction.

The rapidly growing body of literature in the anthropology of reproduction only recently started to ask questions regarding men's perspectives and experiences. The few studies in the field take the medicalization of reproduction as a point of departure. Scholars explore representations of the male reproductive organs and cells in the scientific and popular literature (Martin 1991; Moore 2002, 2003), men as obstetricians and gynecologists (Davis-Floyd 1992), and men's experiences with infertility treatments (Birenbaum-Carmeli, Carmeli, and Casper 1995; Birenbaum-Carmeli et al. 2001; Carmeli and Birenbaum-Carmeli 1994; Goldberg this volume). Research on male partners in pregnancy also has only recently begun to emerge. Such studies include Sandelowski's (1994) work on the experiences of American men with obstetrical ultrasound, as well as Draper's (2002, 2003) and Reed's (2005) studies of men's experiences with pregnancy and birth in the United Kingdom and the United States respectively.

Men's perspectives rarely occupy the analytical focus of studies in the anthropology of reproduction as an issue in and of itself, despite the fact that men do appear in recent ethnographic accounts of reproduction in the United States and Europe. Men are described as being involved in dramas of decision making, for example, whether to undergo amniocentesis (Rapp 1999; Browner and Preloran 1999) or medical spectacles such as ultrasound screenings (Sandelowski 1994; Georges 1996; Draper 2002), birth education courses (Reed 2005; Sargent and Stark 1989), and the birth event itself (Jordan 1993, 1997; Reed 2005).

The emergence of men in reproductive arenas reflects a growing public trend in the United States and Western Europe to consider pregnancy and birth as experiences that can and should be shared with male partners (see Tjørnhøj-Thomsen and Han, both in this volume). Reed's analysis (2005) of the "birthing revolution" shows how the process through which men were invited to take part in birthing developed at the intersection between natural birth movements and the continued hegemony of the biomedicalized model of birth. These changes in birthing practices during the past three decades occurred under the continuing and growing influence of ideas expressed by activists of the international women's movement, in the hope that sharing pregnancy, birth, and childrearing with men will promote greater equality and balance between the sexes. Yet one thing is clear: biomedicine as a social system that manages pregnancy and birth while using sets of authoritative knowledge, procedures, and technologies plays a major role in the attempt to "draw men closer" to reproduction.

The first technology that comes to mind is obstetrical ultrasound scans functioning as "proxies" of embodiment for male partners who supposedly do not have access to the direct embodied experience of pregnancy (Draper 2002:779). Ultrasound, Draper claims, gives the father "the potential . . . to have the same visual access to the baby as his partner, thus equalizing their respective positions as knowers of the baby" (782). She also claims that "ultrasound is an example of a range of contemporary rituals, helping men make and mark their transition to Western fatherhood" (790).

Conversely, accounts by anthropologists and feminist writers call attention to the various tensions, paradoxes, and contradictions brought about when men step into spheres of medicalized reproduction. For example, scholars call into question the "equality" advocated by reproductive technologies. Sandelowski (1994) argues that while men are indeed becoming more involved than ever before in pregnancy thanks to the development of obstetrical ultrasound, ultrasound is making the woman increasingly invisible, because the male partner is given knowledge by the doctor while the woman often is being left out. In the same vein, van der Ploeg (1995) argues, based on data she gathered in Holland, that women are pushed out of the metaphorical status of "pregnant patient" by their male partners and fetuses as depicted by the doctors. Reed's (2005) account of men's birthing experiences reveals that many men walk out of the birthing room feeling ambivalence about the experience and their role in it.

Finally, even *Spiritual Midwifery* (Gaskin 1997), the highly popular book among advocates of the American natural birth movement that emphasizes male partner participation as crucial to successful deliveries, warns (in various places throughout the book) that some male partners lack either the knowledge or the emotional and spiritual ability to help their partners (Gaskin 1977:321–2, 344, 440–1). Such accounts exemplify some of the tensions that the attempt to make male partners equal and full participants in pregnancy and birth may impose on the process of reproduction. This chapter explores these tensions and their sociocultural context.

My findings from six years of fieldwork in Israeli medical institutions, as well as in less strictly medicalized reproductive arenas, confirm that although individual men participate in medical events to different degrees, men in general are becoming frequent visitors to these sites, much like their American and European counterparts. I have seen men accompany their wives to routine medical checkups during pregnancy, especially to ultrasound scans but also to special prenatal tests such as amniocentesis. They often participate in birth education courses and most are present at the birth of their children. Thus, while many women giving birth thirty years ago or more tell of a lonely experience, both medical practitioners and pregnant women in Israel today would agree that male partners participate in the process of pregnancy and birth as they never did before. That more Israeli men feel comfortable making statements such as "we are pregnant" when speaking about the pregnancy physically taking place in their partner's body suggests that the idea of sharing the experiences of pregnancy and birth has become less remote and, for some of them, even desirable.

This shift toward greater participation of male partners in pregnancy and birth—typically "feminine" arenas—is particularly interesting when one considers the growing literature by Israeli sociologists and anthropologists dealing with the central role of the military in the construction of gender identities (e.g., Ben-Ari 1998; Lomsky-Feder 1995; Sasson-Levi 2000; Weiss 2002). Specifically, it has been argued that the hegemonic masculinity in Israel—a state involved in continuous military conflicts—is that of the combat soldier. If this is true, examining Israeli men's involvement in pregnancy and birth may provide a particularly illustrative example of how men negotiate and navigate gender identities within reproductive arenas when those identities are tinted by the military.

The analysis here is threefold. First, I explore the nature of the social expectations placed on men to "participate" in their partner's pregnancies and show how male partners devise rationales for participating in birth education courses while negotiating with these expectations. The analysis then moves to delineate the conceptual and experiential tools men use to make sense of their partner's pregnancy. Finally, I explore the repercussions of some men's attempts to become equal players in pregnancy on their bilateral relations with their pregnant partners. It is my impression that many Israeli men make serious attempts to participate in pregnancy. However, I argue that this attempt to understand pregnancy and to fulfill social expectations to participate may bring a considerable amount of tension and paradoxes into the process of childbearing for both partners. It is these tensions and paradoxes that stand at the center of my analysis.

Birth Education Courses: Arenas of Negotiation

As indicated above, care providers in medical events such as ultrasound scans, prenatal testing, and pregnancy checkups are likely to exhibit hospitality when male partners appear. However, the arena of birth education courses stands out as one aspiring to draw men in almost ideologically. Rather than confining men to the back of the bed (as on the front cover of the gynecology textbook), birth educators are sure to embellish their advertisements and introductory brochures with pictures of smiling men holding either their babies, wives, or both. Moreover, many of the courses given in Hebrew make a point to emphasize that they are designed equally for male partners and pregnant women. For example, one of the courses I observed was advertised under the name "Giving birth together" [*laledet beyahad*]. The back cover of its widely distributed brochure states, "In our course the husband, or the person who accompanies the woman, is as important as the pregnant woman herself." This general dedication to the inclusion of men is one reason I chose to focus my analysis on this specific segment of my data.

But there are plenty of other reasons. For many Israelis, birth education courses have come to signal one prominent station on the way to parenthood. The word "courses" [*kursim*] is used here to refer to a range of organized "educational" activities for pregnant women and their partners, in which they are guided through issues related to their particular "situation." A wide variety of courses exists in Israel, ranging from programs offered by hospitals or midwives, often held in private spaces and possibly even condensed into a weekend in a hotel. One may find courses oriented toward alternative medicine, to conventional medicine, or to integrating both (the latter being the most common). Courses usually include four to seven classes and are held once a week.

In spite of their diverse orientations, all courses share two features. First, although they convey anatomical information (heavily laden with medical terminology, even in holistically oriented courses), this information is augmented by plenty of props, pictures, and videos. In this respect, course instructors contributed vivid illustrations in order to transform medical knowledge into popular understanding. Second, all course instructors attempted to create an intimate and "homey" atmosphere within which women and their partners could feel free to ask questions, and friendly interactions could exist. To facilitate this relaxed atmosphere, the spaces were decorated with wall-to-wall carpeting, a wealth of pillows, and comfortable armchairs. Food and drinks were provided during breaks.

It is important to note that Israeli birth education instructors draw heavily upon ideas, written materials, and strategies developed in the United States. However, the instructors also demonstrate a local version of birth education. This is especially clear when one compares

Israeli birthing courses to Reed's description of American courses (2005:135–60). Reed discusses the two main elements he identifies as part of a "rite of passage" to fatherhood that American courses engender. The first element is the routine stretching and relaxation exercises at the beginning of class, accompanied by background music featuring ocean sounds, which constructs the birthing class as a liminal space (148–49). The second element is the practice of role reversals between men and women participating in the class, which Reed analyzes as a modern version of the couvade ritual (154–57). These two aspects do not characterize Israeli birthing courses. In my observation, while Israeli birth educators attempt to generate a relaxed and friendly atmosphere, their classes were considerably more "academic" than those studied by Reed.

Although medical knowledge is offered and negotiated, birth education courses, in comparison to gynecological clinics and ultrasound rooms, are sites that are somewhat less "strictly medical," in which pregnancy is negotiated within a larger group of people (compared to the doctor-patient-partner triad). Thus, the second reason for focusing on these courses is the comfortable social atmosphere birth educators encourage, which enable men to get out from behind the bed.

A third reason for choosing to focus on birth education courses is that, unlike medical checkups and prenatal tests, they provide a somewhat less "fetus-oriented" perspective on pregnancy. Specifically, studies approaching men's experiences of pregnancy from the perspective of obstetrical ultrasound tend to maintain this technology's emphasis on the fetus. From this "feto-centric" perspective, distance or closure in relation to pregnancy can only be "measured" by distance or closure to the fetus. From this point of view, men emerge as having a "reproductive deficit" (Sandelowski 1994:234), because their "knowledge of the fetus is disembodied and therefore, more disconnected and abstract than hers" (234). However, as Petchesky-Pollack (1987) argues, "feto-centrism" tends to conceal the woman on whom the fetus is dependent. Returning to our specific purpose, if we shift our perspective toward the perception of pregnancy as a malleable physical and emotional phenomenon that happens within and to women, we could start exploring men's experiences with their partners rather than approaching them as disadvantaged "knowers of the fetus." The shift from a feto-centric attitude is especially important in the context of the Israeli pregnancy, where the fetus maintains its status as a nonhuman until birth, both in the legal and public discourse, despite the inculcation of obstetrical ultrasound in the medical arena (Ivry 2009). Thus, birth education courses provide a site where pregnancy is not negotiated through a fetus-privileging technology.

Methodology

The data presented in this chapter is part of a larger, comparative study that explores conceptions of pregnancy in Japan and in Israel (Ivry 2006, 2007, 2010). This study attempts to understand the experiential, medical, and social meanings of pregnancy in these two countries, through a variety of human experiences and sets of medical knowledge about pregnancy. I use a combination of anthropological methods Marcus (1995) calls "multi-sited-ethnography"; I conducted participant observations in prenatal clinics, maternity and birth education courses, and clinics performing prenatal tests, as well as in-depth interviews with OB/GYNs and pregnant women. I also collected pregnancy guides, medical forms, and medical literature. Data was collected in Israel and Japan, in Hebrew and Japanese, respectively.

While trying to understand pregnancy from the perspective of sociocultural comparison, I attentively observed and documented male partners accompanying their female partners in both countries and throughout different stations on the route to parenthood. This aspect of pregnancy became one of the differences that deeply informed my analysis of the meaning of pregnancy in the two countries.

Though it is beyond the scope of this chapter to carry out a comparative analysis of men's roles in pregnancy, observing the social management of pregnancy in Japan—where it is still relatively rare to find men accompanying their partners to pregnancy checkups, and birth education is in most cases offered only to pregnant women as "maternity courses" [*hahaoyagakkyû*]—has drawn my attention to the relative intensity of the involvement of Israeli men in their partners' pregnancies and ways they spoke about and reacted to pregnancy.

I resumed fieldwork in both fields in 2003, feeling that in order to understand women's experiences of gestation, men's pregnancies must be further researched. During the summer of 2006, I again resumed fieldwork to observe any changes in birth education courses and conducted in-depth interviews with sixteen Israeli men of diverse professions from the center and north of Israel (Ivry and Teman 2008). Their narratives highlighted the continuing presence and importance of the issues raised by the male partners I had met in birth education classes during the previous set of observations and on which I focus my analysis here. The insights that arose from observing Israeli men accompanying their partners to ultrasound scans, coping with difficult decisions during genetic counseling, or holding their partner's hand while she underwent amniocentesis all fed into the concerns of this chapter. In fact, every one of these data sets could serve to examine how men navigate their participation in pregnancy. However, birth education classes are the only pregnancy activities explicitly defined and designed for couples.

Thus, this chapter focuses on data collected from participant observation of five birth education courses held in diverse geographical locations throughout Israel between 1999 and 2003. The courses consisted of seven to eight classes lasting two to three hours each. Three courses were conducted in hospitals and two in the private homes of the midwives teaching them. Seven to nine couples participated in each course. Overall, I observed thirty-nine couples, most of whom were first-time parents in their mid-twenties and thirties; all but one were married. To judge from participants' occupations, their social status ranged from lower- to upper-middle-class. The couples were both religious and nonreligious. I took notes in Hebrew, translated them into English, and interviewed instructors for supplementary data. I have changed the names and identifying features of all informants.

In what follows, and as my analytical point of departure, I will treat Israeli birth education courses as social constructs organized along culturally specific reproductive relations, embedded within local reproductive politics (see Ginsburg and Rapp 1991, 1995). That male partners ought to be equal participants in their partner's pregnancy and birth is one belief shared, I dare say, by all participants in birth education courses. However, my observations suggest that not all participants would agree on what "participation" means.

Dragging Men In: Rationales for Participation

The analytical focal point of this section can be illustrated with a story from one of the birth education courses I observed. The course took place at a large medical center in the south of Israel and was taught by Anat, the head midwife of the maternity ward. It was the group's third meeting, and it fell on the same day as the World Cup soccer tournament (*Mondial* in Hebrew, taken from the European title), which was being broadcast on Israeli television. Anat greeted the nine couples who were sitting comfortably on the thick mattresses and pillows arranged around the room. "Good evening," she said with a smile. "I'm glad to see all of you with us. I salute all the men who have come and are missing the Mondial. They must love you a lot, girls, you should appreciate them." "I am not a sucker," responded Kobi, a computer technician in his late twenties. "I record everything on video." Kobi, his wife Ella, and all the other couples, as well as Anat, laughed wholeheartedly.

Anat's praise of the special effort men had made to attend the class reflects the tension within the very expectation that men will participate, and one that manifested itself in different ways in all five courses. Although men participated in almost all the classes, and are considered equal partners in pregnancy and birth and expected to be physically present, birth educators do not take their presence for granted. In fact, birth educators seemed to put as much effort into meeting "male tastes" as they did women's needs. Thus, assuming that the women were listening attentively, birth educators were busy inventing all sorts of techniques and strategies to attract men's attention and keep them alert.

Paula, who has been teaching birth preparation classes in a hospital in central Israel for eighteen years, has developed an interactive style of teaching. She holds their attention by constantly referring to male participants, asking them direct questions, and joking with them. She always opens her first class with a question directed personally at the male partners:

> *Paula*: Eli, why did you come to this birth education class?
> *Eli*: We wanted something more than just reading books.
> *Arie*: Something that would give us an education, that would give us some indication of what is going to happen.
> *Paula*: Do any of the men read the books?
> *Ami*: Well, not much. My wife reads [them] and tells me about it.
> *Avi (responding to the question about reading)*: Not from start to finish, but certainly relevant chapters.
> *Paula (looking at Avi with surprise, and then turning to Gadi)*: Why did you come [to this birth education course]?
> *Gadi*: Massive pressure from [his wife] Sarit.
> *Paula*: Why did you come to this course, Shaul?
> *Shaul*: I want to help my wife.

These men present the three different rationales for participation that I often encountered in the field. The first accepts the hegemony of biomedical knowledge uncritically and assumes that the accumulation of such knowledge is necessary for the ultimate progress of pregnancy and birth. Thus, Eli and Arie, who represent this pattern of thinking, were in the course to become better "educated." Although the majority of women share this view, men and women differ considerably in their patterns of consuming medical information. Women often report reading pregnancy guides from cover to cover and consuming large amounts of magazines and newspaper articles; their partners rarely conceive of the occasions of pregnancy and birth as reading assignments. Yet, becoming the "owner" of a certain critical mass of medical information is crucial to cultivating a sharing male partner, at least for some women and men. This is one of the promises birth education classes hold out to men as they can acquire knowledge without becoming devoted pregnancy readers. Therefore, while for women reading is an integral part of "pregnancing," for some men birth education courses serve as a substitute. It is notable that when Avi admits to more extensive reading (but still only of the "relevant parts"), Paula expresses surprise. Men are not expected to read pregnancy guides.

The second rationale is expressed by Shaul, a thirty-one-year-old Argentinean-born man, who said he wanted to help his wife. Shaul and Joanna had immigrated to Israel two years earlier. Shaul was the only man in his group who was not at all embarrassed by the back rubs Paula taught male partners in order to help relieve their wives' labor pain. While other men giggled and smiled embarrassedly, Shaul practiced diligently on his wife, continuously seeking her reassurance that he was doing it well.

However, when at the first lesson Shaul stated that his purpose was to help his wife, Paula immediately countered his words by inverting "help" to "knowledge." As Paula explained, addressing the male participants with the Hebrew second-person plural, "I want to help you. This is not your natural world, your language . . . The best feeling of satisfaction for me is when you phone after the birth and [say] there were no surprises, low apgar, high apgar, caesarean . . . you knew *everything*." Paula's statement echoes Sargent and Stark's (1989) findings from birth education courses in American hospitals—these courses in fact try to "prepare" the women for medical interventions during birth. In this same spirit, Paula assumes that men need to learn the correct jargon for pregnancy and birth. She does not assume that the medicalized language of pregnancy and birth is "natural" for women either, only that women are better acquainted with this language.

The third rationale, as expressed by Gadi's answer, is to satisfy a social pressure to participate. Gadi expresses an unwillingness to participate, depicting himself as a passive and forced participant, and his wife as a domineering and demanding person strong enough to "force" him to do something against his will. It is notable that rather than the archetypical image of the dominant and even oppressive patriarch, men emerge in Gadi's narrative as subservient and subjugated: the second sex in reproduction. Experienced birth educators are aware of the presence of disenchanted men and attempt to cater to their needs. One pamphlet advertising a course at a northern-Israel hospital states, "even hesitant husbands will find their place in our course." Another pamphlet, "Giving Birth Together," quotes a husband named Eitan: "'My wife dragged me, I was afraid that it was going to be too 'feminine' and boring for me. But on the contrary, I was really into it. The course is not only for women. It is a basic training for fathers. A must.'—Eitan is an officer in the Israel Defense Forces (IDF)."

What message did the birth educators who designed the pamphlet want to transmit by quoting Eitan? First, they wanted to "formally" recognize the fears and unwillingness some men might feel as legitimate. Second, while femininity is equated with boredom in the military-officer's narrative, the birth educators apparently wished to assure the pamphlet's readers that even the most "manly" of men, that is, officers in the IDF, find these classes relevant. In this way, they were using an image that represents Israeli hegemonic masculinity as a stamp of approval for their product. Thus, whereas the equation of femininity and boredom remains unchallenged, there is a subtle implication that the classes use a language common to men and women. When asked about the problem of male partners participating unwillingly, Paula explained that it was worthwhile for a male partner to participate because "I am teaching him a language that is easy for him to learn."

Paula is supposing that the highly medicalized language she uses in her classes will fit a "natural disposition" in men, thus echoing the traditional categorization of men as "rational" and more comfortable with technologies (Reed 2005:212). Ruth, an experienced midwife qualified in alternative medicine who teaches courses at her home, expressed this view on the "guided tour to birthing rooms" she offered during her course. As soon as all the couples had entered the birthing room, she explained the surrounding medical equipment. As part of a particularly detailed explanation of the monitor, she said, "You can see the fetus' pulse [measured] on this monitor. A fetus' pulse rate is usually between 120–170. I am saying this for the men because they like numbers and machines. The first thing they look at when they move into the birth room is the monitor."

Ruth made clear use of male gender stereotypes. In a more general sense, her course was interesting to me, because Ruth saw herself as a supporter of "natural" birth. In her pamphlets, she promised her clients to "present the conventional as well as alternative styles of birthing." Courses like Ruth's reflect an increasing diffusion of ideas from the American natural birth movement into the Israeli public sphere. By the beginning of the twenty-first century, a local natural birth movement was launched in Israel, calling for the legalization of home births. Yet, though Israeli women seem to look suspiciously on antimedicalization messages, medical institutions are increasingly attempting to integrate alternative medical practices into hospital births. Ruth, like other birth educators I met, tried to offer her clients a broad perspective about "the many possibilities that exist today." Nevertheless, she saw "preparing couples for whatever may happen" as her primary duty, and because she knew that most of her clients would give birth in hospitals, she regularly offered them the guided tour of birth rooms. Ruth also believed that men really could help their wives and dedicated a considerable number of hours to teaching them how to massage their partners. Still, when Ruth pictures men in the birth room, she imagines them watching the monitor rather than massaging their wives.

Although birth educators do their best to draw men in, men complain about various aspects of the course. It is assumed that both partners work, and classes are therefore usually in the evening. At the end of a long day's work, some men complain of tiredness. During one class, Yoni, a thirty-year-old lawyer, yawned repeatedly. At one point Ruth asserted, slightly angrily, "Do me a favor: go and make yourself the muddiest black coffee you can and come back." Yoni went obediently and did as he was told. However, in the elevator, on their way down to the first floor, I recorded the following conversation between Yoni and his wife:

> *Tali (in a soft voice)*: You see, you should have taken a nap in the afternoon.
> *Yoni (cynically)*: I should have slept the whole day, shouldn't I?
> *Tali*: But this way you cannot concentrate and do not learn anything.
> *Yoni*: Here you are. You [pointing at me] are yawning now, and Ruth also at some point yawned, but I am the only one she picks on.

Clearly, for some couples the occasion of a birth education class raises implicit and explicit frictions around the issue of the male partner's "participation" and a negotiation about what it means to be a participant. Unlike the American expectant fathers described by Reed (2005), relatively few of the Israeli men I observed enthusiastically participated in the classes. Tali—a graduate student who defines herself as a feminist—assumes there is a lot to learn and sees Yoni's physical presence as not enough. She wants him to participate "fully," which means gaining knowledge about pregnancy. Yoni, for his part, feels that although he is trying his best, he is just being picked on. When classes end slightly later than scheduled, some of the male partners mutter their dismay. Moreover, although classes are usually heavily supported by several visual aids, male partners still complain of boredom. From the above account, it is clear that it is not always easy to draw men into the spheres discussing pregnancy. However, once men do show up, at some point they become engaged in the project of making sense of the bodies of their pregnant partners.

Trying to Make Sense of Pregnancy

While some tensions of sharing a pregnancy are structured into the contradictory social expectations from men, other tensions have to do with a perceptual difficulty. When making sense of pregnancy, an embodied process that does not occur in their own bodies, what is meaningful to Israeli men are the life experiences and images available to them. To illustrate the embodied experience of pregnancy, Ruth gave an elaborate presentation of the anatomy of pregnancy, using an impressive collection of visual props. Her purpose was to explain and illustrate how much strain pregnancy puts on a woman's body:

> *Ruth*: How much amniotic fluid do you have, Miriam?
> *Miriam's husband*: Three liters.
> *Ruth*: If your wife had three liters of water in her belly, she would have walked like this [mimics a heavy backward-bending type of walk].
> *Miriam's husband*: When I was in the army, I carried fifty liters on my back regularly, and I walked straight.
> *Ruth*: But this is not the same thing!! This goes in front, in the belly [participants laugh].

It is notable, first, that while Ruth is trying to use medical logic and language to help men and women make sense of pregnancy, Miriam's husband is drawing on a familiar embodied experience to make sense of his wife's condition. Second, his comparison of pregnancy with his physical experience of soldierhood diminishes the effort of carrying a child, making pregnancy a "nonissue." Third, the fact that this statement was met with laughter rather than anger suggests that the terminologies with which pregnancy was negotiated were common and familiar to both female and male participants. In fact, male partners are not the only ones to use images from the military world to describe reproductive processes (see Goldberg this volume). To give a few examples from other sites of my Israeli fieldwork, a doctor described sperm as "a combatant soldier propagating in enemy territory," a midwife explained that birthing women are "true fighters," and one birth educator even equated pushing a baby to shooting a gun: "You inhale, hold your breath, and then push." In all these examples, the military metaphors were followed by general laughter.

At the same time, many of the Israeli women interviewed felt that pregnancy was not a legitimate excuse for easing up on their everyday tasks. Those who fantasized about reducing pressure at work and at home or, better still, about quitting their jobs toward the end of their terms described themselves as "spoiled." Ultimately, women are expected to take paid maternity leave only after giving birth. Representations of pregnant women as spoiled and capricious are not rare, even in literature for pregnant women, and in such humorous representations, men emerge as subservient rather than "supportive" or "empathetic" in a way that echoes Gadi's description of his domineering wife (see caricatures from Ber and Rosin 1998:33,130,251). Although medical versions construct pregnancy and birth as problematic and dangerous physiological processes that can turn chaotic at any moment and should be monitored closely, Hebrew language, slang, experience, and logic lend themselves well to a trivialization of the physical difficulties of pregnancy, in which women as well as men participate.

In her elaborate anatomical description, Ruth aimed to explain why women "complain so much" during pregnancy, as she felt this might be an important service for women. However, we should pay attention to the technique she used. As Ruth cited numbers and exploited her anatomical charts to illustrate the amount of strain pregnancy places on a woman's body—the increasing pressure a fetus puts on the woman's bladder, as well as heartburn, varicose veins, fatigue, and so on—I could not help thinking that Ruth was medicalizing pregnancy, the same medicalization criticized in feminist literature, as a way to avoid trivializing what she called "the burdens of pregnancy." It was only the authoritative knowledge that was capable of turning mere "griping" into a legitimate inconvenience deserving attention.

Nevertheless, the role Ruth takes upon herself is particularly difficult because, by military standards, carrying "the burdens of pregnancy" seems to be no big deal, certainly nothing to fuss about. Although she (as an authoritative birth educator) challenged Miriam's husband's comparison in terms of pregnancy's position in the body, none of the participants challenged this comparison. No one mentioned that pregnancy is not a package one can unload at the end of the day or questioned the exaggerated number of liters Miriam's husband said represented a soldier's normal load. This indicates that his response was more than a private experience—instead, he called forth the particularly powerful script of the combatant soldier, the ultimate symbol of hegemonic Israeli masculinity. This example vividly shows how the aspiration to include men in the most intimate details of reproduction creates an inner tension. This tension stems from the paradox of the ideal of sharing between men and women in a society with a strong tendency to draw on military images. Measuring pregnancy against military standards is just one technique men use to make sense of pregnancy.

It is significant that one of the characteristics of male narratives throughout the classes was humor. This dimension was almost absent in "women's talk" about pregnancy. The first instance I observed was when Daniela, a midwife teaching at a hospital, stood in the doorway to welcome the couples:

> *Daniela (smiling)*: A belly is the entrance ticket to this class.
> *(Daliya approaches. Daniela strokes Daliya's belly and says)*: What a nice belly! What do you have in there? A developing fetus?
> *Amos (Daliya's husband)*: She's just fat.

On another occasion I recorded the following exchange:

> *Paula (mimics late-pregnancy heavy walking and says to Ayelet)*: You are walking with spread legs—pay attention to the position of your spine.
> *Haim (laughing)*: That's her normal walk.

The transfer of meaning common to these jokes is the nullification of the fertile aspects of pregnancy. When the quality of pregnancy as represented and symbolized by the baby is deemphasized, pregnancy comes to be seen as sheer physical ambiguity, from which it follows that pregnancy is merely like carrying some type of baggage. The above jokes take the nullification of pregnancy to an extreme, which is exactly what makes them humorous.

I repeatedly saw men expressing their puzzlement or resorting to cynicism when confronted by pregnancy. Some felt too much fuss is made about pregnancy and birth, as these are natural and easy processes requiring little intervention. Shahar, a thirty-five-year-old accountant, said, "During my military service, we worked with Bedouins. Once I saw a Bedouin woman giving birth—she had no problem. And we have to study and go through courses." Yoav, a forty-year-old engineer, told me about a birth event he witnessed in Asia: "I saw in Thailand a woman—she gave birth squatting on a banana leaf and then kept on working."

When measured against women in nonmedicalized contexts, Israeli women end up being portrayed as spoiled and requiring excess care that women from Third World countries can do without. All these images portray birth as belonging to the natural or primitive realm of being. However, this is not nature in its grandeur; instead, it is nature as the seemingly simple cycle of life. The Bedouin woman had no problem giving birth, and the Thai woman even resumed her work immediately. It should be borne in mind that Israeli women often refer to themselves as "spoiled," and pregnancy as a nonissue is not a male invention but rather a cultural construct referred to by both genders.

These concepts reached their climax in the following scene, which took place in the birthing room of a Jerusalem hospital during one of Ruth's guided tours. After meeting eight pregnant couples in the hospital lobby and reviewing the hospital's reception procedures, Ruth led us to the birthing rooms. As I wrote in my field notes at the time, Ruth said she wanted to show the couples how they could alter the atmosphere, to create a more intimate feeling despite all the medical equipment. With a whoosh, Ruth sat herself down on the obstetrical chair. "Even if they are going to let you wander around while having contractions, you are most likely to end up here," she said, pointing to the chair. "So we [had] better learn how to manage this chair. This is how you lift the back . . . to assist the woman in pushing the baby out. You see, this chair may be used in creative ways." Then she remembered that she wanted to demonstrate the "traditional" birthing position as well. Sitting on the chair, she tried to lift the stirrups and fasten the screws. However, as she put her legs in the stirrups, they collapsed, making a loud metallic sound. On her first trial, the audience burst out laughing. Ruth continued trying but could not fasten the screws. At some point, the couples started to talk quietly among themselves. And then Uri said to Arik:

> *Uri*: Arik, did you see the flood in Mozambique on TV last night?
> *Arik*: Oh, yeah.
> *Uri*: Did you see that woman?
> *Arik*: She gave birth on a tree.
> *Tsipy*: What?
> *Arik*: Didn't you see? There was a hurricane, and she got stuck on a tall coconut tree. She gave birth there and stayed there for two more days until they got her off the tree when the flood started to ease.
> *(Clang, the sound of the stirrups collapsing again.)*
> *Uri*: We spoil the girls too much. Nurses, massages, beds, tranquilizers, back rubs . . . This woman gave birth on a tree.
> *(Clang, the stirrups collapsing again.)*
> *Uri (to Ruth)*: It's better in a tree.

I argue that the men here are challenging not only the relevance of the specific pieces of knowledge taught in these classes, but also the whole (medicalized) conception of childbirth underlying and organizing the practices of pregnancy and birth. It is important to note that their criticism of medicalization differs profoundly from the familiar feminist discourse that medicalization alienates women from their bodies. In fact, it is quite the contrary: in the men's narratives, the medical organization of childbirth is seen as acting in the interests of "spoiled" women. Most important, the medical model does not necessarily enjoy a special, privileged status in men's efforts to make sense of pregnancy. At least for some men, especially those not engaged in medical occupations, comparable physical efforts from their own lived experience and televised images of "other" models of birth play an equally important role in their attempt to imagine pregnancy.

Involved Men and Their Ill-Defined Role

The case of Tali and Yoni presents an interesting example of the kind of relationship that can be created when the male partner decides to take a greater role in the pregnancy. Tali, who defines herself as a feminist, was quoted as urging Yoni to take a nap in the afternoon so he could concentrate on what was being taught in the birth class. However, later, when Yoni becomes more deeply involved, she takes a different position:

Yoni wanted a child for ages. I took more time. And we [always] said that he would share [the load] with me. He [will] even take half the maternity leave so that I can get back to work earlier. Yoni is the kind of husband that makes my girlfriends die of envy. But on the other hand, when they [men] participate, they also think they are entitled to have a say. With all due respect, I'm the one who's going through this. For example, we said that we were not going to tell anybody that I was in the birthing room. So Yoni asked, "What if your labor becomes longer, and I get tired? What shall we do?" So I said we might call my mother. So Yoni said, "What about my mother?" I said, "No way, this is me giving birth, absolutely not!" He thinks that since he knows what dilation means, he is entitled to make decisions for me.

Yoni is seriously prepared to participate, but this seems to threaten Tali. When her goal has been achieved and Yoni can cite authoritative medical terms, this very knowledge is turned against him. She seems to have adopted a new criterion for eligibility in making decisions, one having to do with the body and experience rather than understanding medical terminology. Yoni and Tali's story demonstrates a central tension inherent to shared pregnancies: the woman's body is where the pregnancy (that is supposed to be equally shared with the male partner) takes place.

Birth educators are aware of the "dangers" of involving men. Paula warned the male partners to "never tell your woman: 'But you vowed not to take any tranquilizers; you wanted a natural birth, didn't you?' She's the one who's in pain." Moreover, all the birth educators I observed seemed to be engaged in the task of inventing roles for men: "Remind your wife that the birth passes," "Be the spokesman for your wife," "Represent your wife to the medical staff," "Remind her to breathe," "Massage her to relieve the pain." Men are expected to participate in pregnancy and birth, but how? In other words, men's social role in pregnancy is anything but well scripted.

When Ruth asked why Tami and Beni had come for a "refresher course" for their second pregnancy, Beni explained that "[w]ith our first son, I tried to use the massages we had learned at the birth education classes on Tami. But at some point Tami bluntly told me, 'Just leave me alone, don't touch me.' So we figured out that this time I should learn how to do it properly." Beni seems to have accepted the idea that massages are necessary for his laboring wife, as well as the role of massager that was offered to him as the "husband's role." His problem was that he did not massage her "properly." When I interviewed Tami after the birth of their second son, she was still seeking a role for her husband. "Birth is not for him. He does not like the sight of blood and does not know what to do, so he videotaped the birth. If he videotapes, that is something for him. Maybe it's my problem that I don't know how to activate him."

Beni was present in the birthing room, but even after the "refresher course" remained a spectator. Tami admitted that Beni is not necessarily the person most suitable to help her while she is in labor: "I have a wonderful sister who could help me." However, it did not occur to her that Beni could be absent from the room when she gave birth. She found techniques to keep him physically present but not overly involved. The video camera keeps Beni far away but in the room to witness the birth of his son, mediated by the lens. From the following scene, it seems that Tami's solution is quite common:

> *Ruth*: Don't forget to take a picture of Mommy and Daddy coming out of the hospital with the baby. This is a standard picture in every family, for the kid as well, so that when Mommy goes to give birth to the next child . . .
> *Noa*: Hanan already sleeps with his camera.
> *Ruth*: Be careful; some fathers find out in the birthing room that they have left the film at home.

It seems that a typical role for men is that of the spectator responsible for documenting the event rather than as a coach. This promotes men to the position of deciding what "deserves" to be documented and what does not, and what is socially acceptable to show to family and friends and what is not. In a way, women are left with the physical labor of giving birth, while men are again assigned roles that have to do with managing and manufacturing external representations.

Conclusion: Toward a Reconsideration of the Shared Pregnancy

What happens to the experience of pregnancy when it is supposed to be ultimately shared by the two partners, as indicated by the statement "we are pregnant"? In other words, what are the social implications of the expectation that men will share their partner's pregnancies? The analysis of Israeli birth education courses suggests that different men react differently to this expectation. Although some might try the roles offered to them—acquiring knowledge about pregnancy or learning how to massage their partners—many remain critical and resistant toward the social pressures to take part in pregnancy and birth and to empathize with their wives.

Juxtaposing Israeli birth education classes with Reed's (2005) account of American birthing classes suggests that the idea of the shared pregnancy and birth has local sociocultural articulations. To reiterate, Israeli and American birth courses are structured differently in that Israeli classes are less about relaxation and role reversal and more about medical information.

In addition, while Reed's American men become disillusioned with the ideas taught in birthing classes only after they leave the birthing room, Israeli men expressed skepticism throughout the course. None of them graduated with the feeling that they could make much of a difference in their partner's well-being during birth (cf. Reed 2005:190). Men's responses ranged between cautious acceptance of the messages taught in the course, to skepticism (more common), to criticism, and even sheer resistance to the ideas underlying birth education. Elsewhere, based on in-depth interviews with Israeli men regarding their experiences of pregnancy, I discuss how this resistance gradually develops throughout the different stages of the pregnancy's medicalized event (Ivry and Teman 2008), a point to which I return below. Thus, whereas the examples here focused on men's responses in birth education classes, they in fact echo the criticism and resistance toward the medicalization of pregnancy and birth I encountered throughout the different sites at which I conducted my fieldwork.

These differences may have to do with two aspects of Israeli social and cultural circumstances that meet here: the local version of medical care of pregnancy and the particular features of Israeli hegemonic masculinity. The local features characterizing the Israeli version of the medicalization of reproduction is clearly illustrated in a growing number of recent works concerned with issues such as surrogacy (Teman 2001, 2003), IVF (Birenbaum-Carmeli 2004; Kahn 2000), genetic testing (Hashiloni-Dolev 2007), routine prenatal care (Ivry 2010), prenatal testing (Remennick 2006), and birth (Morgenstern-Leissner 2005). These works collectively depict a highly medicalized and technologized approach to reproduction supported by state legislation and subsidy. Specifically in the case of pregnancy, Israeli prenatal care emphasizes prenatal diagnosis of inborn fetal anomalies throughout the pregnancy. Thus the minimal state-subsidized routine prenatal care in Israel includes at least three ultrasound scans (one in each trimester), and a second-trimester screening test of maternal blood alfa-feto-protein. Lest any indication of fetal anomaly arise from the latter, amniocentesis is offered to patients of any age and subsidized by the state.

As I have revealed elsewhere, the implications for men are that the more they consider themselves dedicated to their pregnant partners, the more intensively they encounter medical knowledge and procedures, which in turn make them more critical and skeptical about the reliability of medical knowledge and the purity of interests of medical experts (Ivry and Teman 2008.). In short, Israeli first-time fathers-to-be often reach the stage of birthing classes after having experienced a few months of navigating the route of highly medicalized Israeli pregnancy, feeling "there is nothing new that this course can teach me at this stage," as one twenty-eight-year-old electronics technician told me. In a sense, birth education becomes the climax of a process of position forming regarding medicalization that started long before.

As the data presented here reveals, male partners engaged in birth education classes do attempt to make sense of pregnancy. However, not all of them accept the offer to view biomedicine as the ultimate paradigm with which to ponder gestation in spite of the fact that birth educators appeal to gender stereotypes associating men with rationality, pretty much in the same way described by Reed (2005). For some Israeli men, embodied experiences and alternative images of birth play an equally important role in understanding gestation. Moreover, it is notable that the embodied experiences men evoked were of a specific kind; that is, iconic experiences from the repertoire symbolizing Israeli hegemonic masculinity. This suggests that to further our understanding of men's perceptions of gestation, it might be useful to explore the repertoire of embodied experiences that generate local masculinities rather than concentrate mostly on men's experiences with biotechnological devices such as ultrasound.

Thus, with such local masculinities in mind, how do pregnant women look from the perspective of Israeli men? It is clear that when men compare gestation to their own physical hardships, they view pregnancy and birth as a physical challenge. Yet within an unwritten hierarchy of physical challenges, pregnancy does not seem to be very high. Rather, if viewing pregnancy from the Israeli male perspective, pregnancy could possibly be seen as a grotesque fattening of women, one making the latter a target for humor. Thus, once inside the arenas that mark pregnancy, some men come to contest the necessity and importance of the social schemes organizing it—namely, its medicalization. In fact, the critique of the medical institution under whose auspices male partners are called upon to participate might not be so surprising if we consider that the social organization of gestation within medical institutions in itself contributes to the obliteration of the male partner's role in pregnancy and birth. If pregnancy is a physical challenge and doctors and nurses are best qualified to help women with their difficulties, what is the role of men?

The findings presented here suggest that while men are expected to take part in pregnancy, their roles remain largely undefined. During the years of my fieldwork, I sometimes came to think of birth education classes as rituals of sharing in which male partners are given a formal opportunity to express their participation by virtue of attendance. Yet, for some male partners birth education classes remain experiences of coercion into which they are forced either by their pregnant partners or by social expectations. This finding invites further research in the area of Israeli masculinities. Although anthropological literature has long emphasized the dominance of men in Israeli society and explored the various mechanisms through which this dominance is achieved, the experiences of coercion some men report in the arena of reproduction present an opportunity to investigate male experiences of subjugation by women. An exploration of such experiences, I propose, will enrich our understanding of the range of Israeli masculinities and the experiences of men that are forged vis-à-vis these masculinities within domestic as well as medical circumstances.

Returning to this chapter's focus on pregnancy, however, these experiences of subjugation bring us back to the final question: what are the implications of men's participation on the ways pregnancy is experienced and negotiated? I suggest that men's inclusion in the process of pregnancy and birth might actually add rather than remove the tensions in both women's and men's pregnancy experiences. Thus, while potentially romantic and enriching, a shared pregnancy can in fact evolve into a complex and delicate maneuvering within a bilateral relationship.

References

Ben-Ari, Eyal. 1998. *Mastering Soldiers: Conflict, Emotions and the Enemy in an Israeli Military Unit.* New York: Berghahn Books.

Ber, Amos, and Tali Rosin. 1998. *Hamadrich Hayisraeli Leherayon Veleida* [The Israeli Guide to Pregnancy and Birth]. Tel-Aviv: Zmora Bitan.

Birenbaum-Carmeli, Daphna. 2004. "Cheaper than a Newcomer: On the Social Production of IVF Policy in Israel." *Sociology of Health and Illness* 26(7):897–924.

Birenbaum-Carmeli, Daphna, Yoram S. Carmeli, and Robert F. Casper. 1995. "Discrimination against Men in Infertility Treatment." *Journal of Reproductive Medicine* 40(8):590–94.

Birenbaum-Carmeli, Daphna, Yoram S. Carmeli, Madjar Yigal, and Ruth Wessenberg. 2001. "Hegemony and Homogeneity: Donor Choices of Israeli Recipients of Donor Insemination." *Material Culture* 7(1):73–95.

Browner, Carole H., and Maber Preloran.1999. "Male Partners' Role in Latinas' Amniocentesis Decisions." *Journal of Genetic Counseling* 8(2):85–109

Carmeli, Yoram S., and Daphna Birenbaum-Carmeli. 1994. "The Predicament of Masculinity: Towards Understanding the Male's Experience of Infertility Treatments." *Sex Roles* 30(9–10):663–77.

Davis-Floyd, Robbie. 1992. *Birth as an American Rite of Passage.* Berkeley: University of California Press.

Draper, Jan. 2002. "'It Was a Real Good Show': The Ultrasound Scan, Fathers and the Power of Visual Knowledge." *Sociology of Health and Illness* 24(6):771–95.

———. 2003. "Blurring Moving and Broken Boundaries: Men's Encounters with the Pregnant Body." *Sociology of Health and Illness* 25(7):743–67.

Gaskin, Ina May. 1977. *Spiritual Midwifery.* Summertown, TN: Book Publishing Company.

Georges, Eugenia. 1996. "Fetal Ultrasound Imaging and the Production of Authoritative Knowledge in Greece." *Medical Anthropology Quarterly* 10(2):157–75.

Ginsburg, Faye, and Rayna Rapp. 1991 "The Politics of Reproduction." *Annual Review of Anthropology* 20:311–43.

———, eds. 1995. *Conceiving the New World Order: The Global Politics of Reproduction.* Berkeley: University of California Press.

Hashiloni-Dolev, Yael. 2007. *What Is a Life (un)Worthy of Living? Reproductive Genetics in Germany and Israel.* Dordrecht: Springer/Kluwer.

Ivry, Tsipy. 2006. "At the Back Stage of Prenatal Care: Japanese Ob-Gyns Negotiating Prenatal Diagnosis." *Medical Anthropology Quarterly* 20(4):441–68.

———. 2007. "Embodied Responsibilities: Pregnancy in the eyes of Japanese Ob-Gyns." *Sociology of Health and Illness* 29(2):251–74.

———. 2009. *Embodying Culture: Pregnancy in Japan and Israel.* New Brunswick, NJ: Rutgers University Press.

———. 2010. "The Ultrasonic Picture Show and the Politics of Threatened Life." *Medical Anthropology Quarterly.*

Ivry, Tsipy, and Elly Teman. 2008. "Expectant Israeli Fathers and the Medicalized Pregnancy: Ambivalent Compliance and Critical Pragmatism." *Culture Medicine and Psychiatry* 32(3):358–85.

Jordan, Brigitte. 1993. *Birth in Four Cultures: A Crosscultural Investigation of Childbirth in Yucatan, Holland, Sweden, and the United States.* Long Grove, IL: Waveland.

———. 1997. "Authoritative Knowledge and Its Construction." In *Childbirth and Authoritative Knowledge: Cross-Cultural Perspectives,* ed. Robbie Davis-Floyd and Carole F. Sargent. Berkeley: University of California Press.

Kahn, Susan Martha. 2000. *Reproducing Jews: A Cultural Account of Assisted Conception in Israel.* Durham: Duke University Press.

Lomsky-Feder, Edna. 1995. "The Meaning of War through Veterans' Eyes: A Phenomenological Analysis of Life Stories." *International Sociology* 10(4):463–82.

Marcus, George. 1995. "Ethnography in/of the World System: The Emergence of Multi-Sited Ethnography." *Annual Review of Anthropology* 24:95–117.

Martin, Emily. 1991. "The Egg and the Sperm: How Science Has Constructed a Romance Based on Stereotypical Male-Female Roles." *Signs* 16(3):485–501.

Moore, Lisa Jean. 2002. "Extracting Men from Semen: Masculinity in Scientific Representations of Sperm." *Social Text 73:* 91–119.

———. 2003. "Billy, the Sad Sperm with No Tail: Representations of Sperm in Children's Books." *Sexualities* 6(2–4):279–305.

Morgenstern-Leissner, Omi. 2005. "Birthlore and the Law of Birth in Israel." PhD diss., Bar-Ilan University, Ramat Gan.

Petchesky-Pollack, Rosalind. 1987. "Fetal Images: The Power of Visual Culture in the Politics of Reproduction." *Feminist Studies* 13(2):263–92.

Rapp, Rayna. 1999. *Testing Women, Testing the Fetus: The Social Impact of Amniocentesis in America.* New York: Routledge.

Reed, Richard, K. 2005. *Birthing Fathers: The Transformation of Men in American Rites of Birth.* New Brunswick, NJ and London: Rutgers University Press.

Remennick, Larisa. 2006. "The Quest for the Perfect Baby: Why Do Israeli Women Seek Prenatal Genetic Testing?" *Sociology of Health and Illness* 28(1):21–53

Sandelowski, Margarete. 1994. "Separate, but Less Unequal: Fetal Ultrasonography and the Transformation of Expectant Mother/Fatherhood." *Gender & Society* 8(2):230–45.

Sargent, Carolyn Fishel, and Nancy Stark. 1989. "Childbirth Education and Childbirth Models: Prenatal Perspectives on Control, Anesthesia, and Technological Intervention in the Birth Process." *Medical Anthropology Quarterly* 3(1):36–51.

Sasson-Levy, Orna. 2000. "Constructing Gender Identities in the Israeli Army." PhD diss., Hebrew University, Jerusalem.

Schenker, J.G., and U. Elchalal, eds.1998. *Haherayon Hayoledet Vehaleida: Sefer Yesod Bemeyaldut* [Pregnancy and Delivery: A Textbook of Gynecology and Obstetrics]. Jerusalem: Grafit.

Teman, Elly. 2001. "Technological Fragmentation and Women's Empowerment: Surrogate Motherhood in Israel." *Women's Studies Quarterly* 29(3–4):11–34.

———. 2003. "The Medicalization of 'Nature' in the 'Artificial Body': Surrogate Motherhood in Israel." *Medical Anthropology Quarterly* 17(1):78–98.

van der Ploeg, Irma. 1995. "Hermaphrodite Patients: In Vitro Fertilization and the Transformation of Male Infertility." *Science, Technology and Human Values* 20(4):460–81.

Weiss, Meira. 2002. *The Chosen Body: The Politics of the Body in Israeli Society.* Stanford: Stanford University Press.

Chapter 12

MAKING ROOM FOR DADDY: MEN'S "BELLY TALK" IN THE CONTEMPORARY UNITED STATES

Sallie Han

Daniel started each day by placing his hand on his wife Martina's belly and talking to the baby they were expecting: "Good morning. How are you?" When Ryan arrived home at the end of the day, he told stories about what had happened at work. Kevin entertained his wife and their expected child with songs and dances. Interpreting the jabs and kicks he felt when he touched his wife Betsy's belly, Kevin boasted: "I think that the baby knows my voice."

In this chapter, I describe and discuss contemporary concerns regarding men and reproduction, and how they resonate in the everyday lives of American middle-class women and men preparing for parenthood.[1] The focus of this chapter is on men's engagement in activities such as talking, singing, and reading aloud to the expected child in utero, a practice I call "belly talk." Although both women and men in my study engaged in belly talk—indeed, I suggest that belly talk accomplishes important cultural work for mothers and fathers, as kin and kinship become constituted through talk—it is regarded as an especially meaningful practice for fathers. Daniel, Ryan, and Kevin saw such interactions as important opportunities for "hands-on" involvement—both literal and metaphorical—in their partners' pregnancies and with their expected children. Engagement in belly talk enabled these men to meet their own certain expectations, as well as their partners, to share equal, active, and direct participation in the experiences of childbearing and child rearing.

Until recently, there has been no place for men in reproduction—not in the literature on this topic, as scholars note (Gutmann 1997; Tjørnhøj-Thomsen, Goldberg, and Mosegaard this volume; van Balen and Inhorn 2002), or in everyday life, as the women and men in my study described. Scholars today are addressing this gap, as the authors in this volume demonstrate. However, the absence of men in reproduction has not been only an academic issue. In conversations at their kitchen tables and in their nurseries, expectant couples in my study expressed their discontent with men's remove from reproduction, and their desire to include and incorporate men as partners and as parents who participated equally, actively, and directly in childbearing and child rearing. As I describe and discuss in this chapter, belly talk appears to be emerging as a solution to the problem of "making room for Daddy" among American middle-class women and men today.

Methods: Listening to Belly Talk

This discussion of men's belly talk is based on ethnographic research I conducted with pregnant women and their male partners in and around Ann Arbor, Michigan, between October 2002 and January 2004. It draws from a larger project that examines contemporary American middle-class pregnancy practices in anthropological perspective. These practices include attending childbirth education classes, seeking prenatal health care, and shopping, as well as belly talk.

In my fieldwork, I used a variety of methods to collect and analyze data that revealed various aspects of women's childbearing and child rearing experiences. I began with women's own accounts. Working primarily with a core group of sixteen women who were expecting a first child, I recorded more than eighty hours of repeated, in-depth interviews that documented their experiences of pregnancy. I also interviewed eleven expectant fathers together with their pregnant spouses at least once; two of these men were interviewed regularly with their spouses.[2] I analyzed the texts of these interviews as the narratives of individual women and men, as well as examining them for themes common across accounts. To complement the interviews, I observed expectant parents at work and at home, accompanied them on prenatal care visits and shopping trips, and attended baby showers. I also interviewed and observed doctors, midwives, and others providing care and services for pregnant women. In addition, I collected media sources such as books, magazines, and websites to which expectant parents turned for information and advice on pregnancy and parenting.

In interviews, both women and men described engaging in activities intended as contact with the expected child. These activities included talking, reading aloud, singing to, and playing music for the child. They also described communication that involved massaging, poking, prodding, or otherwise touching the pregnant woman's belly and by extension, the expected child within. I use the term "belly talk" to refer to all forms of the contact and communication directed to an expected child (or children) in utero by expectant parties, including parents and/or others interested in establishing relationships or "relating" to the expected child (e.g., siblings, relatives, or neighbors).[3]

It is unclear how common a practice belly talk is and how long it has been practiced in the United States. However, a perusal of advice literature for parents indicates that engagement in the activities I call belly talk has become popular, if only recently. *Pregnancy and Childbirth*, a best-selling book published in 1997, advises expectant mothers and fathers that "[t]here's a new concept referred to as 'prenatal parenting,' which has to do with the influence you can have on your unborn baby's development" (Hotchner 1997:41). No such mention is made of "prenatal parenting" or "prenatal stimulation" in the guides and manuals for earlier generations, such as Samuel R. Meaker's *Preparing for Motherhood* (1956) or Nicholson J. Eastman's *Expectant Motherhood* (1963). Although I have not started a systematic study with grandmothers and grandfathers, I have spoken with few of that generation who recalled engaging in belly talk.

Initially, it was not my intention to examine belly talk. Rather, the focus of my study was on the bodily experiences of reproduction, pregnancy in particular. I made two assumptions that I quickly learned were in error. First, I assumed that talk was not bodily. Second, I assumed that men had little or nothing to say about pregnancy as bodily experience because, after all, they do not become pregnant. I was inclined to view their involvement as secondary and included fathers in my study in order to gather information on the kinds of support they provided (or failed to provide) during pregnancy. Women experienced childbearing, and men merely bore witness to their experience—or so I thought until I began to hear about belly talk, which also prompted me to reconsider what constituted bodily experiences in the first place.

Because this discussion of men's belly talk is based primarily on women's and men's reports describing it, I can claim only limited knowledge about the exact context and entire content of the communications that were made. However, I occasionally observed demonstrations of belly talk when I became the witness to an intimate moment shared spontaneously among an expectant mother, father, and their expected child. As the woman and I were conversing, her husband, who was seated on the floor at her feet, pushed up the bottom of his wife's top and began to talk slowly and exaggeratedly "into" her now-exposed belly, with his lips pressed near her navel. First, he said, "Hello." Then, he said, "I love you." However, I was impressed less by what the man said and more by how he said it. I saw the close physical contact of belly talk as meaningful communication shared among the expectant mother, father, and their expected child.[4]

I also gained hands-on experience with men's belly talk when I learned I was pregnant, approximately nine months after I began fieldwork. As my own belly became more of a physical presence in our life together, I noticed my partner had begun to interact physically with it. At twenty weeks of pregnancy, I could feel the fetal movement, but my husband could not—he sometimes placed his hands on my belly, hoping to feel a kick from the outside. Although he certainly was as involved in the pregnancy as any other man I know, he sometimes expressed to me how "unreal" the pregnancy felt to him. Belly talk became a means for making the pregnancy—and the child we were expecting—real for him.

Such experiences with men's belly talk alerted me both to the limitations of considering it only as speech and to its significance in terms of men and reproduction. Belly talk is comprised as much of body as of language. As I discuss in the following sections, it enables men's equal, active, and direct involvement as partners in childbearing because it allows them to have such bodily involvement in and during pregnancy. Belly talk also involves men equally, actively, and directly as parents to their expected children.

Partners in Belly Talk

Like other expectant mothers in the United States, Greta marked the progress of her pregnancy with the passage of many firsts: the first time she heard her baby's heartbeat during a prenatal visit; the first time she and her husband, Adam, saw their baby's face during an ultrasound screening, when they also first learned that the baby was a girl; the first movements she could feel, and the first movements Adam could feel.

In fact, for Adam, that first baby "picture" from the ultrasound and those first kicks and flutters touched off a flurry of activity. He and Greta, then twenty-three weeks pregnant, picked out a stroller, a paint color for the spare bedroom they planned to remake as a nursery, and even a name for their expected baby girl. They signed up for classes on childbirth preparation, breastfeeding, and infant care, enlisting in weekend courses called "Basic Training for Moms" and "Boot Camp for Dads."

Greta observed that although Adam had been a supportive partner from the start, the level of his interest and involvement in the pregnancy, and especially in their expected child, seemed greater than it had been: "He now talks to her because she's been starting to move around a lot more." Greta also seemed to take pleasure in Adam's stepped-up participation in the pregnancy and his engagement with their expected daughter, both in the form of talk. "Adam says, 'Hi,' and oh, you know, 'Give us a kick.' This morning, I could feel her move, and she's been moving a lot, so I asked Adam to talk to her, and then he did, so she'd kick. So, that's kind of fun."

For the women and men in my study, the bodily experience of pregnancy was central to partnership and to parenthood. Mothers and fathers alike were concerned that men should share bodily involvement in and during pregnancy. Not surprising, pregnant women were particularly articulate about this topic. Kris, a graduate student, described men's experience of pregnancy as only partial because of what she perceived as their lack of bodily involvement. "It's like they get to audit the class—they don't actually have to take the exam at the end," she said. "You get everything out of it, but you don't have to be the one physically going through it." However, bodily involvement in the pregnancy is exactly what her husband seemed to want. "David is telling me to eat more because he wants to see the baby more. Well, I don't want to get too big," she said. "I hope I don't have to get an episiotomy. I hope the kid doesn't get that big."

In awestruck tones, Kevin described both the burgeoning of his wife Betsy's pregnant body and of the baby they were expecting:

Since we've been pregnant, Betsy has been at least 74 percent emotion. I'm not saying this is a negative thing. You're transforming. Her heart moved over, her ribs moved, her pelvis. Her body is moving, her nipples leaking, her breasts enlarging two or three sizes. Her body is transforming. I feel it kicking. I heard the heartbeat many times. Creation is something—and there's a sense of jealousy. There's a sense of—for a man watching the creation of a child, to know that's something that no man will be able to accomplish in life—unless some new technology happens. That's that bond that I got with my mama to this day.

Kevin's awareness of Betsy's bodily experience of pregnancy was not unusual though his articulateness about the minutiae might be. Here, Kevin linked Betsy's emotional changes with her transforming body. Although he is discussing the fact that her physical discomforts are causing emotional discomforts, Kevin is respectful of Betsy's transformation overall. Significantly, it is not only Betsy's bodily experience that Kevin describes here. He also includes his own experiences feeling the kicks and hearing the heartbeat of their expected child.

Because of the ways it remains naturalized as a biological fact and bodily experience, for the men and women in my study, motherhood seemed more self-evident and less complicated than fatherhood. They all understood there were certain kinds of expectations for mothers and certain experiences mothers shared. However, this is not so for fathers. In anthropological terms, fatherhood presented itself as problematic because of its nature—or apparent lack of it, as there is no exclusively male complement in American society and culture, jokes about couvade and sympathetic pregnancy symptoms (such as men's weight gain) aside. With the invention of belly talk, a bodily experience of pregnancy has been invented for men, too. As father-to-be Kevin explained, "I try to compensate because I'm not holding the baby."

The expectation that men should share the bodily experience of childbearing appears to be consistent with the ideal of modern marriage and the idea of conjugality that American social historian John Gillis describes: "The perfect couple now must be everything to one another—good providers, super sexual partners, best friends, stimulating companions—roles that earlier generations turned to others to fulfill" (1996:151). Women and men in my study expressed strong feelings about the connection between partnership and parenthood. As one woman in my study described her plans for breastfeeding and sleeping with her baby in order to promote strong bonds between mother and child, her partner interrupted by saying, "The bonding starts with the man and the woman."

Indeed, all of the men in my study took active part in being expectant. (If they had not, they would not have been willing or able to contribute to this research.) They attended childbirth preparation and even breastfeeding classes. Most made a point of accompanying their partners to prenatal appointments. Several men began making arrangements at their workplaces, such as reassigning projects and saving vacation days, to be able to schedule time off around the birth. One man built a dresser for the child he and his wife were expecting, with woodworking skills he taught himself from books borrowed from the local library. Before their wives became pregnant, all of the men had shared responsibilities at home to some degree. During pregnancy, they all seemed to have stepped up their efforts, especially during the early months, when their wives were coping with nausea and other symptoms, and again during the later months, with the onset of back pain and fatigue.

Interestingly, the women in my study were more vocal than the men about their wishes for more equal, active, and direct involvement from their male partners and for more acknowledgment from others of their participation. For example, expectant mothers seemed to be invested especially in the involvement and acknowledgment of expectant fathers in the medical setting, which figured significantly in women's and men's experiences of reproduction (as I discuss below). At twenty weeks of pregnancy, Nicole said, "I'm not really showing yet. I haven't felt movement up until this week. I'm hoping that when we have our big ultrasound next week that that will do a couple of things—reassure me that things are still going OK and also get my husband involved." Although it obviously annoyed her, she tried to excuse her husband's uninvolvement: "He doesn't come to the appointments because he's very uncomfortable. They just let us sit in the examining room for a long time by ourselves. He was bored and not happy." In fact, Nicole had decided to "spare" him from refusal to accompany her (and herself from disappointment): "I don't even tell him because he doesn't like to go to the doctor himself."

Finding ways to enable and encourage men's involvement in the pregnancy (or in Nicole's case, even to excuse uninvolvement) has itself become a pregnancy practice. Though written for expectant mothers, popular pregnancy books now include advice for expectant fathers. (Presumably, mothers-to-be must pass along the advice—if not the book itself—to fathers-to-be.) In a special section called "Fathers Are Expectant, Too," the authors of *What to Expect When You're Expecting* address the problem of "Feeling Left Out": "So much attention has been focused on my wife since she became pregnant that I hardly feel I have anything to do with it" (Eisenberg, Murkoff, and Hathaway 1996:412). The expectant father is prescribed belly talk as a way to become involved, both with the pregnancy and with the expected child. "Your wife may have the edge in getting to know the baby prenatally because it's comfortably ensconced in her uterus, but that doesn't mean that you can't start to know the new family member, too. Talk, read, sing to your baby frequently" (413).

Such advice underscores the significance of bodily experience in reproduction. First, pregnancy, or more specific the changes that pregnancy engenders in the woman's body, draw attention from others to the woman (and child) and, it can be inferred, acknowledgement from others that mother and baby have a relationship—one from which the man is "left out." Second, such bodily involvement also gives women an "edge" in establishing relationships with their children. Thus, the purpose of advice to talk, read, and sing to the baby is to eliminate this edge and make women's and men's participation as partners and parents equally important. Indeed, women and men in my study were concerned that men received recognition socially as fathers-to-be (equal to what women received as mothers-to-be) and that men were participating in the experience of pregnancy and involved with the children they were expecting. Although such advice is intended to include and involve fathers, it also calls attention to the ways men have been excluded and uninvolved.

Out of Place: American Men and Reproduction in Context

"Men are totally taken out of it," Kevin commented during an interview only three weeks before his wife Betsy's due date. While Americans today are reminded by politicians and the popular press that fathers are "missing in action," Kevin has first-hand experience, at home and at work, with the absence of men in reproduction.[5] He is an African American male whose own father had been largely absent during his childhood, and he is the lone male teacher at a preschool where most of the African American or Latino students are the children of single mothers.

On the one hand, Kevin felt that men's uninvolvement with their children was a failure of personal responsibility. On the other hand, Kevin also asserted this was not just the problem of individuals. "The world expects men to be smoking a cigar," he complained. Other mothers and fathers in my study expressed discomfiture and dissatisfaction not only with what they perceived as men's unequal involvement in childbearing and child rearing, but also with a lack of expectations and opportunities (as well as regard and respect) to support and encourage men's participation as partners and as parents in American society and culture at large. One woman in my study told me she had apologized to her partner for the advice on American men's role during labor and delivery that had been offered jokingly during a childbirth education class—to change the channel on the TV and keep the volume on low. I heard similar comments, also intended to be humorous, during a tour I took at a local birthing center.

Despite changes in institutional practice that barred previous generations of fathers from labor and delivery rooms, the medical setting appears to remain a space where men (other than doctors) have no place. When Kevin decried the lack of expectations for men as fathers, he evoked an image of the "traditional" father of the recent past—the breadwinner "smoking a cigar" while waiting for his wife to finish the woman's work of labor and delivery. Kevin rejected both this style of fathering and the model of masculinity associated with it. Rather than smoking a cigar—which implies passively waiting in a hospital—Kevin and his wife planned for his active involvement to include "catching" their child at birth, which was planned to be in their home. Indeed, Betsy explained that she and Kevin were planning a home birth with independent midwives in order to avoid having what she called an "institutionalized" experience of pregnancy, labor, and delivery. From her perspective, institutionalized care not only "disempowered the woman"—echoing the feminist critique of the medicalization of childbirth (Davis-Floyd 1992)—but also disenfranchised the man. Kevin continued,

> The men are really downplayed. Even in our visits [with the midwives] sometimes—I mean, they cater to [Betsy]. They're supposed to, you understand. But it's almost like, men pacing in the waiting room, the woman in there laboring. That's the Stone Age. I want to be an integral part in the birth of my child. Here in North America, I've seen a lot of proud fathers, but it's usually quote-unquote a woman's thing at birth. It's not. It is a two-person job.

Here, Kevin describes institutionalized practices that keep men uninvolved as "Stone Age," or unenlightened and unevolved. His reference to the Stone Age also recalls the labeling of men (particularly those demonstrating a certain model of masculinity) as cavemen or Neanderthals. However, Kevin also criticizes the non-institutionalized practices of the lay midwives because they made no room for fathers.

Similarly, Brian and Kerri sought prenatal care that equally involved and recognized them as partners. This led to their decision to transfer Kerri's prenatal care from a larger practice of obstetricians to a smaller practice of certified nurse-midwives. Kerri, who was twenty-six weeks pregnant at the time, explained that there were two reasons for the change. The first was her wish for more personalized attention from her care providers. Kerri confided that at age forty, having already suffered one pregnancy loss, plus failed attempts at in vitro fertilization, she had been unhappy with being treated like "just another pregnant woman." The second reason for the change in care providers was Kerri's wish for Brian to be more included. Kerri compared her previous experiences at the obstetricians' office to those at the midwives' office.

> When we were at the first check-up with the midwives, it was interesting just to see how different their way of relating to Brian was, which I was really happy about because he's often felt like, by the practitioners—he's not really included in things. The first time we were pregnant—this was when I had the miscarriage—he went with me to my first prenatal visit. The nurse was taking my blood pressure, and there was no place for him to sit in the room. He was kind of off on the side. The nurse was talking just to me. No eye contact with Brian at all, not including him, not explaining anything to him. That's been pretty much the way he's been treated all through the experience so far. The midwives were measuring me and they said, "Brian, I don't mean to turn my back on you. Come on and stand up here and take a look at what I'm doing." It was just immediately a very different kind of approach, saying, "This is our baby. Even though it's me carrying, Brian is as much of an involved partner here."

Kerri's concern was not only with the care provided to her, but also with the care provided to her husband. At the previous practice, there was a lack of it for Brian, with "no place for him to sit" and "no eye contact." Kerri especially seemed to take satisfaction in the fact that the nurse-midwives recognized the expected child as "our baby." By extension, the pregnancy also was theirs together, rather than hers alone. In fact, Kerri sees both herself and Brian as making equal contributions. She is "carrying," but he "is as much of an involved partner here." Brian himself added: "I think if I was twenty or twenty-five or maybe even thirty—I think I would have a very different approach to it. But it's something that I've looked forward to for so long, and I really feel like this very well may be our only pregnancy."

Significantly, both Kevin and Brian saw themselves as involved equally, actively, and directly in both the pregnancy and the birth. Prenatal care was received not at "her" appointments but during "our visits" with the midwives. Kevin rejects the notion that childbearing and childbirth should be "a woman's thing." Ironically, the "reclaiming" of birth for women has been cause for the celebration of "traditional" midwives in the United States, including among anthropologists (Davis-Floyd and Sargent 1997; Klassen 2001). However, Kevin and his wife Betsy, and Brian and his wife Kerri demand equal recognition for fathers in the experiences of childbearing and child rearing. Kerri attempts even to minimize the difference between her and Brian's involvement, as she refers to the fact that she is "carrying" their child.

Returning to Kevin's reference to the cigar-smoking, breadwinning father, this model of masculinity not only has lost its appeal for Kevin and the other men in my study, it also is no longer attainable for many American middle-class men. Gillis observes that in the United States, "there has been an unprecedented drop in men's real earnings, partly as a result of unemployment, but also a consequence of stagnant or falling wages. A dual income, now increasingly dependent on more than two jobs, had always been a necessity for most working-class people, but now it became the norm for all social classes" (2000:232). For many American couples today, including Kevin and Betsy, simply making ends meet is a "two-person job," as Kevin had described childbirth and child rearing.

Gillis also suggests that "the marginalization of fathers in western countries is a structural rather than a moral problem" and is "linked in important ways to the current restructuring of the global capitalist economy" (2000:227). Specifically, Gillis refers to two related shifts—the relocation of manufacturing jobs to developing areas where cheap labor can be exploited and the increased reliance worldwide on women's labor. In the United States, mothers who work outside the home have become nothing exceptional. However, there exist few structural spaces, in the form of support, for American men as fathers.[6] American sociologists Ann Orloff and Renee Monson observe that "the most salient fact about the treatment of fathers in US social policy is the virtual absence of programs targeting them *as fathers*" (2002:61). Notably, leave policy from work in the United States was enacted later than in most other Western countries and provides fewer benefits for fewer workers. Passed in 1993, the Family and Medical Leave Act provides for up to twelve weeks of unpaid leave only and applies only to companies employing fifty or more workers. Consequently, fewer American fathers take leave, and those who do often take shorter leaves than allowed (Seward, Yeatts, and Zottarelli 2002). Indeed, there appears to be a particular bias against men taking leave from work for family matters (Wayne and Cordeiro 2003). In this context, American women and men continue to regard fathering in terms of morality, and American men's increased involvement as fathers comes in the form not of institutionalized opportunities, but of individualized practices such as belly talk.[7]

Parents in Belly Talk

Both women and men in my study engaged in belly talk. Greta "checked in" with the baby during her morning drive to work. Bridget occasionally told a bedtime story or had her husband, Ryan, tell one. Both mothers and fathers regarded such activities as important for the development of the child and especially their relationship with her or him. As I discuss in this section, belly talk accomplishes important cultural work for American mothers and fathers alike. First, I suggest that belly talk socializes women and men as parents. Second, I suggest that belly talk genders parents as mothers and fathers.

Although language socialization usually is understood in terms of the socialization of children, I suggest that it also can be considered as the socialization of adults as parents.[8] Language has been regarded as an important tool for socializing children—that is, for instructing them in how to use language and how to act appropriately in other arenas (with language facilitating such instruction). It has been assumed that the function of caregiver speech, better known as "baby talk," was to make adult language understandable to young children. However, linguistic anthropologists working in the United States long have demonstrated that caregiver speech has other effects. Linguistic anthropologist Charles Ferguson (1977) observed that baby talk was used with adults as well as children to express affection, offer nurturance, and coax. The effect of baby talk is "to signal the childhood status of participants in the communication situation" (231). Linguistic anthropologists Elinor Ochs and Bambi Schieffelin note that "[e]very social relationship is associated with a set of behaviors, verbal and nonverbal, that set off that relationship from other relationships. Additionally, these behaviors indicate to others that a particular social relationship is being actualized" (1984:301). I suggest that belly talk has the effect of signaling the status of expectant and expected participants in the communication situation. Parents and children become constituted through belly talk, which actualizes their relationships.

Although I have employed here the term "parents" to refer to both mothers and fathers, I suggest that it remains necessary to distinguish between them. The terms "parent," "parenting," and "parenthood" are assumed to be inclusive of women and men and their reproductive roles and responsibilities. They are used as interchangeable for mother/father, mothering/fathering, and motherhood/fatherhood. However, as anthropologists repeatedly have demonstrated, difference with respect to reproduction usually defines women as women and men as men, even as their specific roles and responsibilities differ across cultures (Collier and Yanagisako 1987). In sum, there are no generic "parents," but rather, there are parents gendered as mothers and fathers.

Although expectant parents—including both pregnant women and their male partners—engage in belly talk, it cannot be considered a generic or gender-neutral practice. Rather, belly talk appears to accomplish different cultural work for women and men. It genders mothers and fathers. In her article "Indexing Gender," Ochs demonstrates how mothers become engendered through communicative practices such as speech: "Gender ideologies are socialized, sustained, and transformed through talk, particularly through verbal practices that recur innumerable times in the lives of members of social groups" (1992:336).

For example, establishing a relationship between father and child seems to be the work of mothers-to-be. It is a form of kin work (and gender work) that women perform as female partners and parents. I observed that belly talk sometimes took the form of role-play. However, the role-play appears to anticipate real roles. Martina reported that she had recruited her husband Daniel's help in communicating with their expected child. At twenty-two weeks of pregnancy, she had been advised to sleep on her side because lying on her back could cut off circulation to the baby. However, she admitted that she had difficulty following this advice, and it worried her.

> Sometimes, I fall asleep on my side, and at some point in the middle of the night, I'll wake up. Oh my gosh, how long have I been on my back? This happened a couple of times. Finally, I said, "OK, Daniel, I need you to tell the kid something." So, he goes down, puts his head toward my stomach, and I told him to tell the baby that—who he was because it's not my voice, and it's a very deep voice compared to mine. You know, introduce yourself and then say, "If you ever can't breathe or if Mommy is lying on her back, then kick Mommy really hard so that she can roll over, OK?" So, that was what we told the kid.

In the exchange that Martina describes, Daniel is asked to introduce himself, which both implies and enforces his physical and relational distance from the expected child. However, Martina also seems to perceive distance from "the kid" in that she asks Daniel to talk to her belly in close proximity, which she cannot do. In that sense, Daniel shares a kind of closeness with the belly and the baby that Martina does not.

These kinds of communicative practices communicate more than that "the kid" ought to kick. They also communicate gender. As Ochs observes, "American mothers enter into negotiations with their children over the meaning of children's unclear utterances" and "treat even the tiniest of infants as conversational partners" (1992:355). Certain responsibilities are assigned to and assumed by Martina and Daniel. Mother recruits father to speak to the child about an important matter.

Belly Talk and American Masculinities

Ochs observes that "images of women are linked to images of mothering and that such images are socialized through communicative practices associated with caregiving" (1992:337). I suggest that images of "new" men and "involved" fatherhood are being socialized through men's belly talk. As first-time father Brian remarked, "It's what I want to do, to be reading these books and being involved. It feels totally natural to me."

However, the fathers in my study generally were self-conscious about their own participation in and during pregnancy. "I feel like we must question or have more of an interest in things than the average person," said Brian, who with his wife Kerri had enrolled in not one but two childbirth education classes, plus infant care and breastfeeding classes, which they planned to attend together. Brian and other men in my study saw themselves as different from most men of their own generation as well as their fathers'. When I asked one man about what fatherhood meant to him, he commented on how his father had not been especially involved, had not shared an equal part with the mother, nor had taken an active interest in the children. However, he also insisted that his father had been "a good man."

In his recent ethnography of American fathers, anthropologist Nicholas Townsend (2002) highlights the tensions between new expectations for men to participate equally, active, and directly as partners and parents, and older ones that defined men and fathers as providers. Townsend describes American masculinity as a package deal that includes marriage, children, and a steady job, and fatherhood as a composite of responsibilities—closeness, provision, endowment, and protection. "Of these four," he writes, "men said the most important thing they did for their children was to provide for them" (53). Townsend notes that the other fatherly responsibilities, especially endowment and protection, depend on provision. Despite significant changes in "the nature of the expectation of paternal closeness and involvement" (102), the expectation that men provide still remains more or less intact. As a result, Townsend observes that "being close to one's children and being a good provider are in tension and fathers have to do cultural work to make the case that they are doing both" (56).

I suggest that belly talk is emerging as an important means for American men to accomplish this cultural work. First, belly talk is a means of establishing and enacting emotional closeness or involvement with children that is equal, active, and direct. If closeness is partly a result of the amount of time that fathers and children have together, as the comments of parents in my study suggest, then belly talk contributes to closeness because it enables men to become involved with their children earlier—even before birth. Daniel, a professor at a small college, and his wife Martina, a graduate student who was then thirty-three weeks pregnant, recounted for me a discussion at the Bradley childbirth preparation class they were attending. "Last week, we saw the videos about birth. Somehow it helped me realize that what's in there"—Daniel gestured to Martina's burgeoning belly—"is an actual person that's going to come out and I have to—that we have to relate to it and everything." Other fathers-to-be made similar remarks about the impact that seeing a birth (even if only on video) had in terms of making the impending birth "real" for them. Daniel continued: "Then I realized, well, I can start relating to the baby right now—talking to the baby while it's still in the womb." As Daniel's comments suggest, belly talk also contributes to closeness because it allows men to have "direct action and personal interaction" (Townsend 2002:103) with their expected children.

Belly talk also enables men to meet the responsibilities of providing endowment and protection for their children. Mothers and fathers in my study described their belly talk in terms of bonding with their babies-to-be; that is, establishing emotional closeness as well as familiarizing their expected children with the sounds of their voices, and providing stimulation that pregnancy and parenting books suggested might promote healthy development in children. Based on comparative research, anthropologist Sara Harkness and psychologist Charles Super suggest that this emphasis on "stimulation" is a feature of the particular "ethnotheory" of parenting that can be identified with American middle-class culture (1996). Anthropologist Meredith Small notes that in contrast to Dutch parents, who "believe that regularity, rest, and cleanliness promote intelligent development," American parents "use all kinds of visual and verbal stimuli to catch the baby's attention and encourage it to interact" (1999:53). Ochs and Schieffelin suggest in their work on language

acquisition and socialization that "[t]he primary concern of caregivers is to ensure that their children are able to display and understand
behaviors appropriate to social situations. A major means by which
this is accomplished is through language" (1984:276). They note
that American middle-class parents in particular "make extensive
accommodations to the child, assuming the perspective of the child
in the course of engaging him or her in conversational dialogue"
(281). They observe that caregiver speech of this kind is "highly valued by members of white middle-class society" and "associated with
good mothering" (283). As I suggest in this chapter, belly talk also
has come to be associated with good fathering.

Belly talk has emerged as a pregnancy practice for men at a moment when "wage-earning has become the norm for white middle-class mothers, [and] anxieties about class-enhancing mothering
may have increased. Perhaps every extra IQ point, vocabulary word,
and physical enhancing feature is needed to compete in the flexible,
'post-Fordist' US" (Blum 1999:183). Gillis suggests that "more men
want to be good fathers, but standards of good fatherhood, defined
as breadwinning and secondary parenting, have had to keep pace
with the standards of good mothering, which have increased spec-
tacularly" (2000:233).

Belly talk also emerges from a particular cultural and historical
context that has been described as "a middle-class culture that values planning, control, and predictability in the interests of a 'quality child'" (Petchesky 1987:282). It reveals much about social and
cultural expectations of children and parents in the contemporary
United States, as well as about ideologies of language, which is regarded both as a tool or means for the socialization of children and
a goal or end in itself. As sociologist Viviana Zelizer suggests (1994
[1985]), American middle-class children today are not only regarded as objects of consumption. In the form of proper parental provision of "enrichment" experiences such as music lessons, foreign-
language programs, soccer league, and summer camp, consumption
is seen now as "investment" in the child's future. As evidenced in
belly talk, investing in children can begin even before birth. Readers of the popular book *Pregnancy and Childbirth* are advised that
"[t]here's a new concept referred to as 'prenatal parenting,' which
has to do with the influence you can have on your unborn baby's
development" (Hotchner 1997:41). The book urges expectant parents to "feel free to talk to your unborn baby, play music for her,
read her stories, and massage her" (42). William and Martha Sears,
the husband/pediatrician and wife/nurse authors of several best-
selling American parenting manuals, including *The Pregnancy Book*,

suggest the impact of such parental attentions: "Orchestra conductors have claimed they feel an unexplained familiarity with music their mothers played while pregnant" (1997:224).

The advice to read aloud seems to be particularly popular among those middle-class mothers- and fathers-to-be especially eager to promote an interest in reading and a love of literature. In her discussion of literacy practices among "mainstream" or middle-class families in the United States, linguistic anthropologist Shirley Brice Heath observes that "[a]s early as six months of age, children give attention to books and information derived from books. Their rooms contain bookcases and are decorated with murals, bedspreads, mobiles, and stuffed animals which represent characters found in books" (1996:14–15). This interest in what Heath calls "mainstream school-oriented bookreading" both reflects and inflects ideas about written language, its link to education, and its association with achievement and success.

Thus, like other belly-talk activities, reading aloud to the expected child serves several ends. Mothers- and fathers-to-be might read from traditional children's storybooks such as *Peter Rabbit* or *Winnie-the-Pooh*. Or they might read from a book such as *Oh, Baby, the Places You'll Go!*, an adaptation of Dr. Seuss stories that is, as its subtitle indicates, *A Book to Be Read in Utero*.

As a "1st-time mom to be from New Hampshire," reads a book review posted on a website, "this is a great way to get 'daddy' involved. My husband loves to read this book to our baby." In another review on the same website, a "New Mom from Alaska" raves:

> My husband and I read this book to the "belly" from about week 20 on. My husband recited it each night and around the house up until the day our boy was born. He read it within a few minutes of the birth and my son recognized the voice and cadence immediately. I've also given this away as a baby shower gift, it's a good way to introduce new parents-to-be to silly children's books, and gets you thinking that the "belly" is alive and can respond.

In this review, "New Mom" seems to be raving equally about her husband's involvement with the belly and about the book and its apparent impact. Because of his participation during the pregnancy, the husband has established a relationship with the baby, one recognized immediately at birth.

By engaging in belly talk, then, expectant fathers establish emotional closeness or bonds with their expected children. These bonds also promote children's development, such as the cognitive abilities and social skills for accomplishment later in life. Through

Figure 12.1. "Book Cover,"copyright 1997, from *Oh, Baby, the Places You'll Go! A Book to Be Read in Utero* by Dr. Seuss and adapted by Tish Rabe. Used by permission of Random House Children's Books, a division of Random House, Inc.

belly talk, men educate their children, endowing them not only with the tools they need to build their own future successes but also giving them a competitive "head start."[9] As a result, men can continue to provide for, endow, and thus protect their children from hardship in a global economy in which the once-celebrated breadwinner has failed. In fact, it seems that involved fathers today offer better provision, endowment, and protection for their children because their participation (as partners and as parents) is equal, active, and direct.

Conclusion

In this chapter, I have described and discussed concerns regarding men and reproduction—the problem of making room for Daddy—from the perspectives of American middle-class mothers and fathers. Women and men in my study conceived of men's belly talk as a solution to what they regarded as men's absence from reproduction, as partners and as parents. Mothers and fathers alike described the many ways men were "out of it" in matters of reproduction.

Belly talk allows American men to be incorporated and to incorporate themselves into the experiences of childbearing and child rearing. As partners in belly talk, men share in the bodily experience of pregnancy. As parents in belly talk, men become equally, actively, and directly involved in child rearing, enabling them to meet continuing expectations that fathers provide for, endow, and protect their children. In the context of an American middle-class culture, men's parenting includes "investing" in their children, notably, the promotion of literacy and other educational practices that will enable a child to provide for and protect herself or himself later in life.

Men's belly talk provides an example of how men are defined by their experiences of reproduction. Women and especially men in my study rejected a model of masculinity that was based on men's detachment from experiences of reproduction and disengagement from bodily involvement (i.e., the cigar-smoking, breadwinning father). Instead, they sought validation and valorization of—and through—an American masculinity based particularly in embodied partnership and embodied parenthood.

Although scholars recently have begun to ask and address the question of why not men in reproduction, the women and men in my study have lived it and have created their own solution in belly talk. An examination of belly talk is not only instructive as an example of the issues surrounding men and reproduction, it also demonstrates what we all might learn about reproduction from the expectations and experiences of women and men in their everyday lives.

Acknowledgments

I am indebted to Jason Antrosio, Nicole Berry, Jessa Leinaweaver, and the editors of this volume for their comments and suggestions, as well as to the mothers and fathers who allowed me into their lives.

Notes

1. For the sake of expediency, I interchangeably use terms such as "parent," "father," "expectant father," and "father-to-be," which women and men in my study used to refer to their partners and themselves. Similarly, I also interchangeably use the terms "baby" and "fetus," which parents in my study used, and "expected child," a term I use to highlight the notion of expectancy as well as of kinship. I use all of these terms advisedly, as none of them are neutral or value free but carry particular cultural and social significance.
2. The remaining five women were not interviewed with partners for various reasons. There were difficulties with scheduling interviews with the spouses of three of the women because of their job situations—one worked irregular hours, the second worked two jobs in addition to attending school, and the third had been sent to Iraq as a civilian contractor, returning not even two weeks before the baby arrived. The other two women were single mothers—one was no longer involved with her child's father, and the other had conceived her child using artificial insemination.
3. Equally important, the belly talks back. Belly talk includes interpreting fetal kicks and other movements felt inside the uterus as communications from the expected child.
4. Although belly talk ostensibly is directed to the baby, it also is a communication between father and mother.
5. There is a vast sociological literature that examines what observers call the "crisis" of fatherhood in the United States—a term that describes observed demographic trends such as divorce and single-parent families, as well as popular perceptions regarding both "deadbeat dads" and absent "workaholic" fathers (Hobson 2002).
6. In fact, there is not much in the form of "support" for mothers, as sociologist Arlie Hochschild has documented (1990).
7. The privatization of fathering I describe here is consistent with contemporary American approaches to motherhood, which can be traced to the Progressive Era social policy of the early twentieth century. Policymakers then had been concerned with promoting particular ideas and practices of parenting through "education, not charity," as phrased in their motto (Klaus 1993). Assistance for parents and children come primarily in the form of tax credits to individuals, and state-funded social supports remain rare in the United States.

8. In the case of belly talk, I suggest there also is the process of socializing fetuses as persons and more specifically as children.
9. There appears to be much interest in belly talk as a means for parents to give their children a head start. I was interviewed by *The Wall Street Journal* for a column on this subject (Zaslow 2004).

References

Blum, Linda. 1999. *At the Breast: Ideologies of Breastfeeding and Motherhood in the Contemporary United States*. Boston: Beacon.

Collier, Jane F., and Sylvia J. Yanagisako. 1987. *Gender and Kinship: Essays toward a Unified Analysis*. Stanford: Stanford University Press.

Davis-Floyd, Robbie E. 1992. *Birth as an American Rite of Passage*. Berkeley: University of California Press.

Davis-Floyd, Robbie E., and Carolyn F. Sargent. 1997. *Childbirth and Authoritative Knowledge: Cross-Cultural Perspectives*. Berkeley: University of California Press.

Eastman, Nicholson J. 1963. *Expectant Motherhood*. Boston: Little, Brown and Company.

Eisenberg, Arlene, Heidi E. Murkoff, and Sandee E. Hathaway. 1996. *What to Expect When You're Expecting*. New York: Workman.

Ferguson, Charles A. 1977. "Baby Talk as a Simplified Register." In *Talking to Children: Language Input and Acquisition*, ed. Catherine E. Snow and Charles A. Ferguson. Cambridge: Cambridge University Press.

Gillis, John R. 1996. *A World of Their Own Making: Myth, Ritual, and the Quest for Family Values*. New York: Basic Books.

———. 2000. "Marginalization of Fatherhood in Western Countries." *Childhood* 7(2):225–38.

Gutmann, Matthew C. 1997. "Trafficking in Men: The Anthropology of Masculinity." *Annual Review of Anthropology* 26:385–409.

Harkness, Sara, and Charles Super, eds. 1996. *Parents' Cultural Belief Systems: Their Origins, Expressions, and Consequences*. New York: Guilford.

Heath, Shirley Brice. 1996. "What No Bedtime Story Means: Narrative Skills at Home and School." In *The Matrix of Language: Contemporary Linguistics Anthropology*, ed. Donald Brenneis and Ronald S. Macaulay. Boulder, CO: Westview.

Hobson, Barbara, ed. 2002. *Making Men into Fathers: Men, Masculinities, and the Social Politics of Fatherhood*. Cambridge: Cambridge University Press.

Hochschild, Arlie Russell. 1990. *The Second Shift*. New York: Avon Books.

Hotchner, Tracy. 1997. *Pregnancy and Childbirth: The Only Book You'll Ever Need*. New York: Avon Books.

Klassen, Pamela E. 2000. *Blessed Events: Religion and Home Birth in America*. Princeton: Princeton University Press.

Klaus, Alisa. 1993. *Every Child a Lion: The Origins of Maternal and Infant Health Policy in the United States and France, 1890–1920*. Ithaca: Cornell University Press.

Meaker, Samuel R. 1956. *Preparing for Motherhood: A Manual for Expectant Parents*. Chicago: Year Book Medical Publishers.

Ochs, Elinor. 1992. "Indexing Gender." In *Rethinking Context: Language as an Interactive Phenomenon*, ed. Alessandro Duranti and Charles Goodwin. Cambridge: Cambridge University Press.

Ochs, Elinor, and Bambi Schieffelin. 1984. "Language Acquisition and Socialization." In *Culture Theory: Essays on Mind, Self, and Emotion*, ed. Richard A. Shweder and Robert A. Levine. Cambridge: Cambridge University Press.

Orloff, Ann Shola, and Renee Monson. 2001. "Citizens, Workers or Fathers? Men in the History of U.S. Social Policy." In *Making Men into Fathers*, ed. Barbara Hobson. Cambridge: Cambridge University Press.

Petchesky, Rosalind Pollack. 1987. "Fetal Images: The Power of Visual Culture in the Politics of Reproduction." *Feminist Studies* 13(2):263–92.

Sears, William, and Martha Sears. 1997. *The Pregnancy Book*. Boston: Little, Brown.

Seward, Rudy Ray, Dale E. Yeatts, and Lisa K. Zottarelli. 2002. "Parental Leave and Father Involvement in Child Care: Sweden and the United States." *Journal of Comparative Family Studies* 33(3):387–99.

Small, Meredith F. 1999. *Our Babies, Ourselves: How Biology and Culture Shape the Way We Parent*. New York: Anchor Books.

Townsend, Nicholas. 2002. *The Package Deal: Marriage, Work, and Fatherhood in Men's Lives*. Philadelphia: Temple University Press.

van Balen, Frank, and Marcia C. Inhorn. 2002. "Interpreting Infertility: A View from the Social Sciences." In *Infertility around the Globe: New Thinking on Childlessness, Gender, and Reproductive Technologies*, ed. Marcia C. Inhorn and Frank van Balen. Berkeley: University of California Press.

Wayne, Julie, and Bryanne Cordeiro. 2003. "Who Is a Good Organizational Citizen? Social Perception of Male and Female Employees Who Use Family Leave." *Sex Roles* 49(5/6):233–46.

Zaslow, Jeffrey. 2004. "Son, You're Not Born Yet, but We Need to Talk: Communicating with Your Fetus." *Wall Street Journal*, 29 April, D1.

Zelizer, Viviana A. 1994 [1985]. *Pricing the Priceless Child: The Changing Social Value of Children*. New York: Basic Books.

Chapter 13

Husband-Assisted Birth among the Rarámuri of Northern Mexico

Janneli F. Miller

When an addition is expected in the family, the chief preparation of the woman is to get ready a quantity of beer, calling on her friends to help her, while the husband goes to look for the shaman. When she feels her time is approaching, she retires to some lonely spot, as she is too bashful to bear her child while others are about. She tightens her girdle around her waist, and bears her child sitting up, holding on to something above her, like the branch of a tree. After the little stranger has arrived the husband may bring her a jar with warm water from which she occasionally drinks (Lumholtz 1902:271–72).

Vignette: Isabel and Ramiro's Story

Isabel fell in love with her husband, Ramiro, because he was a good racer. She used to attend footraces with her family, and Ramiro was a frequent winner. He caught her eye and that was it—they both tell me this story one afternoon, giggling at each other. Isabel and Ramiro live on land she inherited from her parents in Basigochi. They have seven children ranging in age from twenty-four to seven years old. Only the three youngest, two boys and a girl, live with them now, as the others are at school or on their own. Ramiro boasts that he is forty-three, while Isabel, with streaks of gray running through her long, dark hair, says she is not sure how old she is. Isabel's mother, Josefina, who lives next door and has joined us, shrugs her shoulders and says she does not know either. Age is a relatively unimportant concept for the Rarámuri—what matters is whether you are still able to work. The softness of Isabel's smile belies her strength and age as she hefts two five-gallon buckets of water and heads inside the newly constructed adobe house.

Shortly after this conversation, Ramiro goes in search of his burro, and we three women retreat into the shade of a nearby shed to shell corn. As we work, Isabel tells me about the births of her children. "They were all born here, in the house." Josefina scowls and says, "Yes, she couldn't go out to the *monte* like I did—these younger women are too weak."[1] Isabel smiles and says, "And now they go to the clinic, but I stayed here, with my husband." I ask Isabel how Ramiro helped her with the babies. "Well, he wanted to, but sometimes he couldn't. The last one, the girl, she was born when Ramiro was out of the house." "Really? You were alone?" "Well, Ramiro was here, but the baby did not want to come when he was around." "Why not?" "I do not know, but as long as he was in the house, the baby did not want to come. Then, when he went out, the baby came right away. I think the baby was shy. She just did not want to come out if Ramiro was there."

Isabel explains how Ramiro helped during her labor. He put a log from a small pine he had peeled in the corner of the house so Isabel could hang on it. He also gave her a cup of warm water to drink. When I ask if they used any herbs, Isabel replies, "They say it is good to use herbs, but I do not know what to use. I don't know the herbs." When the labor pains became strong, she pulled on the log in the corner. She spent almost all her labor walking, stopping occasionally to hang and breathe with the contractions. When I ask how long this labor was, she replies, "Well, it began in the night, and then, you see what time it is now, she was born about this time of the day." I estimate perhaps eight hours of labor for her seventh and last child, and Isabel was probably in her mid-thirties at that time. It is all guesswork, and I realize my questions about time and the length of labor are irrelevant to Isabel. I ask next, "When the baby came out, what position were you in?" Isabel looks puzzled but then tells me that at first she was standing up, near the bed, and then kneeled down. "The baby came out fast. Ramiro went outside, and then the baby came out. She slid down to the blanket, and cried right away." Isabel tells me she leaned over to pick up the newborn, cutting the cord with a sharp knife. I ask about the *gemá*, or placenta. Isabel says Ramiro buried the placenta in the woods, where he had buried all their children's, perhaps a half-hour walk from their house. "Nobody knows where, just Ramiro, and he won't even tell me," laughs Isabel.

Another day I ask Ramiro to give me his version of the birth. He says he helped Isabel with all the births. He learned from his own mother when he was a boy, going with her when she gave birth. He believes it is best for the woman to be upright, which is why he peeled the pine log for Isabel. "My mother would hang on the tree branch, but inside, Isabel didn't have anything to hold on to, so I brought the tree to her!" he says, smiling. He acts as if his wife could not have given birth without him, and when I ask about the baby who was born as soon as he left the house, he says, "I think I scared her." "You scared your wife?" "No, the girl—I think I was too ugly," and I think he is serious until I see the twinkle in his eyes. Ramiro is a charismatic man who likes to laugh and joke, and the fact that his youngest daughter would think her father is ugly delights him. "I don't know," he continues, "children do what they want, who

Figure 13.1. This Rarámuri father assisted his wife with the births of all their children. Photograph by the author.

are we to say?" Finally, I ask him about placentas. "Did you bury the boys' and girls' placentas together or separate?" "Together." "Where are they?" I ask, thinking he'll tell me. "I don't remember," he smiles, adding that if nobody knows where the placentas are buried, nobody can do any harm to the children.

Isabel tells me about the births of her other children while we continue shelling corn. They were all born in the same way, in the house, and usually they came in the night or the early morning. She stood for most of the deliveries, kneeling down at the end in order to grab the babies as they came out. Ramiro was there for each baby, except of course the last one. He made sure the fire was still going and gave her water to drink. The labors were fast, and she had no problems. Josefina cooked and helped with the other children after each baby was born. There really does not seem to be much to talk about—simply, babies get born.

As the afternoon wanes, we finish shelling the corn, which Isabel must soak to make *nixtamal* for tortillas. She does not want me to help her grind it, so Josefina and I sit in the shade while Isabel leans over the *metate* and begins moving the *mano* back and forth, crushing the soaked kernels.[2] I try to find out if Josefina will tell me about the births of her children, but she smiles shyly, only saying, "Yes, they were born in the *monte*." Isabel mentions that Josefina is very shy, so I take the cue and leave the questions for another time. As I walk up valley to my house, I see their youngest daughter, Marcelina, chasing goats from the new *mequasori* (edible greens), laughing as they bleat and run. Ramiro comes over the rise, his burro loaded with wood, and waves at me. Smoke rises from Isabel's fire, and as the sky turns from gold to red, I ponder why Marcelina waited to be born until her father was out of the house. And how Isabel knows.

Introduction

In this chapter, I discuss the birthing practices of Rarámuri women in Northern Mexico, where solitary birth has been practiced for over one hundred years.[3] A few women continue to give birth alone in the same manner depicted above by explorer Carl Lumholtz, and some younger women now attend government clinics. Yet most women still give birth at home with their husbands' assistance, as did Isabel.

My focus here is the practice of husband-assisted birth among the Rarámuri, with an examination of the roles men play in reproduction, including changes due to modernizing influences. Physical reproduction is inseparable from social reproduction, with social processes, including culture change, embodied in moral norms expressed and affirmed through birth practices.

When a Rarámuri woman begins labor today, her younger children are generally removed from the birth site; however, in the not-so-recent past, children accompanied their mothers to the woods and her "birthing tree." Today, women usually confide in their husbands about the impending birth, continuing household duties until the delivery is imminent, at which time most remain inside their homes until well after the child is delivered. The birth of a child is generally an unmarked event in the social life of the Rarámuri, which is seen as a matter of interest only to immediate family members. Children are well loved and considered to be individuals able to make decisions independent of their parents.

Women learn about birth in conversation with sisters and aunts and by observing their mothers, sisters, or other female relatives. Men learn about birth from their wives, not infrequently during the first pregnancy, or from their mothers, when their own younger siblings are born. Knowledge about how to assist women in childbirth is common to all members of Rarámuri society. Indeed, there is no specialized role of birth assistant in Rarámuri culture and no word in the language for such a role. At drinking parties known as *tesguinadas* (the primary social event among the Rarámuri), women may talk quietly about birth. Occasionally during these parties, groups of men and women engage in raucous banter, including bawdy jokes that assume a general knowledge of sexual reproduction from conception to birth. These repartees frequently include overt sexual expression and explicit sex play. Children overhear and participate in these social interactions, thereby learning sexual behavior and mores in a public environment without shame or secrecy. Birthing practices are no exception.

Research Background

Virtually all of the research conducted on birth in Mexico discusses the traditional practice and training of indigenous midwives (Bortin 1993; Castañeda et al. 1996; Davis-Floyd 2001; Faust 1988; Galante and Castañeda 1997; Jordan 1989, 1993; Kelly 1956; Parra 1993; Schwarz 1981). A growing number of studies point to the efficacy of incorporating "traditional" cultural beliefs into the training of birth attendants (Jordan 1989; Kelly 1956; Newman 1981) or

incorporating midwives into primary health care programs (Castañeda et al. 1996; Schwarz 1981), but the assumption is that an at-
tendant at birth is essential to reduce fear and ensure the safety of
mother and child. A secondary assumption is that birth attendants
are female. There is no literature describing birth from a male's
point of view, nor is any attention given to husbands who attend
births. The emphasis on female birth attendants suggests that a desire to be assisted by another woman during childbirth is a cultural
universal. Investigations of female childbirth attendants certainly
contribute to our understanding of the cultural patterning of childbirth, yet births taking place without female attendants indicate a
markedly different sociocultural milieu than those in which female
experts exist.

This discussion of birthing practices of the Rarámuri of Northern Mexico details how the husband's role is central to childbirth
and provides a necessary critique of stereotypical assumptions pre-
dominating our understanding of men's involvement at birth. In
Rarámuri culture, men play a vital and necessary role in reproduction, a role that strengthens the egalitarian nature of the conjugal
relationship, and enables men to reinforce and augment their social
status. The cultural patterning of birth is indicative of individual independence as well as social interdependence.

Methodology

The research upon which this chapter is based was conducted in two
sites over a period of two-and-a-half years, from January 1999 to
September 2001. One research objective was to conduct an ethnographic study of birth among the Rarámuri, including how solitary
and husband-assisted birth reflect cultural norms. To accomplish
this I lived for eighteen months in the Rarámuri *rancho* of Basigochi,
in the Sierra Madre of Northern Mexico. Another research objective was to examine whether birth practices are changing for those
Rarámuri who have migrated to urban areas where they have easy
access to Western medical facilities and potentially more sustained
contact with *mestizos* and government health care workers than
Rarámuri living in the Sierra.[4] To address this, I spent eight months
conducting research among Rarámuri living in Chihuahua City, in
the state of Chihuahua, approximately four hours south of El Paso/
Ciudad Juárez.

Similar research strategies were utilized at both sites, and data
from both is included in this chapter, although to a greater extent

I rely on my village experience. Participant observation and ethnographic interviewing were the cornerstones of fieldwork. I did not presume to be able to attend and observe home births because access to childbirth is restricted among the Rarámuri, but I did attend births at Hospital General in Chihuahua City and a few clinics in the Sierra. I participated in daily life, observed health care interactions in clinics and hospitals, and interviewed Rarámuri men and women and their families, as well as health care professionals, social workers, and other individuals working with the Tarahumara (such as priests, educators, philanthropists, anthropologists, and politicians). I also interviewed two male *owirúame* (traditional healers) informally and extensively during ceremonies, as well as thirteen *mestiza* midwives in Guachochi who were part of the National Social Security Institute rural midwife program.

Fifty structured interviews with Rarámuri women were conducted in Spanish and Rarámuri; half of these interviews were recorded and the rest notated by hand. In approximately two-thirds of these interviews, husbands were present, and their comments were specifically coded and added to those of their wives. Selection of individuals was opportunistic, as some individuals refused to be interviewed.[5] Extensive reproductive histories were elicited from all the women in the *rancho* where I lived, providing me with rich details of births, miscarriages, stillbirths, and other reproductive events, including family planning and sexual histories. I interviewed Rarámuri children to assess their knowledge of birth, conducting several "interview sessions" in the school in Basigochi, with children from the fifth and sixth grades (ages twelve to sixteen), eliciting drawings and stories about birth. Interviews were analyzed according to categories generated by a review of field notes and combined with archival, statistical, and interview data. For this chapter, I concentrate on interview data highlighting men and their roles in the reproductive process. The vignette beginning this chapter and all quotes are taken directly from taped interviews and field notes.

Changes in Rarámuri Lifestyle and Birth[6]

The Rarámuri occupy the southwestern region of the Western Sierra Madre in Northern Mexico, an area frequently called "Copper Canyon" or the Sierra Tarahumara. Five canyons, each deeper than the Grand Canyon in the United States, characterize the region. The Rarámuri are semi-nomadic horticulturalists who grow corn as a staple food, supplemented by beans, potatoes, foraging, and some hunting. They also raise goats and cattle, saving meat for ceremonial consumption and manure to fertilize poor soils. They retreated to this remote country in the sixteenth century, after the Spanish conquest. The first one hundred years after the conquest was an unsettled time, with some Rarámuri converting to Catholicism and some removing themselves from contact with outsiders. The Jesuits retreated in 1767 and were replaced by Franciscans who could not maintain all their missions; thus during the eighteen and nineteenth centuries, Rarámuri were left relatively alone to integrate changes brought by contact. Population estimates suggest an increase from the twenty thousand reported by Lumholtz at the end of the nineteenth century, to a current number nearing one hundred thousand.[7]

At the beginning of the twentieth century, Jesuits returned to the Sierra, successfully intensifying missionizing efforts. They provide education in Spanish and Rarámuri at boarding schools, and established clinics and hospitals, recruiting Western health care professionals for faith-based service deliveries. Catholics financially back diverse development projects, including well digging, craft production and marketing, and tourism. The Church also sponsors local political workshops focusing on human rights. New since the mid-twentieth century are Christian evangelical efforts, similar to those of the Catholics. Also increasing are government-sponsored economic development projects, a burgeoning international tourist trade, wide-scale intensive logging operations that have resulted in the cutting of 90 percent of the old-growth forest since the 1970s, and drug traffickers who occupy Rarámuri farmlands, bringing all the associated violence and covert political and military activities. A severe drought that began in the 1990s has exacerbated these multiple threats to the Rarámuri lifestyle, and by 2000, over four thousand Rarámuri had migrated to Chihuahua City to look for jobs and food, with uncounted others residing in US–Mexico border towns such as Cd. Juárez, Nogales, and Tijuana. Some even cross the border to work illegally in the United States (Miller 2003).

The changes that took place over the twentieth century have resulted in profound challenges to the Rarámuri. Typically referred to as the "most traditional" Indians in North America and portrayed in dramatic photos highlighting colorful skirts, loincloths, and cave dwellings (Fisher, Verplancken, and Williams 1999; Merrill 1996; Verplancken 1999), Rarámuri now find themselves in the lowest rank of Mexican society, simultaneously discriminated against for their lack of Spanish-language skills, education, and industrial work ethic yet romanticized for their traditional lifestyle and ceremonies.

They are in the throes of cultural renegotiation on every front, with change intensified by evangelical efforts undermining traditional religious values and health care workers quick to provide a pill and discourage indigenous medical practices.

What does this mean for birth practices? Two shifts have become evident in the past one hundred years: the transition from women giving birth alone in the forest to moving into their homes, assisted by their husbands; and the changes resulting in health care service availability in the Sierra Tarahumara and the corresponding increase in public education efforts promoting these services.

At the turn of the twentieth century, most women gave birth in the forest. This practice was discussed in the ethnographies of American anthropologists Bennett and Zingg (1935) and John Kennedy (1978, 1996). The first shift came when women moved out of the forest and into their homes to give birth, a transition accompanied by the change from a solitary birth to a husband-assisted one. The shift is evident in two sets of data: my own and that of Dennis and Dorothy Mull (1984, 1985), a doctor/anthropologist team who worked among the Tarahumara. There are several interesting differences between my findings and the Mulls's. It should be noted that the Mull interviews were conducted fifteen years before my own study took place, in a region now known for tourism and development, which is quite different from the area where I worked. Discrepancies between our data may reflect changes in birthing practices over time, but also may demonstrate regional variation. Most important, the practice of solitary birth is similar in both studies: the Mulls record a rate of 23 percent, and my study records 18 percent. The tendency to give birth alone has been relatively stable throughout the intervening years in spite of the increased existence and use of medical services. I believe this is because solitary birth continues to be a culturally congruent behavior. In the Mull data, women were as likely to deliver alone as they were to choose husbands and female relatives to attend them. However, my findings are quite different, as over half of the women I interviewed had chosen their husbands to assist them at birth. I assert that husband-assisted birth is directly related to the changes impacting Rarámuri life.

This shift corresponds with the increased numbers of outsiders (non-Rarámuri) in the region. Rarámuri women are shy and frequently avoid contact with outsiders, especially males, because they are perceived as dangerous due to the collective memory of abuse during the tumultuous colonial encounter. Tarahumara society is commonly referred to as a sex-segregated society, in which women and men perform their activities in different social spheres, and in public women occupy an area physically distinct from men. The physical separation indexes a social code whereby, to ensure their protection, women are highly discouraged from interacting with men who are not kin. The birthing tree in the wilderness is no longer the safe, isolated spot it used to be, as trails and new roads in the area are traveled by loggers, drug traffickers, police and militia searching for marijuana and poppy fields, eco-tourists backpacking through villages, missionaries, and government social workers, as well as health care professionals. As a result, Rarámuri women have moved into the safety and privacy of their homes to give birth.

The second shift in Rarámuri birth practice began in the mid-1980s, with the increased utilization of Western medical services by Rarámuri women. This shift entails a move from husband-assisted home birth to clinic and hospital birth. My data shows more births taking place in the hospital and clinics, which reflects the promotion of Western health care services by the Mexican government and missionaries. The first hospital in the Sierra was built in 1982, only three years before the Mull study, and was three hours away from their research site. In contrast, a hospital was "only" two hours away from the *ranchos* in the Sierra where I conducted research and had been in operation for almost twenty years. It was well known that women gave birth there, a fact apparent in the pictures drawn by the Rarámuri schoolchildren in response to the direction to "draw a picture of where women give birth." Out of fifteen drawings, ten portrayed either a hospital or clinic. The fifteen-year interval between my study and the Mulls's demonstrates Rarámuri women's escalating awareness of hospitals and clinics, including the idea that there are options for delivery.

This second shift is a result of the changes in health care service availability in the Sierra Tarahumara and a corresponding increase in public education efforts promoting these services. In 1998, the World Bank approved two loans to Mexico worth US$725 million to improve the National Social Security Institute, with a focus on providing services to the poorest localities and to enable decentralization of health care delivery. The "Basic Health Care Grant" was renewed for US$350 million in 2001 for a period of eight years (World Bank 2009). The State Development Plan for Chihuahua—created and implemented through the governor's office in Chihuahua—prioritized decentralization of health services, along with a focus on modernizing existing facilities and broadening the scope of the Wide Coverage Plan mobile units, especially in the Sierra (Chihuahua State Government 1999).

Despite these mandates and the international funding, there remains a lack of adequate health care services in the region. Although some residents in remote villages are subjected to monthly visits by health care teams, missionaries, and government workers admonishing and encouraging them to utilize Western health care services, these facilities often do not have medicines or health care professionals in attendance. Rarámuri also listen to repeated public health care messages on the popular local Rarámuri radio station XETAR. On-air educational programs emphatically discourage solitary and husband-assisted home births, as they are blamed for high infant mortality rates. These health messages affect younger childbearing women, who are beginning to give birth in the clinics. Most Rarámuri are well aware of the increasing pressure to discontinue traditional medical practices in favor of Western services. Information in reproductive health messages is based entirely on Western medical conceptions of risk; for example, Rarámuri women learn they are high risk and need to attend the clinic if they are under nineteen and pregnant for the first time, if they have had more than five pregnancies, if they drink *tesguino*,[8] or are anemic or poorly nourished, conditions that apply to almost all pregnant Rarámuri. When women go to the clinics for nonreproductive reasons, health messages are reinforced. Although my ethnographic data reflects some hesitation to use Western medical services at birth, it is fair to say the move to give birth in clinics is a definite trend, especially among younger childbearing women who attended government schools.

Elderly women I interviewed were responsible for 8 percent of women delivering in the *monte*. Twelve percent of women giving birth in clinics and hospitals consisted entirely of younger childbearing women, and 80 percent delivering at home were the middle generation of women, those in their thirties and forties. Thus, younger childbearing women are primarily responsible for the second shift, which I assert as an artifact of the modernizing influence of *mestizo* culture. As Rarámuri women have more sustained contact with *mestizos*, their fear of associating with outsiders lessens; they become familiar in *mestizo* environments, adopt *mestizo* values, and are more likely to adhere to health mandates communicated through public health messages. Many of the younger women delivering in the clinic are married to *mestizos*.

Husband-Assisted Birth among the Rarámuri

Generally, when men assist at birth they bring warm water, deflect unwanted visitors, provide a peeled pine log for the woman to hang on to, and bury placentas. They also take care of the couple's other children, keep the fire burning so that the house and food are heated, and notify relatives and neighbors if more help is needed. Their main function is to support and protect the laboring woman and her newborn. Husbands do not "deliver" the babies per se; instead, the woman does this herself with her husband nearby.

There is really not much else for a helper to do; thus, birth practices are not highly elaborated among the Rarámuri. The specialized role of midwife was not developed because it was not thought necessary. As noted earlier, most Rarámuri learn about birth as children and do not think of it as anything special. Rarámuri women hide their pregnancies and do not often discuss them in public. Some women notify the indigenous curer (*owirúame*) when they are first pregnant so that the *owirúame* can care for her during pregnancy and birth.[9] The *owirúame* tells the couple of any problems he discerns, and they take heed of this direction and act accordingly. If trouble arises during labor, the husband will send a message to the *owirúame*, or he will make arrangements for transport to a hospital or clinic, accompanying the woman the entire time.

Rarámuri men I interviewed knew as much about pregnancy and birth as women did. In fact, most men boasted about how they had helped their wives with the births of their children. A typical comment is one made by the governor of Norogachi: "I helped my wife with each of the births of my children. And we know what to do to make sure we only have babies when we want them. Yes, I know and I help my wife."

Yet this "help" is not the actual hands-on delivery of the baby. Rarámuri women generally kneel down and "catch" the newborn themselves, wiping it off with a clean cloth *rebozo* (shawl) or skirt. The baby is swaddled and put directly to the breast. The placenta is delivered into a bowl or plate and given to the husband, who buries it immediately. Mothers usually cut the umbilical cord with a knife or scissors. Most women have short, uneventful labors of six to ten hours in duration, so the husband's role is to keep others away and provide the woman with what she needs to manage the delivery.

According to the Rarámuri, women and men need to work together to keep the world in balance. Women and men work side by side their entire lives, whether they are herding animals, planting fields, moving a goat pen, or caring for children. A woman's life is incomplete without a man, as is a man's without a woman. Each needs the other to fulfill practical community obligations, such as providing *tónari* (meat and bean stew) and *batari* (fermented corn beverage) for ceremonies, or attending community work parties. In these activities, they embody and express cultural moral ideals. It is no surprise, then, that Rarámuri women choose their husbands as birth assistants and that men brag about their role in reproduction. In almost all the productive work they do, men and women equally share the hardships and pleasantries in life, and thus their reproductive roles are a consistent extension of their social lives.

Core Values Expressed in Birth Practice

Modesty

Husband-assisted birth is congruent with Rarámuri moral norms, including modesty, reciprocity, non-aggression, hard work, generosity, happiness, and good thinking. Some of the female gender-specific traits respected by the Rarámuri are the ability to make good *batari, pinole,* and tortillas, and having a sense of propriety. Men have the additional responsibility of speaking well, educating their children, and controlling their family's behavior to the greatest possible extent. One of the first full sentences I learned to speak in Rarámuri was *Neje we riwérame ju* (I am very shy). In Basigochi, *riwérame* was translated into Spanish as *verguenza,* which literally means shame. *Riwérari* is the noun form of the verb *riwera,* which means to be ashamed or embarrassed, and *riwérame* is the adjective descriptor. I became aware of the term and the moral ethic it indexes during my interviews, when women typically told me they did not attend government-sponsored health clinics because they were very shy. Upon further discussion, they told me it was inappropriate and embarrassing for them to be examined by male physicians (female physicians are rare). To avoid this contact with non-kin males, many women chose not to return to clinics.

If a woman is not modest, she will be the subject of much gossip, which serves as an effective mode of social control in small communities such as the Sierra and the urban communities where I worked. Modesty also involves more subtle behaviors such as eye contact and body language, including volume of voice and quickness of movement. Women are to discourage eye contact with unrelated males. Proper behavior is outlined in public speeches by indigenous community leaders and enforced in daily interactions. For men, the cultural norms of masculinity include hard work and industry, as reflected in some male gender-specific activities like wood cutting, plowing, animal husbandry, tool making, and community leadership. Modesty also applies to men, who strive to embody and express ideals through their daily chores and communal roles and by giving advice to their children. Modest behavior for men implies that intimate acts, including sexual relations and any display of marital affection, are restricted to private moments. This modesty is in contrast to overt, public sex play at drinking parties, which has the additional function of modeling inappropriate actions and serving as a psycho-emotional release of daily tensions (Kennedy 1996:229).

The cultural value placed on modesty—for both men and women—contributes to the practice of husband-assisted birth. Men do not generally make disparaging remarks about their wives, and the self-respect they exhibit in describing how their wives gave birth with ease is one way they can publicly demonstrate a moral marriage. Men are expected to help their wives in all work, and being knowledgeable about reproduction is one way to display the fulfillment of marital obligations. Women, whose closest companions are their husbands, break no cultural taboo by engaging in intimate activities with them. Indeed, as Isabel notes in the beginning of this chapter, the child chooses who will attend the delivery. Women's choices at birth include those with whom they can maintain their modesty. Outsiders are unwelcome at birth, and women first select husbands and then female relatives, including mothers and mothers-in-law. This not only indexes the core cultural value of modesty, but also plays into social obligations inherent in the closely knit communities consisting of extended kin. If the woman does not incur a social obligation by depending on a relative for birth assistance, she will not have to reciprocate, since the cultural ideal of generalized and balanced reciprocity is at work in Rarámuri society. It is simpler, and easier, for her to depend only on her husband, and the practice enables her husband to fulfill one of his social obligations.

Marriage

In Basigochi, the husband–wife team is the basic unit of the social structure. Nuclear family units, including extended family consisting of both affinal and consanguinal relatives as well as fictive kin, are the main source of reciprocal economic support. In the region where I worked, descent is reckoned bilaterally, with patrilocal residence most common after marriage. There are, however, exceptions, as the Rarámuri are fundamentally pragmatic people subsisting in a rugged and difficult landscape. Sometimes newlyweds farm the husband's land but live near the wife's family. Frequently, land from both sides of the family is cultivated, with the couple moving between the two locales according to seasonal work needs.

A monogamous and endogamous marriage pattern is the norm among the Tarahumara, with most of the population marrying in their mid-teens. It is thought to be unhealthy for people to live alone, since solitude makes people sad, and sadness will result in illness or disease. Widows and widowers usually remarry as soon as they are finished grieving. In Basigochi, most young men choose to marry Rarámuri women, but a few younger women were looking for and finding *mestizo* mates. Women who married *mestizos* left the *rancho* behind and went to live in larger towns, adopting *mestizo* dress and customs. I asked several women why they preferred to marry *mestizos* and, in every case, it was because they perceived the *mestizo* men to have better access to economic resources than their Rarámuri counterparts. In essence, they were exchanging their cultural identity as Rarámuri for the economic security of the *mestizo* world. These were the women who were giving birth in the clinics and hospitals, because they were not as fearful of contact with outsiders. Obviously, their marriages also mimicked typical Mexican ideals of male domination and female submission, which, I emphasize, is quite different from the egalitarian gender relations of Rarámuri culture. Mestizo men do not assist their wives at birth, believing birth to be a woman's domain.

Both the choice of a woman's mate as birth assistant and men's pride in their ability to assist at birth are consistent with the kin-based social organization among the Rarámuri, which emphasizes the conjugal pair. An unwritten expectation of the male's responsibility for his family is to provide for her protection as well as material support. Husbands are responsible for protecting their wives from the harm inherent in contact with non-kin, a job that is especially important during the woman's pregnancy and labor, when she is vulnerable. Men who help their wives at birth incur increased social status by adhering to local moral norms dictating that men safeguard the modesty and reputation of the family and provide for his family's security (in this sense, meaning protection from outsiders). By letting community members—and outsiders—know he has helped his wife at birth, a Rarámuri man demonstrates he is able to protect his wife. Rarámuri men gain respect when they take part in birth, and it is not shameful to talk about it because public expression of the fulfillment of a social obligation is part of the moral life of all Rarámuri. In this manner, men's active role in the reproductive process reaffirms not only modesty as a core cultural value, but also the egalitarian and interdependent nature of the marriage bond as an essential feature of Rarámuri social organization.

Knowledge

How do men learn what to do at birth? Most men stated they learned about birth from their parents and wives. Many men boasted that they knew how to help their wives in labor, telling me how they had provided warm water, cut cords, and buried placentas. A few men told me their fathers had taught them how to help during labor and birth. Other men learned from their wives. Although young boys and girls tend to play separately, knowledge about birth is common among children of both genders. When I talked to sixth-grade classes in Basigochi about birth and elicited drawings from them, I found that these children—between the ages of twelve and sixteen—were all aware of sex and birth. Many Rarámuri marry shortly after completing the sixth grade so their level of knowledge about these subjects was not unusual. When I asked how they had learned about birth, they said from their parents as well as older sisters and brothers.

I believe information on these subjects is shared freely within households. I had the opportunity to stay overnight with several different families during my fieldwork. There is a sweet, quiet time after dark when members of the household are in bed but not yet asleep. All family members usually sleep close together in the same room, engaging in conversations before falling asleep and upon waking. During these intimate moments, dreams are shared, personal concerns are voiced, and children may ask about sex, birth, violence, illness, or things that frighten them. This is when female family members also share their experiences about birth. Outsiders do not usually witness these private moments, and I felt privileged to be included. These experiences gave me insights on the intimacy that exists among Rarámuri family members—again emphasizing the strong bond between husband and wife, as well as the everyday nature of talk about sex and birth. Knowledge transmission among the Rarámuri is embodied in practice as much as it is discursive, and men take advantage of any opportunity to learn about birth and to display their wisdom on the matter.

Masculinity and Change

Is male participation in birth related to the Rarámuri ideal of masculinity? In spite of the publicly apparent gender segregation, male and female domains are not as sex-specific as they appear. Both women and men told me they could and frequently do perform tasks typically associated with the opposite sex. Thus, men make tortillas and care for babies, while women plow and cut wood when necessary. As discussed earlier, the cultural ideal of masculinity primarily includes the ideas of hard work, generosity, and proper speech (including modesty), which applies to all members of Rarámuri society. Men must provide for their families, and besides farming, hunting, procuring and caring for animals, and participating in ceremonial activities, this also implies assisting their wives at birth and giving good advice to children. Men who help their wives at birth earn a measure of social respect not given to men who do not. It is not that men whose wives go to the clinic are looked down upon; rather, the men who help at birth have yet another domain in which to demonstrate their adherence to the cultural ideal of providing and caring for their families, therefore gaining an opportunity to win the respect of the community.

The conjugal relationship in Rarámuri culture emphasizes the equality of men and women, as evidenced through the work each contributes to maintaining the household and providing for the children. This cultural value has not changed over time, resulting in a popular conception that women who give birth in hospitals and clinics are "weaker" than women who give birth alone outside or at home. The first shift in birth locale, from outside to inside, does not entail weakness because women still deliver their own children, nor does having one's husband assist at birth imply that a woman is weak. Besides the fact that the woman delivers the child herself, it provides her husband with an opportunity to fulfill his social obligation of protecting her.

However, the second shift into the clinic does imply weakness, an association that applies equally to men and women. Older women note that women these days are not as strong as they used to be, as evident from the vignette at the beginning of this chapter. In fact, the weakness of youth is a widespread attitude, attributed to increased contact and association with *mestizos*, including adoption of their ways. In Basigochi, acculturated Tarahumara are thought to be "less" than Rarámuri who do not associate with outsiders. A complete discussion of culture change among the Rarámuri is beyond the scope of this chapter, but there is a wide range of acculturation, more so in accessible areas. The communities where I worked upheld "traditional" cultural ideals. Those maintaining such norms were more likely to assume leadership roles, even as the power and efficacy of these roles were eroded by the ongoing adoption of *mestizo* ways, including Christianity, wage labor, and utilization of health care services. Generally, older individuals adhere to traditional practices and watch with dismay as younger generations leave traditions behind. Women giving birth in clinics are perceived as being weaker than those staying home, and similarly, men whose wives choose to deliver in the clinic are thought to have failed in their social obligations to protect their wives.[10]

What is interesting is that Rarámuri women continue to give birth at home, alone or with their husbands, even in urban settlements, where they are exposed daily to *mestizo* cultural influences. There is not necessarily a positive correlation between length of exposure to *mestizo* ways and willingness to adopt them. I found that younger Rarámuri were more willing to abandon traditions than middle-aged or elderly individuals, as evidenced by the generational distinctions regarding place of birth in my data. Rarámuri birth practices create and affirm relationships between husband and wife, female kin, and mother and child, independent of where the couple may reside. Desire to adhere to community moral norms is an important facet of the decision of where and with whom to give birth. The fact that husbands help women at birth demonstrates a trust and intimacy in the husband–wife unit that is the foundation of social relations among the Rarámuri. In so doing, women turn to those closest to them for help when they need it. This establishes the enduring social ties needed for practical material and economic security. As the younger generation turns away from this practice, and as more Rarámuri women marry *mestizo* men, one can expect an accelerated erosion of these social ties, which is consonant with increasing dependence on the market economy. It is expected that conjugal relations in this context will increasingly conform to the male-dominated Mexican pattern, an occurrence only hinted at in husband–wife relations today. Rarámuri women and men I knew in both the city and *rancho* were upholding the egalitarian and cooperative nature of their marriage relations, even in the face of increasing social pressures to conform to *mestizo* cultural norms.

The move to clinic and hospital birth has given men less opportunity to demonstrate their social responsibility. Men who assist their wives embody ancestral cultural values and consequently earn increased social status for doing so—male social prestige depends upon fulfillment of these obligations. Although this is generally unmarked, men removed from birth are thought of (by both men and women) as being "less" than men who actively participate. When women end up at the clinic, either by choice or necessity, men are perceived as having failed in their duties to protect their wives from outsiders. In the case of an emergency, husbands can demonstrate their moral conjugal responsibility by arranging and providing for the extra services needed, and there is no blame. But when women choose the clinic—a place implying immodesty and exposure to danger—that choice often reflects either the fact that the man is an outsider (this is frequently the case) or has not fulfilled his obligations to uphold local cultural moral norms and protect his wife. Sometimes this failure is seen as belonging to the woman's father, because her choice indicates her lack of desire to adhere to Rarámuri cultural values, a result of her father failing to give her proper moral advice about staying home to give birth. Her weakness stems from a lack of proper instruction, even though her behavior is her own choice.

Either way, Rarámuri do not generally assign blame. Instead, they factor all behavior into the sum total of an individual's participation in community social relations. A husband may be more or less likely to achieve an active social role in community ceremonial or political life, depending on his ability to protect his wife. Such a failure can, in turn, erode Rarámuri tradition in a muted, but important, manner. Because Rarámuri demonstrate their social status through daily participation in community life, including reciprocal work projects and communal ceremonies, the voluntary adoption of mestizo custom may undermine the ability to take on traditional leadership roles. Over time, this means that fewer Rarámuri men will be available to affirm and uphold these important social roles, an effect evident today in Basigochi as more Rarámuri fall under the influence of Christian evangelicals and discontinue participation in community activities. Clinic birth certainly contributes to this dynamic, but the extent to which it does is difficult to discern at this time.

Conclusion

Ethnographic research on birth among the Rarámuri presented in this chapter highlights both men and women's agency, and provides detailed information on the egalitarian nature of Rarámuri society. Men and women play essential roles in maintaining and affirming—as well as producing and reproducing—key cultural values, one of which is the egalitarian nature of their marriage bond. That men share an equal role in the intimate reproductive moments of family life demonstrates the strength of the male–female partnership and its central place in the reproduction of social life. Much of Rarámuri reality is nondiscursive: it is experienced physically and spiritually in subtle ways ranging from how to stir a pot of steaming corn beer, where to sit at a ceremony, how to shape a perfect tortilla, or where to go to give birth and whom to ask for help. Similarly, men know what their wives need at birth, including how to stoke the fire, whom to call for help if it is needed, and where to bury a placenta. There is no separation between cultural ideologies and practices in the art of everyday living. Rarámuri communicate much about what is important without having to talk about it. Both men and women express and embody the relationship between humans and *Onorúame* (God) in their daily activities and in their mutual performance of these subsistence activities. By looking after the children, cutting wood, harvesting corn, tending goats, building houses, hauling water, planting beans, and doing each task to the best of their ability, men and women embody the egalitarian and cooperative nature of life. In doing so together, they create and maintain a balanced world. Birth is an integral part of it.

Acknowledgments

I want to thank Mark Nichter for originally suggesting that it would be important to write about Tarahumara men's role at birth. This research was supported by a Fulbright Garcia-Robles dissertation grant, as well as Spicer-Comins and Riecker grants from the University of Arizona. Thanks go to the editors of this volume for their gracious encouragement and, of course, heartfelt gratitude is due the Rarámuri men, women, and families who took the time to share their stories and lives with me. *Gara ju ko. Matétele ba.*

Notes

1. Rarámuri translate *gawi* as *monte* (Spanish) for wilderness. This refers to the uninhabited areas around the *ranchos*, as well as the earth and world. Included in the concept is the notion of a "wild" world out of and beyond human control, and inhabited by nonhuman creatures and forces. Power is associated with the undomesticated world, indexing potential and possibility.
2. *Mano* and *metate* are Spanish words used to refer to grinding stones; the *mano* is held in the hands and scraped over the larger bottom *metate*.
3. In this chapter, I interchangeably use the words Rarámuri and Tarahumara. Tarahumara is the Spanish name used to refer to the indigenous group and is more commonly used in popular and travel literature. However, the people prefer to use Rarámuri, which is how they refer to themselves in their native tongue.
4. Mestizo is used in the region to refer to persons of mixed blood who assert a Mexican (non-Indian) ethnic identity.
5. I conducted opportunistic interviews among women while I was visiting larger towns in the Sierra (Creel, Guachochi, San Juanito, and Norogachi), and some of these women refused to be interviewed because they did not know me or feel any need to participate in the questioning. In a few cases, the husband did not want his wife to be

interviewed. I believe this is because of cultural norms associating contact with strangers and outsiders as risky interactions.

6. This section is based on chapters two and three of my dissertation (Miller 2003).
7. This estimated population growth rate is inconsistent with reported high rates of Infant Mortality Ratios (IMR) attributed to solitary birth. The population growth could not have taken place if the IMR was as high as has been reported.
8. *Tesguino*, or *batari*, is a fermented corn drink used ceremonially and in cooperative work exchanges. It is considered sacred and healthy, and most pregnant women participate in social drinking parties, even though they consume little of the beverage (approximately one liter a month in the village I lived in).
9. The *owirúame* diagnoses and cures through dreaming, a process beyond the scope of this chapter, although it is important to note the "supernatural" basis of his knowledge, which differs from that of midwives, who usually provide physical and/or herbal assistance.
10. This also explains why Rarámuri women married to *mestizos* give birth in the clinic—their *mestizo* husbands do not know how to assist during birth. This reinforces the idea that *mestizos*, and Rarámuri who adhere to *mestizo* ways, are somehow less than Rarámuri who uphold cultural ideals.

References

Bennett, Wendell C., and Robert M. Zingg. 1935. *The Tarahumara*. Chicago: University of Chicago Press.

Bortin, Sylvia. 1993. "Interviews with Mexican Midwives." *Journal of Nurse Midwifery* 38(3):170–77.

Castañeda, Xochitl, et al. 1996. "Traditional Birth Attendants in Mexico: Advantages and Inadequacies of Care for Normal Deliveries." *Social Science and Medicine* 43(2):199–207.

Chihuahua State Government. 1999. State Development Plan for Chihuahua, 1999–2004. Office of the Governor, Chihuahua City, Chihuahua, Mexico.

Davis-Floyd, Robbie. 2001. "Special Issue on Midwifery, Parts I & II." *Medical Anthropology* 20(2 & 3).

Faust, Betty B. 1988. "When Is a Midwife a Witch? A Case Study from a Modernizing Maya Village." In *Women and Health: Cross Cultural Perspectives*, ed. Patricia Whelehan. Portsmouth, NH: Bergin & Garvey.

Fisher, Rick, Luis Verplancken, and Kit Williams. 1999. *Mexico's Copper Canyon*. Tucson, AZ: Sunracer Publications.

Galante, Cristina, and Martha Aída Castañeda. 1997. "Mujer-partera: figura central de la salud reproductiva en el medio rural." In *Género y Salud en el Sudeste de México*, ed. Esperanza Tuñón Pablos. México: UNAM.

INEGI (Instituto Nacional de Estadística, Geografía e Informática/ National Institute of Statistics, Geography and Information). 2000. *Anuario Estadístico: Chihuahua*. Edición 2000. Aguascalientes: INEGI.

————. 2002. Census Data for 2000. www.inegi.gob.mx.

Jordan, Brigitte. 1989. "Cosmopolitical Obstetrics: Some Insights from the Training of Traditional Midwives." *Social Science and Medicine* 28(9):925–44.

————. 1993. *Birth in Four Cultures*, rev. ed. Prospect Heights, IL: Waveland.

Kelly, Isabel. 1956. "An Anthropological Approach to Midwifery Training in Mexico." *Journal of Tropical Pediatrics* 1(4):200–205.

Kennedy, John G. 1978. *Tarahumara of the Sierra Madre: Beer, Ecology, and Social Organization.* Arlington Heights, IL: AHM.

————. 1996. *Tarahumara of the Sierra Madre: Survivors on the Canyon Edge,* 2nd ed. Pacific Grove, CA: Asilomar Press.

Lumholtz, Carl. 1902. *Unknown Mexico: A Record of Five Years' Exploration among the Tribes of the Western Sierra Madre, in the Tierra Caliente of Tepic and Jalisco, and among the Tarascos of Michoacan.* New York: Charles Scribner.

Merrill, William. 1988. *Rarámuri Souls: Knowledge and Social Process in Northern Mexico.* Washington, DC: Smithsonian Institution Press.

————. 1996. Book jacket comment for John G. Kennedy's *Tarahumara of the Sierra Madre: Survivors on the Canyon Edge,* 2nd ed. Pacific Grove, CA: Asilomar Press.

Miller, Janneli. 2003. Birthing Practices of the Rarámuri of Northern Mexico. PhD diss., University of Arizona, Tucson, Arizona.

Mull, Dorothy, and Dennis Mull. 1984. "Tarahumara Obstetrics." Paper presented at the 83rd Annual Meeting of the American Anthropological Association, Denver, Colorado, November 17.

————. 1985. "Differential Use of a Clinic by Tarahumara Indians and Mestizos of the Mexican Sierra Madre." *Medical Anthropology* 9(3):245–64.

Newman, Lucile F. 1981. "Midwives and Modernization." *Medical Anthropology* 5(1):1–12.

Parra, Pilar. 1991. "La mujer rural, las comadronas y el sistema Mexicano de salud." *Estudios Demográficos y Urbanos* 6(1):69–88.

————. 1993. "Midwives in the Mexican Health System." *Social Science & Medicine* 37(11):1321–29.

Schwarz, Ronald A. 1981. "The Midwife in Contemporary Latin America." *Medical Anthropology* 5(1):51–71.

Verplancken, S. J., Luis G. 1999. "The Rarámuri, or Tarahumaras." In *Mexico's Copper Canyon*, ed. Rick Fisher. Tucson, AZ: Sunracer Publications.

World Bank. 2009. "Mexico County Brief." http://go.worldbank.org/WUY-JOF0RM0.

World Health Organization. 1976. *Training and Supervision of Traditional Birth Attendants.* Brazazavile:WHO.

————. 2002. "Country Indicators." www.who.int/county/mex.

Chapter 14

STORIES OF FATHERHOOD: KINSHIP IN THE MAKING

Maruska la Cour Mosegaard

I had not told my friends anything. I was afraid they would laugh at me, you know, trying to get something that you can't get naturally, and "Who the fuck would want a child with you, who is out partying all the time? You are not mature enough and you won't be able to handle it."

—Peter

An increasing number of gay men wish to be fathers and parents. In spite of this, homosexuality and fatherhood is often seen as a contradiction, and male (homo)sexuality may be seen as a threat to the family as a universal, moral, and social entity (Weston 1991). The lives of gay men are seen as sexual but not procreative. While their sex lives repeatedly have been explored and challenged in studies of same-sex sex and by queer theory (see Bolton 1992, and Gutman this volume), their fatherhood has been strangely ignored. In anthropological studies of reproduction, and in Danish legal and political debates, homosexual parenthood has been synonymous with lesbian motherhood.[1] This silence surrounding homosexual fathers and fathers-to-be caught my attention, and in the autumn of 2003, I conducted a multisited fieldwork project among gay men in Copenhagen, Denmark.[2]

As I cohabitate with a woman and have considered the possibility of parenthood, I had closely followed the official Danish debate regarding homosexuals' opportunities to parent, and I was struck by how little attention was paid to homosexual men wanting children. Searching for literature for my fieldwork, I had the same impression. Although the corpus of studies on homosexual parenting is growing (see Hayden 1995; Lewin 1993; Sandell 1995; Weston 1991), few seem to focus on gay men having children, and even then, the main focus is on lesbian parents (for exceptions, see Andersen 2003 and Pash 2005). Homosexual parenthood seemed to exclusively concern lesbians, and I wondered if any homosexual men were or were wishing to become parents.

This chapter focuses on how Danish homosexual men who either have a child or wish for one experience and construct fatherhood.[3] I discuss how this form of homosexual fatherhood reproduces and challenges more dominant Western understandings of kinship as informed by notions of gender and sexuality. I analyze homosexual men's reasons for wanting children, then explore the thoughts and practices related to procreation, and the gendered expectations of parenthood that gay men express in searching for a potential women with whom to have a child. This includes a discussion of how these expectations are both lived out through and contradicted by the practice of fatherhood.

Methodology: Telling Family Stories

A central inspiration for my study was American anthropologist David Schneider's 1980 analysis of American kinship, in which he finds heterosexual intercourse, nature, blood, and marriage to be central symbols of kinship in Western societies. As several scholars have pointed out, Schneider does not address how gender is central to kinship (e.g., Collier and Yanagisako 1987; Weston 1991). Contemporary studies of kinship continue from where Schneider left his analysis, and these and other studies of gays, lesbians, and kinship inspired my research (Dalton 2000; Hayden 1995; Lewin 1993; Weston 1991). I meant to explore fatherhood and kinship as both lived experience and as a contested concept embedded in different forms of power relations (Weston 1991), leaving me with the question of how to grasp kinship in contemporary society.

I found storytelling to be both a useful methodological tool in collecting data and a meaningful analytical approach. I was inspired by British sociologist Kenneth Plummer's (1995) theory that stories play a crucial social role in contemporary society, where the most personal and private stories have become the most public property, and the domains of public and private have crumbled. Taking a narrative approach allowed me to analyze personal stories of fatherhood, as well as the official debates about homosexual parenting as stories in which the family as a social category is being defined, contested, and negotiated (Bourdieu 1996). My fieldwork was constructed on two levels: the relationship between a gay man and his close social relations, and the relationship between the private stories and official family stories told in political debate, family law, and the media, and by homosexual organizations. With these levels functioning as analytical constructions, I also found empirical connections between private and official family stories that would refer, reflect, and reject each other. Likewise, "dominant stories," such as those of the nuclear family, exist as a point of reference, which had preservative and controlling tasks while constantly being contested and reinvented in the new families and stories being created (Plummer 1995). A narrative approach thus made it possible to analyze the relationships between private, official, and dominant stories.

Turning toward the methods used, I traced my object of interest, family stories, in different contexts (see Marcus 1995). Interviews with the men in my study became an important methodological approach, but I also interviewed politicians and members of homopolitical organizations, and participated in organizational meetings, analyzed parliamentary debates and legal documents, researched relevant websites, and followed media debates regarding "the family." In addition, I had informal conversations with lesbian parents, visited a fertility clinic, and spoke with staff, as well as lesbians and single women undergoing insemination. All of this gave me insight into the magnitude of stories told about the family in Danish society.

All of the men participating in the research described themselves as potential or current "active fathers," a term used to describe how they as fathers were or would be known to their children. Most of the men participating in my research were members of the Internet-based organization "Aktiv Far" (Active Father). It was founded in the 1990s and acts as an advisory virtual forum for homosexual fathers and to gay men wishing to have children. Through the founder of this organization, I made initial contact and in the fall of 2003, conducted between two to four in-depth interviews with eight different men, with each interview lasting from two to four hours. In addition, I conducted a group interview, with most of the eight men participating. Between interviews, stories were systematically analyzed, and recurring themes were revisited during future interviews. In addition, each man was given a camera to take pictures of his daily family life for a month and asked to draw up his kinship genealogy. All these methods provided me with a visual insight into each man's private family life, and the photographs gave an interesting and somewhat divergent story of fatherhood, one not previously told. Following the men, as well as the official family stories, I had a glimpse of family life in its contradictory and changeable ways.

Politics of Homosexual Reproduction in Denmark

The law is the glue of the community; it is the new means of inclusion or exclusion par excellence (Hastrup 2001:7; also see Dalton 2000). Therefore, it is crucial to cast an eye on Danish family legislation. Not only is it an officially recognized and legitimate definition of the family, but also it provides an important context for understanding family lives in Denmark and has direct consequences for homosexual men wishing to be parents. The political discussions surrounding child-custody cases, access to adoption, and artificial insemination can be seen as family stories in which moral negotiations of social relations are taking place. In these official kinship stories, parenthood and the family as a unit are constantly being negotiated by discussions of what and who makes a "good parent," and how and with whom Danish citizens are supposed to live.

I have followed parliamentary debates regarding homosexual parenthood and the family as an object of legislation. Three issues can be seen as greatly concerning homosexual men and their access to fatherhood. The first is the right of homosexuals, as opposed to heterosexuals, to have children. Under Denmark's current law, gay men have no access to adoption.[4] Because surrogacy is generally forbidden, women, most often lesbians, are gay men's only access to parenthood. In 2007 the state has given lesbian couples, as well as gay men and lesbians wishing to parent together, access to assisted reproductive technologies (ARTs). Until January 2007, access to ARTs was only given to women who were married or living with a man in a heterosexual relationship. Because it was previously illegal for doctors to perform intrauterine insemination (IUI) on lesbians and single, heterosexual women, sperm came either from an active father or an anonymous donor, and IUIs could only be performed in private clinical settings.[5] These clinics have been able to function legally, as nurses and midwives have been permitted to perform insemination. In my visits to one of these clinics and during informal talks with staff, it was clear that many lesbians create families without known fathers. However, Danish gay men, when acting within the limits of Danish law, must always share parenthood with the mothers of their children.

The second issue of concern to gay men is a father's right to have access to his child or children. Currently, shared custody is automatically given to the biological parents, if the parents are married. In cases of conflict and divorce, the mother will most likely obtain sole custody, although political and legal attention slowly has been turning toward fathers. In 2001, it became a criminal offense for a woman to fail to report the identity of her child's biological father. Shortly after, another law was enacted allowing fathers, during the first six months of their child's life, to take legal action in cases regarding doubts about their biological paternity. The men in my study, and many of those looking for a woman with whom to co-parent, expressed great concern about obtaining custody. In some cases, the issue is highly problematic, because gay men's (potential) family constellations can involve several parts, demanding a custody arrangement that cannot easily be divided between two people.

This issue can be seen as a more general concern in Danish society, which has a high divorce rate and a growing number of families with several parents, such as primary, part-time, and step-parents (Dencik and Schultz Jørgensen 2002). As compared to the nuclear family, divorce is an increasingly common feature of "family life" in contemporary Western society. In his study of divorce and remarriage in Britain, Robert Simpson points to how the emergence of this "unclear family"—as opposed to the nuclear family—entails a fundamental reordering of kinship and how people make sense of the relational dimensions of their lives (1994:833). What is common to gay parenthood and the heterosexual divorced family is how family constructions make explicit the difficulties in the interplay between state legislation and private interest. But whereas the divorced family has become an unclear family, the families of many gay men can be unclear from the outset, because they can include both the biological parents and their partners. In this manner, the considerations and negotiations taking place in the creation of these families can be used as a lens on the potential problems of the nuclear family—legally, economically, and emotionally.

The last issue of concern to gay men regards the rights of children as opposed to the rights of their parents. In political debates, "the rights and needs of the child" are discussed in opposition to "the rights of the adults." When, in 2003, the Danish Parliament proposed homosexuals' access to adoption, arguments against pointed to the right of the child to be brought up in a "normal" and "unstigmatized" environment. This was in strong opposition to the individual, as well as the collective, rights of homosexuals to have children. Likewise, a child's "rights to both parents," meaning a mother and a father, is brought up repeatedly in discussions of homosexual parenthood, especially whether a child has a right to have a father, because in practice only lesbians can parent without the other sex. This issue is known more generally from discussions about parenthood, as the absent father has been a repeated theme in European and American culture since the early nineteenth century (Gillis 1996). The concept of active fatherhood can be seen as reflecting this, as the very term refers to a stereotype that does not necessarily reflect the reality of many contemporary families. In this image, fathers are passive and absent, and because mothers are always available they need not be discussed. In a Danish context, then, the ideal family is seen as consisting of both parents, but while families are seen as being able to function without the father, the same cannot be said for families without the mother—she is synonymous with the family.

In summary, the Danish politics of reproduction and kinship are shaped and informed by notions of sexuality and gender. This, in turn, has legal consequences and practical implications regarding access to ARTs, definitions of parenthood, parents' rights and duties toward children, and more generally, questions of inclusion and exclusion into the kinship being defined. Although the boundaries of kinship are being debated and contested at the Danish parliamente, the nuclear family—defined as consisting of two differently gendered parents living in a conjugal relationship—directs the foundation of family legislation. Within this family, motherhood and womanhood seem far more inseparable than fatherhood and manhood (see Collier and Yanagisako 1987; Kahn 2000; Teman 2003). Thus, mothers are seen as being more naturally and closely related to their children than fathers.

Opposing Loneliness by Entering Fatherhood

"To have children is not a right. Certain choices in life simply implicate a renouncement. And when one chooses the homosexual form of life, one has to realize that one cannot have children" (Jespersen 2002:7; author's translation).

Having children and wanting children is seen as a cross-cultural human need. However, when it comes to homosexuals, the picture tends to change. American anthropologist Kath Weston (1991) argues that a lesbian or gay identity has been portrayed as a rejection of the family and a departure from kinship. With this in mind, I asked the men in my study why they wanted to have children and whether they saw having children as conflicting with their sexual orientation. Though all of the men categorically rejected the idea that homosexuality was in conflict with their desire to have children, most of the personal stories included considerations, grieving, and the problems of being a gay father. Homosexuality appeared as a factor that could make fatherhood harder to obtain and less socially acceptable. For Tobias Gartner (all names are pseudonyms), a thirty-year-old man in "quest of" fatherhood (Inhorn 1994), his first thoughts about having children came at a very young age and were strongly related to his awareness of being attracted to men.

> At that time—or when I was around ten, eleven, twelve years old—if anybody had asked me then I probably would have said, Well I think I shall live together with men, or a man, or be attracted by them, but I will not sacrifice, how should I put it, the other—which would be having a child. So in some ways, to me those two wishes are naturally connected, and that is also why very often I get so mad when people tell me that thing about choosing the one thing means letting go of the other.

Tobias expresses an awareness that as a homosexual, he is an object of political discussion. The private story thus breeds on the surrounding official stories. In the telling of Tobias's private story, he can be seen as opposing official family stories expressing attitudes toward homosexuals and parenthood. Many politicians and members of children's rights organizations opposing homosexual access to artificial insemination and adoption discuss how those "choosing a homosexual lifestyle" must realize that such a choice will necessarily implicate not having children (Jespersen 2002:7). Parenthood is instead exclusively reserved for the heterosexual couples. Accordingly, in Schneider's (1980) analysis of American kinship, he finds heterosexual sexual intercourse to be a central symbol in Euro-American kinship consequently excluding homosexuals. Building on this symbolism, Weston states that positioning homosexuals as members of a nonprocreative species is a short step from portraying them as a menace to family and society (1991). Whereas heterosexual intercourse can bring people into enduring association via the creation of kinship ties, lesbian and gay sexuality signifies "unbridled lust and the limitations of individualism" (22). As a result, homosexuals are portrayed as isolated individuals destined for a future of solitude and loneliness (23).

The above stigmatizing image of gay life is also reflected in many of the private family stories. But instead of being an obstacle, a fear of being an elderly and lonely gay man was one of the main motivating factors for wanting children. Christian Andersen, a thirty-seven-year-old hairdresser, described how meeting older gay men motivated his own desire to be a father.

> It was actually because I was cutting [the hair of] a sixty-five-year-old gay guy who was so lonely because he hadn't created his future; he hadn't made anything to come after him. He hadn't created anything to be engaged with or anything that could be engaged with him. And actually it took him a while to realize why. It was because he was gay and had not created a family, he had not made anything for himself.

In some stories, the image of gay life as a lonely one is connected to the idea of the gay man as promiscuous. In these instances, the storyteller has an experience of relationships as short and unstable. Peter Aagaard, the father of a three-year-old girl, portrayed the gay lifestyle as one without responsibilities and strong commitments:

> Nightclubs and such places; it is a wide variety when it comes to age. You have young guys of seventeen to eighteen, and you have older guys of fifty to sixty—in a nightclub! They probably don't have anything else to do. So I thought I don't want to live my life like that—I won't have it like that. Plus, gay men tend to change partners.

Here, the dominant portrayal of gay men is seen as ending up old and alone because of sexual orientation and is used as a major argument for fatherhood. Contrary to arguments in political and popular debates, in which the same story is used to exclude gay men from fatherhood, men in my study included fatherhood as part of the gay lifestyle. Although these men have internalized the dominant story of the gay lifestyle as nonprocreative, lonely, and sexualized, paradoxically, in telling the story of fatherhood, it is the focus of denial (Jenkins 1997). Children are seen as taking gay men away from their lonely lives and opening the gate to an enduring kinship.

In her study of infertile couples, Danish anthropologist Tine Tjørnhøj-Thomsen points out that having children is seen not only as a question of having a home and a family, but also as creating the possibility of being "a part of society" (1999:92; author's translation). For the men in my study, a large part of their stories included how fatherhood brings one into social communities normally not associated with homosexuals, such as baby showers, baptisms, and school and kindergarten classrooms. Their motivations for wanting children can be seen as involving a wish to be part of society.

Simultaneously, the stories involved a close, emotional perspective concerning the wish to bring love and enduring diffuse solidarity into their lives (Schneider 1980).

Having Children—Upholding the Natural Circle of Life

> You get to use love in a completely different way: taking care of someone. They love you unconditionally, and the fun part is that you also love them unconditionally.
>
> —Peter

In the stories of gay men, as in stories of infertile couples, having children has to do with unlimited love, as well as limited time. It involves planning and sharing the future with another, as it has to do with leaving one's past behind. Time was addressed when explaining the motivation to have children, which is also discussed in studies of single motherhood (Kahn 2000) and lesbian motherhood (Weston 1991). Notions of kinship and constructions of relatedness cannot be separated from ideas about time. As Tjørnhøj-Thomsen writes, being "related in time" is what it is basically about (1999:97; author's translation).

In the stories of the men in my study, time played a significant role, not only as a reference to the future, but also to the present and the past. Peter told me how his desire to be a father was related to a growing awareness that his lifestyle of parties, late nights, and hang-overs no longer brought him joy. In changing his life and planning his future, children were part of bringing "aim and meaning": "You put money aside for the pension and you buy your apartment—you plan for the future. But it is no good having a future if you are all by yourself—and that is what I kind of fear." When recalling how he felt when his daughter was born, Peter said,

> I thought it was fantastic. I could really feel that I had entered another period of my life, you know all those big thoughts about life, death, and the universe—all that. I could suddenly feel gray hair beginning to grow, wrinkles, and now I will soon be the one put in the grave. You know—the chain of life. I got that feeling that if I were to be run down by a truck tomorrow it wouldn't matter. Now I have done my part, now she is here.

Peter's story reflects most of those I heard. He relates the birth of his daughter to leaving part of himself behind, having someone who will carry on even after he is gone. This idea of someone to come after him is related in time, through genetic ties, blood, and sperm.

As in many official Danish family stories, the idea of procreation and biogenetic relatedness is strongly associated with the idea of permanence. The stories told by the men in my study differ from Kath Weston's 1991 and 1995 studies of the family constellations among San Francisco homosexuals. In the "families we choose" (Weston 1991) the aspect of time has a different significance. Family ties are constructed with the idea that one chooses kin relations from friends, lovers, ex-lovers, and biological kin. These ties gain strength and permanence through time, not blood.

However, for the men in my study, biogenetics carry certain ideas of timeliness. Although family ties in Weston's study are built on the idea that "what lasts is real" (1995), the men in my study stated that blood ties were real and everlasting. The wish for biological relatedness was a "fundamental need" (Tjørnhøj-Thomsen 1999), and as for Peter, many of the men saw having children as fulfilling their destiny in the natural circle of life. This biogenetic relatedness carries with it the social significance of love as an inheritance of one's birth family. Tobias explained that

> The entire fundamental feeling of having been born into this world, first of all from my mother's side, she is also the one giving birth to me, as something which was valuable and important and entirely—how to put it—unreserved, cared for, that is the strength of my life, and I have always wanted to pass that on. Because I think, unreserved as well—I can do that.

In Tobias's story, biogenetic relatedness is indistinguishable from unlimited love, from enduring diffuse solidarity (Schneider 1980). One constitutes the other. The wish for fatherhood is naturalized (Collier and Yanagisako 1987), and having children becomes the fulfillment of a natural longing. To some of the men in my study, this longing was referred to as something that had always been present—they had always seen parenthood as something that would eventually become a part of their life. For others, the wish for fatherhood grew as they had contact with children, either by working with them or by being closely related through kin or friendship relations.

For many gay men, though, children had not been part of their social life. When asked why his former partner had not initially wanted children, Thomas Andersson, the father of a five-year-old daughter, responded,

> Damn, I think a lot of gays, especially, feel like that, that they don't even consider [fatherhood] an opportunity. I think more and more do, but just eight years ago it was not common to be considering it. Because you didn't hear many stories of someone actually doing it.

Thomas believes the apparent lack of gay fathers held others back from becoming fathers or considering fatherhood. Thomas's statement shows how individuals in both their private lives and desires search for reflection and representation in official stories.

Historically speaking, though gay men have been parents for a long time, procreation has for the most part been the result of heterosexual marriage. In most cases, this meant "coming out" as fathers while hiding their homosexuality (Plummer 1995). Martin Samsø, a fifty-four-year-old man, had two children from his previous marriage with a woman. Looking back, he found he had always been attracted to men but had repressed this attraction, as homosexuality, he argued, was far more culturally unacceptable during his childhood and youth. Thus, different historical periods had different conditions and possibilities for inventing families, just as notions of procreation and kinship differ depending on the cultural context (Carstens 2000). For my study this meant each generation had its own family story to tell.

According to Weston's 1991 study, the increase in gays and lesbians having children should be seen as related to the historical emergence of a visible homosexual community. A growing consciousness of a "gay identity" and the emergence of a gay community made new family forms possible. Keeping in mind the words of Martin and Thomas, this growing consciousness has made room for stories about and the desire for gay fatherhood.

It is worth noting that some gay men have had children as part of a love relationship with a female partner (two of the men in this study had children from a previous heterosexual marriage). In these stories of fatherhood, sexuality becomes far more elastic then the strict dichotomy between homosexuality and heterosexuality. Martin, who had always been more attracted to men, described his relationship with his wife as one of love and affection. In his story, procreation does not only involve reproducing oneself, but also the conjugal relatedness with one's partner, as is central to the heterosexual relationship (Tjørnhøj-Thomsen 1999). His story departs from the stories told by the men in my study whose desire for fatherhood was inseparable from their sexual orientation. In these stories, having children was part of an individual life project, one not necessarily involving a conjugal relationship.

The reasons for wanting fatherhood were related to a life with values seen as inherent in the dominant perceptions of kinship. Avoiding loneliness, reproducing enduring diffuse solidarity, upholding the circle of life—continuing one's self and family bring aim and meaning into life. The desire to be a parent is related to the visibility and acceptance of homosexuals and their parenthood, and thus reflects interconnectedness between private and official family stories.

(De)Sexualizing Procreation

When considering fatherhood, Danish gay men must face the question of how to obtain it. With no access to adoption or surrogacy arrangements, the only options are to find a woman and procreate through ARTs, private insemination (in my study, all private insemination took place in the woman's home), or through intercourse. Although some of the men in my study had initially considered options available abroad, such as surrogacy or adoption, they all ended up searching for a potential mother with whom they would share parenthood. After finding a woman either through friends or through an ad, private insemination was used for procreation. One of the men interviewed, Peter Aagaard, had first considered marrying and having a sexual relationship with a woman, and then divorcing her later. When he brought this up at a group interview, the response was laughter and surprise, as none of the others had or ever would have considered this option. Although the men wanted their own genetic children, they did not want a sexual relationship with the mother.

This line of thinking is contrary to a dominant Danish understanding of kinship, in which reproduction is associated with a sexual act between a man and a woman. With this in mind, I questioned if gay parents' attempts to have a child would also carry sexual connotations, and if so, how they would deal with this given their sociocultural background. As described above, none of the participating men had sexual intercourse with the women involved, and procreation had not included any physical contact between the parents. However, in their stories of procreation, there seemed to be an element of sex, either as an outspoken attempt to distance oneself from it or as a complete silence about insemination.

The former was the case in the story of Christian Andersen, who was searching for a potential mother. In telling me why his first attempt to have a child with a female friend had not worked out, he said that "she just told me the wrong things," that is, how the insemination was going to work. "She never should have told me," he said. "My cream up into her vagina—it is just too vulgar. It means that I have actually fornicated with her." When asked if it was not possible for him to think of the insemination as something merely technological, he replied in a matter-of-fact way that "twenty and thirty years ago, you would have had to have sexual intercourse, be together intimately to have a child. Maybe I am not physically intimate with her, but psychologically I actually feel I am. I have fucked that bitch no matter what."

For Christian, reproduction is associated so strongly with sexual intercourse that it is impossible for him to ignore the sexual connotation, a theme repeated in Peter's story. The mother of his child is lesbian, and the private insemination took place in her apartment. Even though they were in separate rooms and only in contact when handing over the cup of sperm, it was extremely difficult for her to think of him masturbating in her apartment. It was so strongly associated with (male) sexual lust that she would "feel like vomiting," and would open all the windows and complain that "a smell" hung around the apartment for days after.

As pointed out by Helene Goldberg in this volume, intercourse, at least conceptually, seems impossible to separate from sperm. In my study, we see that the male contribution to procreation is equated with sexual lust, as the above example illustrates. For Christian, although physical intercourse does not take place, the meeting of sperm and egg is still conceptualized in sexualized terms, like an unwanted "romance" taking place (Martin 1991). For gay parents, private insemination can challenge and provoke their own sexual identity and desire. Even if not thinking of women as sexual objects, some of the men associated procreation with sexual intercourse. This association is not only conceptual, but also has social and practical consequences, as is seen from Goldberg's 2004 study, where doctors include or exclude infertile men from observing their wives being inseminated. This attempt to practically separate intercourse, and the emotions of love thought to accompany it, was one of the reasons the men in my study preferred to parent with a lesbian. Unlike heterosexual women, lesbians are expected to understand their shared parenthood as not involving a conjugal, erotic love.

(Re)Confirming Motherhood

In Euro-American kinship, parenthood involves partnership as reproduction involves intercourse. Parents are husband and wife, affine kin whose relationship is based on the order of law, meaning they are not blood relatives, but are united in marriage and related through sexual intercourse and reproduction (Schneider 1980). Inherent in this understanding of the family is the notion of male and female, defined by their sexual organs as two different elements united in conjugal erotic love (40). As discussed previously, gay parenthood contests and is challenged by this notion of parenthood and family life, because it does not involve a partnership based on a sexual relationship. However, it can be questioned whether love in some form is not a prerequisite for gay men and women sharing parenthood.

When searching for a potential mother, the shared parental relationship is given great importance. The (potential) mother is seen as a person with whom one has to have a kind of unity based on a balance between closeness and distance. The men in my study repeatedly emphasized a common need for respect and understanding as well as the ability to "agree" with each other. In the same manner, being alike was of value, as it will make it easier to share parenthood—having common interests and the same sociocultural background were important. At the same time distance was to be kept; this was expressed by several men when rejecting women's proposals to live together.

Although most of the men were not living with their children's mothers (although one lived with one of his two daughters, the men spent time with their children every other weekend and one to two days each week). This, however, is a general picture in Danish society, which has an extremely high divorce rate. In the cases of divorce, children tend to live with their mothers (Dencik and Schultz Jørgensen 2002), reflecting some of the basic cultural assumptions about motherhood and womanhood, which were voiced by the men in the study. In many of their stories, the mother, and in some cases her lesbian partner, was the primary home and primary family. Although fathers were not excluded, mothers represented the child's everyday, stable environment, while the father stayed nearby as an extra bonus. As Thomas said, "home" for his daughter was her mother's, whereas his house was being "at Daddy's."

When explaining why this is the case, many of the men interviewed pointed to their "private life." Women and motherhood were equated with the home, but men's lives were related to a life outside the family. This seems to reflect the family pattern that has developed in Western societies, with the gendered division of labor following the capitalist Industrial Revolution. According to historian John Gillis (1996), in this notion of the family women are the primary caretakers, equated with the domestic and reproductive sphere. The main reason the men in my study gave for not living with their children echoes this assumption about motherhood—the woman is "naturally related" to the child. When asked why his daughter lives with her mother, Peter responded,

I think a special intimacy is created within the first year, in connection with the breastfeeding. And I just think I can see, through all times, in all cultures—well, everyone I know, all children I know, all divorced families I know—that it is always the mother who stands for confidence and warmth and love first-hand. In all theories, from Freud to Tibetan monks, you know everyone thinks the same: that the love of the mother is the primary source of love.

In all the private family stories, the reproductive role of the woman was loaded with social significance—pregnancy and breastfeeding create a special bond between mother and child. Thus, a sociobiological relationship exists in which, according to most men, the mother cannot be replaced. According to Peter, this relationship is not only created after birth, but also is a "natural connection in our preconsciousness." In the private family stories, dominant notions of kinship and gender were reproduced in ways found in political and legal stories—in both, the mother is the primary force of the family. To sum up, men's role and rights regarding parenthood are subject to political discussion, while women's role is taken for granted.

(Re)Inventing Fatherhood

In her discussion of lesbian parenting, Kath Weston (1991) points to the male contribution in procreation as a donation that does not necessarily involve the man becoming a father. Weston refers to men who donate sperm but have no wish to coparent with the mother, preferring a more distant relationship with the child, one defined perhaps as an "uncle" or "godfather." Reading the ads in Danish magazines for gays and lesbians, a few men offer themselves as potential donors but do not opt for active fatherhood. However, for the men in my study, this was an unthinkable situation, as donating sperm signified fatherhood, which meant being emotionally as well as physically available for their child. The relationship between father and child was defined as a question of emotion, gender, and biology.

The notion that biological fatherhood is a special bond was present in all the stories. Whereas some saw the relationship between mother and child as the result of a preconscious biological connection, in some stories fatherhood was described in the same manner. Thomas, who was parenting his (biological) daughter with his former partner, explained how he had "an intuitive understanding" of their daughter, one different from his former partner's. He explained this difference with the fact that she physically "resembled" him. This importance attributed to biological relatedness also could be seen in Tobias's photos, as he had chosen to photograph his own hands and feet. When asked why, he responded that he liked these physical features and wished to pass them on. Again, physical resemblance was important.

The importance placed on biological relatedness is reflected in Danish family law, in which the rights of the biological parents are the main foundation of the family. In debates regarding the laws on donor insemination, it is repeatedly discussed as to whether the donors should be anonymous, and the importance for children to know their biogenetic backgrounds is emphasized.[6] Studies of infertility (see Goldberg 2004; Tjørnhøj-Thomsen 1999) show how infertile men considering donor insemination display great fear about their potential relationship with the child, because they will not be biologically related. The story of biogenetic

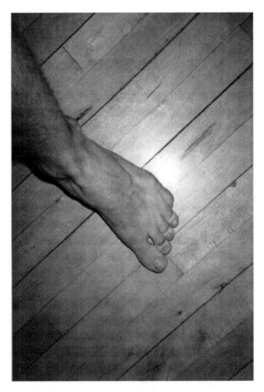

Figure 14.1. A picture of my informant's foot. For him, having a child would mean passing on his flesh and blood. The idea of his child resembling him physically was a thing that mattered greatly to him.

relatedness as synonymous with kinship dominates the private and official family stories.

Although not living with their children and equating motherhood with nurturing and emotional intimacy, all the men in my study emphasized the importance of emotional closeness with their own children. Many of the men understood that this closeness—as contrary to that between mother and child—was created and upheld over time. When I asked how they spent time with their children and how this time differed from that between mother and child, most of the men pointed toward the same activities. Generally, they saw themselves as being very physical, describing themselves as being "wilder" than their children's mothers. Fathers saw themselves as being less concerned than women, who were seen as being "overly concerned" with potential dangers. Finally, several of the men described the father's contribution as inherent to him "being a man," as opposed to the mother "being a woman."

This manner of defining masculinity and maleness as qualities contrasted with femininity and womanhood as described in Schneider's analysis of the differences between the sexes as "a fact of nature on which the family is based" (1980:41). The respondents in Schneider's study said these qualities of masculinity and femininity fit men and women for different activities. This understanding of gender, and its intersection with kinship, can be found in the stories of the men in my study. Fathers were described as being more physically active, playing with their children, and involving them in activities outside the home. Women were described as less physical and more nurturing, and in most stories were responsible for primary infant care and the primary home.

Although this distinction was stated, the photographs and pictures of kinship told a different story, one contesting the intersection of gender and kinship. When discussing parenthood, the men would use available gendered categories, but when practicing fatherhood, they would go beyond and across the gendered boundaries. This became clear as I was writing my fieldnotes:

> As I go through the photos, I am puzzled by the similarity in the chosen motives. While showing different people and locations, the pictures portray the same situations, places, and rituals: fathers picking up their children from kindergarten, taking their sons or daughters to the doctor, to the playground, or going shopping. Children in the kitchen, helping with the cooking and in the dining room, eating. In the bathroom, having their teeth brushed, being bathed, or having a diaper changed. Dressed in their pajamas in the bedroom; being tucked in, or having stories read out loud. Apparently everyday family life takes place at home, also when being "at Daddy's."

It was also striking how all of the fathers portrayed themselves and their children: in situations displaying nurturance, which is still strongly associated with motherhood. Likewise, in conversation, the men pointed out the differences in gendered parenthood leading to different traits and tasks. But while this gendered difference was clearly expressed by the reasons children lived primarily with their mothers, this same difference seemed to be contradicted by the photos picturing everyday family life.

Historically speaking, gay fathers can be seen as part of the development for the demands of fatherhood, emphasizing how they can complete the same parenting tasks as women while also pointing out inherently male qualities. In defining fatherhood, the men challenge the supreme status of motherhood while also defining motherhood and fatherhood as two equally necessary and complementary roles. The former can be exemplified in the story of Jens Konig, who in the first months of his daughter's life had a conflict with her mother. Although the mother believed Jens did not know their daughter as well and therefore did not know how to handle her, he insisted on his ability to take care of his daughter just *as well* as the mother. Even though Jens acknowledged that his daughter spent more time with her mother, it irritated him that the mother would "always know better." In talking to me, he expressed anger and humiliation at being defined as the "second-best parent," thus defending his parental status and challenging the supreme status of motherhood.

Conclusion: Toward New Family Patterns?

How does homosexual fatherhood reproduce or challenge more dominant Western understandings of kinship as informed by notions of both gender and sexuality? There is no straightforward answer, because the families of gay men cannot be seen as radically different from or as a mere replication of the traditional nuclear family. In the stories of gay fathers, the nuclear family as a social category is used as a point of reference, as an ideal picture of kinship that is both wished for and rejected. Gay fathers therefore can be seen as reinventing and reconfirming kinship, as well as others, such as families opting for adoption, couples using surrogacy and donor insemination, foster families, and single-parent or divorced families.

But gay fathers have certain traits distinguishing them from other fathers. Because their fatherhood is not based on an erotic relationship with a woman, they challenge the notion of kinship as based on and symbolized by heterosexual intercourse. This understanding of kinship is also contested by couples using anonymous donor insemination, such as infertile couples or lesbians parenting together, but in these families the sperm donor is unknown and therefore uninvolved. In the family constellations of the men in my study, all the parts implicated biogenetically in procreation are known to each other and related in everyday family life—this is probably what makes these families most radically different from other families. First, they contest the idea that parents have to be lovers. Second, they are far-reaching sociocultural units, because they consist, often in their outset, of several family members being socially, as well as biogenetically, related to each other.

Unlike the contemporary divorced families who eventually become unclear families, gay parents create and negotiate their family constructions even before their child is born. The lives and considerations of gay fathers provide a useful lens on contemporary kinship, casting light on the gendered expectations and practices of parenthood, and basic assumptions underlining the interconnectedness of kinship, gender, and sexuality. Although gay men express a range of gendered expectations to parenthood, they cross the very same gendered boundaries in practicing fatherhood, and thus, alongside other men, as well as women, challenge the supreme status of motherhood. The fathers in my study must therefore be understood as negotiators in the larger kinship debate in contemporary Danish society.

The apparent invisibility that partly surrounds homosexual fathers can be seen as an expression of the more general notion of kinship, in which mothers are the primary force of the family, consequently making parenthood an exclusive lesbian concern. Simultaneously, gay men and lesbians suffer from moralistic judgments in which homosexuality is opposed to kinship and sometimes even perceived as a threat to the family as a social and moral unit. For several reasons, homosexual fathers are surrounded by silence. This silence is being broken by the many stories told by men who parent children and those who are starting to consider themselves as possible parents. They are the tellers of kinship in the making.

Acknowledgments

I thank the men who gave this article life by letting me into their lives and telling me their stories. I also thank Tine Tjørnhøj-Thomsen, Helene Goldberg, and Marcia Inhorn for their useful comments on the content and structure of this chapter. Finally I thank Pia.

Notes

1. When using the terms "gay parenthood" and "gay parents," I refer to homosexual men having children with lesbian women, as was the case for most of the men in my study. I speak of "lesbian parents" when referring to lesbian couples who have had a child through anonymous donor insemination. Generally, "gay parents" can refer to lesbians parenting together without a father being involved or gay men sharing parenthood without a woman being involved. One of the men in my study had a child through private insemination with a heterosexual woman.
2. The definitions of "gay" and "homosexual" are used interchangeably, as the interviewed men used them. However, it is not my intention to reproduce a strict dichotomy between homosexuality and heterosexuality, and I emphasize that some of the men used the terms "bisexual" and "queer."
3. The men participating in this study are all self-defined homosexuals. At the time of my fieldwork, two were trying to become biological fathers, and the rest already had children. One man defined himself as the father of the child biologically related to his former partner.
4. A proposal in favor of foreign-child adoption for Danish homosexuals was voted against in February 2003. However, since 1999, homosexual couples living together in a registered partnership (legal since 1989) have had access to "stepchild adoption." This is most frequently used by lesbians adopting the child biologically related to their partner and conceived through anonymous sperm donation. In some cases, stepchild adoption is used between lesbian partners even when the father's identity is known.
5. Three clinics in Denmark have offered insemination to lesbians and single women. The first opened in 1999, and is called Jordmorklinikken Stork (the Midwife Clinic "Stork"), referring to the midwife who opened it, as well as the bird. According to an old Danish myth, storks bring the newborn child to the parents, a myth referred to in the Danish-English dictionary by the saying that "babies are found under the gooseberry bushes." The clinic opened as a reaction to a 1997 law that forbids doctors from performing inseminations on women not living with or married to a man. The clinic is not defined as a fertility clinic but as a midwife clinic. Likewise, in accordance with the law, the only reproductive method offered by the clinic is IUI.
6. Donor insemination is required by law to be anonymous. Interestingly, fertility clinic staff keep information regarding donors' physical features in order to match them with the (nonbiological) father-to-be.

References

Andersen, Arnfinn J. 2003. *Menn skaper rom for foreldreskap og familie. Farskapets betingelser i en heteronormativ kultur.* PhD diss., Institute of Sociology and Political Science, Trondheim.

Bolton, Ralph. 1992. "Mapping Terra Incognita: Sex Research for AIDS Prevention—An Urgent Agenda for the 1990s." In *The Time of AIDS*, ed. G. Herdt and S. Lindebaum. London: Sage.

Bourdieu, Pierre. 1996. "On the Family as a Realized Category." *Theory, Culture, and Society* 13(3):19–26.

Carstens, Janet, ed. 2000. "Introduction." In *Cultures of Relatedness: New Approaches to the Study of Kinship*. Cambridge: Cambridge University Press.

Collier, Jane Fishburne, and Sylvia Junko Yanagisako. 1987. *Gender and Kinship: Essays Toward a Unified Analysis*. Stanford: Stanford University Press.

Dalton, Susan. 2000. "Nonbiological Mothers and the Legal Boundaries of Motherhood: An Analysis of California Law." In *Ideologies and Technologies of Motherhood*, ed. Helena Ragone and France Winddance Twine. New York: Routledge.

Dencik, Lars, and Per Schultz Jørgensen. 2002. *Børn og familie i det postmoderne samfund*. Copenhagen: Hans Reitzels Forlag.

Gillis, John. 1996. *A World of Their Own Making: Myth, Ritual, and the Quest for Family Values*. New York: Basic Books.

Goldberg, Helene. 2004. *The Man in the Sperm: A Study of Male Infertility in Israel*. MA thesis, Copenhagen University.

Hastrup, Kirsten, ed. 2001. *Legal Cultures and Human Rights: The Challenge of Diversity*. London: Kluwer Law International.

Hayden, Corrine P. 1995. "Gender, Genetics, and Generation: Reformulating Biology in Lesbian Kinship." *Cultural Anthropology* 10(1):41–63.

Inhorn, Marcia. 1994. *Quest for Conception: Gender, Infertility, and Egyptian Medical Traditions*. Philadelphia: University of Pennsylvania Press.

Jenkin, Richard. 1997. *Rethinking Ethnicity. Arguments and Explorations*. Thousand Oaks, CA: Sage.

Jespersen, Per Michael. 2002. "Adoption: Bøsser bruger børn som murbrækkere." *Politiken*, 15 December.

Kahn, Susan Martha. 2000. *Reproducing Jews: A Cultural Account of Assisted Conception in Israel*. Durham: Duke University Press.

Lewin, Ellen. 1993. *Lesbian Mothers: Accounts of Gender in American Culture*. Ithaca: Cornell University Press.

Marcus, George E. 1995. "Ethnography in/of the World System: The Emergence of Multi-Sited Ethnography." *Annual Review of Anthropology* 24:95–117.

Martin, Emily. 1991. "The Egg and the Sperm: How Science Has Constructed a Romance Based on Stereotypical Male-Female Roles." *Signs* 16(3):5–501.

Pash, Diana. 2005. "Kinship in Action: Care and Obligation in Families Headed by Gay Fathers." UCLA Sloan Center on Everyday Lives of Families Working Paper No. 35.

Plummer, Kenneth. 1995. *Telling Sexual Stories: Power, Change and Social Worlds*. London: Routledge.

Sandell, Kerstin. 1995. "Lesbisk mor og homosexuell far—ny variant av styvfamilien." *Kvinnovetenskapligt tidskrift* 1, 16 årgang.

Schneider, David. 1980. *American Kinship: A Cultural Account*. Chicago: University of Chicago Press.

Simpson, Robert. 1994. "Bringing the 'Unclear' Family into Focus: Divorce and Re-Marriage in Contemporary Britain." *Man* 29(4):831–51.

Teman, Elly. 2003. "Knowing the Surrogate's Body in Israel." In *Surrogate Motherhood: International Perspectives*, ed. Rachel Cook and Shelly day Schlater. London: Hart Press.

Tjørnhøj-Thomsen, Tine. 1999. *Tilblivelseshistorier. Barnløshed, slægtskab og forplantningsteknologi i Danmark*. PhD diss., Institute of Anthropology, University of Copenhagen.

Weston, Kath. 1991. *Families We Choose: Lesbians, Gays, Kinship*. New York: Columbia University Press.

———. 1995. "Forever is a Long Time: Romancing the Real in Gay Kinship Ideologies." In *Naturalizing Power: Essays in Feminist Cultural Analysis*, ed. Sylvia Yanagisako and Carol Delaney. New York and London: Routledge.

Contributors

Matthew R. Dudgeon is a medical anthropologist and epidemiologist whose work explores the intersections of gender and medicine through the lens of reproductive health. His research focuses on men's influences on maternal and infant health, as well as men's reproductive health problems, in two K'iche' Maya communities in Guatemala. He has used U.S. data to examine associations with birth control failure and unwanted pregnancy, as well as determinants of health care utilization during pregnancy. Dudgeon is currently rotating through his clinical clerkships as a medical student at Emory University, Atlanta, Georgia.

Helene Goldberg is a social anthropologist affiliated with the Department of Public Health in Guldborgsund, Denmark. Her former fieldwork explored issues of masculinity, kinship, and sexuality, and her work on male infertility in Israel has won several prizes. With Maruska la Cour Mosegaard she has authored the children's book *slottet med de mange værelser* (Turbineforlaget 2008), which introduces the various ways children come into being today in single-parent, heterosexual, and homosexual families; this book is published in Danish and has been translated into Swedish. Goldberg's current applied research focuses on the experiences and perspectives of families with obese children. It is part of an effort to develop health policies aimed at health promotion and illness prevention.

Matthew C. Gutmann is Professor of Anthropology, Ethnic Studies, and Latin American Studies at Brown University, where he teaches courses on gender/sexuality, political and medical anthropology, and social theory. He is the author of *The Meanings of Macho: Being a Man in Mexico City, The Romance of Democracy: Compliant Defiance in Contemporary Mexico*, and *Fixing Men: Sex, Birth Control and AIDS in Mexico*. He is also the editor of *Changing Men and Masculinities in Latin America*.

Sallie Han is Assistant Professor of Anthropology at SUNY College at Oneonta. Her research interests include reproduction, kinship, gender, and the significance of language in everyday experiences of kin and person making. Currently, she is working on a book on pregnancy as a cultural and social experience among American middle-class women.

Nguyen Thi Thuy Hanh is a medical doctor and a Lecturer in Medical Anthropology and Demography at the Faculty of Public Health, Hanoi Medical University. She has done research on health care systems, reproductive health, HIV/AIDS, and disability. Currently, her research focuses on mother-to-child transmission of HIV, focusing on reproductive choices among and health care for HIV-positive pregnant women.

Marcia C. Inhorn is the William K. Lanman Jr. Professor of Anthropology and International Affairs at the Department of Anthropology and The Whitney and Betty MacMillan Center for International and Area Studies at Yale University. She also serves as Chair of the Council on Middle East Studies at Yale and is past-president of the Society for Medical Anthropology of the American Anthropological Association. A specialist on Middle Eastern gender and health issues, Inhorn has conducted research on the social impact of infertility and assisted reproductive technologies in Egypt, Lebanon, the United Arab Emirates, and Arab America. She is the author of *Quest for Conception: Gender, Infertility, and Egyptian Medical Traditions, Infertility and Patriarchy: The Cultural Politics of Gender and Family Life in Egypt,* and *Local Babies, Global Science: Gender, Religion, and In Vitro Fertilization in Egypt.* She is also editor or coeditor of six books in the areas of gender, health, science, technology, biomedicine, and public health. With Soraya Tremayne and David Parkin, she co-edits the Berghahn Book series on "Fertility, Reproduction, and Sexuality."

Tsipy Ivry is a medical anthropologist and Lecturer in Anthropology at the Department of Sociology and Anthropology at the University of Haifa, Israel. Her research focuses on the ongoing interactions between reproductive medicine, local reproductive politics, and personal experiences of self and the body. Her book exploring clinical encounters and experiences of pregnancy in Japan and Israel is forthcoming in 2009. Other publications explore notions of maternal responsibility, doctors' and pregnant women's negotiations around prenatal diagnosis, and male partners' experiences of pregnancy. Her current research focuses on fertility treatments among observant Jews in Israel.

Janneli F. Miller is an applied medical anthropologist and licensed midwife whose work focuses on reproductive health among indigenous women in the southwest United States and northern Mexico. Currently, she is working on a book about the practice of solitary and unassisted birth.

Lisa Jean Moore is Professor of Sociology at Purchase College, State University of New York, where she is also the Coordinator of Gender Studies. Her books include *Sperm Counts: Overcome by Man's Most Precious Fluid, Gendered Bodies: Feminist Perspectives* (with Judith Lorber), and (with Monica Casper) *Missing Bodies: The Politics of Visibility.*

Maruska la Cour Mosegaard is a social anthropologist at KVINFO, the Danish Center of Information on Women and Gender Research. She has carried out fieldwork in Denmark among gay men and their families, focusing on kinship, sexuality, gender, and the policies and rights surrounding reproductive technologies in the country. She has been engaged in both political and legal debates concerning homosexual rights to parenthood, especially focusing on the situation of gay fathers. Currently, she is working with refugee and immigrant women on their integration into the Danish labor market. With Helene Goldberg she has authored the children's book *slottet med de mange værelser* (Turbineforlaget 2008), which introduces the various ways children come into being today in single-parent, heterosexual, and homosexual families; this book is published in Danish and has been translated into Swedish.

Laury Oaks is Associate Professor of Feminist Studies, Anthropology, and Sociology at the University of California, Santa Barbara. Her research has explored the cultural and social dimensions of reproductive politics in the United States, Ireland, and Japan. She is the co-editor with Barbara Herr Harthorn of *Risk, Culture, and Health Inequality: Shifting Perceptions of Danger and Blame* and author of *Smoking and Pregnancy: The Politics of Fetal Protection.* She is currently co-authoring, with Jo Murphy-Lawless, *The Sally Gardens: Women and Sex in Ireland* and conducting with Tania Israel a community-based participatory research project that examines lesbian, gay, bisexual, and transgendered communities' strengths, concerns, and mental health needs.

Tine Tjørnhøj-Thomsen is a social anthropologist and Associate Professor at the Department of Anthropology at the University of Copenhagen. She has done extensive research on infertility, reproductive technologies, and kinship in Denmark, receiving a prize for the work relating to her doctoral thesis on "Stories of Coming into

Being: Childlessness, Procreative Technologies and Kinship in Denmark." Her current research is titled "On the Limits of Reason: New
Perspectives in Anthropological Studies of Magic, Social Technology,
and Uncertainty." It explores the role of magic as a means of managing uncertainty in modern society. She has also carried out fieldwork
in India and currently works in the area of cancer rehabilitation.

Aura Yen is Assistant Professor of medical humanities at a number
of medical universities in Taiwan. Her research has focused on indigenous women's health in China. Recently, she has begun a study of
immigrant health in Taiwan, focusing on women's labor-migration
flows and cross-national marriages.

INDEX

Breinigsville, PA USA
03 September 2010
244825BV00004B/76/P